DISCIPLINED

INQUIRY

UNDERSTANDING AND DOING EDUCATIONAL RESEARCH

DISCIPLINED INQUIRY

UNDERSTANDING AND DOING EDUCATIONAL RESEARCH

R. Tony Eichelberger
University of Pittsburgh

Longman
New York & London

Disciplined Inquiry: Understanding and Doing Educational Research

Longman Inc., 95 Church Street, White Plains, N.Y. 10601

Associated companies:
Longman Group Ltd., London
Longman Cheshire Pty., Melbourne
Longman Paul Pty., Auckland
Copp Clark Pitman, Toronto
Pitman Publishing Inc., New York

Senior editor: Naomi Silverman
Production editor: Carol Harwood
Text design: Jill Francis Wood
Cover design: Kevin C. Kall
Production supervisor: Kathleen M. Ryan

Library of Congress Cataloging-in-Publication Data

Eichelberger, R. Tony.
    Disciplined inquiry.

    Bibliography: p.
    Includes index.
    1. Education—Research—United States.   I. Title.
LB1028.E37   1989   370'.7'8073   88-26596
ISBN 0-582-99864-6

89 90 91 92 93 94 9 8 7 6 5 4 3 2

This book is dedicated to:
Francis J. (Jack) Kelly,
who started me on a lifetime of inquiry;

Rita Bean Eichelberger,
my wife, colleague and co-inquirer;

Erin and Derek Eichelberger,
my children; and

The Eichelberger family of Pekin, Illinois,
who have nurtured me since birth.

Contents

Preface

Given the knowledge explosion, educators have attempted to include more information at each level of education—from kindergarten through graduate school. Too often this educational material is presented as meaningless, abstract pieces of information that must be "learned." The information is often meaningless because it is foreign to students' past experience and is not applied in their daily lives. This is particularly true of science and associated research methodology. As curriculum developers attempt to include the latest findings in these fields (as well as the theories used to describe or explain these findings, such as photosynthesis, nerve impulses, and DNA and RNA), students struggle to find meaning in the complex processes that are so removed from their prior knowledge and experience. Too often teachers and students resign themselves to teaching or learning these "meaningless" terms with the expectation that the meaning will become clearer in future years.

Such a perspective is neither necessary nor useful. The basic principles of science are relatively simple and straightforward and should be understood by high school graduates. The technologies used to implement these principles, such as measurement and statistics, can be complex, requiring years of study and experience to master. This book focuses on the simple, elegant logic used to investigate and gain knowledge about our world and the people in it, rather than the intricacies of the mathematical technologies used in research. That same logic is used by members of a jury to judge the guilt or innocence of a defendant, a mechanic in repairing a car engine, or a teacher in instructing students in math, reading, or social studies.

This book emphasizes the problems that researchers study and the ways different methods are used to investigate different problems. By emphasizing the substantive problem under investigation—such as achievement differences be-

tween boys and girls, the effects of participatory management on staff morale
and effectiveness, or teachers' reactions to an instructional innovation—the logical basis for the procedures that are used can be illustrated more clearly. Research is not a magical process open only to those who have successfully
completed mystical rites of initiation that include total mastery of mathematics.
Research is based on the same foundation of sound, critical thinking needed by
every professional to make informed decisions.

Scientific study includes much jargon, as does dentistry, medicine, education, and every other field. In many ways, learning research methods is similar to
learning a foreign language. You must learn the definitions of some new terms or
symbols, such as that the Greek letter μ (mu) represents the mean of a set of
scores, just as you learn that *rex* means "king" in Latin and *casa* means "house"
in Spanish.

Research requires that a person understand basic mathematical operations
of addition, subtraction, multiplication, and division. If you have not had much
experience or success with mathematics in the past, that is not going to affect
your ability to learn the logical principles of educational research. On the other
hand, the level of mathematics required in most research is minimal. I have tried
to demystify the use of mathematics and show how it directly represents substantive issues, or characteristics.

My primary purpose in writing this book is to help you gain a meaningful
understanding of the central elements of educational inquiry—particularly those
methods for doing empirical research. The relationships among data, theory, and
knowledge are discussed in an applied perspective. The book is applied in both
emphasizing the practical value of educational research and theory, and presenting information and exercises in ways that help in *doing* research. A study comparing two methods for teaching reading is provided in the "Introduction" as a
concrete example of both the substantive and methodological issues that arise in
implementiung and interpreting the results of a study. This example provides a
view of the "forest" before the "individual trees" in each chapter are examined.
It is used throughout the book, along with other studies, to illustrate the principles of inquiry.

In Chapter 1, changes in philosophy of science and associated methods for
gaining knowledge (epistemology) that were used by scholars—from before Plato
and Socrates through the different periods to present perspectives—are identified. The ways in which the interpretation of data are subjective and the relationship between knowledge and truth as currently viewed are discussed also. The
primary purpose of this chapter is to describe present epistemologies of science
and show that conceptions of the world and the rules of evidence for "legitimate" interpretation of information have changed over time and will continue to
change in the future.

In Chapter 2, the essential elements of science and research are identified
and discussed. The central point is that the scientific method is not a series of
steps that can be universally followed, but it is a doubting approach to knowledge
that uses the thoughtful identification of other possible explanations for a given

result and the careful investigation of these alternative explanations. Good research is the result of an accurate, honest reporting of what was done, what was found, and what processes seemed to operate in the setting studied.

In educational research, the rights of participants must be protected. The changing views of individuals' rights in the United States and the guidelines for ethical research behavior have changed greatly in the past 30 years. A brief discussion of these changes and the procedures that researchers must carry out in planning and implementing a study are presented. Sources of more detailed information about ethical practices and institutional requirements for review and approval of research are listed.

An overview of the empirical research process is presented at the end of Chapter 2. Before addressing each aspect of the research process in detail, it is essential that you have some idea of the parts of the inquiry process and how they fit together. Several research studies are used to illustrate the logical and methodological issues addressed in the book.

In Chapters 3 through 9 the following specific elements of research are addressed:

3. Problem and Purpose of Study
4. Reviewing Literature Relevant to a Problem
5. Characteristics of Data
6. Research Design: Issues of Quality and Relevance of Research Results
7. Organizing, Analyzing, and Summarizing Empirical Information
8. Interpreting Results of a Study
9. Content and Structure of the Research Report

The specific topics in each chapter are addressed using practical examples to show how they are applied and why they are needed in the systematic and logical process of investigating a problem. The relative importance of the various methodological and substantive issues are discussed on the basis of the researcher's specific purpose for doing the study. It is important to learn that in science, as in everything else in life, one set of rules cannot be applied in exactly the same way in every situation. As purposes for studies change, the relative importance of elements of research methods, such as sample characteristics, measurement processes, research design considerations, and data analysis techniques, will also change.

In Chapter 10, "Theory, Research, and Practice," the interrelationships among theory, empirical research, and practice are discussed. Most people are unaware of the central position of theory in personal and professional day-to-day decision-making. The main purpose of this chapter is to show, as Dewey has stated, that "There is nothing more practical than a a good theory." The ways relationships between basic psychological research and associated changes in conceptions of the learning process have affected the curriculum, the structure of classrooms, and classroom furniture over the past 85 years are used to illustrate the centrality of theory in practice.

How new models and theories are developed that account for what appear to be conflicting results is illustrated using research results about the effects of teacher expectancy on student achievement. These new models or theories are used by later researchers to test their applicability in new settings.

In my experience, the order of material in this book has worked well for students in learning relevant knowldge and inquiry skills. Reading the last chapter of the book first may provide a more complete understanding of the inquiry process and the relationships among the various elements before addressing the many details of specific research methodology techniques and issues discussed in the earlier chapters.

The rather extensive discussion of positivism, phenomenology, and hermeneutics can be skipped without greatly affecting your ability to understand the remainder of the book. It is included to clarify the present controversy among educational researchers as to whether the social sciences (or the human sciences) should be analytical and nomothetic, or wholistic and idiographic. These latter characteristics are represented by research based on world views and assumptions of hermeneutics or phenomenological sociology, whereas the former are characteristics of positivism. The perspective represented in this book is that research from the various perspectives provides more comprehensive description of the nature of the human condition than that provided by any one perspective alone. Each can be addressed in ways that contribute useful knowledge to educators. For a study to contribute to knowledge, the methods used in a study must be described so that others can judge the evidence used to draw conclusions and make recommendations.

A final comment: You will fail to learn the essential elements of educational research if you only read about them or listen to lectures. You must have some hands-on experiences, with critical feedback from your instructor, before research knowledge and skills can be meaningful. Some useful experiences are the following:

1. Doing an empirical study (even if it is "trivial").
2. Reading a number of research articles critically.
3. Analyzing and synthesizing research articles on a specific educational problem or issue.
4. Doing exercises that illustrate specific methodological principles and how they relate to substantive conclusions such as drawing samples randomly from a population, observing students in a classroom, or interviewing a teacher, principal, student, or parent.

Learning how to do research and use the results obtained by others is not a spectator sport. Most new concepts have to be addressed three or more times before they can be understood. Once you realize this and study these topics, knowledge of inquiry methods will become one of your most useful tools as a professional, citizen, and person.

Acknowledgments

In organizing what I know about disciplined inquiry and putting it into a book, I owe many debts, both intellectual and personal. The faculty in the Guidance and Educational Psychology Department at Southern Illinois University, Carbondale in the late 1960s introduced me to the pursuit of educational knowledge. Colleagues at the Learning Research and Development Center at the University of Pittsburgh in the 1970s worked at the forefront of educational research and development. Since 1971, the faculty in the School of Education, particularly those in Educational Research Methodology, have been valued colleagues who have affected my knowledge of eductional inquiry. Evaluators in the Evaluation Network and the Evaluation Research Society (which merged into the American Evaluation Association), have been active participants in the pursuit of appropriate methods for gaining useful knowledge.

Donald L. Beggs, Francis J. Kelly, and Keith A. McNeil taught me much about measurement, research design, and statistics. As colleagues at the Learning Research and Development Center, William W. Cooley and Gaea Leinhardt helped me translate those methods into meaningful research and evaluation. Allyson Walker and I have struggled to move beyond quantitative, positivistic research to more qualitative, interpretive studies. John Singleton and Rolland Paulston have contributed much over the years in the effort.

The help of my colleagues and friends in producing this book is gratefully acknowledged. David E. Engel, Noreen B. Garman, James Kelly, Jr., Louis A. Pingel, and Irene E. Salazar commented on specific parts of the manuscript. An anonymous reviewer read an early draft of the philosophy chapters and made a number of valuable suggestions. Robert W. Covert and Robert B. Ingle reviewed the book for Longman, making insightful comments and suggestions that I tried to address. Richard C. Cox went well beyond what anyone could expect of a friend and colleague, reading and commenting on the entire manuscript.

Karyl Troup-Leasure did numerous time-consuming tasks, such as obtaining original sources, compiling bibliographies, and producing annotations for the book. As a student, she also used the book in my class and provided a number of valuable comments and suggestions. I appreciate her efforts and those of other students who used the book and helped me identify ways to improve it.

Yvonne Jones put my initial scratchings and numerous rewrites on the word processor, making sure that no errors were made. Her willingness to meet my deadlines, which at times were unreasonable, and her ability to produce readable copy is appreciated. Her work on the book during her weekends, evenings, and other "free" time over the past year is a special gift I cannot adequately repay. She truly made it "her" book. Theresa Dunn, Denise Morrin, Lorraine Mundell, and Reni Pitts typed and copied some parts of the book and helped me keep my sanity by producing many other documents that were needed while this book was being produced.

Shirley Covington, copy editor, and Carol Harwood, production editor, did a superb job producing a final, more readable copy of the book. My thanks to Naomi Silverman for facilitating the entire process of developing the book from initial idea to a final manuscript.

Rita Bean Eichelberger helped me organize and write many of these complex ideas and examples so that readers would more easily understand them. She does much to keep my abstract thoughts and writing as applied and meaningful as possible. Her help and support as colleague and helpmate are gratefully acknowledged and humbly appreciated.

Introduction

The purpose of this book is to help you develop a better understanding of the research process and how research results can be used in educational decision-making. Most students are introduced to the scientific method in elementary school. Often the steps in the scientific method are committed to memory. Some students even do science experiments and measure the outcomes. But students seldom have the opportunity to systematically investigate a question that has direct application in their personal or professional lives. As a result, common misconceptions about the nature and methods of science abound.

What is the scientific method? Is there only one? Is it using the most objective measures to generate numbers? Is it doing experiments? Does it require the use of sophisticated statistics? In this book, issues are delineated and discussed to help you answer these questions in ways that are meaningful in your personal and professional life.

The purpose of all empirical research is to describe accurately what occurs in a specific situation. Anthropologists, historians, and other researchers study situations as they normally exist (or existed). They use theories and data to identify variables that seem to be related. Physicists, chemists, and many psychologists set up contrived situations, called experiments, to test their hunches, or theories. They usually manipulate one variable, called the independent variable, to observe its effect on a second variable, called the dependent variable. In every empirical study, the goal is accurate description of what occurred in the natural or contrived situation in order to develop theories or models of the nature of the human organism, or the human condition. That aspect of the human condition of concern to us is education.

Many educational research texts—especially at the introductory level—indicate that variable A can be identified as a cause of variable B *only* when an experimental study is done. How did astronomers and astrophysicists learn so much about the Moon and planets in our solar system without doing experimental manipulation? How do anthropologists learn about cultures without experiments? As Mill (1906) indicated when he identified the various methods for making causal inference, the experimental paradigm is only one of the possible logical bases for making causal statements from empirical studies.

The research method that is best in any specific study is that which most adequately addresses the research problem studied. To investigate the attitudes of teachers toward the mainstreaming of handicapped children, for instance, a researcher should do a survey of teachers. To investigate the relationships between socioeconomic status and academic achievement, a correlational study is needed. In either case, it is unlikely that an experimental design would be of much value. Thus, in either doing research or gaining knowledge from previous research, the concept of the experiment as the "best" research method tends to be misleading.

Most philosophers of science and researchers today are well aware that you can never prove a particular theory or model is true. All you can do is obtain information that supports, or fails to support, the applicability of a specific theory or model in a particular situation. The confidence you can have in the conclusions reached in a study are determined primarily by (1) the extent to which the procedures used adequately measure the variables being studied, and (2) the ingenuity of the researcher in identifying and "controlling" other possible explanations for the results obtained in that study.

EXAMPLE 1   AN EXPERIMENTAL STUDY (THE GARFIELD SCHOOL STUDY)

To illustrate these points in a practical setting, suppose there were two teachers in Garfield School who wondered which method of teaching reading would be best for their second-grade students. They did not know whether a phonics or a meaning (whole-word) method would be better for teaching beginning reading. The two second-grade teachers in Garfield School decided to investigate the problem empirically in their classrooms. They convinced their principal to allow one teacher to use a phonics approach (Teacher A) and the other teacher to use a meaning approach (Teacher B).

To make the two classes comparable, the principal assigned the 50 second-grade students to the two classes "randomly" by writing each student's name on a slip of paper and placing all the folded papers in a shoe box. The principal then drew one slip of paper out of the box and assigned that student to Teacher A. The second student whose name was drawn was assigned to Teacher B. This continued until all students were assigned to one of the classrooms. In this as-

TABLE I.1 MAT READING ACHIEVEMENT SCORES (IN GRADE EQUIVALENTS)
OF 50 SECOND-GRADE STUDENTS WHO USED EITHER A PHONIC OR MEANING
READING METHOD (HYPOTHETICAL EXAMPLE)[a]

Teacher A (Phonics)				Teacher B (Meaning)			
Student Number	Reading Achievement	Student Number	Reading Achievement	Student Number	Reading Achievement	Student Number	Reading Achievement
1	4.1	14	2.8	26	5.0	39	2.4
2	4.0	15	2.8	27	4.7	40	2.4
3	4.0	16	2.7	28	4.6	41	2.4
4	3.9	17	2.7	29	3.4	42	2.4
5	3.6	18	2.7	30	3.1	43	2.3
6	3.6	19	2.6	31	2.9	44	2.1
7	3.6	20	2.6	32	2.8	45	2.1
8	3.4	21	2.5	33	2.8	46	1.8
9	3.2	22	2.4	34	2.7	47	1.2
10	3.0	23	1.0	35	2.6	48	1.1
11	2.9	24	0.8	36	2.6	49	1.0
12	2.9	25	0.6	37	2.5	50	0.9
13	2.9			38	2.5		

[a]Grade equivalent scores are used in this example because most educators have a good sense of what they mean.
Because of their unique characteristics, a mean grade equivalent is not usually a meaningful number. Why a mean
grade equivalent is hard to interpret is explained in Chapter 5. The grade equivalent score as a norm is used in this
example to illustrate other ways to analyze and interpret results of a study.

signment process, each student initially had an equal chance of being assigned to
either class (and experiencing the instructional method used in that class).

The teachers agreed to spend the same amount of time on reading in the two
classrooms and to assign the same amount of homework each week. If the two
groups did not have equal time for reading, the students who spent more time
studying reading would be more likely to show higher reading achievement at the
end of the school year. This was a control for time as an alternative explanation
for differences between the two classes in reading achievement if it occurred at
the end of the year.

The teachers and principal also agreed to use the results of the reading subtests of the Metropolitan Achievement Test (MAT), which the school district
administers each May, as the primary measure of reading achievement. One reason for using the MAT is that it is a very reliable, objectively scored test of
reading competencies. At the end of the year, the 25 students in each class received the grade equivalent scores on the MAT reading subtest reported in Table
I.1.

Which group did better? This is an extremely complex question that can be
answered in a number of ways. How it is answered depends on the specific question the researcher wants to answer. There is no one "right" way to answer it.

The teachers and principal at Garfield School were interested in determining which type of basal text was best for their second-grade students. This determination can be made (as it usually is) by calculating the mean score for each class. The mean grade equivalent for students using phonics was 2.85, whereas that for the students using the meaning approach was 2.53. A test of statistical significance was used to find that the obtained difference of 0.32 grade equivalent (GE) was not significant. This means that overall the mean difference between the two groups is *not* large enough to say with confidence that the phonic method is better than the meaning method in teaching second-grade students to read.

Another way to think about this is that if a principal assigns 50 children to two groups by chance alone, it is likely that the mean reading scores for the two groups will differ by 0.32 GE or less by chance alone more than 80 to 90% of the time. The differences between the two groups would have to be larger (such as 0.50 GE or more) before we could be confident that the group differences obtained represented real differences in reading achievement between the two groups.

A second way to address the question of whether one method had a greater impact on the class as a whole is to count the number of children in each group who showed average or above average reading achievement for second-grade students. Since this is the ninth month of the school year, the expected score (or norm) would be 2.9 GEs. Thirteen (13) of the 25 students using phonics (52%) scored 2.9 or above. Only six (6) of the 25 students using the meaning approach (24%) scored at these levels. This seems to indicate that phonics would be a better method than the meaning method for the whole class.

But does that statement adequately describe the results of this study? Perhaps one method is better for the high ability students and the other is better for the low ability students. Which method is better for the majority of students in each group? Some other ways that these questions could be addressed in this study follow.

The three students with the highest reading achievement scores all used the meaning approach. They obtained mean MAT scores of 5.0, 4.7, and 4.6, whereas the highest score in the phonic approach class was 4.1. These scores seem to indicate that the meaning approach facilitates reading at the highest level. But these scores (5.0, 4.7, and 4.6) may have been earned by the three highest ability students in the second grade who, by chance, had all been assigned to the classroom using the meaning approach. These students might have done as well, or better, in the phonics classroom. More information would be needed in order to compare the effects of the two approaches on high ability students.

What about the students in either group who did not do well in reading? These students could be defined as scoring more than one grade equivalent below the expected score (or norm). There were three students in the phonics classroom (1.0, 0.8, and 0.6) and five in the meaning classroom (1.8, 1.2, 1.1, 1.0, and 0.9) who scored 1.8 or less. Are these students who could not gain much from the type of instructional approach that they experienced? Would they have done better in the other classroom? There is no way to know that from this study.

There are numerous other questions that people might have as they try to interpret the data in this study. For example:

1. Were the two teachers equally capable and effective with their students? (Always a difficult question to answer.)
2. Were the ability levels of the students in the two classrooms equivalent? (Not even random assignment assures equivalent groups in a study.)
3. Did the MAT equally test the reading skills taught in the two classrooms? (A norm-referenced test seldom does.)
4. Did the phonics group do better on some reading skills, and the meaning group do better on others? (The usual case in most studies.)

These are the kinds of questions that arise in any study. The results in the hypothetical example are typical of studies done in educational research. In fact, this example does not reflect some complexities that arise often in studies, such as: some students get sick or leave the district, one of the teachers is sick and away from her classroom for an extended period, some students are absent for more than 20 school days in a school year, students miss the day of district-wide testing, teachers (or bus drivers) go on strike, one classroom has asbestos removed, and so on. The so-called Murphy's Law seems to apply in all empirical studies: If something can happen, it will happen! In educational research, as in life, truth is often stranger than fiction.

The problems that arise in a study must be taken into account in order for the conclusions from research to be an accurate reflection of what occurred and to allow accurate conclusions to be drawn that are useful in other schools or districts. If the conclusions are not accurate, then the researchers, and readers of the study, will be misled about the effects of the two approaches and make decisions that may be harmful to students. Identifying other explanations (or causes) for the results obtained from a study is an essential element in determining the value of a study. At times these come from a person's experience in the type of situation studied, such as knowing that second-grade students (and teachers) vary greatly in their initial abilities or that some students are likely to be absent frequently. At other times they come from one's knowledge of research methods, such as the technical quality of the MAT as a test of second-grade reading, or the types of data analyses that could be done to answer specific research questions.

The essential point of this book, and a fundamental tenet of scientific research, is that there is no set of steps that a person can follow in every study that will assure its quality. Sir Karl Pearson (1937), who developed the Pearson Product Moment Correlation Coefficient (r), indicated that "the scientific method is one and the same in all branches and that method is the method of all logically trained minds" (p. 15). In a similar vein, P.W. Bridgeman (1944), a Nobel Laureate in physics, said "The scientific method, as far as it is a method, is nothing more than doing one's damnedest with one's mind, no holds barred" (p. 450). All possible explanations for the results of a study (both substantive and methodological) must be identified and systematically investigated with the information available.

Understanding and using the results of science, or empirical research, is essentially the same logical process as drawing conclusions in most other aspects of life. For example:

1. When should children be rewarded in order to facilitate learning?
2. Does reading to your child help the child become a reader?
3. Is the defendant in a trial guilty on the basis of evidence presented?
4. What new car would meet your needs and be your best investment?

There is no single piece of evidence that will allow you to answer any of these questions. For example, cost is certainly an important consideration in buying a car. But other considerations might be: (1) Will the car be used to entertain clients? (2) Will you ride long distances? (3) What is its history of durability? Many people naively expect a single piece of research to answer important educational questions. A study that is well done may provide valuable information, but it must be interpreted within the broad mosaic of previous research, theory, practical experience, and the unique characteristics of the setting in which it is applied.

What may be new to you as you study educational research are the many new terms used by researchers and the precision with which those terms are defined and used. Thinking about a student, your class, your school, your community, your job, or your family in the precise way required to study the many variables and their relationships in a specific situation may be a new experience. But do not conclude that understanding research is fundamentally different from trying to understand information relevant to teaching, administration, or raising a family. Precision is required in order to clarify the important variables or activities in any situation. Does increasing academic learning time increase achievement? Does positive reinforcement of students increase learning? Does positive reinforcement of teachers improve teaching? We cannot study these questions without defining precisely academic learning time, achievement, positive reinforcement, learning, teaching, and the context in which they are occurring.

It should be obvious that something as apparently simple as defining these terms may not be simple. For example, does academic learning time include periods when students stare out the window? Are they daydreaming or thinking about academic issues? Is a teacher's comment reinforcing or punishing for a particular student? Is achievement evidenced only by students' responses to norm-referenced tests?

To learn how to use the information available in research studies is complex, but much has been learned about gaining knowledge from studying the world in which we function. This book has been developed to facilitate your understanding of the research process and how knowledge is gained from research. The most encouraging point for you should be that you already understand the fundamental logic of drawing conclusions from available information.

The relative importance of the various methodological and substantive issues is determined by the researcher's specific purpose for doing a study or your purpose for reading a study. As purposes for reading or doing a study change, the relative importance of the characteristics of subjects in the study, measurement processes, research design considerations, and data analysis techniques will also change. How the purpose for a study and the context in which it is studied affects the procedures used and the conclusions that can be made from a study are central elements of research. In Chapter 10, the interrelationships among theory, empirical research, and practice in education are discussed. The main purpose of this final chapter is to show that, as Dewey indicated (1910), there is nothing more practical than a good theory. Studies of basic psychological research and associated changes in conceptions of the learning process (theory) have affected the curriculum, the structure of classrooms, and classroom furniture over time are used to illustrate the application of theory in practice.

To understand the central issues of educational research, particularly the interrelationships among theory, practice, and research, it would be valuable for you to know intimately the specific context and substance of each study used illustratively in this book. Given the specialized knowledge of professionals in education, each reader cannot be an expert in each area. Thus, a variety of examples drawn from concerns of teachers, principals, supervisors, superintendents, school boards, as well as some from various disciplines, are used to illustrate fundamental concepts. It is important to recognize in each study both the substantive and methodological issues because both are always important in drawing legitimate conclusions from research. Keep in mind that the importance of each methodological procedure used in a study changes when you attempt to use the results in your specific context. As you become a more knowledgeable reader and user of educational research, the artificial distinction between substantive and methodological issues will disappear, because the central concerns in educational research are all fundamentally logical and are based on the applicability of theories and models about human beings and their behavior to new situations that have not been studied.

REFERENCES

Bridgeman, P.W. (1944). Logic of modern physics, *Yale Review 34*, 444–461.
Dewey, John (1910). *How we think*. Boston: Heath.
Mill, John Stuart (1906). *A system of logic*, Vol. 1, London: Longman Green.
Pearson, Karl (1937), *The grammar of science*. London: J.M. Dent.

CHAPTER 1

Philosophical Foundations of Knowledge

How do we know when something is true or when it is false? When we were children, this was a relatively simple question. Our parents, religious leaders, books, newspapers, radio, and television were our sources of "truth." As we grew older, we often disagreed with our parents or religious leaders. Radio and television commentators and newspapers were often blatantly wrong or reported errors. What sources of knowledge can be trusted? How do human beings gain knowledge about the world and how to succeed in it?

Philosophers and other scholars and leaders have searched for knowledge about life from the beginning of human existence. At each period of history, despite minority views, general agreement is reached within a society about what knowledge or truth is and how to reach it. But the nature of knowledge and the methods of gaining it continue to be studied. To understand the methods of science and research used today and the nature of the knowledge that is produced, we must be aware of the methods that have been used in the past. These methods have produced not only the knowledge that leeches will cure most illnesses but also that the sun is at the center of our galaxy and that a certain amount of thrust is needed by a rocket to escape the Earth's gravity.

The primary lesson to be learned from this material is that scholars' conceptions of the world and the rules of evidence for "legitimate" interpretation of information have changed over time and will continue to change. What some may perceive as truth at a particular time, such as the use of leeches or the concept of IQ, is simply present knowledge that is subject to change as new information is gained and new theories and models are developed. To understand and use research, you must be aware of the assumptions that are being made about both the nature of human beings and how we learn, as well as the methods used to gather, analyze, and interpret data.

When present theories are taught as if they are absolute truth, as some supporters of B. F. Skinner and his theory of behavior modification often do, that is because they assume that their present view of man and research methods is final. The following overview of changes in the philosophy of science and their associated epistemologies should convince you that we will continue to learn about the inadequacies of both our present approaches to science and our present knowledge of human beings. Better models and theories will be developed, but will we ever arrive at truth empirically?

CHANGING EPISTEMOLOGICAL PERSPECTIVES

When culture was flourishing in Greece, and before Plato, the Sophists were the scholars who educated the Greek nobles (circa 500 B.C.). Their method of disputation, which questioned everything, required persons to defend their ideas using whatever logic, experience, or debating skill that would support these ideas. The Sophists treated knowledge as relative—that is, "What is true for you is true for you; what is true for me, is true for me." Without some agreed-on method to arrive at truth (knowledge), only such relative truth is possible.

Plato (428–348 B.C.) and his followers viewed human sensations as unstable and unreliable as sources of knowledge. Plato believed in the eternal unchanging nature of ideas, or forms, which are accessible to the mind. The Platonic seeker of truth believes that human beings are born with a predetermined classification of ideas. All that physical sensations can do is remind the seeker of what the soul, or mind, already knows. Thus, Plato describes Socrates leading an uneducated slave to advanced mathematical concepts—leading him without instructing him. By asking specific questions and forcing the boy to examine and correlate his answers, the boy comes to accurate conclusions because this knowledge already exists in all human beings.

Aristotle (384–322 B.C.), Plato's most famous student, did not agree that the world is radically divided between idea and sense. He believed in one reality stretching between the ground of possibility and the apex of actuality. Aristotelian reality insists that the physical world merits investigation. The realist assumes that the world operates on fixed natural laws, which will be discovered by observation and reason. Theory becomes the highest level of knowledge.

The philosophical school that combined the idealism of Plato with the realism of Aristotle is *rationalism*. The rationalist uses deduction from fundamental truths through formal operations to specific conclusions. The operations are based on formal logic and mathematics, but all knowledge must be verified by empirical data from our experiences.

The *empiricists*, such as Francis Bacon (1561–1626) and John Locke (1632–1704), revolted against rationalism, viewing the purely sensory, empirical information that we get from the world as most important for gaining knowledge. The empiricists use inductive methods to develop generalizations from specific sensory data. Rather than using formal logic or mathematical operations, they use human judgment to transform raw data into knowledge.

An apocryphal story that represents the role that the rules of evidence play in gaining knowledge at any particular time describes a meeting of a society of scholars such as the idealists who distrust the senses, or experience, for gaining knowledge. An argument about the number of teeth in a horse's mouth breaks out. When one neophyte recommends that they bring a horse to the meeting and count the horse's teeth, he is thrown out of the society as an incompetent. The neophyte had not accepted the sources of knowledge and rules of evidence that these scholars had agreed best represented "true" knowledge.

At each point in time, researchers and scholars who study a problem from a particular perspective will agree on the sources of knowledge and rules of evidence that are legitimate. The basis for their agreement becomes their philosophy, or philosophy of science. The specific assumptions and detailed rules of evidence of these historical positions are beyond the scope of this book. What you should gain from the study of this book is the assumptions and rules of evidence held by present researchers, so that you can read research critically and improve the quality of education.

The position generally accepted today between rationalism and empiricism was developed initially by Emanuel Kant in *The Critique of Pure Reason* (1787). It strikes a balance between radical empiricism, in which knowledge is generated only by inductive processes from experience, and radical rationalism, which distrusts human senses and uses only formal logic and reason to gain knowledge.

In the past 3,000 years, but particularly over the past 300 years, many changes have occurred in the sources and methods for producing knowledge. Such changes will continue to occur. Thus, we must realize that the knowledge ("truths") we have today will be modified or discarded in the next 300 years, if not sooner.

Each of these positions conceptualizes the world and human beings in different ways. To understand and recognize the philosophical or epistemological foundations of research about the human condition, you must identify the following characteristics. Information is meaningful only in a context of:

1. Assumptions about the source of knowledge (reason, experience, other).
2. Theories or models that describe the human condition studied.
3. Assumptions required by the theories, models, and methods used.
4. Agreed-on methods to collect and analyze information to arrive at conclusions (e.g., mathematics, human judgment, or observation).

The goal of an educated person is to gain understanding of the assumptions, methods, and theories that provide the foundation for whatever knowledge we produce or use.

POSITIVISM, PHENOMENOLOGY, AND HERMENEUTICS

People continue to differ in their views of the nature of knowledge, the sources of that knowledge, and ways to assess the validity or legitimacy of knowledge. The sources of knowledge may be viewed differently by a researcher or educator in different situations. For example, the nature of reading or math achievement may be viewed as "real" in some sense and can be measured with multiple choice test items. In contrast, a driver's avoidance response to a blowing tumbleweed is *not* based on the reality of a harmful object on the road but on the nature of that person's experience of the tumbleweed or on the meaning the person gives to that experience. The driver's previous experience had been that only solid objects, such as rocks or boxes, were on roads and did not include a basis for understanding that a tumbleweed was not a solid object.

In many situations, researchers assume the existence of some variables, such as reading skills, and attempt to measure them in reasonable ways. In other situations, they attempt to describe the nature of experiences that they had or the meaning they give to a situation. The first illustrates realistic studies; the second represents interpretive studies. Realistic studies use an appropriate set of theories, methods, and underlying assumptions. Similarly, interpretive studies use a different set of theories, methods, and underlying assumptions. In the two situations, these are based on different fundamental assumptions and views of the world that are called *philosophies*. Three philosophies that have particular relevance to research methodology today are positivism, phenomenology, and hermeneutics. A discussion of each follows.

A fundamental tenet of *positivism* is: "If something exists, it exists in a quantity and we can measure it." To most of us this is entirely reasonable. If we cannot measure it with any accuracy, how can we relate it to other variables and how can it be included in theories? In this way, a clear demarcation is made between science and metaphysics. Positivists view researchers as objective observers of events that occur in the universe and on which the researchers have no impact.

An experiment in a laboratory with a pigeon in a Skinner box is an example of such an ideal. The only variation in the pigeon's experience is the stimulus that the experimenter controls and the reinforcement (such as food) that is delivered automatically when the pigeon makes the correct response. It may be set up to record all responses and reinforcements electronically so that no human being is ever involved.

Many positivists view the variables they are studying as truly existing in the universe. The relationships they "discover" have always been there. This perspective is the reason the philosophy is called positivism. Positivism, in its most fundamental sense, assumes "not only that there is an external world, but (also) that the external world itself determines absolutely the one and only correct view that can be taken of it, independent of the process or circumstances of viewing" (Kirk & Miller, 1986, p. 14).

Logical positivists view knowledge as only those statements of belief or fact that can be tested empirically—that can be confirmed, or verified, or disconfirmed. Logical positivists assume that variables in the human sciences can be expressed in physical terms such as those used by the natural sciences. This usually leads to breaking aspects of human life that are studied into component parts. For example, reading is made up of vocabulary, grammar, spelling, and comprehension; or a principal's role includes administration, communication, academic leadership, and interpersonal skills. This raises the question of the whole being more than the sum of the parts, such that analyzing anything into its component parts essentially destroys it.

Much has been learned from analytical procedures in the natural and physical sciences as well as in education and psychology. Classifying plants, insects, and animals on the basis of the shapes of their leaves, the number of legs or body segments, or their methods of reproduction has helped to produce much valuable knowledge about plants, insects, animals, and other natural entities.

Physicists and chemists have assumed that chemicals, masses, and forces represent actual things that exist in the universe, and they study them. They develop new ceramic materials that conduct electricity, new rockets to power human beings to the Moon and beyond, microwave ovens to heat our food.

Psychologists have clarified how human beings think, remember, make decisions, and learn. Educational researchers have developed more effective ways to teach reading and math knowledge and skills. Most of our present knowledge is based on nomothetic and analytical methods and procedures. Many educational researchers and social scientists question the validity and value of the positivist's perspective when these theories and assumptions are applied to such human behavior as reading achievement, attitudes, interpersonal relationships, and the meaning that people attribute to their experiences. When scientists study nuclear physics, similar questions arise. Two interesting books, *The Tao of Physics* (Capra, 1975) and *The Dancing Wu Li Masters* (Zukav, 1979), relate issues of nuclear physics to Eastern philosophies, which are not positivistic. How these conflicting perspectives are presently represented in research is discussed at the end of this section of the book.

Phenomenologists use human thinking, feeling, perceiving, and other mental and physiological acts to describe and understand human experiences. To understand the nature of the human experience we must study that experience itself and not an objective external world. A fundamental assumption is that human experiences can be catalogued and described in order to learn how we get meaning from our experiences. Edmund Husserl (1858–1938), who founded this philosophy, called these appearances in our conscious mind "phenomena." Their study is called phenomenology.

To study a phenomenon, researchers must "bracket" all their ideas and theories related to the phenomenon in an attempt to be unbiased reflectors of the human experience. The experience studied is compared with other experiences, real or imagined, to identify the essential features of the phenomenon, such as "red," "horse," "love," "clinical transference," or "learning." These features can be compared with those of other phenomenologists who have been as rigorous in their analysis of the experience, so that basic elements of the experience that are common to members of a specific society, or all human beings, can be identified.

This last point is essential to understanding the philosophical basis of phenomenology, yet it is often misunderstood. On the one hand, each person has a unique set of experiences, which are treated as truth and which determine that individual's behavior. In this sense, truth (and associated behavior) is totally unique to each individual. For example, an experienced driver drives over a tumbleweed on a southwestern highway, but a naive driver swerves to avoid this "solid" object. Some researchers are misled to think that they are using a phenomenological perspective when they study four teachers and describe their four unique views. A phenomenologist assumes a commonality in those human experiences and must use rigorously the method of bracketing to search for those commonalities. Results obtained from a phenomenological study can then be related to and integrated with those of other phenomenologists studying the same experience, or phenomenon. Existential phenomenologists best represent this philosophical position.

Phenomenologists and positivists have a similar goal in the sense that information must be generated in a way that allows both the quality of the study to be assessed and various studies to be analyzed and synthesized so that agreements are reached about legitimate conclusions. The major difference is that the phenomenologist believes that the important aspects of human existence occur within the human mind (an idealist), whereas the positivist believes that knowledge exists primarily outside the human—as observed by an objective, analytical observer (a realist).

A second group of researchers who make the phenomenological assumption that truth lies within the human experience rather than an external, positivistic world and who carry out interpretive rather than realistic studies are phenomenological sociologists and ethnomethodologists. They believe that social sciences are idiographic, rather than nomothetic, and should produce individualized conceptions of social phenomena and personal assertions rather than generalization and verification.

Alfred Schutz (1977) indicated that "the exploration of the general principles according to which man in daily life organizes his experiences, and especially those of the social world, is the first task of the methodology of the social sciences" (p. 233). He assumed that the person who does something is the only one who "knows what he does, why he does it, and when and where his actions start and end" (p. 234). The researcher who studies a number of people in the same situation, such as parents of second-grade children using an innovative math curriculum, may have some ways of organizing their experiences that are similar to others and some that are unique to themselves. From this perspective, both should be important to social scientists, such as educational researchers, as they study this setting.

Ethnomethodologists hold similar views and make essentially the same assumptions about the sources of knowledge and methods for gaining meaningful knowledge. In studies of human decision-making, such as coding data into various categories, Garfinkel (1967) and others were not concerned with the consistency of the coding but with the various ways in which the coders interpreted the coding "rules." They found that such interpretations can be characterized as "et cetera," "let it pass," "unless," and others. These classifications are typical of categories found in such phenomenological studies when people have to make categorical decisions. They are attempts by individuals to organize their experiences by using general principles, and they inform us about human behavior.

These researchers are not concerned with the external world but with the person's experience of that world. They are not concerned with producing generalizable theories but with useful descriptions of individuals' responses to social situations or tasks. The extent to which these studies are truly phenomenological and do provide generalizable models or descriptions are not clear. More information about how these perspectives are presently implemented follows the hermeneutic perspective.

Hermeneutic philosophy, developed by Wilhelm Dilthey and other German philosophers (Rickman, 1979), is the study of interpretive understanding, or meaning. The Greeks initially developed a technique for interpreting legends and other texts that they called *hermeneutics* (Kneller, 1984). Others have used it to interpret the Christian Bible or for applying laws in legal cases (Dallmayr & McCarthy, 1977).

To interpret text it is necessary to understand what the author was attempting to communicate in the text. Historians must know the intended meaning of text when they read documents centuries old from very different cultures. We are all aware that words used by Englishmen in 1450 do not always mean the same thing today—in England or the United States. Dilthey used the phrase "empathic understanding" to describe this process (Rickman, 1967).

The interpretive understanding of hermeneutics usually comes from delineating and interpreting the conditions under which it was produced. More generally, hermeneutic studies interpret the meaning of something from a certain standpoint or situation. Kneller (1984) identified the following hermeneutic themes as they relate to interpretation of meaning more generally:

1. Understanding a human act or product, and hence all learning, is like interpreting a text.
2. All interpretation occurs within a tradition.
3. Interpretation involves opening myself to a text (or its analogue) and questioning it.
4. I must interpret a text in the light of my situation. (p. 68)

As in phenomenology and positivism, hermeneutic studies are done in a rigorous way using methods that are accepted by others who do the same type of research, or scholarship. If this is not done, there is no way to combine, or integrate, the work of various researchers to gain knowledge. It is this agreement on method that primarily differentiates science from the humanities as ways of understanding the world.

Several hermeneutic studies of the same context, such as teaching-learning processes in second-grade classes or the clinical supervision movement, could be carried out from the perspectives of various traditions. In a similar manner, these same situations could be studied from the perspectives of various disciplines, such as sociology, psychology, and economics. Neither of these sets of results could necessarily be synthesized. They are various interpretations, or descriptions, of the same setting. When researchers begin with different theories or assumptions, their work is often uninterpretable to researchers who use other theories or assumptions. Knowledge exists within the particular philosophy, theory, method, and assumptions used to gain that knowledge.

All knowledge is based on preconceived notions about the nature of the universe and those aspects that are most relevant to the present situation. The positivist, phenomenologist, and hermeneutist differ on a number of fundamental assumptions. Similarly, three psychologists, each of whom is a positivist, will observe different behaviors in a classroom because they have different theories of how children learn: one believes in Skinner's behavior modification approach, another believes in Piagetian theory, and the third believes in discovery learning based on the work of Hebb (1949) and Berlyne (1960). To demonstrate how differences among the three philosophies affect educational research an example follows.

STUDYING AN EDUCATIONAL INNOVATION

School districts across the nation, if not the world, need better ways to educate children. Periodically, one or more innovations are identified and widely adopted. One such innovation is the Madeline Hunter Model. If researchers from the different philosophical positions were to study this innovation, what might each do?

A positivist would focus on objective ways to measure important aspects of the model and associated changes in educational processes and outcomes. These could include the number of teachers and children in a school district who are affected by it. They could include the changes in the number of personnel or the types of roles teachers, supervisors, and others carry out, as well as the impact of the model on teacher and student behavior. These changes would include both instructional processes and academic achievement, which would be measured by methods that are as objective as possible. These measures would analyze both the educational processes and achievement outcomes into component parts, such as time spent on each topic, questions asked by the teacher, and the amount of lecture, demonstration, seatwork, and homework as components of educational processes.

An existential phenomenologist might use this context to study the human experience of "change" as it occurs in the lives of these teachers but would not study how the teachers experience the Madeline Hunter Model because that has no meaningful generality to the lives of other human beings. In all likelihood that model will be gone in 10 or 20 years and other educational models will replace it. Reactions of various teachers to the change experience would be categorized and combined, using the method of bracketing to minimize the researchers' biases.

A phenomenological sociologist, or ethnomethodologist, might study how the various teachers implement the model, particularly how they vary in their educational decisions on the basis of the "rules" of this model—much as the coders varied in their use of coding rules. The various "lessons" that students learn as they study the same texts, or work under the same instructional approach, would be other possible interpretive studies that such researchers might study.

Hermeneutic studies are often similar to those of social phenomenologists. They want to know what meaning people attribute to activities, such as those required by the Madeline Hunter Model, and how that relates to their behavior. These researchers are much clearer about the fact that they are *constructing* the "reality" on the basis of their interpretations of data with the help of the participants who provided the data in the study. They often carry out their research much as anthropologists do in their studies of culture. They do a great deal of observation, read documents produced or read by members of the groups being studied, do extensive formal and informal interviewing, and develop classifications and descriptions that represent the beliefs of the various groups.

For example, in a study of teacher reactions to the Madeline Hunter Model, Garman and Hazi (1988) identified eight types of teachers. These include "zealot, enthusiast, game player, passive skeptic, having second thoughts, dissident, early retiree, and malcontent." Their primary purpose was to describe the teacher responses to the model and to articulate the significant education issues and dilemmas that relate to it. This allows the construction of various scenarios of likely future outcomes under various conditions, such as alternative policies that administrators might implement. These scenarios can be particularly valuable to administrators who must decide on policies to use when implementing this or other innovations. If other researchers had different backgrounds, used different methods, or had different purposes, they would likely develop different types of teacher reactions, focus on different aspects of the setting, and develop somewhat different scenarios.

Hermeneutists also believe that social science should not be nomothetic but should provide individualized accounts of a situation in ways that describe the meaning of events to the participants. This cannot be done without a thorough knowledge of the backgrounds of the participants and the contexts in which they exist. Different researchers will emphasize different aspects of those very complex settings that will have somewhat unique results. That is one sense in which the reality is constructed by the researcher and why such studies are called *interpretive*.

The foregoing description of the various philosophical perspectives and the related studies and methods was developed to differentiate the major positions

and their approaches to educational research. As a result, it is somewhat misleading and does not accurately describe research practices of educational researchers or of social scientists in general. Those who work primarily from a positivist
framework also endorse more qualitative and context-embedded interpretive inquiry, whereas no social phenomenologist, ethnomethodologist, or other interpretive sociologist conducts research that is purely interpretive. For example, in
establishing the validity of their constructs, they use procedures that are as systematic and verified empirically as the most positivistic (Miles & Huberman,
1984). Thus, we should think of educational research practices as falling along a
continuum from purely realistic to purely idealistic. Little, if any, research today
rests fully at either end but is a combination of activities each of which falls at
various positions along the continuum.

Another way to think about the relationships among positivism, phenomenology, and hermeneutics is called the table tennis analogy (Singleton, personal
comm.). The positivist and phenomenologist are the two players at each end of
the table; the hermeneutist is represented by the Ping-Pong ball that passes back
and forth between the two players. At times it is difficult to differentiate the
hermeneutist from the positivist, and at other times the hermeneutist is somewhat like the phenomenologist. For more extensive dicussions of these issues, see
Jacobs (1987), McCutchan (1981), and Dallmayr and McCarthy (1977).

IDEALISTS, REALISTS, AND PRAGMATISTS

What exists in the world and what human beings can know about it has been an
ongoing concern of scholars. The idealists took the position that nothing exists in
the absence of someone perceiving it. The issue about whether a tree falling in
the forest makes any noise if no one is there to hear it may seem silly to us today.
Yet, can we ever answer it?

The realists certainly assume that objects exist in the universe but also that
we can never know the essence of those objects. Since 1950, major changes in
theories about the nature of matter have been made. Einstein's theory of relativity was specified in the early 1900s, although little of everyday knowledge today
takes into account his theory of relativity that specifies relationships among mass,
speed, and time. The knowledge about the fundamental composition of matter,
such as a chair or any other physical object, is undergoing continuing change.

It is important to remember that experience does not show us things as they
are. The pictures and feelings in our brain that are triggered by the appearance
of stimuli in nature are constructed from *a priori* structures of theories and language. When we see a wall or an orange, do we know what it is naturally? Most
of us think that we do. In fact, we must have learned the concepts "orange" and
"wall" to interpret and name the stimuli we experience. That is what happens
through any learning process.

Young (1960) described the experiences of people who were blind from
birth and had operations as adults that made their eyes functional. You might

assume that when their eyes became physiologically normal they would see "naturally." In fact, their first response to the new stimuli was one of pain caused by a spinning mass of light and color stimulation that was meaningless to them. With no conception of space that contains objects, these people required a great deal of time to learn to use their eyes. Young reported that such persons could identify familiar objects, such as an orange or a banana, by touch but not through sight alone. Many patients refused to try to use their sight. They had no concepts, or rules, that allowed them to interpret the visual stimuli. Young stated that:

> ... if you can convince him that it is worthwhile, then, after weeks of practice he will name simple objects by sight. At first they must be seen always in the same color and the same angle. One man having learned to name an egg, a potato, and a cube of sugar when he saw them, could not do it when they were put in a yellow light. The lump of sugar was named when on the table, but not when hung in the air with a thread. However, such people can gradually learn; if sufficiently encouraged they may after some years develop a full visual life and be able even to read. (p. 63)

It should be clear that seeing (perceiving) is not an automatic, or natural, process by which whatever exists in the world is translated directly into our minds. The theories, models, and ideologies we believe in, even our religion, affect how we define what we perceive. That is one reason the work of a single researcher making observations in a study is often questioned.

The relationship between knowledge and reality (truth) that is used by many researchers today is that of the pragmatist. John Dewey (1910) was a principal spokesman for this position, which states that all knowledge is produced by human beings and that we can never distinguish between knowledge and truth. In empirical research, this means that if something works in practice then it is true, or we assume that it is true. A truth (knowledge) that is not supported by further empirical study will be modified or discarded.

WAYS OF KNOWING

Why are most public schools in the United States open from September through May? On what basis does a teacher decide how to teach an adult to read? How does an engineer decide on the supports needed for a bridge? In general, schools are open at that time because that is the way it has been done in the past (tradition). Most teaching decisions are based on educational theories and experience. An engineer decides on supports on the basis of controlled trials of materials and designs that test how much weight they will support (systematic study).

These are somewhat simplistic examples of three "ways of knowing" that help clarify the basis on which people draw conclusions, or make decisions. They are as follows:

1. Tradition, or appeal to authority.
2. Personal experience.
3. Systematic study (research).

The primary reason to identify these three ways of knowing is to clarify the basis on which conclusions are drawn. Tradition represents situations in which conclusions are based on evidence that has not been examined critically. Continuing to do something, such as holding school from September through May, because that is the way "it has always been done" is drawing conclusions, or making decisions, based on tradition. Accepting an author's statements or unsubstantiated theories as true are appeals to authority, which are acts of faith, believing in the truth or value of something with no critical examination of the evidence.

Personal experience as a way of knowing uses evidence from the world, but it is anecdotal rather than systematic information. What particular teacher or administrator "learns" from experience is usually idiosyncratic to that individual and her or his unique experiences. The likelihood for being misled is great, in part because of the selective perceptions of all human beings. The particular dimensions, or aspects, of a situation that a person attends will be unique to that individual.

Systematic study, which requires the systematic collection of information (data) from the world, is an attempt to describe this world of ours as best we can. Such study does not result in truth, but when done well it should produce information that can be interpreted with some degree of confidence.

I want you to distinguish the ways of knowing something on the basis of the types of evidence used to draw conclusions, or to make decisions, in a specific situation. By distinguishing among these three types of evidence, we can examine the basis for a conclusion, more easily identify likely sources of error, and make necessary changes more easily as new evidence is obtained. The following example illustrates differences among these three ways of knowing.

When choosing a math curriculum that would be best for the district, a superintendent of schools usually assigns a committee of math teachers and other relevant people to make a recommendation. The committee reviews the materials carefully. They may even ask other teachers to rate each curriculum on a number of characteristics and to vote for the one that would be best for their students. After a thorough assessment, the committee makes a recommendation.

What is that recommendation based on? The recommendation was based primarily on tradition, in the sense that these teachers hold unexamined beliefs about what a "good math curriculum" should contain and on their experiences as math teachers in their district. There was no empirical evidence that one curriculum was more effective with children in their school district (or in any other). Thus, the decision was based primarily on the model of a "good math curriculum" (authority) and their anecdotal experience. The method of systematic empirical study, or science, was not used.

Tradition

Tradition, or appeal to authority, as a way of knowing is the use of tradition, common sense, a model, or other unexamined acceptance of a person's pronouncements, such as those of a teacher, parent, friend, or counselor. For example, Ann Scoville never placed coats on a bed because her parents never allowed it. The reason, which she had never known, was that her grandfather had gotten lice when he was five years old when a coat was thrown on a bed. When the reason for doing something is no longer known, the people who continue to act by the rule are doing it on the basis of tradition. Another example is continuing to hold school only from September through May. Students are at home June through August, even though we are no longer an agrarian society. Many things continue long after there is any good reason for them. The basis for continuing them is classified as tradition because it is essentially an unexamined acceptance of something.

In making decisions, or drawing conclusions, one of the weakest logical foundations for doing anything is an appeal to authority. Just because someone of authority states that a multiple choice test is better than an essay test does not mean that it is true in your situation. You can find almost anything in print if you look long enough. For example, Linus Pauling, a Nobel Laureate in chemistry, has been extolling for years the virtues of large doses of Vitamin C for minimizing the effects of the common cold. Nearly every study of Vitamin C has shown no effects on colds. People who take large doses of Vitamin C for a cold are doing it exclusively on the basis of authority.

Personal Experience

Personal experience as a way of knowing is defined as a personal, internal revelation. Each of us has revelations every day as we come to conclusions about (or classify) people we meet for the first time, or as we gain knowledge from our professional experience. An example of the latter might be a principal who is responsible for implementing a new program in the school. The principal holds some meetings with teachers and may even have formal training sessions, over the year experiencing various problems that arise, identifying responses that work (and those that do not work), and drawing conclusions about which activities or variables are important to the successful implementation of such a program. All these conclusions are based on personal experience, because no information was collected systematically, only anecdotally (what was remembered of experience).

If the principal had systematically varied alternative activities and measured the outcomes as systematically and objectively as possible, the conclusions based on those data would be more believable. Principals rarely have the time, resources, and inclination to do such investigations, however, so that most of their decisions are based on tradition/authority or personal experience.

Systematic Study

Systematic study, or research, is defined as the systematic collection of information to describe as accurately as possible some aspect of our world. Some persons would require that the data collection be objective and have no logical flaws. That is certainly the ideal, but no perfect piece of research has been done in the past, and it is unlikely that any will be produced in the future. We are incapable of producing truth, only knowledge.

Surveys of American attitudes toward either sex education or the performance of the U.S. president are examples of research, as are tightly controlled laboratory experiments with rats or college sophomores. Each empirical study has particular strengths and weaknesses. Even though a study may be poorly done, with logical problems in the conclusions that are drawn, it is still based on systematic study *as a way of knowing*. The data represent, to a greater or lesser degree, aspects of our world.

Every study requires detailed assessment of the procedures used in that study in order to assess the accuracy of the conclusions and their applicability in other settings. The remainder of this book deals with issues and methods that affect the quality of a study and the confidence one should have in conclusions that are reached from empirical research.

In any profession, conclusions must be drawn and decisions made on the basis of all three types of knowledge. Being able to distinguish among the three ways of knowing that we have described is a tool to use in deciding which theories, models, or ideas should be most valuable in a particular situation. Identifying and assessing the evidence and the logic on which it is based are essential to becoming expert in a field. We will never have the necessary knowledge based totally on research and will always use knowledge based on tradition/authority and personal experience. We must recognize the basis of whatever theories, models, or other beliefs that we use so that we minimize the degree to which we fool ourselves.

THEORY IN EDUCATION

The theories, models, and laws that exist in any field provide the framework that enables practitioners to think and communicate with one another. The concepts that we use every day, such as height, weight, intelligence, achievement, speed, and velocity, exist because they fit into some broader theory or schematic that we use to structure our world. When several educators view the same classroom, one sees "on-task" and "off-task" behavior, another sees "rewards" and "punishment," and another sees "coercion" and "self-actualization." Are they seeing different things, or do they use different theories to understand important classroom activities? Perhaps some of each.

In 1936 Albert Einstein wrote:

Physical concepts are free creations of the human mind, and are not, however it may seem, uniquely determined by the external world. In our endeavor to understand reality we are somewhat like a man trying to understand the mechanism of a closed watch. He sees the face and the moving hands, even hears it ticking, but he has no way of opening the case. If he is ingenious he may form some picture of a mechansim which could be responsible for all the things he observes, but he may never be quite sure his picture is the only one which could explain his observations. He will never be able to compare his picture with the real mechanism and he cannot even imagine the possibility of the meaning of such a comparison. (p. 221)

The pictures that an ingenious researcher develops is usually in the form of a theory, or model. A *theory* is a general explanation of the relationships among several variables that are applicable in a variety of settings. Numerous theories of learning have developed over the past 50 years. Thorndike (1903) developed transfer of training perspective about education on the basis of associative learning theory. This changed educators' and psychologists' view of the brain as a muscle to be exercised to that of associating activities to outcomes. This had profound effects on education. At approximately the same time Pavlov (1927), a Russian scientist, showed that a dog could be trained to salivate to the sound of a bell by associating it with food. This began the stimulus-response, or S–R, theory that Watson (1930) and Skinner (1953) modified into what is now called operant conditioning and behavior modification. This theory has a system of assumptions about the human being, accepted principles, and rules of acceptable procedures to study and explain human behavior. Other researchers and theorists have developed various cognitive theories of learning that focus on the internal operation of the human mind. For example, a central tenet in the open-classroom approach to education is that the learner is an innately curious organism who will learn those things that are needed in order to function effectively. These three perspectives—S–R theory, operant conditioning, and cognitive theories—vary greatly in their specificity and development, but all are used by researchers and practitioners to describe and understand human behavior.

A *model* is a description of a phenomenon or theory that accounts for the important properties in a specific setting. The Bohr model of a hydrogen atom with a "solid" nucleus and an electron traveling around it, much as a planet travels around the sun, is a typical physics model. Models of the steps that people go through to solve a problem have been developed to describe problem solving (Kendler & Kendler, 1962).

As with many terms in research, each author may use a somewhat different definition for the terms theory and model. The definitions presented here are fairly broad so that they include the various ways that these terms are used by researchers. These definitions were chosen to help you understand (1) how they are used in research, and (2) why it is important that research be conceptualized concretely from approriate theories or models.

The last point should be clearer if you keep in mind that the theories and models we carry around in our heads are used to describe and understand what goes on around us. It is no less true of teachers, supervisors, principals, superintendents, and other educations as they perform their professional roles. If research does not address the many variables they think are important, in ways that help them form more accurate theories and models, then research is likely to produce little of practical value.

A researcher who wants to study educational problems of poor and minority students must know thoroughly the various theories of learning that others have used before deciding which theory (or theories) appears to be most promising for these kinds of students with the types of problems to be studied. The specific theory or model that a researcher uses to conceptualize a study is determined by the purpose for the study and the value of the theory or model in facilitating a better understanding of that situation.

All theories and models are based on fundamental assumptions. A theory can be applied only if those fundamental assumptions are met in the situation studied. For example, B.F. Skinner's behavior modification assumes that only observable behavior can be used to build a science of human behavior, and that internal states of a human being, such as motivation, values, religion, or cognitive knowledge, do not need to be addressed. Many educators do not agree with that assumption and choose not to use that theory. It is probably no accident that behavior modification models work best on animals and in other situations where the effects of mediating variables may be relatively low.

Without a clear understanding of the theory or model that is used in a study, it is often difficult to identify the assumptions that are required in order for the conclusions of the study to be accurate. In areas where the reader has a great deal of knowledge and experience, it is relatively easy to identify the assumptions that must be met before the results can be used in that setting.

For example, in comparing the effects of a phonic to a meaning curriculum for teaching reading in grade one, it is important that a wide range of reading skills be assessed. Because the two types of curricula make some different assumptions about how human beings learn to read most effectively, a study that looks only at letter knowledge and decoding skills (which are emphasized in phonic curricula) will be biased and misleading. The effects of a decoding emphasis on vocabulary and other reading comprehension skills that are viewed from a meaning perspective as more important outcomes of reading instruction are not well documented at present. When these issues concerning the assumptions made by each approach are clarified, it becomes easier to study them or to learn from past research results.

These are examples of the types of assumptions, methods, and theories that were listed in the first section of this chapter as essential to understanding and using empirical research. Given that theories, variables, and related information are essentially created rather than discovered, it is important to understand that the interpretation of all data is inherently subjective. Even in the "hardest" sciences, such as physics and chemistry, the conclusions drawn from any study depend on the extent to which the assumptions of both the theory and the methods used accurately reflect the situation being studied. In applying results of studies to *new* situations, the extent to which the assumptions are met may be even more problematic.

SUMMARY

Scholars' conceptions of the world and the rules of evidence for producing defensible knowledge have changed over time and will continue to change in the future. Knowledge of education exists within a context of (1) assumptions about sources of knowledge, (2) theories that describe the human condition, (3) methods to collect and analyze information, and (4) assumptions required by the theories or methods.

For the past 50 years or more the prevalent philosophical perspective has been positivism with emphasis on objective, quantifiable data. Some educational research is now being done from phenomenological and hermeneutic perspectives using more qualitative methods and interpretive studies. These two groups differ in the extent to which they assume that something exists in the world (positivism), or that its meaning resides in the human experience of it (phenomenology) or the meaning they attach to it (hermeneutics).

Three ways that human beings believe that something is true are tradition (authority), personal experience, or systematic study (research). The evidence on which a belief is based affects the confidence that we can have of its applicability in our setting. All three ways of knowing will continue to be used. It is important that you know the basis of the beliefs (or knowledge) that you use.

Past knowledge and experience are often creatively used to develop theories about the relationships among important variables in a setting. Each of us uses such theories—often unknowingly—to think about and organize our world and our experiences in it. Such theories are "free creations of the human mind" that require numerous assumptions in order to be used in a specific setting. We must recognize both the theories (or models) we use and the assumptions that they require in a particular situation.

In Chapter 2 science is defined, and essential characteristics of the scientific method are discussed. Ethical principles and procedures for carrying out educational research are delineated. An overview of the research process, as it is presented in Chapters 3 to 8, is also presented.

SUGGESTED ACTIVITIES

1. Review an issue of the two most commonly used journals in your field that include research studies.
   a. Indicate the proportion of articles in each journal that are based on systematically collected and analyzed empirical information (data).

  b. Characterize the nature of the other articles in terms of personal experi-
     ence or tradition/authority as the basis for the conclusion or suggestions in
     those articles.
2. Review a research article in your area of specialization.
  a. Identify the theoretical or conceptual framework that the author used to
     identify the variables that are included in the study.
  b. Identify the discipline base in which that framework has been developed.
     If no framework is indicated by the author, what seems to be the
     framework?
  c. What basic assumptions are made by the researcher? Do they represent the
     philosophy of positivism, phenomenology, or hermeneutics?

RELATED SOURCES

Dallmayr, F.R., & McCarthy, T.A. (Eds.). (1977). *Understanding and social inquiry*. Notre
     Dame, IN: University of Notre Dame Press.
     The editors of this book of readings have compiled fundamental articles on the prob-
lem of *Verstehen*, or interpretive understanding. The five parts of the book are: Max
Weber on *Verstehen*, The Positivist Reception, The Wittgensteinian Reformulation,
Phenomenology and Ethnomethodology, and Hermeneutics and Critical Theory. The
original sources and the editors' introductions provide the best overview of these topics
as they are related to social science inquiry. Original articles by Talcott Parsons, Jurgen
Habermas, Alfred Schutz, Harold Garfinkel, and Paul Ricoeur present the fundamental
beliefs, assumptions, and methods of the various perspectives. Relationships between
philosophical perspectives and inquiry methods are emphasized.
Titus, H.H., Smith, M.S., & Nolan, R.T. (1986). *Living issues in philosophy* (3rd ed.).
     Belmont, CA: Wadsworth.
     This introduction to philosophy addresses comprehensively those issues most central
to developing your own philosophical perspectives. It is written for readers with no
previous philosophical background. The major sections include: The Nature of Human
Nature, The Realm of Values, Knowledge and Science, Philosophical Perspectives, and
Religion: East and West. Taking a historical perspective in most sections, the authors
clearly delineate the changing views and the interrelationships of those views in each
section. Sources of knowledge, nature of knowledge, and validity of knowledge are each
addressed in separate chapters, as are the philosophical perspectives of naturalism, idealism and realism, pragmatism, and analytic philosophy. A chapter on existentialism,
phenomenology, and process philosophy includes biographies and excerpts from Søren
Kierkegaard, Friedrich Nietzsche, Jean-Paul Sartre, Edmund Husserl, Martin Heideg-
ger, and Alfred North Whitehead. It places the present controversy between positivism
and interpretive meaning into a more comprehensive philosophical framework that relates to practical knowledge. It is a very readable philosophy textbook.
Zukav, G. (1979). *The dancing Wu Li masters*. New York: Morrow.
     Zukav leads you through the evolution of quantum mechanics as he experienced the
intellectual and personal aspects of the physicists' search for understanding. He causes
you to question many of your beliefs about reality and the nature of "things." Quantum
mechanics began in 1900 with Max Planck's theory of quanta. Albert Einstein's special

theory of relativity in 1905 began an era of "new" physics, in contrast to the "classical" physics of Isaac Newton. Although this is a book about the new physics and the creative, imaginative conceptions of physicists since 1900, similarities with Eastern philosophies are also discussed. Zukav provides insight not only into physics and science but also into yourself, your conceptions of the world, and your place in it.

REFERENCES

Bacon, Francis (1952). Advancement of learning. In R. M. Hutchins (Ed.), *The great books of the western world, 30.* Chicago: Encyclopedia Britannica.

Berlyne, D.E. (1960). *Conflict, arousal, and curiosity.* New York: McGraw-Hill.

Capra, F. (1975). *The tao of physics.* Berkeley, CA: Shambala.

Dallmayr, F.R., McCarthy, T. A. (ed.) (1977). *Understanding and social inquiry.* Notre Dame, IN: University of Notre Dame Press.

Dewey, John (1910). *How we think.* Boston: Heath.

Einstein, Albert (1936). On physical reality. *Franklin Institute Journal, 221.* (March), 349–382.

Garfinkel, H. (1967). What is ethnomethodology? In H. Garfinkel (Ed.), *Studies in ethnomethodology.* Englewood Cliffs, NJ: Prentice-Hall.

Garman, N.B., & Hazi, H.M. (1988). Teachers ask: Is there life after Madeline Hunter? *Phi Delta Kappan, 69* (9), 669–672.

Hebb, D.O. (1949). *The organization of behavior.* New York: Wiley.

Jacobs, E. (1987). Qualitative research traditions: A review. *Review of Education Research, 57* (1), 1–50.

Kant, Emanuel (1952). The critique of pure reason. In R. M. Hutchins (Ed.), *The great books of the western world, 42,* Chicago: Encyclopedia Britannica. (Original work published 1787)

Kendler, H.H., & Kendler, T.S. (1962). Vertical and horizontal processes in problem solving. *Psychological Review, 69,* 1–16.

Kirk, J., & Miller, M.L. (1986). *Reliability and validity in qualitative research.* Beverly Hills: Sage.

Kneller, G.F. (1984). *Movements of thought in modern education.* New York: Wiley.

Locke, John (1952). An essay concerning human understanding. In R. M. Hutchins (Ed.), *The great books of the western world, 35,* Chicago: Encyclopedia Britannica.

McCutchan, G. (1981). On the interpretation of classroom observations. *Educational Researcher, 10* (5), 5–10.

Miles, M.B., & Huberman, A.M. (1984). Drawing valid meaning from qualitative data: Towards a shared craft. *Educational Researcher, 13* (5), 20–30.

Pavlov, I.P. (1927). *Conditional reflexes.* London: Oxford University Press.

Rickman, H.P. (1979). *Wilhelm Dilthey: Pioneer of the human studies.* Berkeley: University of California Press.

Schutz, A. (1977). Concepts and theory formation in the social sciences. In F.R. Dallmayr & T.A. McCarthy, *Understanding and social inquiry.* Notre Dame, IN: University of Notre Dame Press.

Skinner, B.F. (1953). *Science and human behavior.* New York: Macmillan.

Singleton, J. (1988). Personal communication.

Thorndike, E.L. (1903). *Educational psychology.*

Watson, G. (1930). *Behaviorism*. New York: Norton.

Young, J.Z. (1960). *Doubt and certainty in science*. New York: Oxford University Press.

Zukav, G. (1979). *The dancing Wu Li masters: An overview of the new physics*. New York: Bantam Books.

CHAPTER 2

Science and Empirical Research

VIEWS OF SCIENCE

The sensational breakthroughs in physics and chemistry in the twentieth century, both in the development of better theories and in technological advances such as making steel, ceramics, and plastics, have led many to equate science with both the study of physical phenomena and with the experimental method. This very limited and often misleading view of science is still held by many people.

In professional education, the term *science* is more appropriately used to distinguish empirical investigation from other ways of knowing about the nature of the human condition, such as through music, drama, literature, or other humanities. In the past, history, anthropology, and similar disciplines that did not routinely include quantified data (numbers) in their studies were often classified as part of the humanities. This was a result of the more limited definition of science as an experimental field, and because historical and anthropological writing at times requires relatively large inferential leaps from somewhat limited data. If empirical research and science are equated, then all disciplines that generate knowledge based on systematic collection and objective analysis of empirical information must be considered as science.

To develop a meaningful definition of science and to describe the scientific method in education, it is necessary to know more of the history and essential elements of science. James Conant, in his book *On Understanding Science* (1951) states the following:

> . . . there is no question that one of the necessary conditions for scientific investigation is an exact and impartial analysis of the facts. But this attitude was neither invented by those who first concerned themselves with scientific inquir-

ies, nor was its overriding importance at once recognized. . . . Who were the precursors of those early investigators who in the sixteenth and seventeenth centuries set the standards for exact and impartial scientific inquries? Who were the spiritual ancestors of Copernicus, Galileo, and Versalius? Not the casual experimenter or the artful contriver of new mechanical devices who gradually increased our empirical knowledge of physics and chemistry during the Middle Ages. These men passed on to subsequent generations many facts and valuable methods of attaining practical ends but not the spirit of scientific inquiry. For the burst of new ardor in disciplined intellectual inquiry we must turn to a few minds steeped in the Socratic tradition, and to those early scholars who first recaptured the culture of Greece and Rome by primitive methods of archaeology. . . .

Petrarch, Boccaccio, Machiavelli, and Erasmus, far more than the alchemists, must be considered the precursors of the modern scientific investigator. Likewise, Rabelais and Montaigne who carried forward the critical philosophic spirit must be counted, it seems to me, among the forerunners of the modern scientists. But not only a few hardy skeptics and antiquarians, but also honest explorers and hardheaded statesmen and military commanders were the ancestors of all who endeavor to probe deeply to find new answers to old questions, who desire to minimize prejudice and examine facts impartially. (pp. 22–24)

Conant provides a useful foundation on which to define science. He points out the necessity of precise and impartial analysis of facts. There are many ways that researchers attempt to increase precision and minimize personal bias in their research. These are presented and discussed throughout this book. In the next section, the terms *empirical* and *science* are defined, followed by a discussion of the scientific method.

Empirical, which is an essential characteristic of science, is defined as, "relying on or derived from observation or experiment" (American Heritage Dictionary, 1982). Empirical is used in this book with the broadest interpretation of this definition. Observation is the process of obtaining information (data) from the world. The observations that are obtained could be math achievement scores of fifth graders on a standardized test, fourth-century writings of St. Augustine, teacher-student interactions during a math lesson, teachers' responses to a questionnaire or interview, or any other empirical information. To include experiment in the definition of empirical is redundant, since all information from the world around us is observation. An experiment is one type of observation process and is *not* a defining characteristic of either empirical or science.

Science is commonly defined as, "that which has been documented in a painstaking way so that others can identify the assumptions that are being made, review the methods used, and verify with new data [information] that they obtain" (American Heritage Dictionary, 1982). Science requires empirical investigation, which relies on observations (information) from the universe around us, not just contemplation.

As indicated in the definition of science, the aspect of empirical work that identifies it as science is painstaking documentation. The precise description of what was done, why it was done, and what was found allows both the researcher and others to identify possible flaws in either the procedures carried out or the logic used to draw conclusions from the information obtained. This documentation also is necessary for the outside verification of results. A second researcher can replicate, as nearly as possible, the procedures described to see if similar results are obtained. This replication of a study provides confidence in both the accuracy of the results and their applicability in other situations.

Another important characteristic of science is the concept of falsifiability. If it is not possible to obtain data that would show that a statement is false, such as those relating to the relative effects of two reading methods, the central values of a Japanese subculture, or the meanings teachers give to classroom actions, then the variables in the statement cannot be addressed scientifically. This concept forces researchers to state their theories or hypotheses as precisely as possible so that they can be tested and either verified or rejected.

SCIENTIFIC METHOD

Knowing that all science is empirical and knowing how to determine which types of activities are empirical are useful in classifying activities as scientific, particularly in contrast to tradition, authority, or personal experience. It is important to know whether conclusions, such as those in your professional field, are based on empirical information that has been systematically collected and carefully analyzed, rather than on edicts or unexamined truths from some authority or from a person's distilled experience.

All three types of information are essential in performing any personal or professional role. In all cases the applicability of the conclusions to your setting should be assessed by a careful review of their logical and substantive basis. This is an essential part of understanding and using the results of empirical research and other types of information in your field.

Two major considerations in using research are the relevance and quality of the study. Relevance deals with the characteristics of the study, the conditions in which it occurred, and their relationship to the situation in which you want to apply the results of the study. For example, a special education teacher of learning disabled students in the United States will generally find a study of variables in regular classrooms less relevant than one that deals with similar variables in learning disabled classrooms. It is less relevant because the variables that are most important in a learning disabled classroom will be somewhat different from those occurring in the regular classroom. A study carried out in Japan will be less relevant than one carried out in a U.S. community. The many cultural, governmental, and educational differences often make it difficult to interpret the meaning of such a study in one's own setting.

The quality of a study depends on the methods that were used to gather, analyze, and interpret the data. These determine, to a great extent, the confidence that you can have in the conclusion that Method A is better than Method

B for building vocabulary, or that the attitudes of students and parents about a new social studies curriculum accurately reflect their views. Some of the types of concerns that arise in any study were indicated in our "Introduction" in the example of the two Garfield School teachers who studied a phonics and a meaning approach to teaching second-grade reading.

Even if the students who used the phonics method in that study had done a great deal better in reading than those using the meaning approach, should we be confident that the differences in achievement obtained were a result only of the teaching method? In most cases, particularly outside a controlled laboratory situation, there are many other possible causes of, or alternative explanations for, the achievement differences or the parental attitudes that are obtained. A good researcher tries to minimize the alternative explanations when designing and implementing a study. Other problems that occur or are identified during or after the study, such as the three top students being assigned to the meaning approach, must be described, and their likely impact on the results obtained must be discussed thoroughly and honestly. If they are not, the researcher will draw erroneous conclusions and a reader will be misled about the relationships among the variables studied. When the researcher does not identify problems, the reader must attempt to specify the weaknesses in a study and alternative explanations for the results, often without enough information to make informed judgments.

Most research methods books that deal with science provide a series of steps that comprise the scientific method. Most such books include a disclaimer indicating that scientists do not necessarily follow these steps when they *do* their research although few readers understand the importance of such a disclaimer. Some books include four or five steps in the scientific method; others include seven or eight, depending on their particular purpose. There is nothing inherently valuable in the specific steps, whether there are four, six, or eight, but there does seem to be some value in identifying important parts of the process of empirical inquiry. The following list of activities important to empirical inquiry should be used to gain an appreciation of research as a unified whole and the necessary interrelationships among the various parts of the inquiry process:

1. Identify an important problem that can be meaningfully studied.
2. Hypothesize relationships among important variables.
3. Develop a plan for empirically investigating the relationships among the variables.
4. Collect the information according to the plan (documenting everything of importance that occurred).
5. Organize and analyze the information to address your hypotheses or expectations.
6. Describe your findings as accurately as possible.
7. Draw conclusions from the findings in your study in terms of the specific problem studied for your specific purpose for doing the study.

8. Report other information or ideas gained from the study, particularly as they relate to previous research and related theories or models and to recommendations for further research.

Some researchers, such as anthropologists, would argue that parts one and two, identifying a problem and hypothesizing relationships among the variables, are not essential parts of doing research or that they do not necessarily need to be delineated at the beginning of an ethnographic study. When anthropologists begin to study a culture, they may have no specific purpose or problem in mind and only a rudimentary sense of what they plan to do to carry out their study. They want only to learn what they can from this culture that will improve their knowledge of how cultural variables seem to operate, or how they operate in this one unique culture.

From past research it is clear that such researchers use their previous experience and knowledge to identify, often rather quickly, relationships among variables that seem to be operating. They then develop procedures, such as observing specific cultural events, interviewing members of specific groups, and reading books or documents most relevant to those issues, that will allow them to delve more intensively into the study of them, in order to identify how they seem to operate in this setting and culture.

This is only one example from an infinite array of possibilities of how the activities of researchers do not necessarily follow a linear set of steps from identification of a problem to drawing conclusions. In research, as in all aspects of life, what is learned in doing one step causes some reorganization of many prior beliefs and knowledge that are central elements of previous steps. These reorganized ideas lead to new experiences, which cause further reorganization of our ideas, *ad infinitum*.

In most field research, activities are seldom organized around a specific problem that has been identified before the researcher's involvement in the project. In her description of field research, Leinhardt (1978) aptly begins the process *not* with "Problem Identification" but with "Opportunity Knocks." Much as the anthropologist goes into a new culture, the educational researcher (even the psychologist or sociologist) goes into a field situation, often for other purposes, and identifies a problem that can be studied fruitfully in that setting. Over time the problem becomes more clearly delineated, and new ways are developed for studying it. Or more important problems are identified, and research on the earlier problem is dropped to begin studies that appear to be more valuable.

There is no series of steps that a researcher can implement that assures the quality of an empirical study. The quality of the study is determined by the specific procedures and methods used to carry out the various parts of the study and by the doubting, questioning approach of the researcher, who identifies and investigates all reasonable explanations for the results. Some typical alternative explanations are the unusual nature of the subjects or setting, the quality of the measurement procedures, other activities that occurred when the study was carried out, or assumptions required by the theories or procedures used that are not adequately met in the study. An accurate and honest reporting of the likelihood that other variables in the study may have had an effect on the outcomes or that some assumptions were not met adequately are essential parts of the scientific method. Research, if it is to be useful, must produce accurate, honest descriptions of what was done in a study, what was found, and the extent to which alternative interpretations of the information obtained are reasonable.

ASSUMPTIONS OF SCIENCE

When a researcher gathers empirical information in ways that allow the conclusions to be tested by others, the researcher must make several assumptions. Three assumptions that are fundamental to all empirical research carried out in the positivist tradition as well as to some research from other perspectives are the following:

1. There exists an *external universe* that human beings can know.
2. *Events* in the universe *are determined* by a finite set of causes.
3. The essential elements of *events will recur.*

The reason for these assumptions should be readily apparent. If nothing exists in the external universe or if a researcher can never observe it, we cannot learn through our senses or from our experiences. Empirical researchers would be wasting their time in describing external events if such an external reality did not exist.

In a similar vein, it makes no sense to try to identify causal relationships among variables if there are no causal relationships in the universe. If events are caused in the universe but the causes are so complex as to be infinite, a researcher has no hope of developing theories or models that would accurately represent the situation being studied. No model would predict relationships acccurately if such relationships did not exist.

The third assumption is basic to generalizing the results of a study to other situations or other groups. A researcher is attempting to learn more about a universe and will always study only a small part of the phenomenon, or situation, that is of interest. The two Garfield School teachers, for example, studied the effects of the phonics and meaning methods on the reading achievement of the 50 students in their second-grade classes. If the results obtained that year were different from those for the 50 students the following year, the study would not be very useful.

In an absolute sense, each situation and each instance of time is unique. At each additional second of history, every person is older, babies are born, and people die. Studying any specific situation would be meaningless (or worse) if the assumption that the essential elements of events will recur was not accurate, at least to some degree.

Neither phenomenologists nor hermeneutists necessarily make these three assumptions. Two fundamental assumptions of phenomenologists are the following:

1. There can be no knowledge of things-in-themselves, only of things as they are accessible to human consciousness.
2. Human beings can examine their own experiences of reality and accurately describe them.

The first assumption is a fundamental belief about the nature of human existence and the source of meaningful knowledge. For someone to work from a phenomenological perspective, this is a basic assumption. It is not absolutely essential because someone could do a phenomenological study from the perspective that this is one of various possible sources. It is an assumption commonly held, particularly by existential phenomenologists.

The second assumption is necessary if a researcher is collecting and using these self-reports. If the reports do not accurately reflect the reporters' experiences, then conclusions about those experiences will be erroneous. Some might argue that these are accurate indicators of what people report about their experiences, but this argument appears to be totally circular. Even if their statements are accurate indicators of their statements, how does this relate either to human experiences or behaviors?

These two sets of assumptions of researchers from different philosophical perspectives are listed and discussed to help you recognize that whenever you attempt to gain knowledge, you must make assumptions. The identification of those assumptions is an essential part of doing science, and the recognition of assumptions that are made in a particular situation is an important part of becoming educated. You must learn to recognize the nature of the assumptions that are made and their implications in your specific situation if you are to use research effectively.

EDUCATIONAL RESEARCH

As indicated previously, science and research are synonyms in this book. Research *in education* means to collect new information (or to reanalyze previously collected data in new ways) using systematic methods of empirical inquiry to study a problem in education. To simply gather data systematically and precisely with no intention to address a generalizable problem is not research. School districts, hospitals, and businesses systematically collect very precise information about attendance, beds filled, or gross receipts, but that is not research. Students go to libraries and organize the information they find there into "research" papers that are often focused on a problem such as, "factors that affect early reading." Such literature reviews are not research because new data were not obtained, nor were previously collected data systematically reanalyzed (only summarized). For a systematic data collection and analysis activity to be research requires that it address a generalizable problem. A generalizable problem is one that concerns others in situations similar to that studied. You can study a problem in a way that provides a reasonable answer only for the specific individual studied. For example, a teacher may try a new method of teaching math to a student who is not learning from the text. Even if the method works for this one student in this unique setting, we can have little confidence that similar results would occur elsewhere. More complex procedures are usually needed to assure that results in one setting are applicable to other groups in other settings. If the teacher used it successfully with 10 students over several years, or if several teachers obtained consistent positive results with all their students, we would have more confidence in the new method of teaching math. This is an issue of research design, which is addressed in Chapter 6.

Research is typically classified into basic, applied, and action research (or evaluation). These categories represent three purposes for doing research. *Basic research* addresses fundamental aspects of human existence and is carried out to develop new theories or to test the theories we use to think about a particular aspect of human life. For example, most artificial intelligence researchers attempt to clarify how human beings organize, store, and retrieve information. They use computers to represent the binary switches, like human nerves, that allow electrical messages to travel through nerves to the brain (their underlying theory). There is no application for the knowledge gained by the study other than to describe how the human brain works. Similar basic sociological research occurs when researchers study generic characteristics of organizations or other groups. Basic researchers are *not* concerned, necessarily, with the application of their knowledge. They are trying to develop models or theories that describe the nature of the human condition, that will allow us to predict more accurately the results of specific actions.

Research that is carried out to test the applicability of a theory or model in a specific practical situation is called *applied research*. Nearly all educational research is applied research because of the professional nature of the field. Educational researchers need to know how theories and previous research can be used to understand important educational situations and processes. This allows them to improve the quality or effectiveness of education.

In general, basic research is more highly valued than applied research because of its potential for impact. New theories and models bring new concepts and terms into existence, and people begin organizing their world using these ingenious concepts. Piaget developed the concepts of "concrete-operational" and "abstract" thinking levels of human development. Freud created the ego, id, and superego that many psychiatrists use in their work. Many of us use these concepts to think about mental difficulties we are having or those that close friends and associates are suffering. Some educators look at pupils in classrooms and see reinforcements and punishments occurring. These are terms developed and used by basic researchers to understand human relationships and learning. Thus, basic researchers often have an enormous impact on society as they develop new theories, models, and associated concepts.

Applied researchers do not develop new variables usually but simply test the applicability of theories and models to their situation. For example, testing the relative effects of phonics and meaning curricula in the second grade addresses the applicability of different psychological and linguistic theories of language development in planning instruction for second-grade pupils. It addresses also the relative practical value of the two approaches in teaching second-grade reading skills to pupils.

In the past 20 years, a third type of research-like activity in which research methods and tools are used is *action research*, or *evaluation*, which is the systematic collection, analysis, and interpretation of data to support decision-making. Much of this type of activity is evaluation of educational processes and programs. Evaluation also occurs in specially funded projects that are of relatively short duration, such as three to five years. It is not strictly research, because a generalizable problem or question is not addressed. It is often called "poor" research because the procedures are not carried out in ways that develop confidence in their generalizability to other settings. For example, positive results may occur in the program because one school principal or one project leader may be outstanding. So long as personnel changes do not occur, the decisionmaker is confident that similar results will continue to occur and is *not* concerned about generalizing results to other projects or settings. If the data show that fewer clients have been served over the past few weeks or that lower student scores are occurring in one classroom, a director or teacher may want to make changes that will stop such declines.

Some call this latter type of activity project monitoring, or administration, rather than either research or evaluation. Making fine distinctions between those activities are not that useful in differentiating among basic, applied, and action research. The important distinctions for professionals are between basic and applied research, and action research, or evaluation, in contrast to basic and applied research. In the case of evaluation, or action research, activities may not address generalizable problems and may include project monitoring or other types of administrative data-gathering and reporting activities, which are not in a strict sense research as we have defined it.

TYPICAL EDUCATION STUDIES

Most problems in education can be studied empirically. Many decisions are made with no systematic empirical information—such as the textbook selection process described earlier, when teachers essentially looked over the textbooks and selected the one they believed was most appropriate for their students. There are ways to investigate education issues empirically, but most of us are not socialized into that way of addressing problems. To help you see more uses for empirical processes, some typical education problems and general methods for investigating them are described.

Problems that occur when special education students are mainstreamed into regular classrooms have been indicated by teachers, parents, and students. An educational researcher did an ethnographic study of several classrooms where hearing-impaired children were mainstreamed to identify the nature of the problems and to suggest ways to alleviate them. The researcher spent many hours in classrooms observing teacher and student activities for an entire year and from these observations identified barriers to meaningful integration of the special education children into the classroom. These included communication problems, even though an interpreter was always in the classroom, and the inability (or unwillingness) of the teacher to discipline the hearing-impaired students.

A second type of problem studied is the relative effectiveness of phonics versus meaning approaches to teaching early reading, which has been studied using experiments such as those implemented by the two Garfield School teachers. By gathering detailed information about students' activities in each classroom and the reading knowledge and skills they gained during one school year, conclusions about the relative strengths and weaknesses of the two approaches can be described. These results may be used to decide which type of materials will be used in second-grade classrooms in a particular school district.

A third problem is whether to implement a sex-education program into the middle schools (grades 6 through 8) of a school district. School board members would want to know the opinions of their parents and teachers on that issue. This information could be obtained from questionnaires or telephone interviews of a large cross section of both parents and teachers. The board would also want to know what happened in other school districts when similar programs were implemented there. Did teenage pregnancy decrease among those students who participated in those programs? Did promiscuity of these teenagers increase? The first question can be investigated through school records; the second would require at least a questionnaire, interview, or other data-gathering procedure.

A fourth problem would be studied by a phenomenological sociologist or ethnomethodologist who is interested in the ways in which teachers make decisions—such as assigning students to special education classifications or to specific reading groups. The teachers would describe their rationales for their decision about each student or about selected students. Although there might be formal rules or guidelines for each classification, previous research has shown that people use various processes for decision-making. Garfinkel (1967) called it "ad hoc-ing." The researcher would describe the ways in which the different teachers made and rationalized their decisions.

In these four kinds of studies, as well as in other studies of human processes, the most relevant and meaningful way to collect, organize, and analyze data that best address the purpose for doing the research should be used. No single method or philosophical perspective is inherently better than another. The value of a study resides more in the identification of important questions that can be usefully explored than in the method used to explore it—although the relationship between the problem and the method determines the value.

The central aspect of the relevance and quality of any study is the degree to which the data that are gathered represent the variables or dimensions that are important in this setting. Inquiry deals with substantive issues in a specific situation. There is no particular form or process, such as an experimental design or objective measurement process, that assures the quality or relevance of a study. There is a unique purpose for each study that requires idiosyncratic methods to be used in unique ways to gain knowledge that is most useful in that situation. The research principles described in this book will help you recognize the importance of the methods used in studies you read and identify alternative explanations for the results when pertinent information was either *not* collected or adequately controlled in the study.

Before proceeding to specific aspects of the research process, it is important to realize that all educational research involves other individual human beings. Researchers must treat these people ethically, particularly in terms of protecting their individual rights to privacy, confidentiality, dignity, and self-esteem. Ethical issues that arise in research and how to deal with them seem to become more complex each year. In the following section, some of the major ethical issues are identified and discussed, guidelines that were developed in the 1970s are delineated, and other sources for more detailed information are identified. Ethical treatment of others is an extremely important area that is not addressed adequately in most graduate education programs. If the following section raises your consciousness about how to treat others in your professional or academic life and leads you to learn more about these isssues, it will have fulfilled its purpose in this book.

ETHICS IN RESEARCH

Professionals and researchers who work with other people, or with information that can affect those people, must treat them in an ethical manner. Organizations representing lawyers, doctors, psychologists, and researchers have developed lists of ethical practices—often with case examples to minimize ambiguity in their application. In research with human subjects, fundamental changes in ethical principles have occurred in the past 20 years.

Historically, the value of research results to society has overshadowed concerns about individual subjects. As a result, researchers were often not sensitive to problems their research posed for participants. Kelman (1972) analyzed the relative power of researchers and their subjects, showing that the subject had less power—both in society and in the research setting. For example, much psychological research was done with college freshmen and sophomores by faculty members. Persons in institutions, such as orphans, prisoners, hospital patients, military personnel, and school children, have been subjects of studies in the past—often with neither their awareness nor agreement. Nazi experimentation in their concentration camps is one of the most reprehensible examples of "man's inhumanity to man." At that time, however, *many* experiments with potentially toxic drugs were carried out in prisons or with military personnel by various researchers throughout the world.

One particularly troubling example in the United States was the Tuskegee Study, begun in 1932, in which the U.S. Public Health Service carried out a study of the effects of syphilis on 399 black males in Macon County, Alabama. These poor, illiterate men were led to believe that they were being treated for the disease, but they were not. Their physical condition was recorded periodically to document the effects of the disease over time, and autopsies were performed after death. (For a more detailed account, see Jones, 1981.)

There is, of course, no acceptable defense for such research, even as we try to understand the rationale for doing it. A review of many such studies indicates that they were undertaken, generally, for the good of society. In the Tuskegee Study, harm to the relatively few subjects was outweighed in the minds of the researchers by the potential gain in knowledge that would allow doctors to treat the thousands, or millions, of syphilis patients in following years. Research subjects are often viewed as "heroes"—even when they did not knowingly volunteer as subjects in the study. Researchers see the potential value of their planned research studies and construct "reasonable" rationales for why the benefits outweigh the potential risks. For example, in 1932 there was no antibiotic or other treatment that would cure syphilis. Many (if not all) of the participating doctors may not have had ethical concerns about the lack of treatment given the subjects because they knew of no way to treat them successfully. Today some doctors and many lay persons question treatment of some kinds of cancer because the treatment does not seem to affect the disease, and it causes greater pain and personal humiliation than nontreatment. Other examples of studies that place subjects at risk are cited in the literature by Kelman (1972), Cook (1976), and Borg and Gall (1983). In much of the important social science research there is some risk to the subjects. A description of the study that focused the debate about ethical practices among researchers follows.

EXAMPLE 2   ETHICS IN RESEARCH (MILGRAM'S STUDY OF OBEDIENCE)

A study reported in 1963 by Stanley Milgram was widely discussed in terms of ethical treatment of human subjects. Milgram studied obedience to authority as an explanation for the willing participation of citizens and soldiers in the systematic slaughter of human beings in Nazi "death camps." In his study, 40 male subjects were solicited from communities around Yale University "to participate in a study of learning and memory." They were paid $4.50 for coming to the laboratory (a sum that is equivalent to $20 or more today). The subjects were told that they were studying the effects of punishment on learning. They had an "electric chair" to administer the punishment and a "generator" with a bank of switches from 15 volts to 450 volts (v) of electricity marked in 15 v increments on the control. The switches were identified in the following categories: Slight Shock, Moderate Shock, Strong Shock, Very Strong Shock, Intense Shock, Extreme Intensity Shock, Danger: Severe Shock, and XXX. A number of noises were made and lights lit when switches were thrown to give authenticity to the "electric chair" setup. Each of the 40 male subjects was strapped into the chair and given a 45 v electrical shock to convince them that the chair was wired to the generator and the electric shock punishment was delivered. An accomplice of Milgram's was strapped into the chair. The subject was told to administer a shock to the "learner" for wrong answers and to move one level higher on the voltage (15 v) with each wrong answer, announcing the voltage level each time before administering the shock. The subject was given a list of 10 word pairs and instructed to continue going through the list using the same procedures until all words were learned (which, of course, they never were). When the subject administered the 300 v shock, the "learner" pounded on the wall, but no other evidence of pain was given. The "learner," whom the subject could not see, gave no further responses to the subject's questions about items on the list that he was supposed to learn. The subject was told to consider nonresponse as a wrong answer and to administer the next level of shock to the "learner." If at any time during the experiment the subject indicated an unwillingness to continue, he was encouraged to continue with a sequence of four prods:

1. Please continue, or please go on.
2. The experiment requires that you continue.
3. It is absolutely essential that you continue.
5. You have no other choice; you *must* go on.

The subjects also were given reassurances, if they asked, that the shocks were painful to the learner, but "no permanent tissue damage" would occur.

Milgram found that only 5 of the 40 subjects refused to go beyond the 300 v shock. Nine others refused to continue before delivering the 450 v shock: four after 315 v, two after 330 v, and one each after 345 v, 360 v, and 375 v. Which means that 26 of the 40 subjects continued to obey the authority and carry out their role in the study to completion.

Diane Baumrind (1964) raised a number of ethical issues soon after Milgram's study was published. She questioned Milgram's ability to help the subjects in this deceptive study to overcome negative effects of their participation. She states:

> From the subjects' point of view procedures which involve loss of dignity, self-esteem, and trust in rational authority are probably more harmful in the long run and require the most thoroughly planned reparations, if engaged in at all. . . . I would not like to see experiments such as Milgram's proceed unless the subjects were fully informed of the dangers of serious aftereffects

and his correctives were clearly shown to be effective in restoring their state of well-being. (p. 423)

In his response to Baumrind's criticisms, Milgram (1964) reported that each subject was given a careful post-experimental treatment. Subjects were told that the "learner" had received no shocks. They had a friendly reconciliation with the unharmed "learner," and they had an extended discussion with the experimenter. Each subject was assured that his behavior was normal and that his sense of conflict and tension about administering the shock was shared by other participants. Some participants had additional lengthy discussions with the experimenter, and each received a copy of the comprehensive report when it was completed.

In response to a follow-up questionnaire: 84% of the subjects were glad that they had participated in the experiment, 74% reported learning something of personal importance, and all strongly endorsed the experiment. Other data from the subjects also supported Milgram's claim that, "at no point were subjects exposed to danger and at no point did they run the risk of injurious effects resulting from participation. If it had been otherwise, the experiment would have been terminated at once" (p. 849).

As in most situations where ethics are at issue, there is no one right answer about the ethical practices in this study. Arguments about this research continue today, with many enthusiastic supporters of Baumrind's concerns and many others supporting Milgram's perspective.

In the past 25 years, many changes in the ways educational researchers treat subjects have occurred. Despite the foregoing rather detailed, vivid descriptions of selected studies, changes in ethical research practice must be viewed in the broader spectrum of changing perspectives about ethics in society.

Changes in Perspectives about Ethical Practices

American society has undergone many changes in the past century or two. The social interactions with neighbors expected by rural farmers in 1850 are different in many ways from those expected in 1988. The sexual mores of both teenagers and adults are much different today from what they were 20, 30, or 50 years ago. What is morally or ethically appropriate in other areas has also changed. In business both the personal and legal rule was that the buyer was essentially stuck with whatever he bought once a deal was agreed on. Today buyers get their money back when a product does not perform as promised.

Some people argue that the Watergate Affair, which led to Richard Nixon's resignation as president of the United States, resulted from changing perspectives about ethics. Workers for the Nixon presidential campaign committee broke into the offices of the Democratic Party in the Watergate building in Washington in order to gain a competitive advantage in the campaign over the Democratic candidate, Senator George McGovern. In many previous elections, such illegal and unethical behavior had been perpetrated by members of both parties, but people accepted it as common practice. Nixon and his colleagues compounded their problem, of course, by attempting to cover up the break-in, thus breaking a number of additional laws. After a long, protracted investigation President Nixon was forced to resign, and his successor, President Gerald Ford, pardoned him of any crime.

The details of the Watergate Affair are of interest only to illustrate the changing perspectives of ethical practice. In fact, nothing of value was taken by the thieves, and Nixon won the election in one of the greatest landslide victories in the history of U.S. presidential elections.

Changes in the protection of human rights for children have occurred rapidly in the past 20 years. School officials have had the protection of *in loco parentis* in their responsibility for the children attending their schools. In that role, they often paddled students who misbehaved or carried out other punishments that were similar to those that parents commonly administered. (I was sent into an unlighted closet as an elementary student when I "misbehaved.")

In the early 1970s, the Secretary of Health, Education, and Welfare (HEW), Joseph Califano, placed a moratorium on research with young children (under six years old), and issued new ethical guidelines for doing research with HEW funds. His rationale for the moratorium was that such children were too young to understand what it meant to participate in research and could not give their informed consent to voluntarily participate in a study. Before the moratorium and the associated ethical guidelines, only parental permission was required to do research with children under 18. This is another example of a changing view of children's rights that has increased children's ability to make decisions independent of their parents' wishes.

Today, parents have fewer rights in bringing up their children. For example, judges require children of "faith healers" to be given medical attention when their lives are in danger. Children are required to go to public schools against their parents' wishes. Some parents (and schools) have been sued by their children for not providing an adequate education. These are all occurrences of increased protection of children's rights as valued individual human beings. The Watergate Affair was an expansion of the protection of human rights to the victim, or injured party (the Democrats). These legal decisions reflect changes in perspectives about ethical treatment of others, particularly in protection of individual rights.

With the advent of the computer, laws have been implemented to protect other rights of citizens. The Family Educational Rights and Privacy Act of 1974, commonly called the Buckley Amendment, protects the privacy of educational records. Data from school records cannot be made available in a way that allows an individual student to be identified without the written consent of a parent or the student (if the student is at least 18 years old). The written consent must be dated, specify the records to be released, the purpose for using the data, and who will see the data.

Confidentiality is an important aspect of treating research participants in an ethical manner. Treating others in ways that you would like to be treated (or *they* would like to be treated) is a good foundation for ethical behavior, but it is somewhat ambiguous. The ethical guidelines that HEW, under Califano, produced in 1971 were the first statements of many rules and procedures that guide present research.

Guidelines for Ethical Practices

In the third edition of *Research Methods in Social Relations*, Stuart W. Cook (1976) discussed a number of "questionable practices involving research participants." These practices included the following:

1. Involving people in research without their knowledge or consent.
2. Coercing people to participate.
3. Withholding from the participant the true nature of the research.
4. Deceiving the research participant.
5. Leading the research participants to commit acts which diminish their self-respect.
6. Violating the rights to self-determination: Research on behavior control and character change.
7. Exposing the research participant to physical or mental stress.
8. Invading the privacy of the research participant.
9. Withholding benefits from participants in control groups.
10. Failing to treat research participants fairly and to show them consideration and respect. (p. 199)

The original HEW guidelines included a number of key concepts that more clearly delineate major changes in ethical practices since 1970: (1) when a subject is at risk, (2) procedures necessary to meet a subject's needs, and (3) informed consent. Being at risk is defined as follows:

> An individual is considered to be "at risk" if he may be exposed to the possibility of harm—physical, psychological, sociological, or other—as a consequence of any activity which goes beyond the application of those established and accepted methods necessary to meet his needs. The determination of when an individual is at risk is a matter of the application of common sense and sound professional judgment to the circumstances of the activity in question.

In education, one of the "other" types of harm that can be done to human subjects is to retard their learning. If a child in a study does not learn the content that was taught using an "experimental" or "innovative" method as part of a study, the researcher is responsible to do remediation activities with that child. Before 1970, researchers who used educational materials or procedures that educators believed to be as good as, or better than, those commonly used with these children had fulfilled their ethical responsibilities to the participants in the study.

Today they must be concerned about placing students at risk educationally when they implement innovative educational materials or practices.

The guidelines indicate that, even though the experimental procedures may be established and accepted, if they are carried out for purposes other than *the necessity to meet students' needs*, they place children at risk. Random assignment procedures and other methods used to control alternative explanations in a study or to improve the quality or value of the study in other ways are clear evidence that the research procedures have *not* been implemented simply to meet the students' needs. Operationally, the use of any materials or procedures in a classroom that are not prescribed, or mandated, by the local school board are *not* being used strictly to meet students' needs, and therefore they place children at risk. The ethical researcher must remediate any educational losses that result from the study.

This principle is very difficult to implement in practice, even by those who strongly support it. When a student who participates in a study does not learn adequately what was taught, such as how to calculate square roots or common second-grade vocabulary, it is impossible to know how well that child would have learned these skills using the regular materials and procedures. If a particularly acute learning problem arises with a student in a study, most researchers work cooperatively with the teacher to do whatever they can to help the child learn the needed knowledge or skills. Before 1970, researchers were not required to do anything that would compromise their study, and all remediation occurred after the study was completed. Many researchers today believe that to do harm to any individual is too great a cost for the "dubious" value of the knowledge to be gained from the research. When faced with such a problem, each person makes an individual decision within the guidelines about minimizing possible harm to participants versus maximizing the quality of the study. Guidelines provide a minimum that is expected, if not legally required, in order to act responsibly to protect the rights of other human beings. Most researchers go well beyond the guidelines as they implement their personal and professional codes of ethics.

To minimize risk and to protect the rights of individuals, procedures for obtaining *informed consent* have been delineated. These include the following:

1. A description of the procedures to be used and the purpose for doing the study in language that the subject can understand.
2. Identification of who will be in the experimental treatment (if there is one), and the availability of alternative procedures that might better meet the subject's needs.
3. Identification of possible benefits from individuals' participation in the study.
4. Identification of possible costs or potential harm from participation in the study. (This is similar to a doctor's discussion with a patient of possible harm from medical or surgical procedures before the patient decides what treatment to undergo.)

5. A description of the extent to which records will be confidential, including the methods to be used to protect the subject's anonymity.
6. Procedures that allow subjects to freely ask questions about the study and their participation in it that the researcher answers fully and honestly.
7. A clear specification that the subject's participation is completely voluntary, and that the subject can withdraw from the study at any time without penalty. No coercion should be used to encourage participation that is not strictly voluntary.

These guidelines, if followed strictly, would eliminate the possibility of deception research in which the subject is misled about the purpose or the procedures of the research, such as those in Milgram's study of obedience. This makes some types of important research impossible to carry out. How can we learn about individual or group social behavior without setting up situations and documenting typical behavior? Some argue that such research should not occur, whereas others point out ways that exemptions can be made for particularly valuable studies. In my experience, all researchers want to minimize possible harm that could be done to participants.

Review Procedures

The National Research Act of 1974 requires that all research with human subjects that is funded by the Department of Health and Human Services (HHS) be reviewed by an Institutional Review Board (IRB). Most universities require that all research at the institution, including student and faculty research, be reviewed to ensure that the rights of the participants are protected. In reviewing research proposals, IRBs often recommend alternative procedures for carrying out the research that will fulfill the researcher's purposes and decrease the possible risks to participants in the study. In most institutions, procedures are in place also to exempt from review research with human subjects that involves no risk, such as anonymous research from data in a computerized information system or research activities that are a regular part of the data collection in a school district. Each researcher must become familiar with and use the review procedures of the university or institution in which the research occurs. For more information about review requirements, the U.S. Department of Health and Human Services or the U.S. Department of Education in Washington can be contacted about the latest guidelines for conducting research with human subjects.

Summary

Doing research ethically requires a great deal of sensitivity and extra effort by the researcher. Our consciousness of ethical issues must be raised just as it has been raised in ethical treatment of blacks, women, and other identifiable groups in U.S. society. For example, the procedures that must be followed to gain permission to do research in a school district usually begins by contacting an administrator at the highest level of responsibility in that district—such as the superintendent or associate superintendent. The chain of command that is then followed includes the principals of participating schools, whose support is also needed. After gaining the often enthusiastic support of these administrators for a research project, the researcher finally meets with the teachers who are asked to volunteer as subjects in the study. Many teachers believe that they will be punished if they do not go along with the study in their schools. Because of this, it is usually impossible for a researcher to do research in teachers' classrooms that is truly voluntary after such steps to gain approval for the study have been carried out.

Before doing any research with human subjects, a person must become familiar with the ethical guidelines and principles that apply. Not only should the basic ethical guidelines and rules from HHS or other U.S. agencies be read and understood, but also the specific review procedures that the institution uses must be followed. A mentor who is familiar with both the general ethical principles and an institution's specific review procedures is invaluable in gaining the necessary knowledge and sensitivity to ethical research practices. Borg and Gall (1983), Kimmel (1981), Cook (1976), and APA Ethical Principles of Psychologists (1981) provide extensive discussions of ethical issues arising in research with human subjects. Become familiar with them before doing research with human subjects.

THE EMPIRICAL RESEARCH PROCESS

The remainder of this book addresses the issues that affect the relevance and quality of educational research and how these are integrated to produce knowledge—the knowledge may be only practical, only theoretical, or both. Specific techniques and the language used by researchers in various disciplines are presented and discussed. Numerous examples are given and exercises are included to involve you in the procedures and techniques. It is important that you do many of the exercises because it is impossible to learn what is important in a specific situation from only reading the book.

Before dealing with the specific language and procedures, you need an overall picture of the research process. In this section, the most important parts of the research process are briefly described. How the various parts contribute to the research process and their interrelationships are discussed to provide a picture of the entire process before you begin to examine the individual concepts and techniques. The remainder of this chapter is an overview of the important issues addressed in the following six chapters (Chapters 3 to 8):

3. Problem and Purpose of Study
4. Reviewing Literature Relevant to a Problem
5. Characteristics of Data
6. Research Design: Issues of Quality and Relevance of Research Results

7. Organizing, Analyzing, and Summarizing Empirical Information
8. Interpreting Results of a Study

Problem and Purpose of Study

The question that each researcher must answer in order to plan the best study possible for the purpose is: What specific problem can be empirically studied at this time to help us either clarify some particular difficulty or provide a likely solution for a problem? At present, the inadequacies of our public educational system have been identified as an important problem area by various groups. *A Nation At Risk* (National Commission on Excellence in Education, 1983) identifies the nature and degree of some inadequacies. But what is the problem? Many politicians seem to think that teachers need more incentives, such as money, to teach well. Several states have instituted increased pay scales for teachers, whereas others have mandated career ladders with increased responsibilities and pay for a few selected teachers. Are the problems that these changes are supposed to solve the basis for the well-documented inadequacies? Not likely!

In most cases, we seem to rush toward solutions rather than investigating and more clearly specifying the reasons for the inadequacies. This is true of most educational problems you can identify: dropouts, early reading problems, secondary science and math achievement, drugs, alcohol, or divorce-related problems. Even the two Garfield School teachers described in the "Introduction" were investigating alternative solutions rather than attempting to clarify the nature of the learning-teaching problem.

In that example, the problem was: "Which reading method is best for our second-grade students?" That question can be investigated empirically, but is it the best research question? The teachers' purpose for the study was limited to their school. Because they used only students in their single school, the likelihood that such results would also occur elsewhere is not clear. If their purpose had been to draw conclusions about the relative value of these two programs for second-grade students throughout the United States, then more students and teachers would have been needed to obtain a cross section of U.S. second-grade classrooms.

The "problem" in a research study is the specific issue, or question, that is addressed empirically in the study; the "purpose" for doing the study indicates how the results will be used, or applied, to inform the researcher about that issue in a specific context. As indicated, the problem and purpose essentially determine the types of information that will be needed to adequately address them.

It is important that you realize how problems for research are identified and that researchers have specific purposes for their studies. As you read research to better understand the problems you face in your situation, it is unlikely that the researchers were concerned with precisely your question. If they addressed your question, it was probably not done in a setting exactly like yours. Thus, you must use research results and related theory to learn more about variables that may be operating in your situation. The research will not show you precisely what to do, however. You must interpret the results and their implications for the problem that concerns you.

Reviewing Literature Relevant to a Problem

As soon as a researcher has an idea about a problem, a thorough review of related literature is carried out. Most libraries have numerous journals containing reports of research studies, theories, and other information that may relate to the problem. By becoming familiar with the relevant studies and theories, a researcher learns how others conceptualized the problem in their situations. Some may think about "frequency of behaviors" and associated "reinforcers" and "time out," whereas others use cognitive learning theory.

Academic scholars and other researchers are familiar with these theories and with many related studies, and they use this knowledge to identify the best problem for investigation. Inexperienced researchers must use the literature review to clarify their thinking about the problem or to specify more precisely dimensions of the problem they will investigate. This review usually takes two to six months, depending on the researcher's past experience and knowledge, amount of related literature, the purpose for doing the review, and the complexity of the problem.

In addition to providing a conceptual framework (or theory) for the problem, a literature review allows the researcher to place the knowledge about the problem in an accurate historical perspective. How have others viewed the problem? In what kinds of contexts has it been studied? Which variables seem to be important? What seems to be the most promising next step for studying (or solving) the problem? What is the most important next step that can be made at this time?

Answers to all these questions are obtained from a critical review of the literature. Researchers go through the process of answering these and other questions in order to plan a study. A review of the literature describes the aspects of the literature that are most relevant to studying the problem for the researcher's specific purpose. The logical process that led the researcher to the conclusions about the information found in the literature must be presented meticulously. As a result, the empirical and logical basis for each decision made in planning the study is clearly documented. Whether you are planning to do a study yourself or only want to learn what is presently known about a problem, a systematic review of literature is invaluable.

Characteristics of Data

The kinds of information gathered in a study, from whom, and under what conditions must be clearly understood. The issues related to the quality and value of empirical information in a study fall under the category of measurement. Which information is most reliable and valid is the central issue of measurement. For example, when you collect reading achievement data from students, you must be able to assure yourself (and others) that the data collected accurately represent the students' actual reading skills. How do these scores differ from the teacher's assessment of each student's reading skills? In what ways are the test results better (or worse) than a teacher's assessments? Are there better ways to assess the students' reading achievement for the purpose of this study?

These same kinds of questions arise in all research. The anthropologist uses certain types of information to represent cultural variables, such as transmission of the culture (education). How accurate is the information collected? Does it tend to overestimate some methods of transmission? Would other methods better represent these, or other, education processes in a culture? Measurement theory and techniques address these types of issues so that the researcher and the reader of research can identify as precisely as possible which aspects of a situation are being studied and how well these variables are measured.

Research Design: Quality and Relevance of Research Results

When conclusions are drawn from results of a study, both the researcher and the reader of research reports need to know how much confidence can be placed in them. There are always alternative explanations for the results of a study, as indicated earlier. Some alternative explanations arise from the measures, or tests, used in a study. Other alternative explanations arise from the procedures used to carry out the study. For example, the two groups of students from Garfield School who used either the phonics or meaning reading curriculum may not have been equivalent. The higher scores received by the students who used the phonics method may not have been caused by the materials; they may simply have resulted from higher initial reading skills—or, more precisely, higher initial skills on those areas measured by the test. Another alternative explanation that is not controlled in the Garfield School study is that the phonics teacher may have been a better teacher than the teacher who used the meaning curriculum.

The researcher who studies the ways that teachers make decisions may study a group of teachers who are not representative of teachers in other settings. This is often true of teachers who volunteer to be part of a new program or agree to participate in research studies. The types of questions asked by the researcher and the researcher's responses to what the teachers said may also affect the results obtained from a study.

Whether planning a study or reviewing the research literature, it is important to recognize and be able to assess the effects of alternative explanations for results obtained in a study. Such recognition and assessment are discussed as issues of research design.

Organizing, Analyzing, and Summarizing Empirical Information

The information, or data, in a study must be organized and analyzed in order to address the problem under investigation. This must be done in ways that best address both the problem and the researcher's purpose for doing the study. There are always different methods that a researcher could use to analyze information.

Each method has certain strengths and weaknesses, or advantages and disadvantages. There is no one right way to analyze data.

Historians, anthropologists, and other types of researchers often collect information that is not easily quantifiable. Many of these researchers believe that quantification of the information (analyzing it into components) oversimplifies it such that they lose important information through quantification. In these fields, methods for organizing and analyzing such information have been developed.

In other areas, such as psychology, economics, physics, and chemistry, most research includes quantification and analysis of the numbers. Although some basic knowledge of mathematics is needed to do the analyses, the use of mathematics to analyze data in research is fundamentally logical. Numerous examples are used to help you understand these logical issues and to show how data analysis is used to draw conclusions in studies.

Interpreting Results of a Study

Drawing appropriate conclusions from a single study, or from a review of literature, requires knowledge not only of the particular problem area (such as third-grade instruction, or teaching and learning in general), but also technical, or methodological, consideration. Learning each methodological technique or skill does not automatically result in producing useful knowledge. The relative importance of various aspects of a research method will be different in each study or setting. To place this knowledge in a meaningful perspective, the logic for drawing conclusions is illustrated using various types of studies in various settings.

To draw conclusions from empirical studies, the weight of evidence must support the conclusion. Which evidence is most important in each setting is not always easy to discern. The more you know about a substantive area, the better prepared you will be to weigh the evidence accurately and insightfully. The evidence is never 100% in support of a single conclusion, either in a simple study or in reviewing many studies. At best, research describes from some perspective a particular aspect of this universe in which we live. Researchers or a reader of research must use this descriptive information along with theories and past experience to interpret its meaning in the situation they are in and for the problem they want to address. Research does not produce truth—only information that must be interpreted before it can be used.

SUMMARY

In this chapter, science is differentiated from other ways of knowing, and the elements of the scientific method are listed and discussed. Assumptions used by researchers from various philosophical perspectives are presented to help you recognize how these assumptions are used and why they are needed. The fact that all knowledge exists within a framework of assumptions, which are often untested or untestable, is an important outcome of this material.

Educational research is defined as using systematic methods to study an educational problem empirically. Basic, applied, and action research (evaluation) are differentiated. In a professional field, little basic research is done. Typical educational studies illustrate both the types of problems that are investigated and methods that are most useful in studying each type of problem.

Increased recognition of changing perspectives about ethical treatment of human beings requires that researchers be aware of present guidelines and recognize their responsibilities to participants in studies. The importance of informed consent and the voluntary nature of participation in studies are major changes in research ethics. Before doing research with human subjects, you must know both the general guidelines and the specific institutional requirements in your setting.

Central elements of the empirical research process are discussed. Their organization into the various chapters of this book provide an overview to help you get a picture of the "forest" of educational research before examining the minute details of the "trees" described in the following chapters. Although presented separately in the various chapters, the specific issues and techniques must be considered wholistically in any study. I have pointed out the relative importance of the various aspects of each study and illustrated the interrelationships in the examples presented.

In the next chapter, the importance of clearly delineating your primary purpose for doing a study is emphasized. The statement of the specific problem and the hypotheses (or research questions) to be addressed in a study can be critically assessed only when the purpose for the study is delineated clearly.

SUGGESTED ACTIVITIES

1. Discuss the definition of science given in this chapter. How does it differ from your definition of science? Can social scientists produce scientific knowledge that is as defensible as that produced by natural scientists? How does science differ from the humanities?
2. Identify a research study in a journal in your field. Specify the author's:
   a. Problem statement.
   b. Purpose for doing the study.
   c. Context in which the problem is studied.
   d. Method used to do the study.
   Identify the evidence that the author used to draw conclusions in the study, indicate implications for practice, and make recommendations for future research. Was the evidence adequate for each of these?
3. In the research study identified in Item 2, identify at least two assumptions that the author must have made to draw the conclusions made in the article. If you were to apply the results of the study to your setting, specify two additional assumptions that you must make to apply it with confidence.

RELATED SOURCES

Conant, J.B. (1951). *On understanding science*. New York: New American Library.

Based on a series of lectures Conant gave at Yale University in 1946, this book provides a perspective on science by a scientist who was productive at the time the first atomic bomb was exploded. It is based on a strong historical foundation of past knowledge produced by science and the processes used to produce it. Conant believes strongly in the value of intensive study of specific discoveries from research in order to learn important characteristics of sciences. The four chapters are: The Scientific Education of the Layman, Illustrations from the 17th Century: Touching the Spring of the Air, Illustrations from the 18th Century Concerning Electricity and Combustion, and Certain Principles of the Tactics and Strategy of Science.

Cook, S.W. (1976). Ethical issues in the conduct of research in social relations. In C. Selltiz, L.S. Wrightman, & S.W. Cook, *Research methods in social relations*. New York: Holt, Rinehart and Winston.

Cook describes the nature of ethical issues that arise when involving human subjects in research. The four sections of the chapter are: Why Ethical Issues Arise in Research with Human Subjects, Questionable Practices Involving Research Participants, Balancing the Costs of Questionable Practices Against the Potential Benefits of the Research, and Responsibilities to Research Participants after Completion of the Research. Cook uses many practical examples of typical problems that occur and discusses how to address them when doing research. He indicates why ethical guidelines have changed and discusses the fundamental nature of the ethical issues that researchers must address.

Ennis, R.H. (1961). Assumption-finding. In B.O. Smith & R.H. Ennis, *Language and concepts in education*. Chicago: Rand McNally.

This book is one of the few sources that describes roles that assumptions often play in education. It provides numerous examples of assumptions and how to identify specific assumptions in various situations. Two of the most important types of assumptions, premises and presuppositions, are emphasized. Finding assumptions is an important element of critical thinking as it is presently taught and tested, particularly in secondary schools and colleges. Becoming more aware of your assumptions is an important step in an educational process.

Pearson, K. (1939). *The grammar of science*. London: J.M. Dent.

This book was originally published in 1892. It presents science as viewed by the developer of the Pearson Product Moment Correlation Coefficient (r). It is very informative, theoretically and practically, about science and the scientific method. Pearson also presents some interesting ideas about how the important aspects of science can best be learned. They are not that different from those of James B. Conant presented in *On Understanding Science*. It is interesting to note the similarities in Pearson's views of science nearly 40 years before the organization of logical positivism, which occurred in the 1930s.

Pirsig, R.M. (1975). *Zen and the art of motorcycle maintenance*. New York: Bantam.

This book is one of the most readable descriptions of scientific methods available. Within the broader context of the various philosophical, ideological, and personal perspectives that people take toward life, the characteristics of method that differentiate science from other ways of knowing is discussed throughout the book. Differences between Eastern and Western philosophies that result in differences in ways people relate to their environment—both physical and personal—are illustrated and discussed. An engaging and enjoyable book to read, regardless of your particular reason for reading it.

Stufflebeam, D., & Webster, W.J. (1988). Evaluation as an administrative function. In N. J. Boyan (Ed.), *Handbook of research on educational administration*. New York: Longman.

These experienced evaluators describe educational evaluation that is carried out in public schools. The various types of evaluations, how to conceptualize and carry them out, how evaluation units are often organized, and four major weaknesses of evaluation as it is presently viewed and practiced are discussed. It is the latest attempt to comprehensively review the state of evaluation in U.S. schools.

REFERENCES

American Heritage Dictionary (1982). Boston: Houghton Mifflin.

Baumrind, D. (1964). Some thoughts on ethics of research: After reading Milgram's "Behavioral study of obedience." *American Psychologist, 19*, 421–423.

Borg, W.R., & Gall, M.D. (1983). *Educational research: An introduction* (3rd Ed.). White Plains, NY: Longman.

APA Committee on Scientific and Professional Ethics and Conduct (1981). Ethical principles of psychologists. *American Psychologist, 36*, 633–638.

Conant, James B. (1951). *On understanding science*. New York: New American Library.

Cook, S.W. (1976). Ethical issues in the conduct of research in social relations. In C. Selltiz, L.S. Wrightsman, & S.W. Cook (Eds.), *Research methods in social relations* (3rd ed.). New York: Holt, Rinehart and Winston.

Garfinkel, H. (1967). What is ethnomethodology? In H. Garfinkel (Ed.), *Studies in ethnomethodology*. Englewood Cliffs, NJ: Prentice-Hall.

Jones, J.H. (1981). *Bad blood: The Tuskegee syphilis experiment*. New York: Free Press.

Kelman, H.C. (1972). The rights of the subject in social research: An analysis in terms of relative power and legitimacy. *American Psychologist, 27*, 987–1016.

Kimmel, A.J. (1981). *Ethics of human subject research*. San Francisco: Jossey-Bass.

Leinhardt, G. (1978). Coming out of the laboratory closet. In D. BarTal & L. Saxe (Eds.), *Social psychology of education: Theory and research*. New York: Hemisphere Publishing Corporation.

Milgram, S. (1963). Behavioral study of obedience. *Journal of Abnormal and Social Psychology, 67*(4), 371–378.

Milgram, S. (1964). Issues in the study of obedience: A reply to Baumrind. *American Psychologist, 19*, 848–852.

Mill, J.S. (1906). *A system of logic*. Vol. 1. London: Longman Green.

National Commission on Excellence in Education (1983). *A nation at risk*. Washington, DC: Superintendent of Documents, U.S. Government Printing Office.

CHAPTER 3

Problem and Purpose of Study

People with little or no experience with research usually find the identification of an important problem for study a forbidding, if not impossible, task. Conceptualizing a study by identifying a problem, specifying hypotheses to test or research questions to answer, and planning the procedures for doing a study are extremely complex tasks. This book provides some guidance by describing each part of a study, the function it serves, and how the parts are interrelated. Intensive study of an area and extensive experience doing research are needed to do valuable research. To read, integrate, and meaningfully interpret the research literature can be nearly as difficult. This book is viewed as a first step in developing these skills.

In this chapter, problem statements, hypotheses, and research questions are described, as are the functions they serve in a research study. The importance of clearly identifying the purpose for doing the study is illustrated. An example of an exemplary study shows how the various parts fit together to make a contribution to knowledge. In the final section, important terms such as operational definition, independent variable, dependent variable, treatment, and research hypothesis are defined.

People too often assume that identifying an important problem for study is one of the easiest aspects of doing research. This may be a result, at least in part, of the fact that there is so much controversy in education and so much that we need to know more about. The difficult part of research in the view of many persons usually lies in the technical aspects of using measurement instruments and analyzing statistical data. As you become more knowledgeable, you will find problem identification to be the most creative and important aspect of doing valuable research.

To provide a broad perspective of the types of educational issues, or contexts, that can be meaningfully studied, some typical titles of historical, ethnographic, economic, sociological, and psychological studies that can be done follow:

1. Historical Studies
    a. The Buffalo NAACP's Fight for Equal Schools: 1910–1930
    b. A History of Academic Freedom in Higher Education
    c. Changing Views of Kindergarten: 1900–1980
    d. Progressivism in U.S. Public Schools: 1950–1960
2. Ethnographic Studies
    a. NICHŪ, a Japanese School
    b. A New Guinea Village and School
    c. School and the Cultural Context
    d. Schooling in the Ghetto
3. Economic Studies
    a. National Economic Conditions and Investments in Education
    b. Economics of Multi-School vs. Mega-School Education
    c. Economic Effects of a Graduate Education Degree
    d. Entrepreneurs in Public Schools
4. Sociological Studies
    a. Social Relationships in High School
    b. Effects of Teachers' Organizations on Education Quality
    c. The Relative Effects of Education and Family on Future Success
    d. Social Methods of Control in High School
5. Psychological Studies
    a. Sugar Intake and Learning to Read
    b. Educational Demands and Student Personality
    c. Student Behavior During Assigned "Seat Work"
    d. Personal Psychological Adjustment and Success in Schools

These short titles do not indicate adequately either the problem to be studied or the reason for studying it. They do describe a wide array of problems that could be investigated empirically. Each problem requires more fine-grained hypotheses or research questions. The differences between hypotheses and research questions and the roles they play in planning and carrying out a study are discussed in the following section.

PROBLEM STATEMENT, HYPOTHESES, AND RESEARCH QUESTIONS

It is not difficult to identify a problem that can be investigated empirically. A sample list of such questions follows:

1. What are the differences in math and reading achievement between economically disadvantaged sixth-grade students and other sixth-grade students in urban areas?

2. What changes in instructional processes have occurred in the past 50 years?
3. What types of changes in classroom instruction result from in-service training?
4. What are the effects of mainstreaming learning disabled children on the academic achievement of these children and of the other children in these classes?
5. What are the sources of educational problems in U.S. public schools?

Each of these questions could be investigated by gathering information empirically. Each could be studied without any intervention on the part of the researcher. In regard to the third question, in-service training must occur before anyone can study its effects, but nearly all school districts provide such training to their teachers. Some research questions require interventions, such as experiments in laboratories, where different groups get different treatments.

Regardless of the kinds of information or procedures required in a study, there is a common structure to problem identification that determines to a great extent the value and potential contribution of a study. The problem includes two parts: the problem statement and the hypotheses to be tested (or research questions to be answered).

The *problem statement* specifies at minimum the variables to be studied and the relationship among them. It may also include defining characteristics of the group studied or the context in which it is studied if they are important. The five questions previously listed could function as problem statements. In the first question, the study is limited to "economically disadvantaged sixth-grade students and other sixth-grade students in urban areas."

The problem statement is the focus of a study. All decisions made by the researcher and the procedures used to carry out the study must be those most appropriate for investigating the problem statement. More specific aspects of the problem that will be answered directly with data are specified as hypotheses (or research questions). In a sense, there is so much packed into a problem statement that it cannot be answered directly with a single analysis of data. In the first question, for example, what is meant by "math and reading achievement"? This term often includes math computations, math concepts, math problem-solving, vocabulary, grammar, reading comprehension, and spelling.

What are "changes in classroom instruction" that are to be affected by in-service training in the third question? Some teacher changes are made in the structure of the class period, such as more individualized work, peer tutoring, or student presentation; other changes may be made in how a topic is presented by the teacher, or how the teacher responds to mistakes. The types of changes of interest in a study are usually those that the in-service training was designed to affect. Those aspects of the problem statement that require more detailed analysis become the operational focus of a study and are delineated more precisely in the hypotheses or research questions.

To illustrate, we can use the first question as a problem statement: *What are the differences in math and reading achievement between economically disadvantaged sixth-grade students and other sixth-grade students in urban areas?* (Notice that the problem statement is in the form of a question. It can be either a question or statement.) Some research questions that could be used to address this problem statement are the following:

1. How do economically disadvantaged sixth-grade students differ form other students on mathematics computation skills?
2. How do economically disadvantaged sixth-grade students differ from other students on knowledge of mathematics concepts?
3. How do economically disadvantaged sixth-grade students differ from other students on mathematical problem solving?
4. How do economically disadvantaged sixth-grade students differ from other students on vocabulary?
5. How do economically disadvantaged sixth-grade students differ from other students on grammar?
6. How do economically disadvantaged sixth-grade students differ from other students on reading comprehension?
7. How do economically disadvantaged sixth-grade students differ from other students on spelling?

Specific tests, or other measurement procedures, would be used to assess economically disadvantaged and other sixth-grade students in each of these seven areas of math and reading achievement. The answers to these questions (within the limitations of the procedures used in the study) are then obtained. The results for all seven research questions are synthesized to answer the problem statement. In most studies, the results will be inconsistent so that the answer to the problem statement is a discussion of obtained results. In this example, the economically disadvantaged students may evidence lower achievement in some areas and not in others. They may even score higher on some types of items than the other students.

How does the researcher decide which variables in the problem statement need to be addressed more specifically in a study and what specific research questions, or hypotheses, to address? These are determined primarily by the researcher's purpose for the study. The difference in achievement between economically disadvantaged and other sixth-grade students can be of interest to many different audiences. Teachers, administrators, counselors, and educational psychologists are four professional groups that have particular interest in these differences. Each of these groups has different concerns and needs that require somewhat different information. For example, what teachers need to plan their lessons and associated instruction is different from what the educational psychologist needs to test the applicability of a particular theory. If this study were being done by a psycholinguist, a specific type of educational psychologist, it is unlikely that the linguist would be interested in both the reading and math achievement differences. In general, psycholinguists would need more specific information about reading and nothing about math achievement. A study by such psychologists would require a different set of hypotheses or research questions from those listed. The seven questions are more useful to teachers and others concerned with the education of children.

The purpose of any study is to contribute to the knowledge in a professional or academic area. The goal of the researcher is to do the best study that is possible at the time that will make the greatest contribution to the knowledge needed by a particular audience. The problem may be theoretical or practical, but it must be clearly understood for the focus of the study to be as clear as possible.

The knowledge need for a study should include the following:

1. A clear description of the knowledge need. (What is the practical or theoretical problem?)
2. Identification of the professional or academic audience for the study. (Who will use the results?)
3. The context in which the study is most important. (Where is it most relevant?)
4. How the knowledge need can be addressed empirically. (How will this study contribute?)

The purpose of the study then becomes to answer the knowledge need. To delineate the purpose of a study, the researcher must know the relevant literature and be intimately familiar with the audience and context of the study. Most research is done to answer the researcher's question. That is, teachers can best do research to answer instructional questions, whereas theoreticians do research to answer theoretical questions. Researchers can do *good* research only in those areas in which they are experienced and knowledgeable.

HYPOTHESES OR RESEARCH QUESTIONS?

To address a knowledge need of some professional or academic audience, a study is conceptualized using a problem statement and associated hypotheses or research questions. The decision to use hypotheses or research questions is an important one that depends on many factors. Some authors equate hypotheses with science, pointing out the many experiments done by physical scientists to test important hypotheses. Others indicate the need to describe some situations as comprehensively as possible so that important data are not overlooked by the researcher during the study. In this section, differences between studies testing hypotheses and those using research questions are discussed to clarify their roles in the inquiry process.

It is true that some logical power is gained from the use of hypotheses when they are appropriate. The power of hypotheses in research lies in the use of some theory or model to state before the study begins precisely what should happen if that theory or model is accurate. Then a researcher assesses whether these predicted results occur, thus testing the applicability of the theory in that setting. A short example describes such a situation.

Several basic researchers have found that many animals, including human beings, respond aggressively when they are frustrated. A good deal of theory has been developed about frustration and aggression. As a hypothetical example, let's say some teachers experience such relationships in teaching third-grade children. When their students were frustrated, they tended to hit other children, cry out in class, and be negative in their behavior toward the teacher. To test the applicability of the general theory to young students in classrooms, these teachers designed a research study. One group of students was given a test comprised of items that no third-grade students could answer correctly, which should cause frustration in these students. A second group of students was given an easy test in which most students would correctly answer all items. Students' physical and verbal aggression toward other children and the teacher for the two groups were compared. The problem statement and hypotheses for this study are as follows:

PROBLEM STATEMENT:

> Third-grade students who are frustrated will evidence greater physical and verbal aggression toward other students and the teacher than will similar students who are not frustrated.

HYPOTHESES:

1. Third-grade students frustrated by a very difficult test will evidence greater frequency of verbal aggression toward other students than will similar students who took an easy test.
2. Third-grade students frustrated by a very difficult test will evidence greater frequency of physical aggression toward other students than will similar students who took an easy test.
3. Third-grade students frustrated by a very difficult test will evidence greater frequency of verbal aggression toward the teacher than will similar students who took an easy test.
4. Third-grade students frustrated by a very difficult test will evidence greater frequency of physical aggression toward the teacher than will similar students who took an easy test.

The results of this study would indicate the applicability of the theory about frustration and aggression to third-grade children who take a difficult test that generates frustration. If there are no differences in aggression between the frustrated and nonfrustrated groups, the theory is not applicable in this particular situation. If there is greater aggression by the frustrated group toward either the teacher or other students in any of the four hypotheses, the theory is supported.

The specific ways in which aggression is shown by frustrated third graders can be described from the results obtained in testing the four hypotheses, and insights into the behavior of third-grade children under these two types of testing conditions are gained.

The logical power of the hypothesis lies in our being able to prespecify what will occur in a specific situation based on a particular theory about frustration and aggression. When the results come out as predicted from the theory, there is strong support for the theory. When the results do not support the theory, then its applicability in this situation is questioned. In either case a well-designed study is a strong test of theory when hypotheses can be prespecified.

The study of achievement differences between economically disadvantaged sixth graders and other urban students illustrates that simply stating research questions as hypotheses does *not* improve the logical power of a study or change its fundamental character. The problem statement and research questions could have been stated as hypotheses, as follows:

PROBLEM STATEMENT:

Economically disadvantaged sixth-grade students evidence lower math and reading achievement than other students in urban areas.

HYPOTHESES:

1. Economically disadvantaged sixth-grade students evidence lower mathematics computation skills than other students in the same urban schools.
2. Economically disadvantaged sixth-grade students evidence lower mathematics concepts knowledge than other students in the same urban schools.
3. Economically disadvantaged sixth-grade students evidence lower mathematical problem-solving than other students in the same urban schools.
4. Economically disadvantaged sixth-grade students evidence less knowledge of vocabulary than other students in the same urban schools.
5. Economically disadvantaged sixth-grade students evidence lower skill in grammar than other students in the same urban schools.
6. Economically disadvantaged sixth-grade students evidence lower reading comprehension than other students in the same urban schools.
7. Economically disadvantaged sixth-grade students evidence lower skill in spelling than other students in the same urban schools.

In this example, there is no specific theory about why economically disadvantaged students should evidence lower math and reading achievement. Because there is no controversy about the fact that economically disadvantaged students tend to evidence lower achievement and no theories that imply that these students should evidence higher achievement, the data do not test the applicability of a theory or model. The results can be used to describe achievement differences between the two groups. When controversy exists, with theories and research support that predict various outcomes, a hypothesis-testing situation occurs. Such a hypothesis-testing study would generate more confidence in the results of the study because it would test the applicability of a theory or model used to predict expected outcomes. The results obtained in the study just described provide only a description of differences between economically disadvantaged students and other sixth-grade students and do not test meaningful conceptual hypotheses about controversial issues.

The logical power provided by testing hypotheses can be gained in a study using research questions if a well-delineated analysis and synthesis of the literature produce *specific* expectations for results in a study. By examining previous relevant research and associated theories that might explain the well-documented lower achievement of economically disadvantaged students, expectations about the results a researcher would expect can often be specified. If it is possible, to prespecify precise hypotheses usually allows a more detailed analysis of the results and informs educators (or theoreticians) about specific differences that may have educational implications. For example, to hypothesize about the types of math computations that these children find most difficult, or the specific problem contexts, would deal with new dimensions or variables and would transform the study into hypothesis testing. Issues about the *specific* reading and math problems economically disadvantaged students have with present school curricula and evaluation procedures are controversial, and information about them would be useful to teachers and other educators. To indicate only that achievement will be lower adds no new information. These students' lower academic achievement, in general, is well documented.

In much of the educational and other social science research, such previous research and associated theory have not been developed. The researcher is simply describing the types of differences between the two groups in ways that would seem to be most valuable. As shown, a descriptive study cannot become a hypothesis-testing study by simply restating research questions as hypotheses. In this example, the comparison between the economically disadvantaged and other sixth-grade students is a descriptive study.

In summary, whether the specific relationships to be investigated in a study are indicated as research questions or hypotheses depends on numerous considerations. The first is, of course, the purpose for doing the study. Next is the amount of previous research and associated theory or models. Only when previous research and theory are adequately developed can meaningful hypotheses be specified. The value of hypotheses in a study is the confidence they provide for conclusions drawn in a study. If a researcher can predict precisely how the economically disadvantaged sixth-grade students will differ from other urban sixth-grade students in math and reading and then obtain exactly the relationships that the theories predict, convincing evidence of the predictive value of the theory is obtained. To identify a theory that is consistent with the data obtained after a study is completed is not as convincing, because the researcher's previous literature review did not identify it as most promising for describing the situation to be studied. Once data are collected and results are obtained, a person can easily develop a rationale, or theory, for how it occurred. Only when that theory accurately predicts results in new situations can we be confident of its value, or applicability.

The difference is akin to using a theory to predict an eclipse of the sun two years before it is to occur, and developing or selecting a theory after an eclipse of the sun occurred that explains how or why it occurred. In a similar vein, do you have more confidence in an investment adviser who predicted the October 1987 stock market drop a few weeks before it occurred or someone who produced creative, detailed explanations for the drop in November or December, months after the drop had happened? The ability to predict future outcomes accurately represents the increased value, or logical power, of the theory or model used to predict the results obtained, such as with hypotheses, compared to *post hoc* explanations for obtained results.

CONCEPTUALIZING A RESEARCH STUDY

The need for a researcher to specify the purpose of a study is not broadly recognized. Many people believe that once an important problem is identified, such as the need for improved vocabulary instruction or increasing the achievement of economically disadvantaged students, the data obtained in a study will describe it comprehensively so that all persons concerned with the problem (teacher, principal, counselor, or psychologist) will have the information they need. Thus, a good study should meet everyone's needs. In fact, just the opposite is true. A good study has a clearly delineated purpose that will best meet the needs of one audience for one situation or type of problem.

Some fundamental assumptions about the nature of data and knowledge are embedded in this erroneous belief. As indicated previously, information needed by a teacher will be different from that needed by a principal or psycholinguist. Studies that contribute to our fundamental knowledge of a theory *may* be applicable by some practitioners if they have the background and know the language well enough to understand the information provided. Even then the teacher or other practitioner must take huge inferential leaps from relatively limited basic research data to application in a practical setting. This must be done cautiously, because educators are dealing with the lives of other humans.

Another assumption is that a researcher can describe comprehensively what exists in the world. If one research study is to meet the knowledge needs of several audiences, then the data must address the situation in ways that each audience requires. It is important to keep in mind that the world is infinite. Each concept, variable, or measure addresses only selected aspects of this infinity. For example, important aspects of reading comprehension are different for elementary school teachers, linguists, psycholinguists, employers, and trainers of army enlistees. It is the height of arrogance, or incompetence, to believe that one study will adequately address the knowledge needs of various audiences. Each audience may obtain some interesting or useful information, but a study should be designed to make the most valuable contribution to the knowledge of only one audience. Many do not do that!

To illustrate the points made in this chapter, excerpts from an actual study follow. The author first demonstrates the importance of the general problem of learning vocabulary and its relationship to intelligence and reading comprehension. Next she gives the background for the specific problem that she will study. The audience (professionals concerned with vocabulary instruction), context (fifth-grade classrooms), general procedure (identify behaviors that characterize the process when it is successful and when it is not as successful), the purpose of the study (to improve vocabulary instruction) are each identified or clearly implied. Then the specific problem statement to be addressed and the research questions to be answered in the study are listed.

In reading the excerpts from McKeown's study, identify those aspects needed to conceptualize a research study and their interrelationships in this particular study. Look to see that the research questions are the most important questions for her audience and purpose. In a well-designed and well-planned study, answers to the following questions are clear to the reader.

1. What is the problem that is addressed?
2. Where is it most relevant?
3. Who will use the results of the study?
4. How will the study contribute to this audience in this context?

The problem and purpose of the study are the most important aspects of it and drive all other activities in doing the study. Be able to identify the tight logic in this study. Are there still holes in the logic for you as you read it?

EXAMPLE 3   CONCEPTUALIZING A RESEARCH STUDY (McKEOWN DOCTORAL DISSERTATION)

The Acquisition of Word Meaning from Context by Children of High and Low Vocabulary Ability*

A good vocabulary is commonly regarded as a mark of an educated or intelligent person. Indeed, there is a strong statistical relationship between vocabulary knowledge and intelligence. The extent of the relationship is such that vocabu-

*Doctoral Dissertation by Margaret G. McKeown, University of Pittsburgh (1983). Sections reprinted with permis-

lary measures are used as indicators of overall intelligence level and as predictors of school success. The importance of vocabulary as a predictor is partly a reflection of its role in another area; that of reading comprehension. Although the specific connections between vocabulary knowledge and reading comprehension are not fully understood, it is well accepted that a strong, and under at least some conditions, causal, relationship exists between them (Beck, Perfetti, & McKeown, 1982; Davis, 1944, 1968; Kameenui, Carnine, & Freschi, 1982). Given the implications that vocabulary knowledge carries, it is not surprising that educators have long sought to impart a good vocabulary to their students. Vocabulary-building activities are common in classrooms at every level, with the most pervasive example being the vocabulary strand that appears in virtually all basal reading series, which are the backbone of the reading curriculum in American elementary school classrooms.

Questions about vocabulary, such as how many and which words do people know, what is the role of vocabulary in academic development, and how is vocabulary best learned have been pursued since at least the work of Thorndike (1917) early in this century. Thorndike proposed that the best way to expand vocabulary was through wide reading. Since then there has been much debate about the investigation of whether vocabulary development is best enhanced by instruction that focuses on meanings of specific words, on word elements, on the use of context clues, or instruction that merely allows for wide reading on a diverse array of topics. Although the topic of vocabulary and vocabulary instruction experienced somewhat of a hiatus around mid-century (Calfee & Drum, 1978), it is now once again an area of active research interest.

Currently, much vocabulary research is focused on understanding the relationship between vocabulary knowledge and reading comprehension. This means not only asking if knowing or learning words leads to comprehension, but under what conditions does it do so and what brings about those conditions. This orientation demonstrates a consideration of cognitive functions that underlie and enable vocabulary learning.

Background and Statement of Problem

The current period of research in verbal comprehension has been heavily influenced by information processing, which can be considered as steps by which information is acted upon by an individual. These steps include recognizing and encoding presented information, activating related information that is already in memory, comparing this new information to what is stored, and then creating a representation of the meaning of the information newly encountered (cf. Newell & Simon, 1972; Pellegrino & Glaser, 1982; Trabasso, 1972). Within an informa-

---

sion. This study earned the best dissertation award from the International Reading Association in 1983. Some editorial changes have been made to emphasize specific points and to conserve space. McKeown's references appear at the end of the chapter in the reference section.

tion-processing framework, the acquisition of vocabulary is not simply familiarization with definitions. Rather it is a complex verbal process that involves the recognition and establishment of relationships between concepts, the classification of concepts into superordinate categories, and the expansion and refinement of knowledge about individual words (cf. DiVesta, 1974; Palermo & Molfese, 1972).

Within the complex process of vocabulary acquisition lies the potential for wide variation in individual vocabulary performance. Factors such as how well words are known, what is known about them, and the process of acquiring knowledge about words have been found to differentiate successful and less successful verbal comprehenders (Curtis, 1981, Note 1; Sternberg & Powell, 1983; van Daalen-Kapteijns & Elshout-Mohr, 1981; Werner & Kaplan, 1952). For example, Curtis (1981) found that high and low scorers on a multiple-choice vocabulary test differed not only in the numbers of words whose meanings they could correctly identify, but also in the amount and quality of information they possessed about words that both groups knew.

Drawing from information-processing theory and empirical work, the instructional goal of enhancing vocabulary knowledge should not be one of merely providing word meanings, but also of helping students to discover relationships between words, to apply words in new situations, and to build skills for learning words independently. The achievement of such goals suggests two directions for vocabulary research. One is strongly and directly instructional, the investigation of teaching methods or techniques that bring about improvement in vocabulary skill. The other direction of research is the investigation of processes that enable vocabulary learning and determine one's success as a vocabulary learner. . . .

This study presents a vocabulary learning situation in which a child responds to a series of contexts designed to tap components of the process of learning vocabulary from context. These vocabulary learning situations are presented in order to learn what behaviors characterize that process when it is successful and when it is less successful. Analysis of successful and less successful processes should reveal the amount and quality of information children of varying ability levels obtain from context and how they make use of the information in inferring word meaning. The outcome of such analysis addresses instructional issues either by suggesting what children need to learn in order to use context effectively, or the kind of information about words and the contexts in which they appear that needs to be communicated directly if instruction is to be maximally effective. . . .

PROBLEM STATEMENT:

This study is designed to investigate the relative importance of selected skills in the process of acquiring word meanings from context in children of varying vocabulary ability.

RESEARCH QUESTIONS:

1. Do students with higher vocabulary ability differ from students with lower vocabulary ability in the selection of contextual constraints they use as clues to the meaning of an unknown word?
2. Do students with higher vocabulary ability differ from students with lower vocabulary ability in their ability to test the contraints selected to evaluate possible meanings?
3. Do students with higher vocabulary ability differ from students with lower vocabulary in the ability to coordinate two contexts to constrain word meaning?
4. Do students with higher vocabulary ability differ from students with lower vocabulary ability in the ability to test the coordinated constraints to evaluate possible meanings?
5. Do students with higher vocubulary ability differ from students with lower vocabulary ability in the ability to discriminate contexts that are helpful from those that are nonhelpful for constraining word meaning?
6. Do students with higher vocabulary ability differ from students with lower vocabulary ability in the ability to assign correct meaning to a new word after exposure to contexts containing direct clues to meaning?
7. Do students with higher vocabulary ability differ from students with lower vocabulary ability in the ability to recognize appropriate use of a newly acquired word in novel contexts?

As in many well-done studies, the specific audience and the context in which members of the audience will apply the results is not directly specified by McKeown. In this study, the clear and relatively comprehensive description of the problem that is being studied and the researcher's primary purpose for studying it identify the audience who will find the study most useful. The focus on educators concerned with vocabulary instruction as the primary audience is shown most directly in the seven research questions that McKeown lists. These are clearly questions about variables that affect students' learning of vocabulary that have instructional implications. They do, of course, have theoretical implications also, but if she had been primarily concerned with addressing theoretical issues she would have used different questions.

The seven research questions address relationships between vocabulary learning and reading comprehension that McKeown had previously identified. In each question, the difference in use of context or constraints between higher and lower vocabulary ability students to understand the meaning of a word (reading comprehension) are assessed. The entire study is focused on that relationship, and it is designed and carried out to investigate best those aspects of that relationship that are most likely to affect vocabulary development of fifth-grade students as they carry out their educational studies.

A number of terms have been used in this chapter that have not been adequately defined. In the following section, terms most relevant to the study of problems, and the research questions or hypotheses used, are defined and examples of their uses in research are discussed.

DEFINING TERMS

An important aspect of all communication is agreement on the meaning of words or symbols used. Most terms have precise meanings when used in research. Some of the most important are the following:

- Independent variable
- Dependent variable
- Treatment
- Variable
- Research hypothesis
- Null hypothesis
- Operational definition

Definitions and descriptions of these terms as they are used in research follow.

When an independent variable is manipulated in a study, as was done by the two Garfield teachers who used the phonics and meaning approaches to teaching reading, the terms are defined by the materials used or the treatment students experienced. The independent variable, instructional method, was manipulated in the Garfield study by assigning half of the students to the phonics treatment and half to the meaning treatment. The *operational definition* of the variable in this study (instructional method) is the total of all differences between the phonics and meaning treatments that the two groups experienced. When these treatments occur over several months in regular classrooms, it is impossible to describe all differences in the reading-relevant experiences of the two groups. The researcher can specify only the textbooks, other materials, and procedures used to operationalize each approach. These descriptions become the operational definitions for the phonics and meaning treatments that the researchers implemented to vary the instructional method for these two groups of students.

The meanings of the terms *independent variable* and *treatment* are often confused. The *independent variable* is the aspect of a situation that is manipulated in a study. The researcher's purpose is to assess the effects of the independent variable on the *dependent variable*. In the Garfield study, researchers assessed the effects of the kind of instruction students experienced (phonics or meaning) on their levels of reading achievement (dependent variable). The students' reading achievement should depend on which aspect of the independent variable they experienced.

The *treatments* experienced by a participant in this study is the specific reading instruction (phonics or meaning) the student experienced. The differences in the two treatments are the variations in the independent variable that are of primary interest to the researcher. Instructional methods could be varied in a number of ways. For example, three groups could be used in the study and a third treatment could include the eclectic reading method that teachers in that school district normally use. The independent variable, instructional method, would vary across three treatments, rather than just the two used in this study.

A *variable* in a study is any dimension or aspect that varies. In Example 3, students vary in vocabulary ability and in the other seven dimensions that were measured. Researchers study the degree to which scores, or variations, on one variable (vocabulary) are related to scores on the other seven variables. In the Garfield study (Example 1), the gender of the teachers did not vary; both teachers were female. The gender of the teachers was a constant in this study.

Another important distinction is that between research and null hypotheses. A *research hypothesis* states the relationship between variables that the researcher expects to obtain in a study. All hypotheses stated in this chapter have been research hypotheses. For example, the following research hypothesis describes the researcher's expectations:

> Third-grade students frustrated by a very difficult test will evidence greater frequency of verbal aggression toward other students in their classroom than will similar students who took an easy test.

A *null hypothesis* is one that states that there is no effect or no impact in the study. A null hypothesis is the hypothesis that is usually tested by a statistical test of significance in a study. The foregoing research hypothesis restated as a null hypothesis is as follows:

> There is no difference between third-grade students who are frustrated by a difficult test and similar students who took an easy test in the frequency of verbal aggression toward other students in their classroom.

Most readers find it easier to read research hypotheses in a study rather than null hypotheses. The research hypothesis is consistent with the related research and theory described in the study. A null hypothesis is simply part of the technical process of testing the results for statistical significance. The process used to test hypotheses and the underlying logic are described in Chapter 7.

Readers of research need definitions in order to precisely identify the procedures used in a study, the results that were obtained, and the meaning of those results. In any study, there are two types of definitions for all important terms: conceptual and operational. The conceptual definition is like a dictionary definition in that it gives the meaning of a word or term. For example, reading achievement can be defined as the level of skill in comprehending the meaning of written or printed material. A person's vocabulary is defined as the sum of words used by, understood, or at the command of that person. The operational definition of a term in a study, such as phonics method or reading achievement, is the process used to implement or measure it in that study. Reading achievement is often defined operationally as the total score earned on the reading subtests of the Metropolitan Achievement Test (or some other commercial test).

In a research report, terms are usually defined conceptually in the "Introduction" or "Review of Literature." When the methods for carrying out the study are specified, the important terms, or variables, to be addressed in the study must be operationally defined. The most important terms are usually those in the research questions or hypotheses that will be answered or tested directly with data in the study. To study the achievement of economically disadvantaged students, the terms italicized in the research question that follows must be operationally defined before anyone can answer the question accurately.

How do *economically disadvantaged sixth-grade students* differ from *other urban sixth-grade students* on *mathematics computation skills*?

The three terms to be operationally defined are the following:

1. Economically disadvantaged sixth-grade (urban) students.
2. Other urban sixth-grade students.
3. Mathematics computation skills.

Students will be identified as *economically disadvantaged* if their custodial parent is receiving Aid for Dependent Children (ADC) or other government welfare aid as indicated on official government records, or if a parent reports less than $12,000 in annual family income on a questionnaire administered at the beginning of the school year.

All sixth-grade students who attend more than 100 days of school in sixth-grade classrooms of the Pittsburgh Public School District (PPSD) are defined as urban students in this study. The *other urban students* are all such PPSD students who are *not* classified as economically disadvantaged students.

Mathematics computation skills are defined as the skills measured by the mathematics computation subtest of the California Achievement Test, Level 6, Form A. The students' standard scores on this subtest will be used to indicate their levels of mathematics computation skill.

Such operational definitions are needed by the researcher and by the readers of the research report to determine the characteristics used to classify a student as economically disadvantaged, as sixth-grade urban students, and according to his or her mathematics computation skills. Without such definitions, it would be impossible to determine which students were economically disadvantaged and which were not, and each student's level of math computation skills.

The operational definitions used in any study represent the researcher's best effort to implement the concept or variable precisely and accurately in that setting. Each of the three foregoing operational definitions has weaknesses that should raise questions or concerns in your mind. For example, are the data used to classify students as economically disadvantaged accurate? Are the government lists up to date? Will parents honestly report their family income? Do they know it? Do all students in the PPSD schools live in an urban situation? Are the mathematics computation subtests of the CAT appropriate measures of these skills for both groups of students? Are some important computations skills *not* measured by these subtests? Are these tests biased against the economically disadvantaged students?

Such questions can be raised in most studies as researchers attempt to implement and study complex concepts or issues. The extent to which the operational definitions do not adequately represent the terms they are defining is the extent to which confidence is lost in the conclusions reached in a study. For example, if the procedure used to classify the sixth-grade students as economically disadvantaged results in many of the students being misclassified, the differences in achievement will not represent differences between economically disadvantaged and other urban students. If the math computation subtest does not include skills that are important to teachers or other educators concerned with math instruction, the results of using this subtest will be of little or no value to them.

The selection of the operational definitions in a study always requires compromise. A comprehensive operational definition is never possible, so the researcher must make choices on the basis of the researcher's primary purpose for doing the study. Thus, a commercial achievement test may be adequate for answering teachers' questions but not adequate for addressing those of a psychologist or counselor. The operational definitions are chosen to produce the best study for the audience and the researcher's specific purpose for doing the study. When these are not clearly in the researcher's mind, a good, tight study is unlikely to result.

Given the various kinds of definitions and different ways that variables can be specified, how should problem statements, research questions, or hypotheses be stated? Some authors say that research questions and hypotheses should include all operational definitions of terms. From the relatively simple example just given, it should be clear that this is not possible, even though some person may believe it to be desirable.

In all writing, the primary goal should be to communicate what you have in mind as precisely as possible to your readers. This is never easy, in part because we vary so much in our background knowledge, relevant experience, and interests. In stating problems, hypotheses, and research questions, it is important to remember that the researcher is using this study of a specific situation to draw conclusions about many other situations. Therefore, the problem statement should be an accurate indication of the relationships between two or more variables that are generalizable to other settings. In studying the differences between economically disadvantaged and other urban students, the dependent variable of the most generalizable interest is "reading and math achievement," which is specified in the problem statement. Those aspects of the dependent variable that are most valuable to the audience of the study (educators concerned with math and reading instruction), are the dependent variables in the research questions or hypotheses:

- Math computation
- Math concepts
- Math problem solving
- Vocabulary
- Grammar
- Reading comprehension
- Spelling

In Example 3, the McKeown study, the problem statement was "to investigate the relative importance of selected skills in the process of acquiring word meanings from context in children of varying vocabulary ability."

The research questions allowed a detailed analysis of the independent variable, selected skills in acquiring word meaning from context. The first three research questions from the dissertation are listed to illustrate this fact.

1. Do students with higher vocabulary ability differ from students with lower vocabulary ability in the selection of contextual constraints they use as clues to the meaning of an unknown word?
2. Do students with higher vocabulary ability differ from students with lower vocabulary ability in their ability to test the constraints selected to evaluate possible meanings?
3. Do students with higher vocabulary ability differ from students with lower vocabulary in the ability to coordinate two contexts to constrain word meaning?

Those elements of the independent variables that are used in each question are underlined above. The dependent variable (knowledge of word meaning) remains the same in each case. Research questions or hypotheses in a study are usually more detailed aspects of either the independent or dependent variable in the problem statement. In some cases, aspects of both the independent and dependant variable are more finely delineated in the research questions or hypotheses.

The differences in vocabulary ability that define the two groups that are studied do not represent an *independent variable* because we cannot manipulate it. It is a *classification variable*. Another classification variable we have used is the economic level of a student's family (economically disadvantaged compared with all others). This distinction is particularly important when a researcher tries to study variables that can be manipulated. To find out that economically disadvantaged students do not achieve as well as other students does not help to alleviate the problem. We cannot change disadvantaged students into advantaged students. Other classification variables that often occur in studies are race, sex, age, intelligence, religion, personality type, level of education, socioeconomic status, and other demographic characteristics. At times it is important that the researcher know whether the variable studied is an independent or classification variable.

The more specific aspects of variables that are of most interest to an audience are usually identified from an extensive review of relevant literature. By examining what other researchers have done and identifying the theories and models that seem most promising, the researcher is able to identify the dimensions of the problem that seem most fruitful to investigate. These important aspects of the problem become the basis for the research questions or hypotheses of the study. They also affect greatly the methods that are used to study the problem.

SUMMARY

The purpose for doing a study determines to a great extent everything else in the study: the problem statement, research questions, variables, measures, design, data analysis, and interpretation of results. The purpose usually includes the knowledge need, audience, context, and contribution of the study. The problem statement is the relationship among variables that the audience in that context needs to know more about. The contribution of the study is to provide the most meaningful information to investigate the problem statement.

Differences between hypothesis-testing and descriptive (or research question) studies are described and discussed. The logical power of prespecifying hypotheses or expectations and then testing them is illustrated.

Important terms used in doing research are defined: independent and dependent variables, treatment, research, null, and statistical hypotheses, and operational definitions. Distinctions between operational definitions of independent and dependent variables that commonly occur in research are identified. Characteristics of groups that cannot be manipulated, such as gender, race, age, or socioeconomic status, are classification variables.

To identify the most appropriate problem statement and hypotheses (or research questions) in a study, you must be familiar with past research and associated theory. This usually requires an extensive review of related literature that takes up to six months to complete. Important characteristics of a review of literature in a research study and how to do a good literature review are addressed in Chapter 4.

SUGGESTED ACTIVITIES

1. Read a research article of your choice.
    a. Identify the author's purpose for doing the study.
    b. Identify the primary audience for the study and the knowledge need that is addressed.

    c. Specify the problem statement and research questions (or hypotheses) that are addressed in the study.

    d. If possible, identify the theoretical or conceptual framework for the study and the primary disciplinary base(s).

    e. List the major conclusions reached in the study and the evidence on which each conclusion was based.

    f. List questions that you have after reviewing the article.

2. Discuss the relationship between McKeown's purpose for doing her study, the problem statement, and the research questions. Do these research questions address those variables that most concern teachers as they plan their vocabulary instruction? Are there other variables that would have been useful to investigate?

3. Identify a research article in your field. Specify the problem statement in the study. Identify the independent and dependent variables that were used in the study. Specify the operational definition of the dependent variable. Specify the operational definition of the independent, or classification, variable.

RELATED SOURCES

Borg, W.R., & Gall, M.D. (1983). *Educational research: An introduction* (4th ed.). White Plains, NY: Longman.

    The first chapters of this book provide a good foundation in the logical basis for conceptualizing a study. Various kinds of educational problems and issues are used to illustrate the use of hypotheses and research questions to carry out research. The book provides one of the most comprehensive lists of relevant sources of any introductory text on eductional research methods. Mistakes commonly made by researchers, which the authors list, are useful as you plan your own research or read empirical studies. It is a classic text in the positivist tradition, emphasizing objective measurement and experimental manipulation.

Castetter, W.B., & Heisler, R.S. (1984). *Developing and defending a dissertation proposal* (4th ed.). Philadelphia, PA: Graduate School of Education, University of Pennsylvania.

    This short (75-page) booklet provides a succinct overview of the logic of educational inquiry. The various parts of a research plan are described with several illustrations of each. The sections on significance of the study, role of the problem statement, and review of related literature are particularly valuable. A number of techniques researchers can use to develop their plans for studies are included. The centrality of the problem statement in the inquiry process is emphasized. The title is somewhat misleading because there is much more to developing and defending a dissertation (or thesis) than the issues addressed in this book. Mauch and Birch (1983), which is described at the end of Chapter 9, provide a more comprehensive discussion of how to complete a thesis or dissertation successfully.

Selltiz, C., Wrightman, L.S., & Cook, S.W. (1976). *Research methods in social relations* (3rd ed.). New York: Holt, Rinehart and Winston.

    Produced for the Society for the Psychological Study of Social Issues, this introduction to research methods has been a classic for more than 20 years. It addresses the many substantive issues and methodological procedures central to doing social research.

The first three chapters: Why Do Research?, The Logic of Analysis, and Selection and Formulation of a Problem, provide a broad background and many practical examples of social problems that have been studied. The role of hypotheses in the process and associated issues of falsifiability are emphasized. The examples, which are from psychology and social psychology primarily, provide a clear and understandable description of the logic of empirical research. It is somewhat more technical and uses more jargon common to the academic disciplines of psychology and sociology than does this text on disciplined inquiry in education.

REFERENCES

Beck, I.L., Perfetti, C.A., & McKeown, M.G. (1982). Effects of long-term vocabulary instruction on lexical access and reading comprehension. *Journal of Educational Psychology, 74*, 506–521.

Calfee, R.C. & Drum, P.A. (1978). Learning to read: Theory, research, and practice. *Curriculum Inquiry, 8*, 183–249.

Curtis, M.E. (1981). *The relationship of word knowledge to verbal aptitude.* Unpublished paper, Pittsburgh: Learning Research and Development Center, University of Pittsburgh.

Davis, F.B. (1944). Fundamental factors of comprehension in reading. *Psychometrika, 9*, 185–197.

Davis, F.B. (1968). Research in comprehension in reading. *Reading Research Quarterly, 4*, 499–545.

DiVesta, F.J. (1974). *Language, learning, & cognitive processes.* Monterey, CA: Brooks/Cole Publishing Company.

Kameenui, E.J., Carnine, D.W., & Freschi, R. (1982). Effects of text construction and instructional procedures for teaching word meanings on comprehension and recall. *Reading Research Quarterly, 17*, 367–388.

Newell, A., & Simon, H.A. (1972). *Human problem solving.* Englewood Cliffs, NJ: Prentice Hall.

Palermo, D.S., & Molfese, D.L. (1972). Language acquisition from age five onward. *Psychological Bulletin, 78*, 409–428.

Pellegrino, J.W., & Glaser, R. (1982). Analyzing aptitudes for learning: Inductive reasoning. In R. Glaser (Ed.), *Advances in instructional psychology, 2*, Hillsdale, NJ: Lawrence Erlbaum Associates.

Sternberg, R.J., & Powell, J.S. (1983). Comprehending verbal comprehension. *American Psychologist, 38*, 878–890.

Thorndike, E.L. (1917). Reading as reasoning: A study of mistakes in paragraph reading. *Journal of Educational Psychology, 8*, 323–332.

Trabasso, T. (1972). Mental operations in language communication. In J.D. Carroll & R.O. Freedle (Eds.), *Language comprehension and the acquisition of knowledge.* Washington, DC: V.H. Winston.

van Daalen-Kapteijns, M.M., & Elshout-Mohr, M. (1981). The acquisition of word meanings as a cognitive learning process. *Journal of Verbal Learning and Verbal Behavior, 20*, 386–399.

Werner, H., & Kaplan, E. (1952). The acquisition of word meanings: A development study. *Monographs of the Society for Research in Child Development, 15* (Serial No. 51, No. 1).

CHAPTER 4

Reviewing Literature Relevant to a Problem

Trying to learn more about a problem or situation that concerns you usually involves reading research and other related material that you can find in libraries. As students in elementary and secondary schools, we have all written "research" papers based on information contained in such sources. These reviews usually address important historical or academic topics. Learning to identify and obtain materials relevant to a topic and synthesizing the information obtained is an important part of education.

In some cases, an issue of personal concern requires a review of literature. An example of this occurred when my son, Derek, was born with a depression in his chest that was exaggerated more when he breathed. The doctor told us not to worry but to keep an eye on it. Derek had a number of respiratory problems during his first year. Someone indicated that an operation might help him. Before making that decision, I went to the medical library at the university where I worked and learned all that I could about "inverted sternums" and operations performed to correct it.

A new operation had been developed only five or six years earlier that seemed to hold much promise. Several articles reported the steps in the operation and the results that were obtained with young children. It looked encouraging, so we took Derek to a cardiovascular surgeon who recommended the operation. The ability to read the research literature did not make me an expert on the medical treatment of inverted sternums, but it did help me to ask relevant questions, better understand the answers, and make a more informed decision about Derek's operation.

Many personal and professional decisions are informed by reading relevant literature. Seldom does a crisis such as the inverted sternum arise that requires a systematic, comprehensive review of literature for a personal problem. The skills needed to do a formal review of literature are extremely valuable, however, in making sense of the research and related literature for personal or professional problems. When people are confronted with such problems, they seldom put forth the effort to do a systematic, comprehensive review of relevant literature—even though it would allow them to obtain a better understanding of the personal or professional problem that concerns them. In many cases, such a review would also save time in the long run because less time would be needed when similar problems arose in the future. One of the most surprising aspects of learning principles of research is how practical and useful they are in other aspects of our personal and professional lives. This is illustrated in the following section where functions of a review of literature relevant to a proposed study are listed and discussed.

FUNCTIONS OF THE LITERATURE REVIEW

Different authors delineate different lists of functions for a review of literature. The list of functions that follows is a relatively short list of important functions that a literature review should serve in order to enhance a researcher's understanding of a problem and how best to study it. A review of literature is carried out to accomplish the following:

1. Learn the history of the problem.
2. Become familiar with the theoretical background of the problem.
3. Assess the strengths and weaknesses of previous studies.
4. Identify promising ways to study the problem.
5. Develop a conceptual framework and rationale for the present study.

It should be clear from this list of functions that the more you know about a problem area from previous study, especially the relevant research and theory, the less time and effort will be needed for the review when a specific study is planned. In most cases, it takes a student three to five months or more to complete a comprehensive review of literature needed to plan a thesis or dissertation study.

A review of literature is usually started as soon as a general problem area is identified. The researcher may have a specific study in mind and tentatively identify a problem statement, even some research questions. The researcher is aware, however, that these are likely to change as a result of what is learned from the review. Only after the researcher knows as much as possible about the problem can the best problem statement and hypotheses (or research questions) for the study be identified.

Learn the History of the Problem

In reading about the problem and ways that others have studied it, the researcher learns how others have thought about the problem: its disciplinary base, theoretical conception, and the changing ways that it has been addressed over time. The relevant period to be reviewed may be relatively short, five to ten years, or it may be a century or more. Too often the naive researcher thinks of the problem in too focused a fashion and is not able to identify the broader problem that the specific problem represents. Psychologists and sociologists have studied individual or group behavior and produced theories that can be used to represent most situations that occur in education. Educators who are unfamiliar with the appropriate psychological and sociological theories and the associated research may initially think that little or no previous work exists that is relevant to their problem. This has never been the case in my experience. It is probably never the case. In fact, the final function in the foregoing list is to develop a conceptual framework for the study of this problem. That is a creative, generative process and not simply the selection of a framework from two or three alternatives that are clearly delineated by other authors. A researcher must develop a framework for a study. There is always some research and theory that are relevant.

Some people argue that learning how others have viewed and studied the problem will stifle creativity and decrease the likelihood that meaningful insights will be gained. Without rejecting this view totally, it is much more likely that previous work will not be repeated unintentionally and that nonproductive methods will be avoided as a result of doing a comprehensive literature review. When the researcher knows what others have done, particularly when that work is critically analyzed and synthesized, the probability that the study will make the best contribution possible is greatly increased.

Even those naturalistic observers of cultural events who want to represent accurately the cultural variables they are studying emphasize the importance of being well grounded in the anthropological discipline and having extensive experience in making naturalistic observations of similar variables (Spindler, 1982; Wolcott, 1981). The researcher needs a strong foundation in the theories that are relevant to the problem studied in order to interpret accurately the meaning of the results obtained.

As other functions of a literature review are discussed, it is important to remember that a review of literature is an integrated whole that is focused on the specific problem that is to be studied for a particular purpose. The list of five functions given earlier is an aid to learning the various roles a literature review serves in planning a research study. With learning the history of the problem listed as the first function, the other functions could be viewed as aspects of this history that must be learned and used in planning the study, or each of the other four functions could be viewed as having important historical aspects. In general, these functions are fulfilled concurrently in a review and are not used as organizing concepts. In the discussion of the five functions, clear boundaries between them cannot be maintained. Depending on the problem, the various functions will differ in their importance, and the literature must be used to fulfill additional functions. Light and Pillemer (1984), in their book *Summing Up*, present a more comprehensive list of functions for the review of literature and how to organize and write the review.

Become Familiar with Theoretical Backgrounds

The importance of both the disciplinary and theoretical bases for a problem have been mentioned in this chapter and in earlier sections of the book. The theoretical frameworks used by researchers to conceptualize their problems are usually identified in their research reports. The relevant theoretical sources are identified in these bibliographies so that others can study them in greater detail. When you obtain and read these sources, other relevant studies are identified that must also be read if you are to understand the evidence that supports or questions the validity of a theory and its applicability to the problem that concerns you. This is true regardless of whether you plan to do a study or only want to read about it, regardless of whether the problem is of personal, professional, or theoretical interest.

The primary reason for understanding the relevant theory and the associated disciplinary base is that research is always conceptualized from theory (even when we are not aware of the theory). For example, is learning to be based on reinforcement and punishment (Skinner, 1953), or is it to be described by the requirements of the learning tasks to be accomplished (Block, 1971)? Are students at concrete-operational or formal levels of thinking (Piaget, 1977)? Are these distinctions important for this study? If these are *not*, what are the important distinctions?

Not only is theory needed in order to state a problem in a way that will be most meaningful to others, it also describes or implies the interrelationships among the variables that occur in this setting. Theory provides a basis for understanding how or why specific relationships exist. The purpose is to unify our understanding of the infinite world, emphasizing parsimony, or simplicity, in that knowledge. Persons' beliefs in the applicability of different theories to teaching and learning often generate controversies that are very important to educational practitioners. One of the latest educational controversies is the placing of special education students in regular classrooms. (This is usually called *mainstreaming* such students.) Mainstreaming is done for a number of reasons, but one often cited is the harmful psychological and developmental effects that many professionals believed resulted from placing students in special education classes. Present theory about development of one's self-image and the effects of a negative self-image on cognitive and psychological development is one of the strongest reasons for mainstreaming these students to the greatest extent possible. At present, there is little evidence of increased functioning of these children nor of the impact this practice has on the teachers and other students in the classroom. Much research is presently occurring, in part because of fundamental disagreement about the applicability of certain theories to special education students and their placement into regular versus special education classrooms. Such research will show which theories seem to explain best the effects of mainstreaming. New theories may need to be developed.

Later in this chapter examples of literature reviews are presented and discussed. Ways that theories are used to provide frameworks for thinking about, or conceptualizing, the interrelationships among important variables that occur in a setting are illustrated. Decisions about which theories are most appropriate and useful in addressing a specific problem for a clearly delineated purpose require intimate knowledge of the alternatives and the research evidence on which the theories are based. Gaining such knowledge is a primary purpose for reviewing the literature.

Assess Strengths and Weaknesses of Previous Studies

One of the strengths of empirical research is that it describes actual events that occur in nature. It is not simply armchair musings that may or may not apply to anything real. Present theory, measurement devices, and other technologies of research have limitations and biases that we cannot at present know or understand. That fact should not lead to despair of gaining knowledge from systematic study. The knowledge that has been gained in the past century promises even more valuable knowledge from empirical research in the future.

Cumulative gains of science have often been made from critical analysis of previous work. Orville and Wilbur Wright were able to fly after crashing their motorized airplane off a hill in North Carolina by analyzing that experience as well as the failed attempts of others. By pulling the plane along a flat runway, they were able to move fast enough to provide the lift needed by their 600-pound motorized plane to stay aloft for 874 feet.

The skills needed to analyze the strengths and weaknesses of a study are addressed throughout this text. The technical knowledge of measurement, research design, and statistics provides many of the tools needed to analyze the quality of a study. There is nothing magical or mystical about using these research tools to systematically assess the strengths and weaknesses of the evidence in order to logically draw conclusions from data. The basis for such analysis is fundamentally in the knowledge of the situation, which includes both the relevant theories and practical experience, and the ability to think clearly and logically about the data obtained in an empirical study.

The relative strengths and weaknesses of previous research must be identified in order to assess their implications for the problem being addressed. Empirical studies relevant to a problem are never perfectly consistent in their findings or implications. Many researchers, for example, have studied the relative effects of phonics and meaning approaches to teaching reading. The studies are carried out in various types of settings (private, public, urban, suburban, or rural schools) with various types of students (gifted, remedial, high SES, low SES, regular classes, special education classes, etc.) at various grade levels (prekindergarten through twelfth grade). In some studies, students using phonics materials do better on some reading skills; in others, those using the meaning approach do better than students using phonics materials on these same skills. Three such studies carried out in regular third-grade U.S. classrooms would usually have similar inconsistencies in the learning outcomes of students using these two approaches.

How can the results be most meaningfully synthesized? What implications (if any) do they have for your third-grade classroom?

It is not very informative or useful to simply report that inconsistencies were found in the literature. It provides no help in understanding your problem. The task in the review of literature is to draw conclusions from the literature about issues important to your situation. In doing research, you need such conclusions to conceptualize, plan, and carry out your proposed study. Some of the types of conclusions you must make follow:

1. Which theory(s) is most appropriate for conceptualizing this problem in this setting?
2. Which variables *must* be included in the study? Which ones should be controlled? Which can be ignored?
3. Which research method is most promising for studying this problem for this purpose (e.g., case study, survey, ethnographic, historical, experimental)?
4. Which instruments or procedures would be most appropriate to operationally define important variables?

These are decisions that must be made in a study and the researcher must have a firm foundation and rationale for each decision made. To use the empirical literature, a researcher assesses the quality and relevance of each study or source. Assume that you are planning a study of the relative effects of phonics and meaning instructional approaches on the reading skills of third-grade students in regular classrooms, such as those in Example 3, the Garfield School study. Studies of third-grade students in regular U.S. classrooms will be more relevant (all other things being equal) than will studies of various kinds of students, such as gifted or remedial, or studies of students in fifth- or ninth-grade levels. The relevance of a study is determined by the degree of similarity between that study and your specific situation on dimensions that are important to your problem or concern. The characteristics of conclusions just listed are most relevant to this study because there is extensive evidence that the learning of reading by other types of students, or similar students at other ages (grade levels), is meaningfully different from that of regular third-grade students. If your setting is in a higher SES suburban area, studies of similar students in similar settings will be more relevant than studies of urban or rural students.

The quality of a study is determined by the confidence one may have in the conclusions reached in that study. Many problems can exist that raise doubts about the conclusions reached in a study. Some of those described earlier in this book are the following:

1. The operational definition of economically disadvantaged may leave many such students defined as *not* economically disadvantaged.
2. The subtest used to measure a variable, such as math computation skills, may be biased or inadequate.

3. The two Garfield School teachers may not be equally effective teachers.
4. The two groups of students taught by the phonics and meaning approaches may not be equivalent or even similar.

Each of these problems results in a researcher producing results that do not accurately represent the situation and problem studied. For example, if either condition three or four existed in the Garfield study, the obtained differences in the scores of the phonics and meaning groups may have been caused by these differences in the teacher's ability or in the differences between the students' initial abilities, rather than by the type of instructional method used.

Such alternative explanations for results are present in each study. By examining critically the procedures used in the various studies that are relevant to your concern, you can weigh the evidence, identify the most appropriate alternatives, and draw conclusions *based on previous evidence* that are most appropriate for your situation.

It is never easy to analyze various studies objectively. Each of us has our own beliefs and biases. When one interpretation of results requires major changes in the tentative plans we have for doing the study, most of us will try harder to find evidence against that interpretation in contrast to evidence that supports it. The major value of the technical aspects of research methodology is to protect us against ourselves, producing a more accurate interpretation of what was found in research and what it means in this setting.

More specific procedures for analyzing and synthesizing previous research are addressed in later sections of this chapter. Many of the skills needed to do this well, particularly the technical skills, are covered in the remainder of this book. Analyzing and synthesizing research and related literature are two of the most difficult tasks for students learning to do research. As with other aspects of research, extensive experience is needed to do them well. The same is true for gaining knowledge from reading research.

Identify Promising Ways to Study the Problem

As indicated, two of the most important decisions to make based on the review of literature are (1) the general method or approach for studying the problem and (2) the specific procedures to use in the study. By analyzing strengths and weaknesses of previous studies as well as their results, you can identify procedures or measurement instruments that appear to work particularly well in your type of setting and those that appear to have major flaws. In most studies, more than one measure should be used to assess important variables. The weaknesses of one measure can be overcome by using a second measure of the same variable. For example, the reading subtests of commercial tests, such as the MAT or SAT, do not include specific vocabulary that was emphasized in a group of classrooms. In addition, other types of reading comprehension not assessed by multiple choice tests are of particular interest to a researcher. Other tests or measures of vocabulary and reading comprehension can be developed and used in the study. When results are consistent across several measures of the same variable, such as reading comprehension, the researcher can be more confident that the results accurately reflect the nature and degree of change on that variable.

Other studies may identify possible sources for a historical study that a researcher had not previously considered. Aspects of a situation that make it more difficult to carry out a good study are often identified in previous work. For example, letters sent to prison parolees at their designated mailing addresses are often not received because many addresses are inaccurate. Receiving mail at the address, even when it is correct, can be problematic (there is no mail box, or mail is left on the porch or in the hall).

The result that always occurs in a study is that the researcher will be surprised in one way or another. For example, who would imagine before a study begins that some fifth-grade students would answer correctly all 80 items on a commercial IQ test? When that occurred on the pretest, the measure was less useful for assessing the increases that resulted from repeated testing. No positive changes are possible for such students. The surprises usually result from inappropriate assumptions about a situation. Knowledge about many of these assumptions can be gained only from personal experience, but many others can be indicated from previous research in similar settings with similar groups of people.

Information gained by previous researchers about aspects of their studies that did not work out (and their ideas concerning why the problems occurred) indicates procedures to avoid as well as procedures that seemed to work well. The review of literature should provide such help in planning a study.

Develop a Conceptual Framework

A final product of the review of literature is the framework that is used to understand and conceptualize a problem or issue. As indicated previously, this may be a comprehensive model that includes all relevant variables in the situation. More often it is a listing of the most important variables that must be addressed in a study of the problem and the associated rationales for the inclusion of those variables. Three examples of different types of conceptual frameworks and associated rationales are presented and discussed in this section.

Each of the following three examples contain sections excerpted from actual studies. In the original dissertation, these sections immediately followed a detailed analysis and synthesis of related literature. The documentation for the statements made in these summaries was specified in the review of pertinent research.

In Example 4a, Israelite (1981) indicates that the linguistic development of deaf children is similar to but slower than that of hearing children. Difficulties children have in learning the passive voice are described. The fact that sentence context seems to affect learning of the passive voice by young children is indicated. Therefore, studying the influences of specific sentence contexts on deaf students' learning of passive sentences should make a contribution to knowledge.

EXAMPLE 4a   DOING A LITERATURE REVIEW (ISRAELITE DOCTORAL DISSERTATION)

Direct and Indirect Antecedent Context and the Comprehension of Reversible Passive Voice Sentences by Deaf Readers*

Summary of the Review of Literature

The preceding review of the literature has focused on the written language abilities of deaf children, acquisition of the passive voice by deaf and hearing children, and the influences of context on the use of the passive voice by deaf and hearing children. A major finding has been that the linguistic development of deaf children parallels that of hearing children, although rate of acquisition is significantly reduced. Other major findings are detailed in the following summary.

Researchers and educators over many years have consistently concluded that the linguistic abilities of deaf individuals, as demonstrated by their reading and writing skills, are severely impoverished. They have suggested that a major cause of the language problems of deaf individuals is delayed syntactic development. Deaf children acquire syntax in a manner similar to hearing children but at a greatly retarded rate. Syntactic abilities appear to improve with age. Although hearing children have acquired most aspects of standard English syntax by 8 years of age, many deaf children have knowledge of only the simplest structures at age 18. Deaf children may never fully understand complex syntactic structures.

The passive voice is an especially difficult structure for both deaf and hearing children to acquire. Hearing children may not develop full control of the passive voice until adolescence. Young hearing children process passive sentences using a subject-verb-object comprehension strategy, which results in an incorrect active interpretation. As linguistic abilities develop, this strategy is discarded. Deaf children also utilize the subject-verb-object strategy when interpreting passive sentences. However, this strategy is generally maintained throughout adolescence and probably into adulthood as well.

Researchers have shown that linguistic and extra-linguistic contexts influence the comprehension and production of passive sentences by hearing children. Results of investigations pertaining to the use of the passive voice by hearing children have demonstrated that linguistic contexts that focus attention on the starting points of passive sentences facilitate assumption of the passive perspective. Young hearing children have benefitted from direct antecedent contexts that explicitly mention the starting points of target passive sentences.

---

*Doctoral Dissertation by Neita Kay Israelite, University of Pittsburgh (1981), pp. 40–42. Reprinted with permission.

The effects of context on comprehension of the passive voice by deaf children have been examined in a limited manner. Deaf children have demonstrated significantly higher levels of comprehension when truncated passive sentences are presented in story contexts. The influences of specific sentence contexts that focus attention on the starting points of passive sentences have not been investigated.

Israelite identifies those elements that are important to the study and why they are important. She does not list them but discusses the most relevant conclusions from the literature that should be addressed in any study of the effect of context on deaf children's understanding of passive sentences. The rate of acquisition is also identified as important. In her study, she uses various types of contexts, including direct antecedent and truncated passive sentences in story contexts, to assess their effects on the comprehension by deaf children at various age levels (8 to 18).

In the next example, Weaver (1976) presents a similar but more detailed summary of the literature for her study of the effects of sentence anagram training on reading comprehension. She notes that certain intrasentence organizational skills are highly related to reading comprehension. She also cites evidence that the sentence anagram task (which she uses in her study) should train students in those skills. In addition, her own pilot testing of the procedure was successful within specified limits. Next, an assumption that is central to her study is specified: The extent to which improved sentence anagram performance reflects increased sentence organizational skills is expected to be reflected in increased reading comprehension. She indicates also the differential transfer effects on the various types of comprehension tests that she expects.

EXAMPLE 4b   DOING A LITERATURE REVIEW (WEAVER DOCTORAL DISSERTATION)

Sentence Anagram Organizational Training and Its Effect on Reading Comprehension*

Summary and Rationale for the Current Study

It was suggested that although decoding skill and vocabulary knowledge are necessary for reading comprehension, they are not sufficient to guarantee that comprehension will occur. Evidence was presented indicating that certain intra-

---

*Doctoral Dissertation by Phyllis A. Weaver, University of Pittsburgh (1976), pp. 30–32. Reprinted with permis-

sentence organizational skills, those that enable readers to use syntactic cues, are closely related to the quality of reading comprehension. Readers who organize text into meaningful units appear to be better comprehenders than those who read one word at a time, and comprehension of poor readers improves when text is presented in a preorganized format. It was thus hypothesized that specific training in organizational skills may enhance reading comprehension.

Evidence was cited that suggests that the sentence anagram task is a suitable task through which to train organizational skills. The task appeared suitable because sentence anagram performance correlates positively with reading comprehension, and because sentence anagram solution is facilitated when words are prearranged in phrases. Results of pilot testing indicated that the sentence anagram task is well suited for training organizational skills since organizing words into phrases and clauses appears to be necessary for solution of long sentence anagrams. That is, short (5 to 7 words) sentence anagrams can be solved in brief periods of time without first organizing the words into groups, but attempts to solve longer (10 to 15 words) sentence anagrams in relatively brief time periods appear to "overload" short-term memory unless the words are grouped into phrases or clauses. Thus, it was speculated that if organizational skills were trainable, then systematic sentence anagram organizational training would facilitate sentence anagram solution. Further, insofar as improved sentence anagram performance reflects an improvement in general organizational skills, this improvement was expected to be reflected in the quality of reading comprehension. Finally, since organizational skills are only one of a number of subskills on which comprehension depends, and since tests of comprehension typically depend on more than one subskill, it was expected that sentence anagram training would have differential transfer effects on various types of comprehension tests.

Four different tests of comprehension were used: a cloze comprehension test, a timed sentence recognition test, a prompted verbatim recall test, and a passage-question comprehension test. It was hypothesized that the effects of training would be reflected most on the timed sentence recognition test because it required more subskills in common with the sentence anagram task than the other tests of comprehension. Similarly, it was hypothesized that the effects of training on the cloze test would be less apparent than on the timed sentence recognition test but more apparent than on the prompted verbatim recall test. Finally, since the passage-question comprehension test required the fewest number of subskills in common with the sentence anagram task, transfer-of-training effects were expected to be the least evident on it.

---

sion. Weaver's references are included in the reference section located at the end of the chapter. This dissertation received the International Reading Association Award for best dissertation in 1976.

In her study, Weaver compared students who received sentence anagram training with similar students who received no training. She tested her expectations about both the overall effects of such training and the relative training effects on the various tests that were derived from previous research and theory.

Eddins (1981) studied variables that might affect attrition of at-risk black students who were admitted to a four-year university with grades and Scholastic Aptitude Test (SAT) scores that were below those required for regular admission. From her review of literature, she developed a model of the interrelationships among variables that seem to affect attrition of such underprepared minority students. She tested her model (based on previous research and other theories) with data collected over several years at one university. Her model is a relatively comprehensive conceptual framework that she needed to gain a better understanding of why these students leave school and what changes in the university situation might decrease their attrition rate.

Given the large number of attrition studies in the literature, Eddins found that the dimensions she identified (types of schools, types of students, variables controlled, and indicators used in the studies) explained, or accounted for, the apparent inconsistencies in the results of the studies. When these differences in the studies were taken into account, the variables (or constructs) and indicators that appeared to have the greatest impact on attrition were identified. These were then organized into the model given in Figure 4.1 that she tested in her study.

EXAMPLE 4c   DOING A LITERATURE REVIEW (EDDINS DOCTORAL DISSERTATION)

A Causal Model of the Attrition of Specially Admitted Black Students in Higher Education*

... In reviewing the literature on student attrition, considerable support for the hypotheses that the constructs of family background, high school attended, entry ability, and on-campus academic behavior have an influence on the attrition and performance of students in higher education was indicated. Even though differential findings were often reported in the research, many of these differences may be attributed to variations in the schools (e.g., black institutions, integrated institutions), types of students, (e.g., white students, black students, specially admitted black students), emphasis on controlling for the effects of other possible variables (e.g., entry ability), and the specific indicators used in measurements of the variables (e.g., income, parent education, measured ability, demonstrated ability).

---

*Doctoral Dissertation by Diane Dixon Eddins, University of Pittsburgh (1981), pp. 28–29, 31–33. Reprinted with permission.

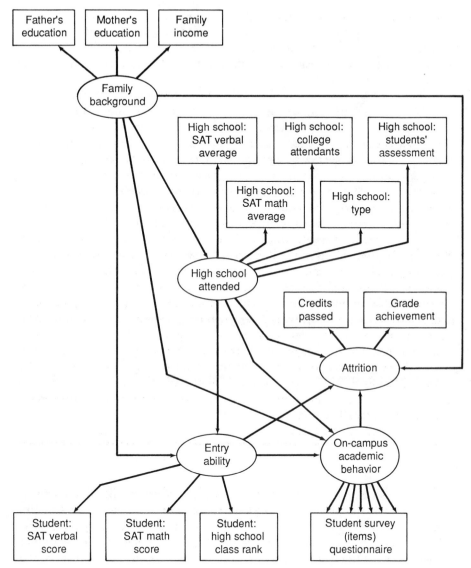

Figure 4.1. Indicators of Proposed Causal Model on Black Student Attrition

... The review of the literature also indicated that the influence of these constructs in terms of each other and student attrition should be considered. Reported findings often suggested multiple causal or relative influences between these constructs and student attrition, the importance of taking into account student ability levels was cited. Other studies implied that students' family background has its primary impact on attrition through its influence on students' high school attended and entry ability. It was reported that students from lower socioeconomic levels attend "poorer" schools and exhibit lower levels of entry ability. Studies on students' high school attended suggested that the students' school has a direct influence on attrition in terms of its preparation of students for the expectations and demands of college and an indirect influence in terms of its effect on entry ability.

Entry ability was given as having the most influence on student attrition with high school performance often reported as having the single most influence on students' academic performance. However, these entry ability levels were sometimes presented as being related to students' family background and high school attended. These same factors were also suggested to be related to students' on-campus academic behavior. It was suggested that this academic behavior reflects students' ability to successfully meet the academic demands of the university, and this ability for successful academic integration was reported to be influenced by students' background and entering characteristics.

. . . The model presented in this study was derived on the basis of these findings. The literature presented considerable evidence for the hypothesized relationships. The proposed model for this study is presented in Figure 4.1. It is a causal model that describes the hypothesized relationships among constructs or latent variables. In this model the latent variables are: (1) family background; (2) high school attended; (3) entry ability; (4) on-campus academic behavior; and (5) attrition. These variables were measured by indicator variables that are given in the rectangular blocks in Figure 4.1. In the figure, for example, the latent variable entry ability is measured by three indicator variables; (1) student SAT verbal score; (2) student SAT math score; and (3) student high school class rank. A one-way arrow pointing from one latent variable to another suggests a nonreciprocal causal relationship.

The relationships Eddins identified were not previously listed in the literature. She had to develop this new model from previous research and models other researchers had proposed. This example is filled with the types of conclusions that a researcher must make about the findings of previous research and their implications for the specific problem and setting of concern in the study the researcher is planning. Others who read research to draw conclusions about a personal or professional issue with no plans for further study must draw similar types of conclusions, but these readers are usually not concerned with how best to study the problem.

As these excerpts indicate, the conceptual frameworks and associated rationales for different studies vary in many ways as a result of numerous factors. Three of the most important are (1) the nature of previous empirical research and theory development that has occurred, (2) the extent to which the present study is conceptualized within a theoretical framework, and (3) the researcher's specific setting and purpose for doing the study.

All three examples are well grounded in theory. One tests a relatively comprehensive model, another tests the effects of training sentence organizational skills, and the third compares various contexts for helping deaf children to comprehend passive sentences. The specific variables that are important to study in all three examples were identified from previous empirical studies and associated theories. The conceptual framework is the final result of a well-done review of literature and a necessary part of planning the best study possible at this time for this purpose.

FINDING RELEVANT LITERATURE

Reviews of literature in various disciplines and professions use various sources and are carried out in various ways. The sources and procedures emphasized in this section are used by most educators and psychologists when they are preparing to study a problem. Some sources and procedures used by historians and enthnographers are presented also.

As indicated in previous sections of this book, you must know how others have conceptualized an issue, what they have done to study it, what they have found, and what their findings imply for your particular situation. To obtain the detailed information needed, you must first find out where it is reported. The location of specific studies is found in numerous ways. Reference lists or bibliographies in books, dissertations, and articles are excellent sources of research reports and other literature related to the topic addressed in that book or document. If you depend on these reference lists alone, it is likely that you will miss much of the relevant literature. Reference books that list the location of articles, usually by the subject or topic addressed, are available in each discipline and profession. Researchers and other scholars search these references early in their study of a problem or issue so that their reviews include all the relevant literature they can find. The first step in this process is identifying key terms that comprehensively address your problem or topic.

Identifying Key Terms

Begin a review of literature as soon as you identify a general problem area. Because the major references, or indexes, are organized by subject, you need a list of subjects related to the problem area to begin. In a study of the practice effects of repeated testing some relevant terms would be practice effect, repeated testing, reliability of tests, test wiseness, achievement tests, and intelligence (IQ). Compare these terms with the *Thesaurus of ERIC Descriptors*, which lists the terms used in the *Education Index* and *Current Index to Journals in Education*. A similar thesaurus or index of key terms exists for other reference books, such as *Psychological Abstracts*.

References or Indexes

The *Education Index* and *Current Index to Journals in Education (CIJE)* list articles that appeared in selected education journals during a specific period. The *Education Index* includes lists of articles published in hundreds of education journals, books, and other education-related publications. It begins in 1929, listing articles by both author and subject until 1961; for eight years (1961–1969) articles were listed only by subject. Since 1969 articles have again been listed by both author and subject. The index is published monthly and is usually bound into volumes of 10 or more years.

To identify articles related to a problem area, use the key terms and read the titles of articles listed. Collect at this time the bibliographic information that you will need for the reference style to be used in writing your paper, such as the American Psychological Association's *Publication Manual* (1983). This information includes at least the author, the year of publication, the title of the article, and the publishing information. It is best to list only one article on a three-by-five-inch or a four-by-six-inch index card so that you can write a summary of that article on the card. It is often difficult to identify the relevance of an article from the title, and more unrelated than related articles are usually found—particularly in the beginning of a literature search.

The *CIJE* has been published by the Educational Resource Information Center (ERIC) since 1969. It indexes more than 800 education and related journals monthly and is cumulated semiannually. The Subject Index is used to identify articles relevant to the problem areas. Each article has a number with an EJ prefix that is used to organize the articles in the Main Entry Section of the *CIJE*. The main entry description includes not only the necessary bibliographic reference information but also a short abstract of the article.

When you have identified a list of promising articles, you can obtain the journals and other publications containing them from an appropriate library. The bibliographies in the most recent articles are often the most useful for identifying other articles. They are also an aid in deciding which articles you should read next.

For the years 1969 to the present, the *CIJE* is a more comprehensive index than the *Education Index* and includes short abstracts of each article. For these reasons, it is usually best to search the *CIJE* first and then search the *Education Index* for previous articles. There are numerous other citation indexes, such as *Research in Education, Social Science Citation Index, Sociological Abstracts, Exceptional Child Education Resources,* and *Educational Administration Abstracts.* Borg and Gall (1983) describe many other reference sources in great detail.

Lists of sources relevant to historical research are more extensive and vary by the area of the world and the era to be studied. A less formal and focused review of literature is carried out in a historical study because literature and records from the past provide the basic data for the study. If you plan to study education at the turn of the century, however, you need background knowledge about the societal context at the time. You also need a thorough grounding in the specific field of study, such as administration, learning, or instruction. In a similar manner, ethnographers must be familiar with anthropological and other social science research and theory to decide on the focus of an inquiry (Wilcox, 1982).

One of the most detailed lists of sources for historical study was compiled by Wood Gray and his colleagues in the *Historian's Handbook* (1964). It includes guides and bibliographies on numerous topics for most areas of the world. One of the most useful is the *Reader's Guide to Periodical Literature*, which has been published since 1900 and lists articles from hundreds of journals and other periodicals.

A final comment concerns the use of computers for searching the literature. Most indexes are computerized today, and procedures are available to search them. Using this tool is not trivial. Identifying the combination of key terms that will identify the most relevant articles and not omit important articles requires much knowledge and experience. The first computer search carried out by most people will either identify several hundred citations or only one or two—neither result is of much use. Most universities have systems that allow students and faculty to do their own computer searches of appropriate indexes. This is an important and useful skill to learn, but like most other valuable skills, it takes much time and effort to become proficient.

Reviews of Literature

Another important source of background knowledge and research articles is reviews of literature. In education the *Review of Educational Research (RER)* includes only reviews of literature on specific issues or problems. The *RER* is published quarterly by the American Educational Research Association. When the *RER* began in 1930, only reviews on specific topics edited by selected authors were published. Since 1969, it has accepted review articles on a submission basis and includes about six reviews of research on various topics in each issue. If the *RER* includes a review of your topic in a recent issue, the body of the review provides meaningful discussion of the topic and the bibliography includes a long list of up-to-date research and other related articles.

Three handbooks of research on teaching (Gage, 1963; Travers, 1973; Wittrock, 1986) contain reviews of research on teaching-related topics. Each gives a historical and theoretical background for research on teaching, paradigms and methods for doing (or understanding) research, and what is known about teaching in various subject matter areas.

Another valuable source to read over early in a search of relevant literature is the NSSE *Yearbooks*. Each year the National Society for the Study of Education commissions two yearbooks to be developed. A committee is charged with planning the yearbook and identifying the most appropriate authors for the chapters. Most areas of education are addressed about every 10 years. The topics are usually broad: Youth, Classroom Management, Education and Women, Teacher Education, Staff Development, Learning a Second Language, Ecology of School

Renewal, and the Gifted and Talented. There are usually 10 to 12 chapters on specific aspects of the topic in each yearbook.

It is usually valuable to read the most relevant chapters of a yearbook that relates to your problem area—even if it is 10 years old. The publication process results in a state-of-the-art synthesis of research and theory by one of the most knowledgeable scholars in each specific area. Both research and theory are published and integrated much more quickly than is possible by other processes. Material in these chapters is usually years ahead of other publications. Some new views presented are never readily accepted in the mainstream of scholarship, but the chapters are generally well documented and the bases for the conclusions and recommendations are open to scrutiny. The more recently that your topic is addressed in an NSSE yearbook, the more immediate value it should be to you.

Another valuable source of literature is dissertations, which include relatively comprehensive reviews of literature with extensive bibliographies. Dissertations are listed in *Dissertation Abstracts International*, which has been published since 1938. Nearly 400 institutions in the United States and Canada provide dissertation abstracts. Section A, which includes education, covers the humanities and social sciences.

After you compile a promising list of articles and publications, you must read the individual articles and write a good summary, or abstract, on your note cards for later use in organizing and writing the actual review. In the following section, aspects of the article to be noted and suggestions for organizing the information on cards are presented.

SUMMARIZING RESEARCH ON NOTE CARDS

Before discussing the literature review further, I must make one admonition. Never depend on a secondary source! Authors who write about the research or theories of others usually have different interests or backgrounds that lead them to overemphasize certain aspects and deemphasize or leave out other aspects of the work. After only a few experiences of reading original works after reading descriptions of the same work by other authors, you will confirm the value of this admonition. The inconsistencies are usually obvious to the most casual reviewer. Do the extra work needed to find the original article, and confirm that the secondary source has reported it accurately.

Each person seems to have a personal method for organizing the information obtained from a review of literature. Some use sheets of paper, others use three-by-five-inch cards, and still others use four-by-six-inch cards. Spiral-bound notebooks are not often used because after all the information has been collected it must be organized by topic in order to write the review. That organization often changes as more is learned from the literature. An article is often moved from one topic area to another in such situations, so no more than one article should be described on each piece of paper or card that is used.

It is useful to place a code in an upper corner of the card (or paper) that indicates the key term or topic the article addresses. These terms will later be located in specific sections of the review of literature. The code allows you to easily sort the cards by the key terms without rereading the summary.

It is important also to write a precise bibliographic reference that includes the call numbers (if any) at the top of the card. If parts are left out, it can be time-consuming to find the source again. This can be one of the most frustrating aspects of reviewing literature in a library where the resources are used extensively or are not replaced accurately and quickly. Get everything you need from an article the first time you have it. You may not have a second chance for weeks —particularly if that journal is sent out for binding.

The content included on note cards for research articles includes the following important elements:

1. What is the problem addressed in the study? Include context and purpose.
2. What general and specific procedures were used in the study?
3. What did the researcher find (results)?
4. What conclusions were made?
5. What implications or recommendations were made that are relevant to your problem (if any)?

There is not much space on a three-by-five-inch card, so you must paraphrase most information and summarize it succinctly. Short quotations can be placed on the card, but longer ones may require a second card. A few articles may be so pertinent to your study that you will need to reread them at various stages in your review and writing. It is usually best to copy them, but *also* make a bibliographic card for them.

Answers to the questions in the foregoing list should emphasize those aspects that are most relevant to your problem. It is important that you accurately represent the work of the researcher from your view. It is best to include in these sections material that comes from, or represents, the study. I find that a sixth section at the bottom of a card is useful for comments or questions about specific aspects of the study. Be clear and precise in what you write on these cards because it may be weeks or months before you will read them again. What may be clear to you as you write each card can be uninterpretable two months later.

The procedures and findings are most important in a review and require the most detailed information. Specify the general method used (survey, observation, or experiment) as well as specific procedures, the number and characteristics of the subjects studied, how they were selected, treatments and measures used (if any), procedures or research design used, and other aspects of the study that seem relevant.

Report in detail the findings that were obtained. As you attempt to describe the overall results of previous studies, you will need these details for interpretation. Often the number of studies that supported each variable are counted to give a quantitative summary of the weight of empirical results. It is often useful to include important tables of findings on the card so that they can be included directly in the review.

Conclusions drawn in a research article are often not adequately documented by the findings in the study. As a reviewer, you must draw your own conclusions from the study and point out the problems with the researcher's conclusions—or with the likelihood that the results obtained will occur in your setting.

Implications and recommendations are often useful starting points to think about your own problem. Some researchers generate insightful recommendations based on their study and their knowledge and experience in that setting. Other studies can be erroneous or poorly documented. They are always thought provoking and useful, however, in gaining a greater understanding of your problem and how to study it.

Most style manuals require that the page numbers where quotations or tables appear in an article be included in the citation. Include these page numbers at the time you copy the quotations. In general, people tend to use too many quotations in a literature review. It is weak logically to appeal to the authority of the author or book. There is usually a solid logical or empirical basis for what is being said in most quotations, and you should document that basis with appropriate evidence.

Summarize other kinds of articles using cards of the same size you used for research articles. The five headings, or questions, given earlier for note cards are not relevant for theoretical or other nonempirical articles. Develop other headings that will help you in focusing on the relevant contributions of these articles.

Throughout the process of doing a review of literature much is learned about the problem or issue of concern. Combining the information in ways that allow accurate description of the literature and insightful conclusions about its meaning for the situation of concern is the ongoing goal of the reviewer. The critical analysis is the tool, or procedure, that facilitates an integrated synthesis of the material. This synthesis becomes the foundation of the conceptual framework, such as those described earlier in this chapter. Some excerpts from reviews of literature are used in the next section to illustrate the level of detail needed in studies and the logical ways the information is used to draw synthesizing conclusions.

ANALYSIS AND SYNTHESIS OF RESEARCH

The analysis and synthesis of research are seldom addressed in most research methodology texts because they are complex skills requiring knowledge of both research methodology principles and substantive knowledge of the problem and context studied. As indicated previously, everything covered in this book can be used to analyze research critically. To read and summarize research adequately, you must know what types of information are used in what ways to analyze and synthesize the literature.

In Example 5a excerpted from the review of literature for Israelite's study of deaf children, you should notice that the studies are not described comprehensively, yet much detail is given about important variables. These variables include ages when specific language skills are learned by hearing and deaf children, the specific skills studied, how these skills relate to passive sentences, and the use of subject-verb-object strategy to comprehend language. This latter concept is the hypothesized reason why deaf students have great difficulty with passive sentences. It is one of the hypotheses, or beliefs, that Israelite's study tests directly.

There is very little analysis specified in this example. Israelite summarized the evidence that was the basis for her rationale because the evidence overwhelmingly supported her synthesis of the literature. In other words, there was little counterevidence in the literature; Israelite was able to synthesize and explain the results of the relevant studies in the literature. It is also important to notice that she had to creatively develop the synthesis and rationale. Although she quotes several authors, she selected from a number of findings, conclusions, and recommendations those that were most relevant to her study. When reading reviews of literature, it often appears that the reviewer is simply summarizing the statements and conclusions of others. Students become upset when they do their first literature review if the studies they read do not have the types of summary statements and conclusions they have seen in other literature reviews.

EXAMPLE 5a ANALYSIS AND SYNTHESIS OF EMPIRICAL RESEARCH (ISRAELITE DOCTORAL DISSERTATION)

Direct and Indirect Antecedent Context and the Comprehension of Reversible Passive Voice Sentences by Deaf Readers*

... Acquisition of the Passive Voice by Deaf Children

In the following section, the limited literature available on comprehension and production of passive voice sentences by deaf children is reviewed. Schmitt (1968) compared the performance of deaf children aged 8, 11, 14, and 17 and

---

*Doctoral Dissertation by Neita Kay Israelite, University of Pittsburgh (1981). Sections reprinted with permission. Israelite's references are included in the reference section at the end of the chapter.

hearing children aged 8 and 11, using a passive sentence to picture matching technique. Deaf children up to 14 years of age experienced great difficulty on comprehension and production tasks, with many 17-year-olds still not demonstrating full mastery. Hearing children demonstrated superior performance at all age levels.

Using the same materials and procedures, Power (1971) studied the comprehension and production of reversible, nonreversible, and truncated passives. One hundred deaf subjects were divided into five age groups: 9–10, 11–12, 13–14, 15–16, 17–18. The major results of this study, which were also reported by Power and Quigley (1973), indicated that students at all ages performed better on comprehension tasks than production tasks. When the authors accepted 75% of the items correct as the criterion for acquisition of the passive voice, the following data were generated for the oldest group:

1. Nonreversible passives were understood by 65% of the subjects.
2. Reversible passives were understood by 60% of the subjects.
3. Truncated passives were understood by 35% of the subjects.
4. Passives were correctly produced by 40% of the subjects.

It should be noted that only a slight difference was found between reversible and nonreversible passives. Deaf children appeared to make use of the subject-verb-object strategy when processing passive sentences. Nonreversible passives were the easiest structures for the children at each age level; reversible passives were ranked second in level of difficulty. Truncated passives presented the most difficulty for all children. Power and Quigley suggested that deaf children often use the passive marker in the agentive phrase as the only indicator of passive voice. When this phrase is deleted, as in truncated structures, the ability of deaf children to interpret passive sentences is greatly reduced.

Tervoort (1970) found similar results in a study of the comprehension of the passive voice by 43 Dutch children aged 10–18 and four hearing controls. Formation of the passive voice in Dutch and English is comparable. The task involved the selection of sentences that correctly described stimulus pictures. Response choices included active and passive sentences. Hearing children achieved perfect scores on the test. Deaf children across age groups scored 80% for active items and 56% correct for passive items. The proportion of correct responses made by deaf subjects increased markedly with age. Subjects under the age of 13 achieved a mean average score of 27.5% correct; subjects over the age of 13 achieved a mean average score of 74% correct. Tervoort explained that deaf children master simple active sentences relatively early in their development and tend to use them almost exclusively thereafter. In passive sentences, however, the roles of the noun phrases are reversed, thus rendering habitually used strategies inadequate. He recommended that teachers present passive sentences in natural contexts where the conceptual focus is the object of the action.

Summary

The results of studies of the acquisition of the passive voice by deaf children parallel much of the literature on acquisition of the passive voice by hearing children. In general, correct usage of passive structures by deaf children increases with age. Nonreversibility facilitates correct interpretation as a function of semantic knowledge. Unlike hearing children, deaf children have great difficulty with truncated passives due to the deletion of the agent phrase.

Young deaf children also utilize the subject-verb-object strategy when processing passive sentences. Although hearing children replace this mechanism with more appropriate strategies at an early age, deaf children usually maintain this strategy into adolescence and likely into adulthood as well. Tervoort (1970) suggested that comprehension may be facilitated when passive sentences are presented in natural contexts in which the object of the action is the conceptual focus of attention.

In this example, Israelite precisely specified the ages of the subjects in each of the three studies. In the first study (Schmitt, 1968), 17-year-old deaf children did not comprehend passive sentences as well as 8- or 11-year-old hearing children. Power and Quigley (1973) studied reversible, nonreversible, and truncated passive sentences. Deaf children from 9 through 18 were studied. The results that had clear implications for Israelite's study were specified after the overall results were presented. She noted that Power and Quigley reported that a passive marker in the agentive phrase had a major effect on comprehension. This important finding was also studied by Israelite. Tervoort (1970) reported findings that presenting passive sentences in natural contexts improved comprehension.

Each of these issues was important to Israelite as she tried to learn which contexts would help deaf students comprehend passive sentences. Her primary purpose was to improve instruction for deaf students, so these were the variables and issues that concerned her most.

In Example 5b, Weaver studies the effect of sentence anagram organizational training on reading comprehension of elementary students. Those critical analysis statements that she makes are italicized. The problems that are caused by the aspects of the studies that she criticizes usually follow the statement. Many reviewers make appropriate critical statements but do not indicate why they are a problem or what aspect of the problem concerns them. Weaver's comments and conclusions are always focused on her problem and the study she plans to do.

EXAMPLE 5b   ANALYSIS AND SYNTHESIS OF EMPIRICAL RESEARCH (WEAVER DOCTORAL DISSERTATION)

Sentence Anagram Organizational Training and Its Effect on Reading Comprehension*

... Organizational or Syntactic Skills and Reading Comprehension

Research on organizational skills and reading comprehension bears directly on the questions posed in the current study. For this reason, the research presented in this section will be reviewed in greater detail than that reviewed in previous sections [of the dissertation].

An early investigation (Gibbons, 1941) suggested that good and poor readers differ in their ability to perceive the relationships among phrases in a sentence and thus differ in their comprehension of sentences. Gibbons related third graders' performance on a "disarranged phrase test" to their comprehension of the sentences from that test and to their reading ability as measured by the Gates Standardized Reading Test. The disarranged phrases tests consisted of 15 sentences that "varied in difficulty and structure" (p. 42). The phrases in each sentence were listed in column form in mixed order. The children were asked to arrange the phrases to form a good sentence. "The sentence completion and question tests were used to measure the ability to comprehend the sentences used in the disarranged phrases test" (p. 42). (It should be noted that the exact nature of these tests was not made clear in the article reporting the study.)

In the same article, Gibbons reported case studies to illustrate the differences among good and poor readers. The poor readers had problems with decoding as well as with comprehension and performed poorly on the disarranged phrases, sentence completion, and question tests. The good readers made fewer errors on the disarranged phrases test and, despite the errors they did make, were able to understand the sentences. Furthermore, the good readers, according to Gibbons, showed "an awareness of the effect of such words as of, to, but, or, ... [etc.] ... and were better able ... to select a phrase with which to begin a sentence" (p. 45). Gibbons also reported that 25 students were divided into two groups according to their scores on the disarranged phrases test. The groups, matched on intelligence, were significantly different in performance on the sentence comprehension tests and the standardized reading test. With intelligence partialled out, the correlation coefficient between the disarranged phrases test and the sentence comprehension test was 0.89; that between disarranged phrases test and general reading ability was 0.72. Gibbons concluded that

---

*Doctoral Dissertation by Phyllis A. Weaver, University of Pittsburgh (1976), pp. 16–25. Reprinted with permission. Weaver's references are included in the reference section located at the end of the chapter.

... the ability to see relationships between parts of a sentence is an essential factor in understanding the sentence and is also related to the ability to read as determined by a standardized reading test. (p. 46)

A limitation of Gibbons' study was the lack of control for differences in decoding skills. Consequently, the reported correlation coefficients may have been influenced by decoding skills in addition to the ability to see relationships between parts of a sentence.

More recently, several researchers have suggested that some difficulties in reading comprehension, apart from those caused by decoding, may be accounted for in terms of a difference between the readers' method of organizing textual "input" and the organizational patterns required for comprehension. These readers, labeled "difference poor," apparently read word by word instead of organizing the input into meaningful units such as phrases (Cromer, 1970).

To study the effects of organizational patterns on comprehension, Cromer (1970) compared three groups of readers identified according to IQ, vocabulary, and reading comprehension test scores. One group called "difference poor" readers were junior college students who had "adequate intelligence, language skills, vocabulary skills, etc., but still had difficulty comprehending reading material" (p. 472). A second group, the "deficit poor" group, had adequate intelligence and language skills, but were deficient, relative to the difference group, in vocabulary skills. Half of a third group, the "good readers," was matched with the difference group on both IQ and vocabulary scores; the other half was matched with the deficit group on IQ scores only. All students read a set of passages under four different input conditions: regular sentences, single words, meaningful phrases, and fragmented word groupings. For all conditions, the passages were presented on drums, allowing each reader to control the rate of presentation. Following each passage, the students answered five multiple choice comprehension questions.

Performance on the comprehension questions supported Cromer's hypothesis that comprehension for the difference group, but not for the deficit group, would improve when the passages were preorganized into meaningful phrases. In fact, under the phrase condition, the difference group did as well as their matched good readers did under any input condition. Cromer interpreted these findings as support for an organizational component that is related to reading comprehension. *It should be noted that (a) these interpretations were based on performance of mature readers and may not be generalizable to school-age children, and (b) a survey of research on reading did not reveal a replication and extension of this study using younger subjects.*

Oakan, Wiener, and Cromer (1971) assessed the relationship of organizational skills to passage comprehension in good and poor readers in the fifth grade. Passages were presented in "good" and "poor" printed (visual) and taped (auditory) input conditions. The poor auditory conditions were created by taping a fifth-grader who read with many errors; the recording was transcribed for the poor visual condition. Comprehension was measured by questions following each passage. Good readers answered more questions correctly than did poor readers. The good readers performed best under the good auditory input conditions. Furthermore, under the good auditory input condition, good and poor readers performed equally well. The authors concluded that good decoding is not a sufficient condition for good comprehension and suggested that a "significant amount of the comprehension difficulties of the poor readers may be attributable to the manner in which the input is organized" (p. 71).

The studies on organization summarized thus far (Gibbson, 1941; Cromer, 1970; Oakan et al., 1971) offer support for the positive relationship between processing textual materials in phrase groupings and quality of reading comprehension. In addition, several closely related studies point to the use of syntactic cues to improve the quality of reading comprehension. Weinstein and Rabinovitch (1971), for example, investigated the relation of grammatical structures to reading ability. Two groups of fourth graders, good and poor readers, were asked to recall sentences in which root words had been replaced by nonsense stems. The sentences were presented on a tape recorder, thus eliminating decoding ability as a possible confounding factor. The sentences were of two types, syntactically structured (e.g., "When they sivoled the veg, they hanashed zalfly") and syntactically unstructured (e.g., "Azlfly they when, veg the hanashed, sivoled they"). Good and poor readers were compared according to the number of trials needed to reproduce the sentences correctly.

The good readers learned the structured materials in fewer trials than the unstructured material; the poor readers showed no differences in learning the structured and unstructured material. Furthermore, good and poor readers had equal difficulty learning the unstructured material. The authors interpreted these results to mean that the difference between the two groups of readers lies in their ability to utilize information inherent in the grammatical structure of a sentence. *These results cannot be generalized to comprehending English text, since no reading was involved in the experiment and nonsense words were used.* Still, the results of this study indicate that a syntactic variable is in some way related to comprehension.

Denner (1970) also suggested that a syntactic deficiency is present in some poor readers. Denner compared average and poor readers on four tasks developed by Farnham-Diggory (1967). The "enactive" task determines whether the children know the meanings of certain simple verbs, nouns, and prepositions by asking them to follow simple commands such as "jump high." The "pictograph" task determines whether children can associate the same verbs, nouns, and prepositions with appropriate pictures. The "logograph" task tests the children's ability to associate the same words with logographs (graphic symbols for each word). . . . The "synthesis" task tests the children's ability to read a logographic sentence and then do what the sentence commands. . . .

Denner's subjects, poor readers in first through fifth grade (excluding second grade), average readers in first grade, and potentially poor readers in a Head Start class, did not differ significantly on the enactive, pictograph, or logograph tasks. Significant differences among groups were reported, however, on the synthesis task. The average first graders performed as well on the synthesis task as they did on the other tasks; they synthesized the meanings of individual logographs and were able to carry out a "unified act." The poor readers attempted to carry out the action implied by each individual logograph, but failed to carry out a unified act. Denner suggested that the poor readers "do not read sentences but a series of individual words; and the sentence meaning is some conglomerate of individual word meanings rather than a unified contextualized conception" (p. 886). Denner interpreted the results as evidence of a syntactic deficiency in the poor and potentially poor readers in his study. *However, since logograph sentences are not always complete (e.g., "Clap over book" instead of "Clap your hands over the book"), the synthesis tasks may not be an accurate measure of syntactic and integrative skills.* Thus, these results should be interpreted cautiously.

Guthrie's (1973) findings contradict those of Denner (1970) and Weinstein and Rabinovitch (1971). In Guthrie's study, poor readers were matched with young normal readers on reading level and IQ, and with older normal readers on chronological age and IQ. Poor readers were generally inferior to normal readers, both young and old, in comprehension of materials for which they had an adequate sight vocabulary. The students were compared on their performance on a "maze task." In the maze task, a modified cloze procedure, the students read a passage in which approximately every fifth word was replaced by a slot with three alternative words from which to choose. In the slots were nouns, verbs, modifiers, and functions words. The alternatives were of three types: (a) the correct word; (b) a syntactic alternative which was in the same form class (e.g., noun, verb) as the correct word, but was not meaningful in the sentence; and (c) a lexical alternative that was in a different form class from the correct word, but was semantically compatible with the context of the passage. Poor readers in this study selected fewer correct alternatives than the normal readers, but no significant differences were found among the three groups in the types of errors they made. From these data, Guthrie concluded that good and poor readers do not differ qualitatively in their use of syntactic cues during silent reading.

. . . The majority of studies reviewed in this section support the notion that certain organizational or syntactic skills are necessary for good reading comprehension. In order to accomplish this higher-order text processing, the reader uses the structural relationships within sentences as cues to facilitate reading in meaningful word groups. In fact, reading in higher-order units implies using syntactic cues.

The need to train these organizational skills to enhance reading comprehension has been suggested (Cromer, 1970; Gibbons, 1941), but a survey of research on reading indicates that no controlled, systematic training has been attempted. The study reported here attempted to train certain intra-sentence organizational skills in the context of a sentence construction (sentence anagram) task.

Weaver's review is focused on a specific problem. The aspects of each study that she chose to emphasize or criticize had direct application to understanding the problem or planning the study of the problem. For example, her note that Cromer studied mature adults and that she found no similar study of young children was made *because* she planned to study elementary school children. Weinstein and Rabinovitch (1971) used nonsense words and Denner (1970) used logograph sentences, so their findings may not apply to English text (that Weaver will study).

Near the end of the review Weaver states: "From these data, Guthrie concluded that good and poor readers do not differ qualitatively in their use of syntactic cues during silent reading." Authors make numerous statements in their articles. A reviewer must make clear, as Weaver does in this case, the basis for any statement by an author that they report. If Weaver had left out the introductory phrase, "From these data," a reader would not know why Guthrie came to this conclusion. The sentence also implies that Weaver agrees that Guthrie's conclusion was appropriate.

SUMMARY

The purposes for reviewing literature may be personal, professional, or academic. The skills needed to meaningfully organize and interpret relevant literature, particularly research studies, are essentially the same for the various purposes. Identifying sources of relevant literature, taking notes from research studies and related literature, and analyzing and synthesizing it were presented and discussed.

The functions that an integrated, focused review of literature serves when a researcher plans a study were discussed to show how a good literature review is an integral part of a well-planned study. Methods of analysis and synthesis that lead to well-documented conceptual frameworks and associated rationales for a study were illustrated with several excerpts from actual studies.

In the next three chapters, the technical issues of measurement, research design, and statistics are presented. Application of the methods and principles in quantitative, qualitative, and historical studies are illustrated and discussed.

SUGGESTED ACTIVITIES

1. Visit the library at the university. Locate and become familiar with the following:
   a. Card Catalogue (or computerized version)
   b. *Education Index*
   c. *Current Index to Journals in Education* (CIJE)
   d. *Thesaurus of ERIC Descriptors*
   e. *Research in Education* (RIE)
   f. *Encyclopedia of Educational Research*

    g. *Mental Measurements Yearbook*
    h. *Review of Educational Research*
    i. *Dissertation Abstracts International*
2. Identify at least five research articles that are related to a problem of interest to you. Analyze and synthesize the five articles. Identify at least one relationship between two variables that was obtained consistently in the articles. Identify a relationship between two variables that was *not* consistently obtained in the studies.

RELATED SOURCES

Barzun, J., & Graff, H.F. (1985). *The modern researcher* (4th ed.). San Diego: Harcourt Brace Jovanovich.

    This introductory text for the study of history is relevant for all researchers. Examples from many fields illustrate both theory and practice in research. Valuable sources of historical information are described. It is particularly relevant to this chapter because procedures a historian uses either to document the authenticity of written documents or to assess the accuracy of their contents are invaluable to researchers in reviewing relevant literature. All aspects of the inquiry process are described, and the logical basis for drawing conclusions from available evidence is emphasized. It is particularly informative because quantification and the use of statistics are not addressed, yet the fundamental logical issues are the same in all types of inquiry.

Light, R.J., & Pillemer, D.B. (1984). *Summing up: The science of reviewing research*. Cambridge, MA: Harvard University Press.

    These authors believe that the best way to improve new research is to improve our ability to synthesize the information that already exists. The development of meta-analysis, a quantitative procedure for summarizing experimental results, has provided researchers with another valuable analytic tool for reviewing results of past research. The chapters of this book include: Organizing a Review Strategy, Quantitative Procedures (Meta-Analysis), Numbers and Narrative, What We Have Learned, and A Checklist for Evaluating Reviews. Procedures for doing meta-analysis are described and explained, but the authors keep the results of these quantitative processes in an appropriate perspective. That is, that meta-analysis provides *one* way to summarize quantitative experimental studies, which are a subset of the previous research and scholarship that is relevant to a particular study. *All* relevant information must be used to adequately describe present knowledge about a specific problem or issue and how best to study it. This book assumes some graduate research knowledge and experience, using some technical jargon throughout, but it is an outstanding presentation of the techniques and provides good advice for summarizing relevant literature.

REFERENCES

American Psychological Association (1983). *Publication Manual of the American Psychological Association*, 3rd ed. Washington, DC: American Psychological Association.

Block, J.H. (1971). *Mastery learning: Theory and practice*. New York: Holt, Rinehart and Winston.

Borg, Walter R., & Gall, Meredith E. (1983). *Educational research* (4th ed.). White Plains, NY: Longman.

Cromer, W. (1970). The difference model: A new explanation for some reading difficulties. *Journal of Educational Psychology, 61,* 471–483.

Denner, W. (1970). Representational and syntactic competence of problem readers. *Child Development, 41,* 881–887.

Eddins, D.D. (1981). A causal model of the attrition of specially admitted black students in higher education. Unpublished Doctoral Dissertation, University of Pittsburgh.

Farnham-Diggory, S. (1967). Symbol and synthesis in experimental reading. *Child Development, 38,* 221–231.

Gage, N.L. (Ed.). (1963). *Handbook of research on teaching.* Chicago: Rand McNally.

Gibbons, H.D. (1941). Reading and sentence elements. *Elementary English Review, 18,* 42–46.

Gray, Wood, (1964). *Historian's Handbook.* Boston: Houghton Mifflin.

Guthrie, J.T. (1973). Reading comprehension and syntactic responses in good and poor readers. *Journal of Educational Psychology, 65,* 294–299.

Israelite, N.K. (1981). Direct and indirect antecedent context and the comprehension of reversable passive voice sentences by deaf readers. Doctoral Dissertation, University of Pittsburgh, Dissertation Abstracts International, *42,* 4791-A.

Light, R.S., & Pillemer, D.B. (1984). *Summing up: The science of reviewing research.* Cambridge, MA: Harvard University Press.

Oakan, R., Wiener, M., & Cromer, W. (1971). Identification, organization and reading comprehension for good and poor readers. *Journal of Educational Psychology, 62,* 71–78.

Piaget, Jean (1977). *The development of thought.* New York: Viking.

Power, D.J. (1971). Deaf children's acquisition of the passive voice. Unpublished Doctoral Dissertation, University of Illinois.

Power, D.J., & Quigley, S.P. (1973). Deaf children's acquisition of the passive voice. *Journal of Speech and Hearing Research, 16,* 5–11.

Schmitt, P. (1968). Deaf children's comprehension and production of sentence transformations and verb tenses. Unpublished doctoral dissertation, University of Illinois.

Skinner, B.F. (1953). *Science and human behavior.* New York: Macmillan.

Spindler, G. (Ed.). (1982). *Doing the ethnography of schooling.* New York: Holt, Rinehart and Winston.

Tervoort, B. (1970). The understanding of passive sentences by deaf children. In G.B. Flores D'Arcais & W.J.M. Levelt (Eds.), *Advances in Psycholinguistics.* Amsterdam: North-Holland.

Travers, Robert M. (1973). *Second handbook of research on teaching.* Chicago: Rand McNally.

Weaver, Phyllis A. (1976). Sentence anagram organizational training and its effect on reading comprehension. Doctoral Dissertation. University of Pittsburgh, *Dissertation Abstracts International, 37,* 1312A.

Weinstein, R., & Rabinovitch, M. (1971). Sentence structure and retention in good and poor readers. *Journal of Educational Psychology, 62,* 25–30.

Wilcox, Kathleen (1982). Differential socialization in the classroom: Implications for equal opportunity. In G. Spindler (Ed.), *Doing the ethnography of schooling*. New York: Holt, Rinehart and Winston.

Wittrock, M.C. (Ed.). (1986). *The handbook of research on teaching* (3rd ed.). New York: Macmillan.

Wolcott, H.F. (1981). *Anthropologists at home in North America: Issues in the study of one's own society*. Cambridge: Cambridge University Press.

CHAPTER 5

Characteristics of Data

Researchers collect, analyze, and interpret various types of data. Those in different disciplines tend to use different types of information. Historians use written documents primarily. Anthropologists act as participant observers, keeping extensive field notes and tape recordings of their experiences. Sociologists may act as participant observers or do precise statistical analysis of sociometric censuses or other data. Psychologists tend to use psychometric tests and other quantified data. There is some overlap among the disciplines because researchers will do whatever is needed to study their problems best. Education issues, as other practical issues of human life, include characteristics that are commonly studied by researchers in all the various disciplines. It is difficult for educators to eliminate any of the important variables as they try to understand education problems that affect their work. Therefore, various types of information are needed about numerous variables. The study of education cannot be unduly limited to only certain types of data, such as those studied by psychologists.

QUALITATIVE AND QUANTITATIVE INFORMATION

Many authors classify data as qualitative or quantitative. The essential difference between the two is that quantitative data are numerical (concerned with quantity), whereas qualitative data are nonnumerical (concerned with quality or meaning). This distinction is often used to reflect other issues of method and precision in a study. For example, qualitative data are often referred to as subjective, whereas quantitative data are said to be objective. Subjective data, in this sense, are viewed as biased, determined by the whim of the researcher, whereas objective data are unbiased. Examples of objective data are those that could be obtained by machine (such as a speedometer reading, a galvanic skin response, or scoring a multiple choice achievement test).

Other authors point out the inadequacies of quantifying data. Historians, anthropologists, and other researchers who are concerned with meaning in a situation or patterns among numerous variables point out the errors and biases produced by quantifying data. They argue that the whole is more than simply the sum of the individual parts.

This issue is at the center of the controversy about whether the external environment determines the observation, or whether legitimate alternative views or descriptions of the environment are possible. A complex skill, such as reading comprehension, is not comprehensively measured by the reading subtest of a commercial norm-referenced test. A score of 54, particularly when contrasted with a 48 or 34, may mislead researchers or teachers rather than inform them about reading comprehension. At other times, comparing those scores may be valuable and informative.

Some authors equate qualitative research with nonpositivistic, or interpretive, research (Cox & West, 1986; Erickson, 1986). These authors view the important quantitative/qualitative distinction at fundamental levels of beliefs about the nature of human beings and the sources of useful knowledge. They place qualitative researchers as clearly in the wholistic camp who are trying to gain an overall understanding of the situation studied (*verstehen*) rather than documenting the "existence" of specific, easily verified dimensions, or characteristics, of the situation.

These various meanings of terms arise often when one reads the results of research. In no sense is one set of definitions correct and others erroneous. Nor is one approach inherently more scientific or of higher quality. There are many ways that knowledge of the universe and our existence in it can be studied. Each contributes to our knowledge.

Much has been written about the inadequacies of the analytical method of breaking complex skills, such as reading comprehension, into component parts that can be measured with some precision. It is important to understand both the strengths of this approach and the weaknesses of the illusion of precision. There are also weaknesses in the more wholistic approaches of history, ethnography, and other fields that use more qualitative data. These are discussed and illustrated throughout this chapter to help you understand the strengths and weaknesses of each approach. Before the more specific aspects of measurement and the reliability and validity of data are addressed, the meanings of *objective* and *subjective* are clarified.

OBJECTIVE AND SUBJECTIVE DATA

The most common distinction between the terms *objective* and *subjective* as they are used in research is that objective methods are free from bias whereas subjective methods are not. Problems arise when some procedures are identified as inherently objective and others as inherently subjective. For example, multiple choice test items are often identified as objective, whereas observing in a classroom is called subjective.

Many people believe that a machine is inherently neutral and unbiased and that therefore data produced by a machine must be objective (unbiased). The easiest counterexample is the scoring of multiple choice tests. The test developer writes a series of test items with several choices for each item, one of which is the "correct" answer selected by the test developer. Respondents to the test select their answer for each item and mark them on answer sheets, which are scored by a computer. The machine has no intentions, theories, emotions, or beliefs, and gives credit for only the answer identified as correct by the test developer. Is the test objective? Is it free from bias? No! An example test item illustrates the problem.

The following test item is often used to test students who read this book:
A review of literature should begin:

1. As soon as a general problem area is identified.
2. After an initial problem statement is written.
3. After the problem statement and associated hypotheses (or research questions) are stated.
4. After a tentative plan for the study is formulated.
5. After the study is completed in order to interpret the meaning of the findings.

Which answer is correct? Various authors and researchers argue for 1, 2, or 3. This book indicates that 1 is usually the best answer. When taking other multiple choice tests, each of you has more than likely experienced similar subjective choices of the best, or correct, answers to multiple choice items. It is the selection of the correct answer that may result in errors or bias in the scores and not the process of marking the answer sheet and assigning the number correct for each respondent, which is done by machine.

Educators who develop new science curricula in elementary schools often disagree with the answers keyed as correct on commercial tests. When such tests are mandated, the developers are often relieved that students do not obtain high scores on such "erroneous" multiple choice tests that are scored consistently and reliably by machines.

In a similar sense, Scriven (1972) indicated that a single individual viewing the relative merits of the TV pictures produced by two TV antennas would provide more useful data than would a number of electronic meters precisely measuring signal output by the two antennas. This is a result of the fact that measured differences in output may not have a noticeable effect on the picture as seen by human beings. If the purpose is to assess the relative value of the two antennas for home television viewing, the human being has proven to be a reliable and valid instrument for assessing TV reception. When two or more viewers give similar ratings, confidence that the results are accurate and unbiased is gained. In gathering, analyzing, and interpreting data, accuracy and a lack of bias are always the primary concerns. Some uses of the terms *objective* and *subjective* tend to obscure that point.

MEASURING VARIABLES

Researchers collect information in various ways. Anthropologists live in a community for a long period observing, asking questions, taping cultural events, and gathering other information related to important variables or questions. Psychologists and sociologists send out questionnaires to estimate attitudes of teachers toward the handicapped. Educators may compare IQ and achievement scores of students at various grade levels. Historians assess the changes in theories and textbooks used from 1900 to 1930 to see how theory affects pedagogy. Each of these studies requires the measurement of skills and attitudes or the assigning of actions or writings to certain classifications or categories. The procedures used to collect data are all processes of measurement.

Measurement is the process of assigning classifications (or numbers) to characteristics of persons, objects, or events according to specific rules. This definition applies to information gathered in historical or ethnographic studies, where numbers are seldom used, as well as in laboratory and experimental studies, which use quantitative data primarily. Measurement is the process by which characteristics of the environment and the people in it (empirical information) are transformed into useful data.

MEASUREMENT SCALES

Different types of measures result in different types of measurement scales, which are categorized into four types: (1) nominal, (2) ordinal, (3) interval, and (4) ratio. The four types of scales represent four kinds of classification: (1) with or without numbers (nominal), (2) ranked data (ordinal), (3) equal interval data (interval), and (4) equal interval data with a meaningful zero (ratio). (See Table 5.1 for specific examples of each type of scale.) The type of scale determines the mathematical operations possible with that type of data. Frequencies can be counted with nominal data. Ranks can be ordered with ordinal data, but direct mathematical manipulation usually is not meaningful. Additions and subtractions are meaningful with interval and ratio data. Multiplications and divisions can be meaningfully interpreted only with ratio data.

Classifying each tree as deciduous or evergreen and counting the number of each type of tree in a 10-acre plot is an example of a nominal measure. Neither type of tree has more "treeness" than the other type, so an ordinal scale is not possible. The frequencies (numbers) that are obtained do form a ratio scale because the difference between four trees and five trees is the same as the difference between one tree and two trees (i.e., one tree). The zero on the scale is

TABLE 5.1. MEASUREMENT SCALES

1. *Nominal*: Names something, or places in a category; classifies.
   a. Sex (male or female)
   b. Trees (oak, maple, locust, . . .)
   c. An act of reinforcement (teacher praises student)
2. *Ordinal*: Orders categories or classifications on a continuum; forms ranks.
   a. Position academically in graduation class (10 out of 243).
   b. Rank of city by population (25th largest in United States).
3. *Interval*: Equal intervals between numbers [i.e., the same distance on the scale 1–3 vs. (27–29)] represents the same amount of the underlying variable; no meaningful zero point.
   a. Temperature on Fahrenheit or centigrade scale.
4. *Ratio*: Numbers represent equal intervals *and* zero means that none of the variable is present (zero is meaningful).
   a. Distance in feet (or meters).
   b. Height in inches (or centimeters).
   c. Kelvin temperature scale (0° K represents absolute 0).

meaningful in that it represents *no* trees. The meaningful zero point means that ratios formed by the scale are meaningful. That is, if there are four deciduous trees and two evergreen trees, the ratio of 4:2 means that there are twice as many deciduous trees as there are evergreen trees in this plot.

When no meaningful zero point exists, such as with a centigrade temperature scale (where 0° C is simply the temperature at which water freezes), ratios of temperatures are not meaningful. That is, 100° C is not twice as hot as 50° C, nor is 2° C twice as hot as 1° C. In fact, it is difficult to comprehend what ratios of centigrade temperatures represent. Using a Kelvin scale, where 0° K represents the total absence of molecular movement, the temperature represents amount of molecular movement. On this scale, 100° K represents twice as much molecular movement (theoretically) as 50° K because it is a ratio scale.

All physical measures, such as height, weight, and velocity, are measured with ratio scales. In each case 0 represents the total absence of the characteristic. As a result, ratios that are formed can be meaningfully interpreted.

Most measures in education, such as achievement tests, interest inventories, IQ tests, aptitude measures, and personality inventories, have no meaningful zero point. A score of 64 on a geometry test does not represent twice as much geometry knowledge as a score of 32. The 32 additional points earned by the person with a score of 64 may represent one skill, or it may represent 32 (or more) skills. An instructor can develop a test on which either no one will answer a single item correctly or nearly everyone will get all items right. Standardized norm-referenced tests, such as the Metropolitan Achievement Test (MAT) or the Stanford-Binet intelligence test, have no meaningful zero points either. In a strict interpretation of the four types of scales, measures of cognitive or personality characteristics of people, such as the MAT, are no better than ordinal measures. That is, they allow you to rank people in terms of more (or less) of the characteristic

**TABLE 5.2. GRADE POINT AVERAGE AND RANK
IN GRADUATING CLASS OF TOP 15 SENIORS**

Grade Point Average	Rank
5.00	1
4.98	2
4.96	3
4.95	4
4.90	5
4.85	6
4.75	7
4.70	8
4.66	9
4.65	10
4.64	11
4.63	12
4.62	13
4.61	14
4.60	15

measured, but, as explained, the differences of 8 units between scores of 2 and 10 versus 24 and 32 on a math test do not represent the same amount of the underlying variable, which is math knowledge. On an IQ test, the knowledge or ability needed to move from an IQ of 100 to one of 105 is much less than that needed to move from 145 to 150 on the same test.

Test scores are generally treated as if they were interval scales because the errors that result when this assumption is made do not seem to be large. Conclusions reached using statistical techniques requiring interval data, such as tests of significance, have generally held up over time. So, educators and researchers continue to treat them as interval measures, even though they are ordinal.

The primary difference between ordinal and interval scales is that additions and subtractions are meaningful with interval scales but are not with ordinal ones. Finding differences in ranks, such as those in Table 5.2, gives no information about differences in the underlying variable on which the ranks are based, such as grade point average. Subtracting rank 2 from rank 5 gives a difference of 3 on the ordinal scale, just as subtracting rank 11 from rank 14 gives a result of 3. The first difference represents a difference of 0.08 grade points (4.98 − 4.90), and the second represents 0.03 grade points (4.64 − 4.61). This illustrates that subtracting (or adding) numbers on an ordinal scale does not result in numbers that can be meaningfully interpreted.

Scores are obtained on each of these types of scales for many purposes. Teachers, administrators, parents, and students need achievement information to estimate how the teaching-learning process is going. School boards need demographic information on their communities to make budgeting and planning decisions for the future. Researchers gather process and outcome information to identify variables that are important in the learning process.

All qualitative data, whether they are based on positivistic assumptions or not, would be classified as nominal data because they are fundamentally non-numerical. When numbers are used for classification purposes, such as coding females as 1 and males are 2, or identifying three groups in a study as groups 1, 2, and 3, the numbers have no inherent meaning. They are used as symbols to represent and identify categories. Any symbols, such as A, M, and E, would serve the same purpose.

Anthropologists, historians, and other social scientists usually use more than classifications. For example, a culture may have ranks within the leadership of its tribe or religion. Identifying persons by their rank can be done numerically, with the numbers forming an ordinal scale.

For more than a decade, a number of historians have been developing methods of quantitative history. There is at present at least one journal of quantitative history, *Historical Methods*. Few disciplines are *totally* either quantitative or qualitative in their methods. The four types of measurement scales are useful in classifying data in a study, which provides some initial guidelines about the type of mathematical operations that can be used.

DESCRIPTIVE STATISTICS

When a set of data is gathered for any purpose, some kind of simplification, or summary, of the data is needed if the scores are to have meaning. When a math test is given in a fifth-grade class, a score is generated for each of the 20 students. If a score of 73 is obtained, what does that mean? There is no way to know without more information. If the mean score was 54, the highest score was 83, and the lowest was 37, you know that 73 is well above average but not the highest score. There is still much ambiguity about the specific position of the score. Statistical techniques have been developed to simplify and summarize sets of data.

Statistics are the mathematical techniques for gathering, organizing, analyzing, and interpreting numerical data. Statistical techniques allow you to describe a set of data, such as the fifth-grade test scores, in order to compare the entire set of data with other sets of data, or to determine the position, or meaning, of a score within the set. The characteristics of a set of scores that are particularly useful to know are the average score and the variation among the scores. In the foregoing example, the mean of 54 was the arithmetic average of these scores. The range from 37 to 83 indicates that the scores vary across 47 points on the score scale. If a different class had a mean of 60 with scores ranging across 32 units, you would know that it is more homogeneous and appears to have slightly higher scores on the average. The various statistics used to indicate the average are called *measures of central tendency*, and those describing variation are called *measures of variability*.

Measures of Central Tendency

The three most common measures of central tendency are mean, median, and mode. The *mode* is the most frequent score. The *median* is the point on the score scale at which 50% of the scores are above and 50% are below. The *mean* is the arithmetic average. For the scores 1, 5, 5, 5, and 9, the most frequent score (mode) is 5, the median is 5, and the mean is 5. When a set of scores is symmetric with one mode, the mean, median, and mode are the same. For a second set of scores (1, 5, 5, 5, 34), the mode is 5, the median is 5, and the mean is the sum of the scores (50) divided by the number of scores (5), which equals 10. The mean is higher than the median because it is affected by the value of *each* score. The 1 is 4 points below 5, whereas 34 is 29 points above 5. Changing the 9 in the first set of data to a 34 in the second set had no effect on the mode or median but raised the mean 5 points. The median is unaffected by the value of scores at the two ends of the distribution, whereas the mean is affected by the value of *every* score.

That is the reason why the average income in the United States is reportd as the median income. At present, 50% of working Americans earn $18,000 or less per year and 50% earn more than $18,000. Assuming that the median income is $18,000 per year, if the mean were used to indicate the average income, it would be in excess of $30,000, because many Americans earn more than $100,000 per year and some earn more than $1 million. These high salaries raise the mean income to a much higher value than the median.

Calculating the Mean and Median. As indicated, the calculation of the arithmetic average, or mean, score for a set of scores is relatively straightforward. The formula for calculating the mean is the following:

$$\overline{X} = \frac{\Sigma X}{N}$$

where

$$\Sigma X = \text{the sum of all scores in the set}$$
$$N = \text{the number of scores in the set}$$
$$\overline{X} = \text{arithmetic average, or mean}$$

The median can be calculated easily so long as there are no duplicate scores. It is the middle score in a set containing an odd number of scores, and it is midway between the two middle scores when the set contains an even number of scores. Given the set of 4 scores 1, 3, 5, and 7, the median is said to be midway between 3 and 5, which is 4.0.

For the set of numbers 3, 4, 4, 5, and 54, the median for this set of scores is *not* precisely 4.0 because there are two 4s in this set. To calculate the median requires assumptions about basic concepts that are universally used in measurement. First, by definition, the median is precisely the point on the score scale where half the scores fall above and half fall below. With 5 scores, the midpoint

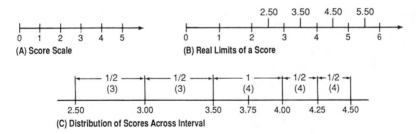

Figure 5.1. Score Scale, Real Limits, and Distribution of Scores Across an Interval of a Score Scale

of the set of scores is the point where precisely 2.50 scores fall below and 2.50 scores fall above.

On many education scales, such as math tests, the only scores possible are the integers 0, 1, 2, 3, . . . , 100. Persons cannot earn 15.2 or 32.761 points. Yet we assume that the scales form a continuum from 0 to 100 (or whatever the highest score possible). This means that there are no holes or empty spaces in it. In Figure 5.1A the first 5 points on a continuous scale are represented. Each score, such as 3, 4, or 54, represents one unit on the score scale. Thus, 3 represents the distance on the scale from 2.50 to 3.50, and 4 represents the distance from 3.50 to 4.50. The points 2.50 and 3.50 are called the "real limits" of the score 3, whereas 3.50 and 4.50 are the real limits of score 4 (see Figure 5.1B). The scores obtained are assumed to be equally distributed across that unit, so half of score 3 falls between 2.50 and 3.00, and the other half is equally distributed from 3.00 to 3.50. The same is true for the two scores of 4; they are equally distributed between 3.50, the lower real limit (LRL) and 4.50 the upper real limit (URL) (see Figure 5.1C). To logically identify the median point on the scale, we must figure out precisely where 2.5 (or $2\frac{1}{2}$) of the scores fall below (and above).

One score (3) falls between 2.50 and 3.50, and 2 scores (4) fall between 3.50 and 4.50. Assuming that the 2 scores are equally distributed, one 4 falls between 3.50 and 4.00. Half of the other 4 falls between 4.00 and 4.25, and the other half between 4.25 and 4.50. Thus, the point below (and above) which 2.50 scores in this set of scores fall is 4.25, which is the median (Md).

A formula that can be used to calculate the median in any set of scores is:

$$Md = LRL\ (Md) + \frac{\text{number of scores needed to reach median}}{\text{number of scores in the interval}}\ (\text{size of interval})$$

To use this formula, you must first divide the number of scores in the set of scores by 2. In our example there were 5 scores, so we need the point where 5/2, or 2.5, scores fall below. Starting from the lowest score, there is 1 score (3) in intervals below the score containing the median. Therefore, the lower real limit (LRL) of the interval where the median falls is 3.50. The number of scores in this interval needed to reach the median is another 1.5 scores, and the numbers of scores in the interval from 3.50 to 4.50 is 2. The length of the interval is 1 unit. Placing these numbers in the formula:

$$Md = 3.50 + \frac{1.5}{2.0}\,(1.0) = 3.50 + 0.75 = 4.25$$

The calculated median, 4.25, is the same as that identified logically in the foregoing discussion.

When a set of scores is symmetric and there are no duplicate scores in the interval containing the median, the mean and median will be precisely the same value. When scores are skewed in one direction or another, the mean and median will differ. Because the mean is adversely affected by the value of unusual scores, such as the 54 in our example, the median is usually a better index of average with skewed (nonsymmetric) distributions.

The mode, or most frequent score, is used more often to describe distributions than it is used as a measure of central tendency. For example, the distributions in Figure 5.2A all have a single score that is obtained most frequently. These are called *unimodal distributions*. The first two are symmetric, and the last two are skewed. Distributions with two scores that are more frequent than those around them are called *bimodal distributions* (Figure 5.2B); those with more than two modes are called *multimodal distributions* (Figure 5.2C). The precise mean-

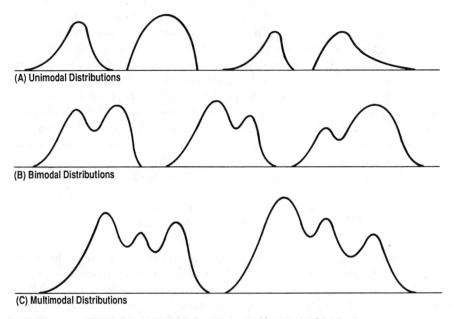

(A) Unimodal Distributions

(B) Bimodal Distributions

(C) Multimodal Distributions

Figure 5.2. Unimodal, Bimodal, and Multimodal Distribution

ing of mode would require the frequencies of the scores in bimodal and multimodal distributions to be equal. In practice, the terms are more commonly used as illustrated in Figure 5.2. Distributions with two "humps" are called bimodal, and those with more than two are called multimodal.

The purpose of using measures of central tendency is to describe the data either to interpret the scores within the distribution or to compare the distribution of scores with other distributions. Measures of variability are used for the same purposes.

Measures of Variability

Four useful indexes of variability are (1) range, (2) quartile deviation, (3) standard deviation, and (4) variance. Each gives a description or indication of the amount of variation in a set of scores. The *range* is the difference between the highest and lowest scores. It is usually the most inconsistent index because it depends on only 2 scores in a distribution: the highest score and the lowest score. In the foregoing example, the set of data, 3, 4, 4, 5, and 54, ranges over 51 units on the score scale ($54 - 3$). Some authors define the range as (high $-$ low) + 1. This includes the real limits of a score ($54.5 - 2.5 = 52$) and is the actual number of points on the score scale across which the distribution of scores ranges (3 to 54).

The *quartile deviation* describes the range of the middle 50% of the scores in a distribution. The definition of the quartile deviation is:

$$Q = \frac{Q_3 - Q_1}{2}$$

where

Q_1 (first quartile) = point below which 25% of the scores fall
Q_3 (third quartile) = point below which 75% of the scores fall
Q = quartile deviation

From the formula it is clear that Q represents half the distance on the score scale that the middle half of the scores ranges across. Because this index is unaffected by scores at the ends of the distribution, it is used with the median (Q_2) to describe skewed distributions.

The *variance* (S^2) and *standard deviation* (S) are used with the mean ($\overline{X}$) to describe symmetric distributions. The variance is defined as:

$$S^2 = \frac{\Sigma (X_i - \overline{X})^2}{N}$$

where

X_i = individual scores (1 through N)
$\overline{X}$ = mean for the set of scores
N = number of scores in the set
Σ = means to sum whatever follows

TABLE 5.3. VARIANCES AND STANDARD DEVIATIONS FOR A SYMMETRIC AND NONSYMMETRIC DISTRIBUTION

(A) Symmetric Distribution:			(B) Nonsymmetric Distribution:	
X_i	$X_i - \overline{X}$	$X_i - \overline{X}^2$	X_i	$X_i - \overline{X}^2$
1	−4	16	1	36
3	−2	4	3	16
5	0	0	5	4
7	2	4	7	0
9	4	16	19	144
$\Sigma X_A = $ 25	0	40	$\Sigma X_B = $ 35	200

$$\overline{X}_A = \frac{\Sigma X_A}{N} = \frac{25}{5} = 5 \qquad\qquad \overline{X}_B = \frac{35}{5} = 7 \qquad S_B^2 = \frac{200}{5} = 40$$

$$S_A^2 = \frac{\Sigma(X_i - \overline{X})^2}{N} = \frac{40}{5} = 8.0 \qquad\qquad S_B = \sqrt{40} = 6.32$$

$$S_A = \sqrt{S_A^2} = \sqrt{\frac{\Sigma(X_i - \overline{X})^2}{N}} = \sqrt{\frac{40}{5}} = \sqrt{8} = 2\sqrt{2} = 2.828$$

   The numerator in the formula is based on the deviation of each score from the mean, $(X_i - \overline{X})$. A characteristic of the mean is that the sum of these deviations, $\Sigma(X_i - \overline{X})$, always equals zero (0). That is, in fact, what the arithmetic average represents—the point where the total value of the scores above that point equal the total value of those below that point. The variance uses the square of the deviation, $(X_i - \overline{X})^2$, in order to use the deviation scores as an index of score variability. The example in Table 5.3 illustrates the use of this definition with two simple sets of data. In Example A in Table 5.3, the sum of the squared deviation scores equals 40, and there are 5 scores. The variance equals 40 divided by 5, which is 8.0. The standard deviation is the square root of the variance, which equals $\sqrt{8}$, or 2.828.

   In other words, the variance (S^2) for a set of scores is the average squared deviation from the mean of all scores in that distribution of scores. Strictly speaking, the standard deviation is not an index of the average deviation of the scores around the mean, but that is the type of variability the standard deviation represents. Rather than 2.4, which is the average deviation of the 5 scores around the mean $(4 + 2 + 0 + 2 + 4 = 12; 12/5 = 2.4)$, the standard deviation of 2.828 is slightly higher.

   To show the effect of disparate, or unusual, scores on the mean and variance of a distribution of scores, Example B in Table 5.3 results from a change of 9 in Example A to 19 in Example B for the scores of 1, 3, 5, 7, and 19. The mean value increases from 5 for Example A to 7 for Example B, the variance from 8 to 40, and the standard deviation from 2.828 to 6.32. Unusually high or low scores, which occur in any nonsymmetric or skewed distribution, adversely affect the standard deviation and variance. With high scores, the standard deviation, S_x, is inflated, just as the mean, $\overline{X}$, is increased. In these types of situations, the median and quartile deviation provide better descriptions of the average score and the variability in the distribution of scores than do the mean and standard deviation.

When there is a symmetric distribution, such as a normal curve, the mean and standard deviation can provide particularly accurate and useful information.

Normal Distribution

Many characteristics of people are distributed much like a normal distribution. For example, height, weight, and IQ are approximately normally distributed in the general population of the United States. An illustration of the normal distribution, represented in Figure 5.3, shows the proportion of scores that fall within each portion of the normal distribution.

The standard normal distribution is used to describe any normally distributed set of scores. It is formed using the formula:

$$z = \frac{X_i - \overline{X}}{S_x}$$

The standard normal score, z, represents the number of standard deviations that a specific score is above or below the mean in a distribution of scores. In the example in Figure 5.3, a score of 54 in a normal distribution with a mean of 48 and a standard deviation (S_x) of 4.0, falls 1.5 standard deviations above the mean. The z value of 1.50 is used with a normal distribution table to identify the proportion of the scores that fall below the score of 54. If a set of scores is *not* normally distributed, changing the raw scores to z scores does not transform them into a normal distribution, and such tables provide no information about the scores in this distribution.

In the normal distribution (Figure 5.3) 0.3413, or 34.13%, of the scores fall between the mean and one standard deviation above or below the mean. Slightly more than two-thirds of the scores fall within one standard deviation from the mean (0.6826). Approximately 95% (0.9544) of the scores fall within two standard deviations (or z scores) from the mean. Nearly all scores (0.9974) fall within three standard deviations of the mean. One of the primary uses for the normal distributions is to calculate the proportion of scores that fall below (or above) any score in a normal distribution by transforming the raw score, (X_i), to a z score.

For the example in Figure 5.3, the z score of 1.50 in a normal distribution would have 43.32% of the scores between that score and the mean (see Figure 5.4). Another 50% of the scores fall below the mean. Thus, the percentage of scores below a score of 54 in this normal distribution would be 93.32%.

Measures of Relationship

Most people know the following facts:

1. Academic achievement is related to socioeconomic status.
2. Student achievement is related to teacher effectiveness.
3. Creativity is only somewhat related to IQ.

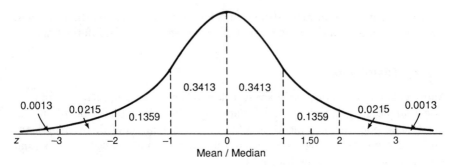

Figure 5.3. Normal Curve

A central element in becoming an "expert" in something is knowing precisely the nature and degree of relationships among important variables. Whether you are a principal, nurse, doctor, teacher, or parent, through education and experience you learn such relationships as that teacher satisfaction is related to involvement in decision-making, that symptoms are related to type of disease, and that learning is related to time spent studying. How is the degree of relationship between two variables measured or estimated?

Numerous indexes of relationship have been developed over history. Two indexes used today with nominal and interval, or ratio, types of data are, respectively, the phi coefficient (ϕ), and the Pearson Product Moment Correlation Coefficient (r). The phi coefficient is used with two classifications for each of two variables, such as gender (male/female) and college graduate (yes/no), which are nominal data. The frequency of each of the four classifications is placed in a two-by-two contingency table. The phi coefficient represents the degree to which

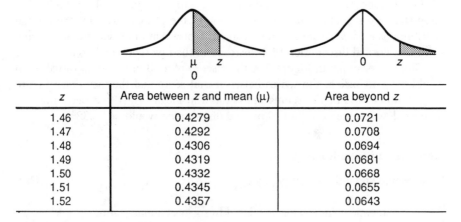

z	Area between z and mean (μ)	Area beyond z
1.46	0.4279	0.0721
1.47	0.4292	0.0708
1.48	0.4306	0.0694
1.49	0.4319	0.0681
1.50	0.4332	0.0668
1.51	0.4345	0.0655
1.52	0.4357	0.0643

Figure 5.4. Excerpt from a Standard Normal Distribution Table

College Graduation

		Yes	No
Male	A	15	B 5
Female	C	8	D 12

Gender

$$\phi = \frac{AD - BC}{\sqrt{(A + B)(C + D)(A + C)(B + D)}}$$

$$\phi = \frac{180 - 40}{\sqrt{(15 + 5)(8 + 12)(15 + 8)(5 + 12)}}$$

$$\phi = \frac{140}{\sqrt{156400}} = \frac{140}{395.4} = 0.354$$

Figure 5.5. Relationship between College Graduation and Gender (A Hypothetical Example of Phi-coefficient Calculation)

college graduation is related to sex within the group of people studied. Figure 5.5 illustrates the relationship between gender and college education and the calculation of the phi coefficient.

The data in Figure 5.5 show that a higher proportion of the persons studied were men who graduated from college, which indicates that gender is related to college education. The degree of that relationship is indicated by a phi coefficient of 0.354. The phi coefficient (ϕ) can be used only to calculate the relationship between two classifications of two variables.

The Pearson Product Moment Correlation Coefficient (r) was developed by Karl Pearson at the turn of the century to assess relationships between variables that are measured on continuous scales using interval or ratio measures. Essentially, it measures the extent to which a person's score on one variable (such as IQ) is in precisely the same relative position within a group of scores as is that person's score on a second variable (such as math achievement). Although many different mathematical formulas can be used to calculate this correlation coefficient, the one that is most descriptive of what it measures is:

$$r = \frac{\Sigma(z_x z_y)}{N}$$

where z_x is the person's standard score on variable X, z_y is that person's score on variable Y, and N is the number of pairs of scores (people).

The three values of all correlation coefficients that describe the limits of relationships between the variables are $+1.00$, -1.00, and 0.0. These are:

$r =$ 1.00 when every person's score is in precisely the same position on the two variables.

$r = -1.00$ when every person's score is in precisely the same relative position on the two variables (same z), but one is above the mean and the other is below the mean.

$r =$ 0.00 when there is no relationship between the scores on the two variables.

The value of r obtained in a situation, such as 0.36 or 0.85, indicates the degree of relationship between two variables. The sign, plus or minus ($+$ or $-$), indicates the direction of the relationship. That is, when people with high scores on one variable also have high scores on the other variable, and persons with low scores on one variable also have low scores on the other variable, the relationship is positive and the correlation coefficient (r) will be positive ($+$). When high scores on one variable go with low scores on the other variable and vice versa, r will be negative ($-$) and the relationship is called negative. Thus, r values of 0.86 and -0.86 represent the same degree of relationship between two variables but differ in the direction of the relationship. Table 5.4 illustrates the calculation of the Pearson Product Moment Correlation Coefficient (r) for two hypothetical variables, X and Y, that represent a perfect positive relationship ($r = 1.00$).

QUALITY OF DATA

In measuring information for any purpose, you must be concerned with whether the measurement process results in classifications or scores that accurately represent the characteristic you want to measure. Are these the achievement levels of these students? Do the teachers give these amounts of reinforcements in their classrooms? Do these principals actually spend this much time on each of these activities? Does this material in the textbook represent a change in pedagogy or theory? When anyone is concerned with obtaining the best information for answering a question, two fundamental issues must be addressed. A first issue, which was mentioned in Chapter 4 and is addressed substantively in Chapter 6, is: What are the best sources of such information? These sources may be books or journals, or they may be particular people, such as teachers, students, parents, administrators, or school board members. A second issue is: How can I assure the highest quality of the information (data) that is gathered?

Issues of data quality are addressed primarily as issues of the reliability and validity of the measurement procedures used to gather the data. *Reliability* of a measurement process means the consistency of results when using that process. If two observers go into the same classroom at the same time and use the same observation instrument, they should get the same results. If they do not, then the results are not perfectly reliable. There is always some error in a measurement process, so there will be some lack of consistency in the results. A reliability coefficient, or index, estimates the degree of inconsistency, "noise," or random error in the measurement process.

TABLE 5.4. RELATIONSHIP BETWEEN VARIABLES X AND Y

X	$(X_i - \overline{X})^2$	z_x		Y	$(Y_i - \overline{Y})^2$	z_y
1	16	−1.414		14	16	−1.414
3	4	−0.707		16	4	−0.707
5	0	0.000		18	0	0.000
7	4	0.707		20	4	0.707
9	16	1.414		22	16	1.414
$\Sigma X = $ 25	40			$\Sigma Y = $ 90	40	

$$\overline{X} = 5.0 \quad S_x = \sqrt{\frac{40}{5}} = \sqrt{8} = 2.828 \qquad \overline{Y} = 18.0 \quad S_y = \sqrt{\frac{40}{5}} = \sqrt{8} = 2.828$$

$$z_x = \frac{X_i - \overline{X}}{S_x} \qquad z_x = \frac{1 - 5}{2.828} \qquad\qquad z_y = \frac{14 - 18}{2.828} = \frac{-4}{2.828}$$

$$= \frac{-4}{2.828} \qquad\qquad z_y = -1.414$$

$$z_x = -1.414$$

$$r = \frac{\Sigma(z_x z_y)}{N} = \frac{(-1.414)\,(-1.414) + (-0.707)\,(-0.707) + (0) + (0.707)\,(0.707) + (1.414)\,(1.414)}{5}$$

$$r = \frac{2.0 \quad + \quad 0.50 \quad + \quad 0 \quad + \quad 0.50 \quad + \quad 2.0}{5} = \frac{5}{5} = \underline{1.00}$$

Validity addresses the extent to which a measurement process measures what you want it to measure. This characteristic of a measurement process is not inherent in the process, as is reliability, but depends on the purpose you have for the data and the way the data are used. For example, one level of the Metropolitan Achievement Test (MAT), a commercially available test with national norms, measures reading objectives usually taught in grades 5 and 6. The MAT is valid for comparing achievement of students in a typical U.S. classroom with that of other typical U.S. fifth- or sixth-grade students who use typical reading curricula. The MAT was used to evaluate the effects of a remedial sixth-grade reading program in a local school district. The teachers in the program were asked to identify all MAT test items that addressed topics studied that year in the remedial program. They identified *no* items. That means the test covered nothing that was taught that year in the remedial program. It was totally invalid as a measure of what students learned from that class; so it could not be used to evaluate the effects of the remedial program. Thus, a measure can be valid for one purpose and invalid for another.

The relationship between reliability and validity is represented by several targets in Figure 5.6. Think of the dots on the targets as scores that result from repeated attempts to measure a characteristic of a person, object, or event. If there is no consistency in the scores (Target A), the measure is neither reliable nor valid. This represents excessive random error in the measurement process. A measure can be consistent (as in Target B) but still not measure what you want to

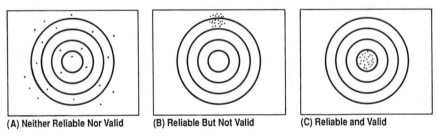

(A) Neither Reliable Nor Valid   (B) Reliable But Not Valid   (C) Reliable and Valid

Figure 5.6. Relationship Between Reliability and Validity

measure. The use of the MAT to evaluate the remedial reading program is an example of this. It is very reliable, but it did not measure what was taught. Only when there is consistency in the scores (high reliability), and the scores represent precisely the variable you want to measure (Target C), is a measurement process valid.

Distinctions between reliability and validity of qualitative data are not as clear-cut as they are for quantitative data, although the concepts are applicable. That is, the procedures used to classify written responses on a questionnaire into specific categories may not be reliable. Different persons might place them in different categories, or the same person might classify them in different categories at different times. In a similar manner, historians' methods would not be reliable if similar classification problems occurred in their studies.

The extent to which the data produced by these classification processes accurately represent the variables studied denotes the validity of the data. In the two preceding examples, the variables addressed by the questionnaire could be teachers' attitudes toward mainstreaming handicapped children, whereas a historian could be studying changes in pedagogical theory from 1900 to 1930. In each case, the procedures used could produce consistent types of information that could be reliably classified but that would not accurately represent the attitudes or changes in theory. When questions are asked in certain ways, teachers will respond differently than if they are asked in different ways (or in different contexts). The historian could obtain consistent but invalid data if the textbooks searched were not representative of pedagogical theory from 1900 to 1930.

In qualitative studies, as in all studies that attempt to describe a situation without assigning treatments or characteristics to subjects, the quality of the data is determined by the selection of sources for the information (books, students, teachers, etc.), the procedures used to obtain information, and the methods used to transform the information into data that can be used to study the problem. The selection of sources, or sample, to be studied is discussed in Chapter 6 because of its impact on the conclusions that can be drawn from a study. The quality of data and the degree to which that data represents the variables addressed in any study are, of course, important determinants of conclusions that can be made legitimately from a study and of the settings to which they are applicable. The ways in which measurement, research design, and statistical issues contribute to drawing legitimate substantive conclusions in a study are presented in Chapter 8. In the next section of this chapter, we address more specific ways to study issues of reliability and validity.

Reliability

Researchers have learned how to develop instruments and procedures in ways that maximize reliability. When quantitative data are produced, mathematical indexes can be used to estimate the reliability of the measurement process. When qualitative data are produced, these quantitative indexes often cannot be used. The logical issue addressed by the quantitative index, however, is relevant to qualitative data. Researchers who use qualitative data have been aware of the issues for some time and have developed some procedures to maximize the reliability of their data. New ways of assessing the quality of the data that are produced in such studies are presently being developed in history and ethnography. Mathematical procedures used to estimate various aspects of reliability and some examples of those procedures follow.

Three types of reliability that address somewhat different concerns about a measurement or testing process are the following:

1. Stability of data over time.
2. Internal consistency of data.
3. Equivalence of alternate test forms.

When most educators think about the reliability of a measure they usually think about the stability of data produced over time by that measure. That is, if we measure a person's IQ at two different times, do we get the same score? The difference in IQ scores from one administration to a second administration of the test represents the chance factors that may affect the IQ scores, or the random error in the measurement process. Getting too little sleep, having a death in the family, or guessing well on items that you do not know may affect your IQ score. If a test or other measure is greatly affected by chance factors, the reliability of the measure will be low. If the scores over time are consistent, then the reliability of the measure will be high.

How is the stability of a measure assessed? A measure, such as an IQ test, is given twice to the same group of people. The correlation between the scores on the first and the second administration is calculated (see Table 5.5). If a measure is perfectly reliable, the correlation, called a *reliability coefficient*, will be 1.00. If it is perfectly unreliable, the correlation will be zero (0.00). The closer the reliability coefficient is to 1.00, the more reliable is the measure. As shown in Table 5.5, the concept of reliability as measured by the correlation coefficient does not apply to the consistency of each person's score but to the consistency of a set of scores. A perfectly reliable measure is operationally defined as placing each individual's score in precisely the same position relative to others in the group each

TABLE 5.5. CALCULATION OF RELIABILITY COEFFICIENT

Person	Score (Time 1)			Score (Time 2)		
	X_1	$(X_1 - \overline{X}_1)$	z_1	X_2	$(X_2 - \overline{X}_2)$	z_2
1	9	4	1.414	12	4	1.414
2	7	2	0.707	10	2	0.707
3	5	0	0.000	8	0	0.000
4	3	−2	−0.707	6	−2	−0.707
5	1	−4	−1.414	4	−4	−1.414
		0			0	

$$\Sigma X_1 = 25 \qquad \Sigma X_2 = 40$$
$$\overline{X}_1 = 5.0 \qquad \overline{X}_2 = 8.0$$
$$S_1 = \sqrt{\frac{40}{5}} = \sqrt{8} = 2.828 \qquad S_2 = \sqrt{\frac{40}{5}} = 2.828$$
$$z_1 = \frac{X_1 - \overline{X}_1}{S_1} = \frac{9-5}{2.828} = 1.414 \qquad z_2 = \frac{X_j - \overline{X}_2}{S_2} = \frac{10-8}{2.828} = \frac{2}{2.828} = 0.707$$

$$r = \frac{\Sigma(z_1 z_2)}{N} = \frac{(1.414)(1.414) + (0.707)(0.707) + (0)(0) + (-0.707)(-0.707) + (-1.414)(-1.414)}{5}$$

$$r = \frac{2.0 \quad + \quad 0.50 \quad + \quad 0 \quad + \quad 0.50 \quad + \quad 2.0}{5} = \frac{5}{5}$$

$$r = 1.00$$

time the measure is administered. Any change in the group of scores as a whole, such as the change from a mean of 5 to a mean of 8, as illustrated in Table 5.5, is assumed to be a systematic change brought about by (a) common experiences, such as classroom instruction, between the two administrations of the measure, (2) differences in conditions of the two test administrations, or (3) some other *systematic* aspect of the situation. These systematic differences in the scores relate to validity, which is discussed later, rather than reliability. Reliability addresses only the random, or error, variation in a set of scores, not systematic differences in groups of scores.

A second type of reliability, *internal consistency*, is addressed when a measure assesses only one topic, or body of knowledge, and is administered only once. Achievement or knowledge tests in one academic area, such as math, is a typical example of such a measure. Internal consistency is estimated by dividing the single measure into two measures and comparing the respondents' scores on the two measures. For example, a 30-item test could form two tests by treating the even-numbered items as one 15-item test and the 15 odd-numbered items as a second test. The correlation between the scores that students earn on the two subtests indicates the internal consistency of the test as a whole. If in Table 5.4 the first set of 5 scores were for the 15 even items and the second set of 5 scores were for the 15 odd items, the calculation of the internal consistency reliability index is exactly like that given in Table 5.5. This process is meaningful only when all the items on a test are supposed to measure the same content or body of knowledge, as on tests given students who have studied the same content in an academic subject.

Such tests can be divided into two equal parts in any one of a number of ways. Odd and even are often used to get similar numbers of easy and difficult items when easier items are at the beginning and more difficult items are at the end of a test. Because this estimate is for tests half as long as the test actually taken (15 versus 30 items), the Spearman-Brown prophecy formula is used. This formula uses the split-half correlation to "predict" the reliability of the longer test. The formula is:

$$r_{SB} = \frac{2r_h}{1 + r_h}$$

where

r_{SB} = the Spearman-Brown reliability estimate

r_h = the obtained correlation between the half-tests

A split-half correlation of 0.54 for two 15-item half-tests indicates that a 30-item test would have a 0.70 reliability, for example.

Another way to estimate the reliability of a test from a single administration is the Kuder-Richardson formula. The KR20 is used when each test item is scored dichotomously, such as correct (1) or incorrect (0). The KR20 formula is:

$$KR20 = \frac{k}{k-1} \left[1 - \frac{p(1-p)}{S_x^2} \right]$$

where

k = number of items on the test,

p = proportion passing each item, and

S_x^2 = variance of the total test scores.

The KR20 is an estimate of the average correlation of all possible split-half combinations that could be obtained from this test.

All estimates of the internal consistency of a test are affected by the homogeneity of the content tested by the specific test items as well as the length of a test. They should not be used when respondents' speed in answering items affects the score. Authors who provide a more comprehensive discussion of internal consistency measures are Borg and Gall (1983), Nitko (1983), Thorndike (1951), and Gronlund (1985).

The third type of reliability, which deals with the *equivalence* of alternate forms of a test, is logically the same as stability over time, except that different test items are used in the two forms. Alternative, or parallel, forms of tests (such as the MAT or SAT) are developed by commercial publishers so that students cannot memorize answers to specific items when tests are given at the beginning and end of the same year, or over even shorter periods. The two forms are assumed to measure precisely the same knowledge or content. An additional constraint is that the two forms must have precisely the same mean and standard deviation when given to the same people. Reliability is measured by administering both forms of the test to the same people at approximately the same time (so that additional learning or other chance factors do not occur). A correlation coefficient is used as the reliability coefficient, as in the first two situations.

The specific type of reliability estimate that is most appropriate in a particular situation depends on the characteristics of the situation (e.g., only a single test can be given) and on the use that is made of the data. Given the availability of computers, the specific formula that is easiest to use is often determined by the computer program. It is important in using these formulas that you know the assumptions on which they are based and the relative advantages and disadvantages of one procedure compared to others. Most basic measurement texts provide such information. Thorndike's chapter in *Educational Measurement* (1951) is one of the most comprehensive presentations of reliability estimates, even though it is somewhat dated.

Validity

The validity problems that arise in one situation are usually different from those in another situation. The most common situations are identified by four types of validity: (1) content, (2) construct, (3) concurrent, and (4) predictive. When knowledge of some content, such as academic achievement, is measured, there are concerns about content validity. When a construct such as IQ, dogmatism, or liberalism is measured, issues of construct validity are addressed. When a volatile variable, such as anxiety is assessed, considerations of concurrent validity arise. When a measure is used to predict some future behavior, such as predicting college success with the Scholastic Aptitude Test (SAT), or using a test of art aptitude to predict success in art, issues of predictive validity are relevant. In a specific situation, a person is interested in only one type of validity for a measurement process or instrument.

There are many ways that a person might try to maximize the validity of a measurement process or to obtain an accurate estimate of it. The difficulty index and the discrimination index are used either to maximize validity in the development of a measurement process or to assess it most accurately (and convincingly) after it is used. To simply carry out these steps will *not* assure the validity of a measure in a specific situation. Each situation is unique and may require extraordinary procedures to obtain some assurance of the validity of measure. Bridgeman's (1944) description of science (Science is doing your damnedest) is most appropriately applied to documenting the validity of a measurement process. Whatever can be done to document (produce objective evidence) that the measurement process is measuring what you want it to measure should be done to estimate its validity.

In developing or using any test made up of items that can be scored individually, such as achievement tests, personality inventories, aptitude tests, or IQ tests, the characteristics of each item can be usefully investigated. Two indexes commonly used are the difficulty index and the discrimination index.

The Difficulty Index. The proportion of students who answered an item correctly is called the *difficulty index*. If everyone answerd an item correctly, the index would be 1.00. If everyone answered it incorrectly, the difficulty index for that item would be 0.00. Most items fall somewhere between those extremes. Items with difficulties of 0.50 provide the greatest discrimination power in a test, whereas those near 0.0 and 1.00 do not discriminate between those who know the content and those who do not.

The Discrimination Index. The *discrimination index* for a test item estimates the extent to which an item differentiates students who score high on the test from students who score low. This is often calculated by selecting the highest 27% and the lowest 27% of the scores on the test. The discrimination index (D) is the difference in the proportion of higher-scoring students who answer the item correctly and the proportion of lower-scoring students who answer the item correctly. Assume that there were eight students in both the higher and lower groups and that all high-scoring students answered the item correctly but only four of the lower-scoring students did. The discrimination index for this item would be 1.00 (8/8) − 0.50 (4/8), or 0.50. The discrimination index can range from 1.00 (when all students with high total scores answer the item correctly *and* all those with low total scores answer the item incorrectly) to −1.00 (when exactly the opposite occurs).

The discrimination index helps to identify poorly written or misleading items in a test. Items with low or negative discrimination indexes (0.30 to −1.00) should be reviewed. Modifying the language of the item or changing the alternative answers will often improve the item. At times such items have to be eliminated. Items with low difficulty indexes are often good items, but they test concepts that the students did not learn. This can be useful for identifying content that was not taught in ways that enabled students to learn it or for identifying poorly written test items. Several authors in Thorndike (1971) provide guidelines for developing good test items and measuring their reliability and validity.

The following subsections discuss some examples and guidelines to illustrate the logical issues and procedures often used to assess validity in the four types of measurement situations. Remember that this list, as all other lists of categories, does not comprehensively address all situations. It is only a tool to help you understand validity and its application in various types of situations.

Content Validity. The primary concern is that *the measure appropriately represent and accurately assess the behaviors, knowledge, or skills that make up the content to be assessed.* This concern is often addressed informally on the basis of expert judgment. For example, if you are developing an end-of-unit test in social studies, you may ask other social studies teachers familiar with the material taught to look over the test. You may even ask a representative of the publisher or a university professor of social studies to review both the material and the test to assure that the test is accurate, appropriate, and fair. This type of validity is often called *face validity* because the material is only looked at or read over and judgments are made on what is observed. Some researchers differentiate face validity from content validity. In most cases, their rationale is that face validity is a more comprehensive and wholistic assessment of the measure's validity.

A more in-depth review of a test would include analyzing students' scores on the measure and interviewing the students (and teacher) after the test was administered. Also, relationships between students' scores and their previous achievement in the course could be obtained. Poor test items could be identified by noting those that most students answered incorrectly or by comparing students' scores on each item with their total score on the entire test, using the difficulty and discrimination indexes described earlier.

Another method for addressing content validity is to develop a table of specifications for the content to be taught. The topics, objectives, or skills addressed by the curriculum and taught in the class are identified and listed. The level or type of skill that students are expected to learn are indicated for each item listed. The Taxonomy of Educational Objectives (Bloom, Englehart, Furst, Hill, & Krathwohl, 1956) is often used to classify the level of skill. A typical example is given in Table 5.6. Next, the proportion of the course (or curriculum) that addresses each level of each skill listed is calculated. A test is developed with items that test these levels and skills with the same emphasis as the content that was taught.

This is the method used by commercial publishers when they develop a standardized, norm-referenced test, such as the Stanford Achievement Test or the Iowa Test of Basic Skills. They identify the curricula used by 80% or more of the U.S. students at the grade level(s) for which the test is intended. The objectives included in each curriculum are listed, and taxonomy levels or other methods of classification are specified for each. Test items written for the many objectives are combined into several objective test forms, and norms are developed. Teachers can use a similar procedure to maximize the content validity of their tests *before* they administer them. This should decrease student and teacher concerns

TABLE 5.6. TABLE OF SPECIFICATIONS FOR A TEST OF KNOWLEDGE OR ACHIEVEMENT (CONTENT VALIDITY)

Topics, Objectives, or Skills	Level or Type of Knowledge[a]			
	Knowledge	Comprehension	Analysis	Evaluation
1. _____	10	5		
2. _____	1	2		1
3. _____		1	6	6
4. _____	2	1		
. .				
. .				
. .				
N. _____	1		1	2

[a]Bloom et al., 1956.

that the test was unfair or that it did not address appropriately the content taught.

Construct Validity. The validity of a measure of a construct, such as dogmatism or IQ, is addressed in part by including tasks or characteristics representative of that construct in the measure, but that does not assure that this measure actually measures the construct. In the past decade, for example, many critics of the IQ construct have argued that IQ measures are primarily reading achievement tests.

Documenting construct validity is essentially doing a research study, gathering and analyzing relevant evidence concerning the degree to which the construct is being measured. One way to investigate, or document, the construct validity of an IQ measure is to calculate the correlation between IQ scores obtained from the measure and reading scores of some identified group. These are often quite high (e.g., $r = 0.60$ to 0.85). Perhaps IQ and reading achievement are essentially the same. If that is not true, what evidence would show that an IQ measure is assessing IQ and not reading achievement?

A method that has been used to assess construct validity is to compare the pattern of relationships between a new IQ measure and measures of other variables, such as math achievement, creativity, reading achievement, and musical aptitude, with the pattern of relationships obtained with other IQ measures, such as the Stanford-Binet Intelligence Scale (Terman & Merrill, 1973). If the pattern of relationships with scores from this IQ measure is like that obtained with the Stanford-Binet measure, and if the IQ scores obtained from the new IQ measure are highly related to IQ scores obtained from the Stanford-Binet IQ measures, that would be convincing evidence that this is a valid measure of IQ and not simply a reading test.

An example of typical patterns of correlations between the Stanford-Binet test (a well-documented and generally accepted measure of the IQ construct) and various skills and aptitudes, as well as of those between the new IQ test and these same skills and aptitudes is reported in Figure 5.7. Even though the correlations are not precisley the same for the two measures of IQ, the patterns are very similar. Both have high correlations with reading, somewhat lower with math, and the least with creativity. Also, the correlation between the two IQ measures ($r = 0.87$) is higher than any other correlation for either IQ measure. This does not *prove* that the two IQ measures are assessing exactly the same construct (not even a correlation of 1.00 would do that), but it does provide evidence that it is more likely to be measuring a construct such as IQ than something else, such as reading achievement.

The relationships between reading and each of the variables in Figure 5.7 (as well as others that might be relevant) could be calculated and compared with the patterns of the two IQ measures. If these patterns are all similar, then the three tests would appear to be measuring the same construct. If the pattern of relationships for reading differed in any meaningful way with those of the IQ tests, it would be evidence that IQ is different from reading achievement.

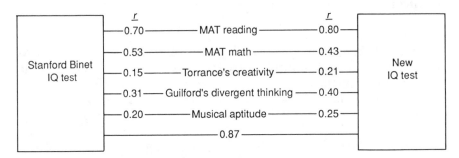

Figure 5.7. Correlations Between Two IQ Measures and Various Skills and Aptitudes

Construct validity is fundamentally a research problem. The researcher must decide which variables, or which relationships, are most relevant to the validity of the measure. These decisions are based on theory and previous research. As results are obtained between the IQ measure and other variables (such as creativity, reading, musical aptitude, etc.), new questions about the construct validity of the measure may arise that will require additional testing. The study of these relationships will continue until the weight of evidence supports the construct validity of a measure or provides convincing evidence that the measure does not assess that construct.

Concurrent Validity. In measuring a volatile variable, such as test anxiety, it is meaningless to give one measure of test anxiety this week and a second measure next week. For example, immediately after a teacher states, "Your semester grade will be determined by the score on this test," the test anxiety of most students will be extremely high. A week later, after receiving a high grade, a student's test anxiety will likely be relatively low. *In this type of situation, two measures of the same variable (test anxiety) must be given concurrently in order to assess the validity of a test anxiety measure.* A person could be wired for a galvanic skin response (GSR), which is a measure of sweaty hands, at the same time that the person was taking a questionnaire on test anxiety.

The correlation between scores on the two measures indicates the degree to which they are assessing the same variable. Because the GSR is generally accepted as a good measure of anxiety, the questionnaire results must be very similar to the GSR results in order to have confidence that it is measuring test anxiety.

A similar method would have to be developed by anyone attempting to demonstrate the validity of a measure of any volatile variable. As indicated, investigating and documenting the validity (or lack of validity) of a measure is a complex logical problem that must be solved creatively in every unique situation. Each is essentially a research project requiring convincing evidence that supports or questions the validity of a measure.

Predictive Validity. Many measures are used only to predict future behavior and are not used as assessments of any particular skills or knowledge. Examples are aptitude and interest measures, such as musical, scholastic, or mechanical aptitudes, or vocational interest inventories. The primary concern of the user of such instruments is *how well they predict future behavior.* The Scholastic Aptitude Test (SAT) and the American College Test (ACT) are the two primary tests used to predict success in college of high school seniors.

The predictive validity of the SAT deals with how well SAT scores predict college success. It is used both for counseling purposes for the student and selection purposes for college admissions officers. If a student scores low on the SAT, a counselor may tell the student that few people with that score (e.g., less than 5%) graduate from a four-year college. As a result, this student may choose to go to a community college. How was the prediction of less than 5% made by the counselor?

Several thousand high school seniors take the SAT in a given year. Their scores vary across the range of scores possible on the SAT (or ACT). Researchers follow many of those students to see how successful they are in college. They may do this for several years and get results for thousands of students. The predictions that are reported are essentially descriptions of those results. What proportion of those students who scored in the top 20% on the SAT, for example, were successful academically in college? What were their average grades?

As a result of such studies and modifications made in the SAT and ACT, the higher students' scores are on either of these tests, the more likely they are to be successful in college. That is the essence of predictive validity for any measure of future behavior.

One of the logical difficulties in developing the SAT predictions is that many colleges will not admit students with low SAT scores. Because few (if any) persons at the low end of the SAT scale are allowed to attend four-year colleges, there is little empirical evidence about what level of success they might have achieved in college. To develop better predictive information, some colleges may admit students with low SAT scores in order to empirically confirm the predictions. Without such information, inferences are made from results of students' success in community colleges or other post-secondary schooling.

Measurement Theory

The fundamental theory about the measurement of most variables in education is surprisingly simple and logical. It states that each observed score, or measurement (X) is made up of a true score (T) and an error score (E). Mathematically, the equation is:

$$X = T + E$$

In most measures of human behavior, the error is assumed to be random. This assumption results, theoretically, in a normal distribution of observed scores (X)

if a person was measured an infinite number of times with the same measure and no change in the person's true score occurred.

If we could measure the standard deviation of this theoretical distribution, which is precisely what test developers attempt to do, we would obtain the standard error of measurement (SE meas) for this measurement process. This standard error is directly related to the standard deviation and reliability of the measure. The formula that describes these relationships is:

$$\text{SE meas} = S_x \sqrt{1 - r_{\text{reliability}}}$$

This shows that the more reliable a measure, the smaller is its standard error of measurement. The larger the standard deviation of a set of scores, the larger is the standard error of measurement.

Because the error in a measurement process is assumed to be random, the normal distribution is used to estimate a person's true score from the observed score. When a person receives an IQ score of 105, for example, the test publisher may indicate that there is a 68% chance that the person's true IQ is between 102 and 108 and a 95% chance that it is between 99 and 111. These statements are based on the assumptions of random error in the measurement process, and the standard error of measurement of this measure *for this person* is precisely 3.0.

A third assumption that was made in these statements is that the observed score is our best estimate of a person's true score. This places the observed score (105) in the center of the normal distribution with a standard deviation equal to the standard error of measurement, which in this case was 3.0 (see Figure 5.8).

The use of statistics to make these types of statements is always based on assumptions that are not precisely met in the situation in which they are used. They are essentially estimates that are often very useful—particularly when you know what they represent and the assumptions that must be met in order for them to be accurate. A person's IQ score or any other score on a measure is at

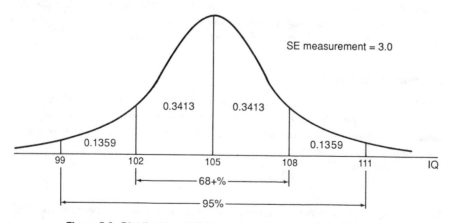

Figure 5.8. Distribution of IQ Scores for a Person With an IQ of 105

best an accurate estimate of the person's position on that characteristic. An IQ score of 105 indicates an average, or slightly above, IQ. More accurate specification is rarely possible—or needed.

Because the standard error of measurement is directly related to the reliability of a test, it usually provides little additional information. A relatively low SE meas (or a high reliability index) indicates that there is relatively little random error in a measurement process. For example, if two math tests are equally valid for your purpose, the one with the lower SE meas (or higher reliability) will have less error in the scores produced and provide more accurate estimates of the variable measured.

TYPES OF MEASUREMENT PROCEDURES

Educational researchers try to study various types of variables in education settings that may have some effect on the process or outcomes of education. Psychologists tend to study human characteristics and other variables relating to growth and development of persons in education settings. The persons may be teachers, students, administrators, counselors, parents, siblings, coaches, bus drivers, ministers, relatives, and so on. The types of variables may be: (1) content oriented, such as math, reading, social studies, or science; (2) psychological, such as motivation, interests, attitudes, values, conservatism, self-concept, or locus of control; (3) physiological, such as body type, height, weight, blood pressure, or sugar intake; or (4) behavioral, such as talking, listening, reading, giving rewards, or being punished.

Sociologists deal with group behavior, which may be leadership, isolation, or other group dynamics. Group behavior may deal with the structure of school district management or with communication linkages within or between schools. The ways these structures and linkages affect teachers' effectiveness or satisfaction are some of the most important variables in education.

Ethnographers study aspects of the unique cultures of schools, classrooms, or stages of growth and development. Lancy (1976) studied the language of elementary school children. He identified the meanings of words such as *work, homework, IPI* (individually prescribed instruction), *teach*, and *learn*. Singleton (1967) described a school in a Japanese community from an anthropological perspective.

A historian might study the variables that affect any of these issues at specific periods. Other issues of particular interest to historians are the causes of changes in the structure or operation of educational processes in a society. These changes often go well beyond the limits of formal schooling.

All educational researchers must use measurement procedures to classify aspects of a situation into data for analysis. It may tend to be qualitative data if the researcher is a historian or ethnographer trying to describe complex processes or to determine the meaning of occurrences in a setting. It may be more quantitative when psychologists, sociologists, or economists test the applicability of specific theories from their disciplines to particular education settings.

Researchers use many kinds of instruments and procedures to gather data. Those used most often by educational researchers are the following:

1. Observations.
2. Interviews and questionnaires.
3. Achievement tests.
4. Measures of personal characteristics.

Reliability and validity issues are important to assuring the accuracy and value of data obtained from any measurement process. The specific aspects of the measurement procedures that affect the data and ways to assure the most reliable and valid data vary by procedure and setting. To illustrate these points and provide a more comprehensive understanding of reliability and validity, each type of measurement procedure is discussed.

Observation

Whenever a researcher participates in and studies a situation, observation occurs. The researcher may be a participant in a gang or an employee of a school, or may be an observer in a classroom with an instrument on which marks are made systematically every five seconds. Observation may include using a tape recorder to record a meeting, a counseling session, or a confrontation between two gangs on a playground. All such observations provide information, or data, but they may vary greatly in quality from one situation to another.

According to Selltiz, Wrightsman, and Cook (1976), observation is a tool of science to the extent that it does the following:

1. Serves a formulated purpose;
2. Is based on dimensions grounded in previous research and theory;
3. Is utilized systematically;
4. Is subjected to reliability and validity checks. (p. 252)

Observation allows you to record behavior as it occurs, rather than depending on retrospective procedures and self-reports weeks, months, or years later. Some problems can be investigated adequately only in this way; examples are teacher-student interactions, communications among students or teachers, or the steps people go through to build a model.

Observations have three primary uses in research, as (1) initial exploration of a setting or problem, (2) supplementary information in a study, and (3) primary data in a study. Rosenshine and Furst (1973) suggest using classroom observation as the first step in identifying variables that might affect the learning of students. Most researchers observe the subjects and context of a study, and the observations are made in an experiment to assure that everything occurs as planned and to identify potential problems that may affect outcomes. More systematic observation may occur when such a problem is identified and more information is needed. Nearly all classroom effectiveness research uses classroom observation, which may include videotaping, to collect primary data about the extent to which certain procedures are used in each class and how they relate to other classroom activities. Nothing provides a better description of what the student experiences in each class.

The observer may be a participant observer, such as sociologists who study street-corner gangs or other closely knit groups. The other members of the group do not know that the observer is a researcher because that might cause the group to act differently or the observer might not be accepted. A classroom observer is not usually a participant observer. This person usually has a form on which to record occurrences of prespecified behaviors in the class. Other observers may fall somewhere between the "incognito" participant observer and the "obtrusive" outside observer who sits apart from the class and marks on a form.

When unstructured observations, such as those of a participant observer or anthropologist, are used, some ways to increase reliability and validity are to record data as soon as it is possible to do so. If an observer does not do this, new activities and ideas will cause some data to be forgotten or modified in memory. A second method is to differentiate observations from interpretations. For example, the observation that "Boggs (the leader) ordered 'Stinky' to clean up the clubhouse," is different from the interpretation that "he exerted his authority and control in order to humiliate Stinky." Only after making numerous observations in various settings are meaningful interpretations of observations possible. Spradley (1979), an anthropologist, recommends that an observer keep four kinds of field notes:

1. Condensed accounts of activities or conversations observed.
2. Expanded accounts of activities or conversations recorded as soon as possible after each field session or observation.
3. A field work journal of experiences, ideas, fears, mistakes, confusions, breakthroughs, and problems that arise during field work.
4. A provisional running record of analysis and interpretation of observations and other field work data. (pp. 75–76)

The interpretations of observations include all data obtained in a setting. The consistency of observation data with data obtained in other ways is an ongoing check of the reliability and validity of both the observations and the other data. One caution about prematurely rejecting more qualitative, or subjective, data for more quantitative, or objective, data was illustrated by Trend (1978). In studying a program that provided aid in obtaining housing for persons on welfare, observations of anthropologists located in program offices were consistently different from the quantitative results obtained by data analysts from program outcome indexes. In the final report, *both* the qualitative observations and the quantitative results contributed to a more complete and accurate analysis of program activities and client outcomes. Much would have been lost if the quantitative analysts of the more "objective" data had succeeded in getting the anthropologists fired, as they attempted early in the project. Both types of information are needed in most studies.

There are numerous ways that the reliability and validity of observation data can be investigated and systematically documented. In some settings a second observer can be used or the observer can question informally another participant, such as a gang member, to assess the accuracy of the observations.

In a structured observation, the observer uses a predesigned form or checklist. When structured observations occur, there is greater use of quantitative data. Whether quantitative or qualitative information is produced, however, the following procedures will improve its reliability.

The categories or classifications that are used, such as "management statement" or "instructional statement," must be defined as precisely and clearly as possible. When an observer must make a decision about how to classify a behavior, the observation process becomes less reliable. In addition to stating clear and precise definitions that have been confirmed in previous observations, training and practice for the observers are needed for adequate reliability among observers.

It is difficult, generally, to obtain 80% or higher agreement among observers in a classroom or in a playground, but with a few clear and simple categories, more than 90% agreement can occur. Less than 70% agreement may occur when many complex categories are used. There are always unique aspects of a situation or unique purposes for doing the study that affect the types of categories needed and the level of reliability possible in an observation process.

Several sources provide help to researchers in designing structured observation instruments and methods for calculating reliability. *Mirrors of Behavior* (Simon & Boyer, 1967) is a 17-volume set of observation instruments that have been used. The types of categories and methods for recording actions in a setting are illustrated and discussed. Medley and Mitzel (1963) and Evertson and Green (1986) did extensive reviews of observation research on teaching and provided valuable information for designing observation forms and methods for estimating the reliability of data produced by the observations.

A simple method for calculating the percentage of agreement between two observers is to divide the number of agreements in classifications by the larger number of events recorded by one of the observers. In formula form this is as follows:

$$\text{Percentage of agreement} = \frac{\text{Number of common classifications}}{\text{Larger number of classifications recorded}} (100)$$

This formula may overestimate the reliability of the observation process because it uses only the data on the two observation forms at the end of the observations. For example, two observers may report four "management statements" during the observation period, so there is agreement that four management statements were made during the period. In fact, three of the teacher's statements were classified as management statements by the two observers, but each put a statement into this category that the other had put into a different category. Most observation forms do not list the specific statements classified. There is only a space to make a mark when such a statement is made, and the reliability of the observation process is thus overestimated.

These examples should make it clear that the potential reliability and validity problems for an observation process in any setting are extensive and probably unique to that setting. The best ways to estimate them are determined by your purpose for doing the observation and the ways you organize and interpret the results. In reading research that uses observations, it is important to know precisely what was being observed, how it was being observed, the reliability of the observation process, and the methods used to maximize the validity of the observation process. If you are not sure of any of these you must interpret results based on the procedures with caution. This does not mean that they are meaningless or fundamentally flawed. As with all other information that is gathered to understand a problem or to delineate possible solutions, they must be used within the framework of the consistency and inconsistency with other data, theories, and relevant information.

Interviews and Questionnaires

Interviews and questionnaires are used by researchers in all disciplines for many purposes. An interview can be described as an oral questionnaire. Oral history is a method that has been used by historians for centuries. Clinical researchers, such as social workers or counselors, can best obtain a person's perceptions, feelings, beliefs, and other cognitive and emotional variables through interviews and questionnaires. Psychologists use many types of questionnaires and often study adults or children who have limited reading skills by using interviews. An interview allows the researcher to pursue a person's response for more or better data about the issue under study. When it is useful to do so, anthropologists use structured interviews as well as questionnaires in much of their work.

To interview someone for a study requires more skill and training than most people realize. For a person to answer questions honestly and accurately, the situation must be supportive and the respondent must trust the interviewer. It is often important for the interviewer to have had extensive previous experience and a trusting relationship with the respondent, particularly if interview questions require the respondent to take risks. For other kinds of demographic information, such as a work history or income level for persons who are unemployed or earn very little money, a stranger who is perceived as a professional who is doing the interview for professional purposes may elicit more honest responses.

Developing and using questionnaires takes skill and experience. Researchers frequently believe that because they know what types of information are needed, writing the specific questions or items on a questionnaire should be relatively simple. This perspective misrepresents the purpose and difficulty of the task when using questionnaires in research. The two major concerns are that the research will contribute to knowledge and the data will be reliable and valid.

To contribute to knowledge, the items in the questionnaire must address as comprehensively as possible the problems, or controversies, that are to be studied. This requires clear delineation of the underlying theories and the dimensions of the theories that past research has identified as important for this problem in this setting. Researchers cannot assume that their practical experience and past education provide adequate knowledge to list all questionnaire items needed, or to structure them in ways that will allow the most important issues to be addressed.

When developing a questionnaire to compare in-class and pull-out remedial reading programs, my colleague and I listed the controversies that could be identified from the literature so that we could organize the parts of the questionnaire and the specific statement of each item of the issues so that answers to the controversies could be identified as clearly as possible (Bean & Eichelberger, 1985). A number of additions and changes had to be made in the questionnaire from our initial drafts, but we assured ourselves that the most important data would be produced by the questionnaire.

The quality of the data obtained is another difficult issue. What appears to you to be a straightforward question may often not be clear to the respondent. For example, we sent a questionnaire to teachers in various schools and asked them to draw a diagram of the shape of their classroom and to estimate its length and width. We inadvertently sent a second questionnaire containing that same request to these same teachers several months later. Many of the second classroom diagrams were grossly different in shape and size from those these teachers had sent previously. We were amazed that such a simple and objective fact was not reported accurately. A natural response to such a situation is to "blame the victim" and conclude that the respondents are dumb or incompetent. That is neither accurate nor useful. It is the researcher's job to develop a questionnaire that is easily understood and relatively simple to respond to, which requires much pilot testing.

Questionnaires must be developed over time by relating them to the literature and obtaining responses from members of the population to be studied. It is difficult to know the types of problems someone might have with specific items in an interview or questionnaire without previous experience with the group to be studied. A pilot test of the instrument or procedure with people from the population to be studied is absolutely essential.

When people are asked to provide information about themselves, there are a number of reasons why such self-reports may not be valid. Answers that would be embarrassing or degrading, such as a man's sexual feelings when the interviewer is an attractive woman, or an annual income of less than $10,000, are seldom given by respondents. Or a person may have a good reason for not answering a specific question and be unwilling to tell you why. For example, a neighbor of mine would not indicate on the census that he owned his house. In the first place he did not consider it any of the government's business, but later he told me there was a legal judgment against him. If they found out he owned the house, they would take it away from him.

There are also many questions that people are unable to answer. A friend may ask, "Why did you say that to Marie at the party last night?" At the moment you may have had a "reason" but were unaware of what it was. The causes of human behavior are extremely complex and ambiguous, even to the person displaying the behavior. Individuals vary tremendously in their knowledge of how they feel and why they behave the way they do. Such variation produces errors and inconsistencies in questionnaire and interview data that are hard to identify.

Achievement Tests

In education, assessing the knowledge and skills of students is usually related to most other activities. Teachers often obtain this information informally through observation, questions and answers in class, and grading student papers. These are an integral part of the diagnostic/prescriptive process of teaching. Both teachers and students need to know what the students are learning and what they are not learning. The issues of reliability, validity, and others that affect the quality and representativeness of data apply to these informal processes, as well as to the formal tests that are taken after each unit in a textbook or at the end of a semester or year. These formal achievement tests usually relate directly to the objectives in the curriculum that is taught. They are often criterion-referenced or domain-referenced tests.

In most school districts, students also take norm-referenced tests, such as the Metropolitan Achievement Test (MAT), Stanford Achievement Test (SAT), the Iowa Test of Basic Skills (ITBS), or some other standardized commercial test. These tests are developed to address the most important knowledge and skills in the major academic areas, such as math, reading, social studies, study skills, and so on that are included in the curricula used in most schools. Norms are developed in each academic area by testing a large, representative sample of students at appropriate grade levels. These norms, or average scores earned by similar students, are used to assess a student's academic status in comparison to all similar U.S. students.

Both types of information are used by educators and students as feedback on their academic status. Educators can use such information to improve the educational processes, and students can use it to identify particular weaknesses on which they should work.

Issues important to each type of measure, or test, are discussed in order to learn more about these various types of measures and to gain further insights into the conditions that affect the quality or relevance of data in a particular situation. First, the ways norm-referenced measures are developed and norms are established and the characteristics most important to these measures are discussed. Second, criterion-referenced and domain-referenced measures are defined and ways to develop and assess the characteristics of these measures are discussed.

Norm-Referenced Measures. In this pluralistic, competitive society parents and educators want to know how well their children are doing academically. A number of different methods have been devised to locate the particular knowledge or skills of each child in comparison to a relevant group. In schools, letter grades are used in each subject area to report achievement levels. Standardized tests in reading, math, social studies, and other academic subjects are commonly used in elementary schools to locate a child's achievement level in the U.S. population. How such tests are developed and the types of norm-referenced scores that are most useful follow.

To identify the levels of academic knowledge or skill of U.S. students at a particular grade level, a test that covers the most common objectives taught at that grade level is developed. It is then administered to a sample of students who are representative of U.S. students at that grade level (as well as to those in adjacent grade levels). Developers of the most common achievement tests first identify the skills or objectives taught in that particular grade level by systematically reviewing the most common curricula used in that grade level. A table of specifications, as illustrated in Table 5.6, is prepared to delineate the proportion of skills at each knowledge level for each objective that are addressed by the curricula.

Teachers and other experts in the subject matter to be tested (reading, math, social studies, etc.) are paid to write multiple choice test items for specific objectives. Several forms of the norm-referenced test are identified after some preliminary testing and further development. Most tests are developed for students in more than one grade level, such as from the fourth month of second grade (2.4) through the ninth month of third grade (3.9), so that fewer tests are needed.

Norms are developed by systematically identifying tens of thousands of students at each of several grade levels who take the test under precisely defined conditions. These conditions in common include the following:

1. Directions
2. Practice exercises
3. Time limits
4. Test items

When a test is administered under such precise conditions, it is called a *standardized test*. These precisely defined, or standardized, conditions allow students' scores that are obtained at different times in different places to be compared. Answering 25 items on the test correctly will be equally difficult for all students regardless of when or where they took the test, because it was administered in precisely the same way each time. No one was given more help or greater opportunity to answer the test items correctly during any administration of the test. This allows the comparison of any student's score with the scores obtained from the tens of thousands, or hundreds of thousands, of students who comprised the norming sample.

To develop norms most publishers administer the standardized test to half the norming sample in the fall of the school year and to the other half in the spring of the year. Several types of norms are developed for each testing period.

The most common are percentile ranks, standard scores, stanines, and grade equivalent scores. Norms are simply descriptions of the scores obtained by the norming sample. The value of norms to you depends on the extent to which they represent a population that is relevant to the person whose score you want to interpret, and on the fact that the norms were obtained within the past 10 years or so. An important consideration is the nature of the curriculum studied by the respondent. If it is not similar to that used to develop the norm-referenced test, a student may not have had the same opportunity to learn the specific objectives, or content, that is tested. A student introduced to that content may learn it well and earn much higher scores.

The recency of the norms is important because the content of curricula taught in the schools changes rapidly. The content of norm-referenced tests is quickly outdated, and the associated norms become meaningless.

One of the most informative types of norms is the percentile rank, which indicates the proportion of scores (or persons) that fall at that score or lower. For the person who answered 25 test items correctly, that raw score may have a percentile rank of 65, indicating that 65% of U.S. students at that grade level who were in the norming sample answered correctly 25 or fewer items on the test. This type of score is called the *national percentile rank* because it represents the percentage of students in the national norming sample who obtained such scores.

Most test publishers also provide a *local percentile rank*, which represents the percentage of pupils in the local school district who obtained that raw score or lower on the test (or subtest). If the student was in a high-achieving district, the local percentile rank for a raw score of 25 might be 42, or 38. If the student was from a relatively low-achieving school district, such as a major urban district like New York City or Chicago, the local percentile rank for a raw score of 25 might be 78, or 85.

Percentile ranks are useful in that they describe the percentage of students in the same grade level who obtained the same, or lower, score. The national and local percentile ranks provide a description of a student's achievement relative to all U.S. students at the grade level and to other students in the same school district, respectively. Percentiles form a rectangular distribution, however, and cannot be analyzed statistically to compare individuals or groups. A score that can be used to carry out useful comparative analyses is the standard score.

Standard scores on norm-referenced tests are transformed scores, often with a mean of 50 and a standard deviation of 10. The raw scores obtained by the norming sample are transformed so that the standard scores are approximately normally distributed. The standard score (SS) can be meaningfully interpreted by indicating the number of standard deviations a particular raw score is above or below the mean. For example, an SS of 40 represents a raw score that is one standard deviation below the mean ($\overline{SS} = 50$, $S_{ss} = 10$). The percentile rank can be obtained from any normal distribution table ($z = -1.00$).

Another norm that is commonly used is the stanine, which divides a normal distribution of scores into nine parts as follows:

Stanine	Percentage of Scores	Percentile Rank
9	4	more than 95
8	7	89–95
7	12	77–88
6	17	60–76
5	20	40–59
4	17	23–39
3	12	11–22
2	7	4–10
1	4	less than 4

Stanines were developed primarily because most people do not understand the concept of error in measurements. All measures include some error. For example, in measuring academic achievement each student obtains a raw score (the number of items answered correctly). This raw score is transformed to a specific percentile rank (PR), standard score (SS), or grade equivalent. When interpreting a child's test performance, it is common to view a PR of 92 as meaningfully greater than 90 or an SS of 56 as meaningfully greater then 52. These scores are, in fact, within the standard error of the test, which is usually about 3 raw score points.

Stanines are used to minimize such overinterpretation of norm-referenced test scores. They are also used to decrease competition among students and parents—particularly in the top two stanines (8 and 9) where the highest-achieving 11% of the students fall. In some states, California, for example, no score more precise than the stanine can be reported.

Grade equivalent scores have been the most commonly used norms with elementary school achievement tests. They are developed by administering the test in the fall and spring to students in two or three grade levels above and below those for which the test was developed. A test that spans the fourth month of grade 2 (2.4) through the ninth month of grade 3 (3.9) would be administered to grades 1 through grades 5 or 6. Because few children below grade 1 can read or do mathematics, it is not possible (or ethical) to obtain meaningful achievement scores.

The median raw scores are obtained from the scores of all students during the two (or more) testing periods and are placed on a graph, such as that in Figure 5.9. A smooth curve is drawn through these medians so that each raw score can be transformed to a specific grade equivalent. In this hypothetical example of a 40-item test, only 11 median scores are actually obtained during the second and eighth months of the school year. A raw score of 2 is the median of the scores of 10,000 or more students in the second month of grade 1 who took the test. Thus, a score of 2 equals a grade equivalent of 1.2. Similarly, a raw score of 10 equals a grade equivalent of 2.2, and 15 is the median score that theoretically would be obtained by pupils at the fifth month of second grade (2.5). Such a score is interpolated from the data obtained near the beginning and end of second grade. At the top end of the scale, a raw score of 39 becomes a grade equiva-

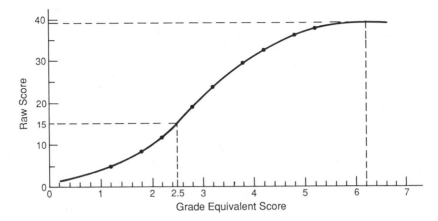

Figure 5.9. Median Raw Scores (*X*) and Associated Grade Equivalent Scores

lent of 6.2. Such a score is extrapolated from the grade 5 data. Most grade equivalent scores are either interpolations or extrapolations that depend on numerous assumptions. The most apparent assumption is that growth in academic achievement is consistent and positive. This may be true for groups, but it is probably not true for individuals. (It is certainly not for some individuals.)

Most people do not understand that a grade equivalent score is only the median raw score that was obtained (or is assumed to be obtained) by students at a particular time in school. The median, by definition, means that half the students scored above that raw score and half below it. Therefore, it is expected that half the students in a particular grade will obtain grade equivalent scores above the norm and half in that same grade will obtain grade equivalent scores below the norm.

I always shake my head in amazement when the leaders of a remedial program state as an objective that 100% (or 80%) of the participating students are to score at the norm or above. If such programs are successful, the test developers would need to renorm their tests to have 50% of the students score below the norm (or grade equivalent score of grade and month of their school placement).

These four types of norms can be developed for any population that can be used as the norming population. Most commercial publishers report both national norms (representing the entire U.S. population) and large-city norms, which are usually based on the 20 largest urban school districts. The Iowa Test of Basic Skills is also normed for Iowa because that test is mandated by the state for use by their school districts. In the next section, criterion-referenced tests are described. Most large school districts that have developed criterion-referenced tests for their academic curricula have also developed norms based on the achievement of previous students in their district who took the tests.

Criterion-Referenced Measures. Robert Glaser (1963) is generally credited with identifying and developing the concept of criterion-referenced tests, or measures that "provide explicit information as to what the individual can and cannot do" (p. 519). Such tests were developed as essential parts of the teaching-learning process in curricula that assume a hierarchical order to the objectives. These curricula assume, for example, that students must learn to add two-digit numbers before they can add three-digit numbers; or that students must learn to add two-digit numbers before they learn to subtract two-digit numbers. When such hierarchical assumptions are used to develop a curriculum, short tests (four to six items) that measure a specific skill (e.g., adding two-digit numbers without carrying) can be used to quickly inform the teacher about a student's achievement level on that objective.

These criterion-referenced measures were an essential part of curricula, such as Individually Prescribed Instruction (IPI), Westinghouse Project PLAN, and Individually Guided Education (IGE), that were developed as "teacher-proof" educational programs. IPI was supposed to change the role of a teacher from that of a clinical instructor to that of a resource manager. The student's score on a short curriculum-embedded test (CET) was to determine the assignment of the student's next academic activity (i.e., do more remedial work or move on to the next section of the text).

The idea of teacher-proof curricula has been dropped, but the technology of criterion-referenced testing has continued. It is recognized as valuable to be able to identify how well a student knows something or to determine that the student has some level of skill. How that can be done accurately and appropriately has not been universally demonstrated. What may work well in assessing reading skills in grades 1 through 3 does not work well in a college writing class. Techniques that provide valuable information in third-grade math are meaningless in trigonometry. Short CETs provide valuable information to teachers and students in elementary classrooms but are highly inefficient at higher grade levels.

As a result of these conditions, there is no singular definition of criterion-referenced measurement (Nitko, 1983). The most common element of the various definitions of criterion-referenced measurement is that test items are directly related to an objective or skill that a student is trying to learn.

Such measures seem to be most useful when the knowledge or skills to be gained can be precisely specified. The military has used the concepts successfully to help new trainees to gain a minimal level of competence in relatively simple tasks. Some school districts have had some success in using such tests to identify students who need more help in time to provide the additional help.

A related concept, domain-referenced measurement, involves tests of a well-defined domain of behaviors. A domain may include the addition of one-, two-, and three-digit numbers, including both problems that require carrying and those that do not. Broadening criterion-referenced measurement to include a number of behavioral objectives within a specified domain has not led to many new insights. As a result, most authors prefer to use the term *criterion-referenced* to cover all such measures that are based on prespecified knowledge and skills, such as those in most education curricula.

Most criterion-referenced tests are given to demonstrate the extent to which the student has mastered the content taught in the class. Mastery testing is one form of criterion-referenced testing that is tied to a particular educational approach. Some school districts, such as those of Pittsburgh, Pennsylvania, and Dallas, Texas, have developed tests at each grade level that are tied directly to the objectives taught in each academic area at each grade level. Many teachers in each district toiled numerous hours to write the necessary items for such tests. In Pittsburgh, these criterion-referenced tests are given every seven weeks to all students. The scores are used to monitor the progress of students and to modify the instructional procedures to assure that all students gain the necessary skills. Such tests can also be used by district administrators to identify teachers and principals whose students are not doing as well as expected. Caution must be advised in this use of such scores. We do not know why some students do better than others. We do know that conditions that do seem to affect student achievement, as measured by these tests, occur both inside and outside the schools. Theories based only on in-school or in-class variables can describe only part of the situation. These theories require the assumption that all relevant variables can be assessed in the school. Such assumptions should be investigated before you use the theories.

Methods for assessing the quality and relevance of the data from tests were developed when the goal of testing was to discriminate among respondents taking the test. Criterion-referenced tests were developed to assess the level of knowledge or skills of each respondent without regard to how others scored on the test. The basic concepts of reliability and validity are, of course, applicable to criterion-referenced measures, but some of the methods appropriate for norm-referenced tests cannot be applied directly to the criterion-referenced tests.

The points made below address the issues briefly. Specific techniques to use in particular situations and the issues to be considered in those situations are described by the various authors in the references cited.

The reliability of relatively short measures (four to six items) cannot be assessed easily using test-retest or split-half procedures. Numerous items could be used to test most objectives, such as learning to add two-digit numbers. The specific items used to assess that objective are a small subset of all possible items. Items that are particularly easy or particularly difficult might be selected. Thus, reliability could be measured by using an alternate form that contains test items with other two-digit numbers. If students obtain essentially the same score and they remain in the same relative position, there is evidence of reliability in the short test.

If students' scores are different on the two tests, particularly if their classification is different (i.e., "mastery" versus "nonmastery" of the knowledge or skills), the validity of the tests must be questioned. Validity can be assessed using a simple two-by-two table. In the example shown in Figure 5.10, 100 students completed two six-item tests dealing with the addition of two-digit numbers. On Test I, 80 of the 100 students answered more than four items correctly, which indicates mastery of the material, and 20 of them answered four or fewer items

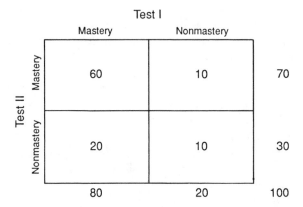

Figure 5.10. Mastery versus Nonmastery of Two Six-Item CETs on Addition of Two-Digit Numbers (N = 100)

correctly, which indicated that they had not mastered this skill. On a second test of this same skill that included six other two-digit addition problems, only 70 answered more than four items correctly. Even more important, there was inconsistent classification of 30 of the 100 students. Twenty of the 80 students who evidenced mastery of the skills on Test I did not do so on Test II. Ten of the 20 who did not evidence mastery on Test I did so on Test II. This implies that inappropriate instructional decisions might have been made for 30% of the students if only Test I had been used, which does not provide much confidence that the use of either test is valid for making instructional decisions for individual students.

The foregoing example should broaden your knowledge about reliability and validity. Validity always addresses the uses that are made of the data obtained in the measurement process, whereas reliability addresses only the consistency of scores within a set of data. The classical methods for calculating reliability that are illustrated in the first part of this chapter are most appropriate for large tests (30 or more items) that attempt to discriminate between respondents in their knowledge of the content tested, such as norm-referenced tests. When test scores are used to make specific decisions about individual students, the consistency in those decisions (or classifications and misclassifications) must be addressed more logically on the basis of the specific situation. There should be similar concerns about longer tests such as end-of-unit or end-of-year tests, whether they have been developed by the publisher of the curriculum materials or by the instructor.

It is always best to make decisions that affect a student on the basis of a number of different types of evidence about the extent to which that student is learning the material. There is evidence that some students have difficulty with in-class paper and pencil tests but can use the concepts in practical settings. It is important to remember that one test, even a long one, is only one sample of a student's behavior on this selected set of problems or test items.

The fact that a test is developed as a criterion-referenced test does not mean that norms cannot be developed. The school districts in both Dallas, Texas, and Pittsburgh, Pennsylvania, have developed norms for their districts on the criterion-referenced tests that were developed for their specific academic curricula at each grade level.

Measures of Personal Characteristics

Researchers in education often want to know how different kinds of people learn, or which kinds of people learn best, or which kinds of personal characteristics affect important education processes. There is some evidence that children with higher IQs tend to be more successful in U.S. schools. Intelligence, or IQ, is a personal characteristic that educational researchers have studied extensively. Other cognitive characteristics are aptitudes, attitudes, values, goals, and interests. Demographic characteristics, such as age, socioeconomic status, number of siblings, size of extended family, religion, and ethnic background, have also been studied extensively. These characteristics are often obtained from questionnaires and interviews. Because these characteristics are so important to the study of education, the ways they are commonly defined and measured are described in this section.

Intelligence. For centuries people have known that individuals differ on many characteristics such as size, shape, complexion, reaction time, sense of humor, and numerous cognitive attributes. Individual differences on reaction time and discrimination ability have been studied since the early 1800s. Galton (1869) delineated characteristics of genius in his book, *Hereditary Genius*, and later developed tests of mental abilities. Cattell studied individual differences among college students on reaction time, discrimination, and various mental tests (Cattell & Ferrand, 1896). He was discouraged to find out that scores on these tests did not relate to college grades, and he concluded that such simple tests could not indicate academic promise or mental ability. Binet believed that more complex tasks, those resembling mental requirements of daily life, were needed on tests that would differentiate mentally retarded children from those with normal intelligence (Carroll, 1978). The test that Binet and Simon published in 1908 included a series of tasks that increased in difficulty in ways that represented typical intellectual tasks of children at different chronological ages. The test items required an understanding of language and the ability to reason. The types of tasks developed by Binet and Simon were used to measure intelligence in various countries and languages and form the basis of the present Stanford-Binet IQ Test.

Because these tests were administered individually, they were impractical as screening devices for large numbers of people. When the United States entered World War I, an easy way to assess mental ability was needed. The army Alpha Test was developed. It used a multiple choice format and could be administered in 25 minutes. A second test, the Group Examination Beta, was developed for recruits who did not have adequate English skills. These tests produced scores that were indicative of the concept, mental ability. Intelligence Quotient (IQ) was developed by Stern (1912) to indicate a child's rate of growth in mental ability.

Over the past half century, most mental ability, or IQ, tests provide two scores, such as linguistic and quantitative, or verbal and mathematical. Carroll (1978) indicates that: "The concept of 'intelligence' or 'scholastic aptitude' came into general acceptance, but the notion that intelligence or scholastic aptitude reflected largely the effects of native endowment in interaction with schooling was apparently slow in coming" (p. 9).

This short, sketchy history of intelligence-related concepts and how they are measured emphasizes that most educational concepts have a very meaningful history. As we study or use these concepts, a detailed knowledge of that history is extremely valuable as we sort out relationships among variables. Too often a generally accepted test of human characteristics is mindlessly used to measure variables with little knowledge of the variables or the alternative definitions and methods of measurement.

Important differences exist between mental age, intelligence, IQ, and scholastic ability. A detailed knowledge of those differences and the relationships among these concepts is needed by educators, who must use these concepts daily. The specific information is well summarized by Carroll (1978) in his chapter, "On the Theory-Practice Interface in the Measurement of Intellectual Abilities," that was written for the National Academy of Education's 1978 volume, *Impact of Research on Education: Some Case Studies*, edited by Patrick Suppes.

Interests, Attitudes, and Values. In a similar manner, researchers investigate the relationships between various human characteristics, such as interests, attitudes, and values, and education. Each of us has a definition of each of these terms and various theories or models about how they relate to, or affect, human behavior. Different psychological theories are based on different world views. Operant conditioners, such as B. F. Skinner, restrict their variables to those that can be observed by others. Interests, attitudes, and values do not fit well into their models. Cognitive psychologists who use information-processing theories also tend to focus on the substance of information storage and retrieval. To them, interests, attitudes, and values are at most context variables. Maslow's theory of motivation (1968) has been used by teachers to plan their instruction in ways that students will find meaningful and interesting. Maslow's theory uses the concepts of interests, attitudes, and values as central elements of human behavior.

Education, as a complex human activity, is more than the relationships among variables delineated by researchers and scholars. And it is certainly more than those variables derived from a single discipline, such as psychology. In response to the increased emphasis on behavioral objectives and systems analysis (or information-processing models), the Association for Supervision and Curriculum Development (ASCD) titled their 1977 yearbook, *Feeling, Valuing, and the Art of Growing: Insights Into the Affective* (Berman & Roderick, 1977). The authors of various chapters emphasize affective outcomes of education, such as interests in particular subjects and attitudes toward education and learning. What are these interests and attitudes, and how can we measure them?

Nunnally (1967) defines these terms so that distinctions between them are clear. *Interests are preferences for particular activities.* This definition is usually interpreted as how people prefer to spend their time. The statement, "I would rather read than listen to classical music," indicates that a person is more interested in spending time in reading than in listening to classical music.

Attitudes concern feelings about specific social objects, such as physical objects, organizations, societal institutions, educational processes or policies, kinds of people, government agencies, and so on. Attitudes are generally categorized as positive or negative. A person may have a positive attitude toward education in general and a negative attitude toward the educational processes used in the local schools. The Gallup Poll regularly assesses the attitudes of U.S. citizens toward the president. Educators try to develop positive attitudes toward learning in their pupils. In that sense, the attitude is a desired outcome of education. A person's attitude toward self is called a self-concept, a construct that is often used in explaining human behavior.

Values deal with preferences for "life goals" and "ways of life" in such areas as esthetics, economics, politics and government, morality, and religion. Long-lasting beliefs or a preference for a capitalistic economic system versus socialism or communism are values rather than interests or attitudes. A person may hold the moral value that honesty in business relationships is an essential. Another may view fundamentalist Christian beliefs about the existence and characteristics of God and the literal meaning of the Bible as important religious and personal values.

Interests, attitudes, values, and other personal characteristics are usually measured with some type of self-report instrument. Statements are often written that indicate a certain interest, attitude, or value. A scale is formed that will differentiate respondents on the particular interest, attitude, or value that is being measured. Selltiz, Wrightsman, and Cook (1976) identify two criteria that are commonly used in selecting items. First, the items must elicit responses that are related by theory to the variable that is measured. An item such as, "I enjoy reading a required English book more than doing math problems," relates directly to both interest in reading and interest in mathematics. The item, "The National Association for the Advancement of Colored People (NAACP) is a positive force in U.S. society," relates directly to a person's attitude toward the NAACP.

The second criterion is that the item must differentiate among persons who fall at various places on the interest, attitude, or value scale as measured by the instrument. Several researchers developed different methods for measuring attitudes that are applicable for interests, values, and other related concepts. The two major types of scales are the Thurstone, or differential, scales, and the Likert, or summated, scales. There is nothing magical or mystical about developing either of these types of scales or any other measure of interests, attitudes, or values. Effectively applying the two criteria we have discussed will result in scores that represent the variable of interest.

Thurstone Scale. L. L. Thurstone (1925) first developed a method which provides scores that approximate an interval scale. The steps in the procedure are: (1) Gather or write several hundred statements that are related to the attitude (interest, value, or other personal characteristic) that is to be measured; (2) have numerous competent judges (50 to 300) independently classify the statements into 11 groups, from most favorable to least favorable, with the middle, or sixth, group containing neutral statements; (3) assign the scale value to each statement (1 to 11) as determined by the median position (or group) to which it was assigned by the judges (statements that are not consistently rated by the judges are not included in the scale) and (4) select approximately 20 or more statements that evenly range from most unfavorable to most favorable as a measure of the attitude represented by these statements. Respondents are asked to check each statement on the resulting scale with which they agree. The respondent's score is the mean (or median) of the scale values of all the items checked. Those statements marked by an individual should have approximately the same scale values, assuming that the person has an attitude about the variable that is addressed. If most respondents select statements that vary greatly in their scale values, that indicates that the development of a scale has not been successful.

Before such a scale is used in a study, its validity must be investigated. The second criterion discussed earlier is essentially the basis for the validity of a measurement instrument. That is, does the instrument clearly distinguish those who have positive attitudes (or interests) from those who have negative attitudes? If it measures values, such as support for capitalism, does it distinguish people with strong capitalistic values from those with who do not hold such values? To test the validity of a measure of conservatism, the instrument could be administered to members of a conservative organization, such as the John Birch Society or the Heritage Foundation, and to those from a liberal organization, such as Americans for Democratic Action (ADA). The scores earned by members of the John Birch Society should be fairly homogeneous and be grouped near the conservative end of the scale. The scores of members of the liberal organization should be homogeneous and fall near the liberal end of the scale. If other groups that fall between those two extremes were also measured, their scores should fall where they are expected to be on the conservative-liberal continuum.

As indicated earlier in this chapter, assessing the validity of any measurement instrument or process is relatively straightforward. If the instrument is to measure something, such as attitude toward education, then what is the evidence that indicates that it is actually measuring it? Whatever creative way that you can conceive to investigate that question so that you (and others) are convinced that it does measure it in the setting with the specific people who responded to the measure is the essence of validity. Everything in research must make sense!! It must be defensible—even to your harshest critics. The fact that a scale of conservative-liberal values may differentiate adults from widely disparate groups may not convince us that it is a valid instrument for seventh-grade students in Chicago, New Orleans, or Honolulu. This point is often overlooked—even in respected journal articles. Readers of such research see authors cite data from unrelated populations in support of the validity of a measurement instrument. This often occurs in special education research, where the reliability and validity of all types of measures are provided for the general population, with no evidence of their applicability to a special population. As a result, the underlying logic of reliability and validity is misunderstood.

A Thurstone scale for measuring interests, attitudes, and values can be used effectively only when the variable is unidimensional. If it is not unidimensional, the judges are not able to form a single scale from the relevant statements. Most interests, attitudes, and values are extremely complex. For example, a person may be conservative on fiscal matters and liberal on human rights. Others may have positive attitudes toward the basic education areas of reading, mathematics, social studies, and science but a negative attitude toward art, music, and drama. A better way to measure such complex variables was developed by Rensis Likert in 1932.

Likert Scale. The Likert scale is called a summated scale because a person's responses to all items on the measure are summed for a total score. The Thurstone scale provides a score for each item, and a person's score is obtained from the scale values of the items with which the person agrees. It is called a differential scale. Developing a Likert scale requires that numerous statements about the interest, attitude, value, or other personal characteristic be gathered, as was done in developing a Thurstone scale. Statements representing the many relevant aspects of the variable to be measured are selected using expert judgment and testing with appropriate respondents. The respondents indicate whether they strongly agree, agree, are undecided, disagree, or strongly disagree with each statement. The five alternative are assigned scores of 1 to 5. The responses of each person are summed to give a total score for the variable measured. The developer must, of course, determine whether a positive or negative response will be scaled higher and assure that a score of 5 on each item represents the same direction.

Obtaining reliability and validity estimates for a Likert scale is done the same as for Thurstone scales or the other kinds of measures described earlier. Statements are initially selected that are directly related to the interest, attitude, or value to be assessed, and the total scores from the scales are compared to other indicators of that particular variable for these same respondents. The degree to which results are consistent with what is expected is the degree to which the scale is a valid measure of that variable.

SUMMARY

In this chapter concepts related to the quality of data from various types of measurement processes were described and their application in practical settings discussed. The use of these procedures allows us to measure these variables as well as is humanly possible at this time. When the assumptions required by the theories and methods seem to be appropriate in our setting, we can have a great deal of confidence in the results. From these successful applications, it is tempting to assume that other applications of these procedures will provide accurate, meaningful results.

Such beliefs are more likely to occur when measures that provide quantitative data are used and statistical analyses are carried out in ways that provide overly precise scores, such as 3.25 versus 3.10 versus 2.03. In all applications of measurement processes, it is important to keep in mind that the world in which we exist is infinitely complex and that the variables we use to think about and understand it are, as Einstein said, "free creations of the human mind." Most human and educational variables, such as self-concept, ego, reading comprehension, attitude toward science, and mathematical problem solving are extremely complex. Any test, or measure, of these variables is only a small sample of the possible skills, knowledge, or examples of the variables we want to measure. That is true of the several reading comprehension or math computation items on a norm-referenced test, the 40 or more items on an IQ test, or the statements used in a measure of interests, attitudes, values, or other personal characteristics.

The researcher and the reader of research must investigate the extent to which the measure is accurately assessing the variable that is addressed in a particular study. A number of ways to investigate and document the reliability and validity of measurement processes were presented and discussed in this chapter. To memorize these somewhat simplistic and limited examples and to define them as the parameters of reliability and validity is to misunderstand the chapter and the message of this book.

That message is that the issues of reliability and validity of measurement processes, and more generally of quality and relevance of the information (or data) used in a research study, are essentially the same in all empirical research. Even though precise methods of calculating mathematical indexes of reliability and validity have not been developed and may never be developed for historical research, participant observation, or other more qualitative research methods, the fundamental issues are still important and the logical basis for investigating (documenting) them is essentially the same.

As you study educational research or science in the broader perspective, the straightforward and simple logic for obtaining evidence that helps to answer important questions remains the same. The mathematics and associated technical theories and tools may be extremely complex, requiring years of study and experience to learn. Educational practitioners do not have to become sophisticated researchers, however, to understand the logical process of research and to read critically research that is relevant to their personal and professional lives.

When researchers fail to document the quality or value of their procedures and to demonstrate their applicability in your setting, you should read their results with much caution. On the other hand, useful knowledge always requires some inferential leaps because other researchers will not study your specific problem in the same type of setting in which you work. You must find a middle ground between overly critical assessment of all research because it cannot document that it is precisely true and applicable to your setting, and the uncritical acceptance of all research as precisely accurate and applicable. Knowledge of measurement processes, the variables measured, the persons measured, and the setting where the measurement was applied are central elements for understanding and using educational research.

SUGGESTED ACTIVITIES

1. a. For the material below, count the number of e's in each line and record that number on a sheet of paper. Count each line *only* once. Add your results to get a total count.

   It will be argued here that questions of attitude congruence can be of at least two distinct types: absolute or relative. These types have attendant differences in analytic models and, therefore, also have different implications for data analysis. The term *absolute congruence* applies to the simple observed proportion of agreement between respondent pairs. The term *relative congruence* applies to the family of agreement indexes which, although functions of the absolute index, are formulated relative to chance expectations. Differentiating between these indexes is a general problem pertaining to any form of cross classification for the purpose of measuring agreement.

   b. Repeat the activity, but count in the opposite direction (from right to left, rather than left to right). Are the numbers the same? Compare your counts with others in the class, or others in your family.

   c. Are the errors in this measurement process random, with equal numbers of scores above and below the true score in each line? In the total?

2. Develop a 10-item test to measure adults' attitudes toward education. Administer it to at least 10 people. Identify each respondent by age, level of education, and political party. Are the scores related to age, level of education, and political party? Calculate the mean score and the median score for this sample of 10 subjects. Which is higher? What does this tell you about the scores?

RELATED SOURCES

Erickson, F. (1986). Qualitative methods in research on teaching. In M.C. Wittrock (Ed.), *Handbook of research on teaching* (3rd ed.), (pp. 119–161). New York: Macmillan.

According to Erickson, the "chapter reviews basic issues of theory and method in approaches to research on teaching that are alternatively called ethnographic, qualitative, participant observational, case study, symbolic interactionist, phenomenological, constructivist, or interpretive." He emphasizes the discontinuities in assumptions between positivist/behaviorist research and nonpositivist/interpretive research. Assumptions, data collection, data analysis, and reporting of interpretive research are illustrated using numerous examples.

Evertson, C.M., & Green, J.L. (1986). Observation as inquiry and method. In M.C. Wittrock (Ed.), *Handbook of research on teaching* (3rd. ed.), (pp. 162–213). New York: Macmillan.

The authors comprehensively address observation as inquiry and method. The many important observation studies and publications listed are placed in a meaningful historical perspective. Present issues in the use of observation data for both decision-making and research are discussed. Although primarily based on positivistic perspectives, an attempt is made to describe observation issues in interpretive and other types of constructivist perspectives. An extremely informative overview for anyone planning to do systematic observation.

LeCompte, M.D., & Goetz, J.P. (1982). Problems of reliability and validity in ethnographic research. *Review of Educational Research, 52*(1), 31–60.

The types of problems that arise and methods used to minimize them in ethnographic studies are discussed. The authors relate these issues to the classical threats to validity identified by Campbell and Stanley (1963). For researchers who are concerned about the quality or value of their conclusions, this article is one of the most fundamentally sound and practically relevant available.

Nitko, A.J. (1983). *Educational tests and measurement: An introduction.* New York: Harcourt Brace Jovanovich.

A readable introduction to classical measurement techniques with many practical examples for meaningful application in education. It provides much historical information about both the people who made important contributions and the methods that have been developed for measuring important educational variables. One of the most comprehensive measurement texts available at the introductory level.

Scriven, M. (1972). Objectivity and subjectivity in educational research. In L.G. Thomas (Ed.), *Philosophical redirection of educational research.* Chicago: National Society for the Study of Education.

Scriven describes fundamental confusions about the terms *objective* and *subjective* as related to research. His discussion of the philosophical foundations and the methodological applications was used in the definitions and descriptions provided in this text. Scriven's examples demonstrate that the logical bases for expanding the use of methods that had previously been classified as *subjective*, such as those described by Erickson (1986), are not necessarily biased and inaccurate. As are many philosophical essays, this chapter is difficult to read with understanding. But, it is one of the few discussions of objectivity and subjectivity that is developed from a firm philosophical perspective.

Thorndike, R.L. (Ed.) (1971). *Educational measurement* (2nd ed.). Washington, DC: American Council on Education.

This entire volume provides a comprehensive description of measurement procedures and issues of their use in education. The first section of this book is of particular value to teachers as they develop tests for their subject areas. It includes principles for writing good test items and methods for developing and validating testing instruments.

REFERENCES

Bean, R. M., & Eichelberger, R. T. (March 1985). Changing the role of reading specialists: From pull-out to in-class programs. *The Reading Teacher,* pp. 648–653.

Berman, L.M., & Roderick, J.A. (Eds.). (1977). *Feeling, valuing, and the art of growing: Insights into the affective.* Washington, DC: Association for Supervision and Curriculum Development.

Binet, A., & Simon, T. (1908). Le developpement de l'intelligence chez les enfants. *L'Anee Psychologique, 14,* 1–94.

Bloom, B.S., Englehart, M.D., Furst, E.J., Hill, W.H. & Krathwohl, D.R. (1956). *Taxonomy of educational objectives: The classification of educational goals. Handbook 1: Cognitive domain.* New York: McKay.

Borg, W. R., & Gall, M. E. (1983). *Educational research: An introduction* (4th ed.). White Plains, NY: Longman.

Bridgeman, P. W. (1944). Logic of modern physics. *Yale Review, 34,* 444–461.

Campbell, D. T., and Stanley, J. C. (1963). Experimental and quasi-experimental designs for research on teaching. In N. L. Gage (Ed.) *Handbook of research on teaching.* Chicago: Rand McNally.

Carroll, J. B. (1978). On the theory-practice interface in the measurement of intellectual abilities. In P. Suppes (Ed.), *Impact of research on education.* Washington, DC: National Academy of Education.

Cattell, J. M. & Ferrand, L. (1896). Physical and mental measurements of the students of Columbia University. *Psychology Review, 13,* 618–648.

Cox, R. C., & West, W. L. (1986). *Essentials of research for health professionals* (2nd ed.). Laurel, MD: RAMSCO.

Erickson, F. (1986). Qualitative methods in research on teaching. In Wittrock, M. C. (Ed.), *Handbook of research on teaching* (3rd ed.). New York: Macmillan.

Evertson, C. M., & Green, J. L. (1986). Observation as inquiry and method. In M. C. Wittrock (Ed.), *Handbook of research on teaching* (3rd ed.). New York: Macmillan.

Galton, F. (1869). *Hereditary genius: An inquiry into its laws and consequences.* New York: Appleton.

Glaser, R. (1963). Instructional technology and the measurement of learning outcomes. *American Psychologist, 18,* 519–521.

Gronlund, N.E. (1985). *Measurement and evaluation in teaching* (5th ed.). New York: Macmillan.

Lancy, David F. (1976). The beliefs and behaviors of pupils in an experimental school: Introduction and overview. Pittsburgh: Learning Research and Development Center, University of Pittsburgh.

Likert, R. (1932). A technique for the measurement of attitudes. *Archives of Psychology,* No. 140.

Maslow, A.H. (1968). *Toward a psychology of being.* New York: Van Nostrand Reinhold.

Medley, D. M., & Mitzel, H. E. (1963). Measuring classroom behavior by systematic observation. In N.L. Gage (Ed.), *Handbook of research in teaching.* Chicago: Rand McNally.

Nitko, A.J. (1983). *Educational tests and measurements: An introduction.* New York: Harcourt Brace Jovanovich.

Nunnally, J. (1967). *Psychometric theory.* New York: McGraw-Hill.

Rosenshine, B., & Furst, N. (1973). The use of direct observation to study teaching. In R.M. Travers (Ed.), *Second handbook of research in teaching.* Chicago: Rand McNally.

Scriven, M. (1972). Objectivity and subjectivity in educational research. In Lawrence G. Thomas (Ed.), *Philosophical redirection of educational research.* Chicago: University of Chicago Press.

Selltiz, C., Wrightsman, L.S., & Cook, S.W. (1976). *Research methods in social relations* (3rd ed.). New York: Holt, Rinehart and Winston.

Simon, A., & Boyer, E.G. (Eds.) (1967). *Mirrors of behavior.* Philadelphia: Research for Better Schools.

Singleton, John (1967). *Nichū: A Japanese School.* New York: Holt, Rinehart and Winston.

Spradley, J. (1979). *The ethnographic interview*. New York: Holt, Rinehart and Winston.

Stern, W. (1912). *Psychologische Methodern der Intelligenz—Prufung*. Leipzig: Barth.

Terman, L.M., & Merrill, M.A. (1973). *Stanford Binet intelligence scale*. Chicago: Riverside.

Thorndike, R. L. (1951). Reliability. In E.F. Lindquist (Ed.), *Educational measurement*. Washington, DC: American Council on Education.

Thorndike, R. L. (1971). *Educational measurement* (2nd ed.). Washington, DC: American Council on Education.

Thurstone, L.L. (1925). A method of scaling psychological and educational tests. *Journal of Educational Psychology, 16*, 433–445.

Trend, M.G. (1978). On the reconciliation of qualitative and quantitative analysis: A case study. *Human Organization, 37*, 345–354.

CHAPTER 6

Research Design: Issues of Quality and Relevance of Research Results

INTRODUCTION

People do research or read studies for various reasons. Personal, professional, and academic reasons were addressed in Chapter 4. Anthropologists, historians, and other researchers study situations as they normally exist (or existed). They use theories and data to identify variables that seem to be relevant. Physicists, chemists, and many psychologists set up contrived situations (experiments) to test their hunches or theories. They usually manipulate one variable, the independent variable, to observe its effect on a second variable, the dependent variable. In every empirical study, the goal is accurate description of what occurred in the natural, or contrived, situation studied. Many researchers develop theories, or models, of the nature of the human organism, or the human condition, that are based on the empirical results. That aspect of the human condition of concern to us is education and the variables that are related to it.

People read research to gain insights into a problem, often to identify or develop solutions to it. For example, 10 years ago I read studies about inverted sternums and how to treat them so that I could decide what to do about a depression in my son's chest that was a birth defect. Professionally, I read numerous evaluation studies to see how other evaluators solved problems similar to those I face in documenting effects of a summer international studies program on academically gifted adolescents. As a professor in a university, I try to develop models and theories about evaluation from the study of several hundred evaluations and from my experience to help me and other evaluators understand the evaluation process and its effects on decision-making. In all three situations (personal, professional, academic) my two primary concerns are the following:

1. Are the conclusions accurate and based on trustworthy evidence? (Quality of the study)
2. How applicable are these findings in my situation? (Relevance of the study)

How trustworthy the evidence is depends on issues that are primarily methodological—that is, the reliability and validity of the measurement processes, the logic of the design of the study, and the appropriateness of the statistical techniques used (if any). Reliability and validity issues for various types of data were discussed in Chapter 5, and inferential statistics are addressed in Chapter 7. This chapter is concerned with issues of research design that deal with the two questions of quality and relevance of a study.

The primary goal of research is to obtain the most accurate and valid information that provides convincing evidence about a problem or issue of concern to the researcher. An important element of research design is to ensure that other variables are not affecting the relationships among variables of interest. For example, the two teachers from Garfield School, described in the "Introduction," implemented an experiment to determine the relative effects of phonics and meaning approaches to teaching reading. They attempted to control the influence of other variables by (1) making the groups comparable, (2) spending the same amount of time on reading, and (3) using the same objectively scored reading test. If their methods were successful (which is always impossible to ascertain totally), these three variables did not affect differentially the reading achievement scores of the two groups. As a result, we can have more confidence that the reading achievement differences between the two groups were caused by the differences between the phonics and meaning treatments. Any aspect of the situation that questions this causal relationship decreases our confidence that the higher reading achievement by the phonics group can be attributed to the instructional method they experienced. One such uncontrolled variable is the teaching abililty of the two Garfield teachers in our example. This design flaw decreases the quality of the study because we are not as sure that the differences in reading were a result of the different instructional methods.

The control of such alternative explanations for results is essential to developing conclusive findings in any empirical research, including those in history and anthropology. Some methods that are commonly used are discussed later as issues of *internal validity*. Internal validity deals with the extent to which the conclusions in a study accurately describe the relationships among variables that occurred in the study. That is, is Variable 1 related to Variable 2? Or, in the Garfield example, did the differences between the phonics and meaning approaches cause the differences in achievement? Are the conclusions in a study valid descriptions of the relationships among the variables studied?

The second major concern deals with the applicability of the findings to another situation. Even though a study may be an accurate description of the situation studied, are the results likely to generalize to your situation? How relevant are they to *your* question or situation?

In the second-grade example at Garfield School, although there is some ambiguity about the best interpretation of the results, how confident would you be in implementing the phonics approach in a class of gifted second-graders? Normal fifth-graders? Learning disabled third-graders? Each of these situations requires you to make inferences (judgments) about the applicability of findings in one situation to a somewhat different situation. The greater the similarity of the two situations, the more confidence you have that the findings in one situation will apply to the second situation. These judgments tend to be based more on substantive knowledge about both the situation studied and the situation to which you want to apply the findings than it does on methodological knowledge or skill. The issues related to the applicability of findings are identified as *external validity* concerns. That is, to what extent are these results applicable (generalizable) to other situations, variables, or groups? (See Bracht & Glass, 1968.)

The considerations that affect the applicability of findings to a new situation can be organized within the following three dimensions:

1. Population
2. Variables and Measures
3. Setting

The relative importance of specific characteristics in any study depends on your interests or purposes for understanding the relationships among the variables. If you are having trouble teaching some of your students to read, for example, studies of phonics versus meaning approaches to teaching reading are unlikely to provide easy solutions. The studies may provide new ways for you to think about how second-graders learn to read and help you identify possible modifications in your instruction that you can try in your classes. The Garfield study would be more useful to teachers or administrators who are deciding on the type of reading curriculum they want to implement in second grade. The variables that are most important to the analysis of a study and its applicability in a new setting depend on your knowledge of the subject area and the context in which the study was done. Authors of texts on research methods (like this one) are not likely to know your field well enough to specify the study characteristics on which you should focus. In-depth expertise, or awareness of the fine-grained details of a situation, is needed in order to gain the useful knowledge available in research. The primary contribution of this text is to present logical principles that apply to issues of validity of conclusions (internal validity) or to judging the quality of a study. Examples of research are used to help you gain insights about their applicability to new situations (external validity). These examples are understood best when they are from a reader's personal area of expertise and experience.

Your purpose for reading a study will usually be different from the researcher's purpose for doing the study. Therefore, the specific details emphasized by the researcher are often not the ones that are most important in your situation. That does not decrease the internal validity of the study, but it may decrease its value to you in applying the findings to your setting. Several examples of such considerations were indicated as analyses of research in Chapter 4—particularly Weaver's review.

The results of the second-grade study indicating that the phonics method resulted in higher reading achievement may not be applicable to gifted second-graders. A reading specialist would know that the gifted students already have the majority of decoding skills emphasized in the phonics approach. It is unlikely that gifted students would gain more reading skills from a phonics method even though average second-graders would. The substantive knowledge about the reading skills of gifted second-graders is needed to judge the applicability of the results from that study to gifted second-graders.

INTERNAL VALIDITY

In most studies, researchers try to estimate the nature or degree of the relationships among variables. The two second-grade teachers at Garfield, for example, investigated whether phonics or meaning instruction resulted in greater reading achievement for their students. The logical bases for concluding that the differences in instructional method (Variable 1) cause differences in reading achievement (Variable 2) is straightforward. Three conditions must be met if a researcher in any discipline is to conclude that Variable 1 is a cause of Variable 2. The researcher must show the following:

1. Variable 1 occurred before Variable 2
2. Variable 1 is statistically related to Variable 2 (r is not 0)
3. Other variables did not cause the observed differences in Variable 2

The logic of the first condition is obvious. For example, if we measured reading achievement in two classes of comparable students at the beginning of a school year (before students used either the phonics or meaning approach), we could *not* attribute differences in reading achievement to the type of reading method that they were going to use that year.

The second condition requires that a relationship exist between Variables 1 and 2. In general that means a correlation exists between the two variables. Correlation coefficients are not calculated in experimental studies, but a statistically significant difference on the dependent variable between the two (or more) groups indicates that a statistical relationship exists. In the Garfield School example, if students in the phonics class had obtained significantly higher reading achievement scores on the average, a statistical relationship would exist between type of instruction (Variable 1) and reading achievement (Variable 2).

The condition that is most difficult to document conclusively in a study is the elimination of *all* other variables as possible causes of obtained differences on Variable 2. For example, the two Garfield teachers were probably *not* equally competent in teaching. And the two groups were probably *not* initially equal (despite random assignment of students to the two classes). Anthropologists, historians, and educational researchers have a difficult time controlling, or explaining away convincingly, such alternative explanations in their research. But it is always an issue that must be addressed by any researcher.

Control of Alternative Explanations

The term *control* has a special meaning in research. A variable in a study is controlled if it cannot be an alternative explanation for the results obtained in a study. When the second-grade students in Garfield School spent the same amount of time studying reading, time could not be an explanation for differences in reading achievement at the end of the year. Time was controlled in this study. If the two groups of students taught by the teachers were equivalent at the beginning of second grade on all reading-related characteristics (such as IQ, initial reading achievement, socioeconomic status, etc.), these student characteristics could not be possible reasons, or explanations, for the higher reading achievement of the phonics group at the end of the year. Students in each group with above average IQs or initial reading skills would tend to gain more from the instruction than students with lower IQs, so the overall effect of IQ on reading achievement was present in the study. But if there were equal numbers of high, middle, and low IQ students in each group, IQ would not affect reading achievement scores in a way that would produce higher reading achievement for either the phonics or meaning group. If the two groups did not differ on a characteristic, then it could not be an explanation for differences between the two groups on the dependent variable. It was controlled in that study.

As indicated, the need to control alternative explanations for relationships between variables is important in all empirical research. The methods used to gain control over alternative explanations are unique to each discipline and situation. Discussions of some typical alternative explanations and methods for controlling them in psychological, sociological, and other research settings where variables can be actively controlled or manipulated follow.

Seven types of alternative explanations, or threats to internal validity, that often occur in research were identified by Campbell and Stanley (1963). They are not intended as a comprehensive list of all possible situations that might arise, but they are useful in identifying typical alternative explanations that occur in studies and in learning more about how researchers control them. The terms used, like most terms in research methods, have some descriptive value as English words. Keep in mind, however that they are defined much more narrowly by researchers than by the dictionary or by our use of these terms in everyday conversation.

When gathering information in a study, the universe and the people in it are constantly changing, both internally and externally. In this infinite dynamic setting, researchers attempt to describe important characteristics of the world and relationships among those characteristics that are important to them. Changes may be occurring naturally, or other variables may confound our efforts to identify relationships. Campbell and Stanley (1963) classified the most common confounding variables, or alternative explanations, into the following categories:

1. History: Other events occurring at the same time.
2. Maturation: Natural growth and development.
3. Testing: Effects of pretesting.
4. Instrumentation: Effects of a biased measurement process.
5. Regression: Regression toward the mean.
6. Selection: Lack of comparable groups.
7. Mortality: Loss of subjects.

History. When a relationship between two or more variables is studied or the effects of some school or class program are investigated, other events are occurring that may affect the study. A seventh-grade music teacher may want to assess the effects of a new music appreciation program on the students. In the second week of the program, a popular singer gives a concert at the school that generates much interest and excitement among the students. Which changes in the students' music appreciation can be attributed to the music appreciation program and which to the concert? There is no way to figure it out accurately because the two "causes" are confounded. One way to control for such historical events is to use the new program with only one or two classes and not with others. Both those who experience the new music appreciation program and those who do not would experience the same events (such as the concert) that occurred during the time that the new music appreciation program was used. The differences in music appreciation between the two groups of comparable students should represent the effects of the new program. This example represents the logic and strength of the experimental method, which is illustrated in Figure 6.1.

In a second example, a social psychologist is studying the effects on children of being classified as gifted and assigned to the same classes with 20 other gifted students. The psychologist is particularly interested in the effects on the children's relationships with other students, both those in the gifted class of 21 students and other students in the school. After three months of study, the psychologist may find that rather profound and consistent changes in those relationships have occurred for 18 of the 21 students but can find no consistent changes in relationships for the other three. The psychologist investigates the other activities of these three students during the previous three months (those during the same period of history) and finds that all three are involved in religious classes after school. Thus, a possible explanation for the lack of change is identified. This is another form of control—explanation based on data or theory.

Maturation. When studies occur over time, particularly over long periods, changes will naturally occur in the organism, agency, or institution studied. Many of these changes will confound relationships that are being investigated. For example, a coach could implement a new weight-lifting program to develop increased strength in a high school football team. The amount of weight each

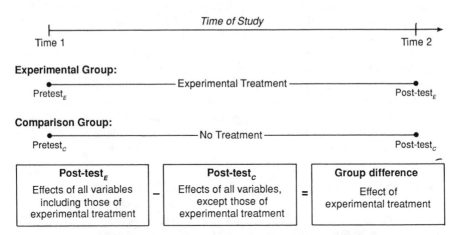

Figure 6.1. Experimental Control of Alternative Explanations

player could lift at the beginning of the year and the amount each could lift at the end of the year were measured. What was the effect of the training? There is no way to know because the high school boys were all becoming bigger and stronger as a result of natural growth during their teens. The use of a comparison (or control) group, such as used to control effects of history, would also control for the effects of natural processes of maturation.

If the coach wanted to know how much better the players performed after the systematic weight-lifting program than what they may have done normally, some players would be excluded from the program but allowed to lift weights as they normally would. They become a comparison group and not a true control group because they would be doing other types of weight lifting. The use of one or more comparison groups allows the coach to compare the systematic weight-lifting program to other training methods and to control for maturation effects. In education we seldom use true control groups because we cannot eliminate totally the variable that is studied. In this example, a control group would do *no* weight lifting. In medical studies, a control group gets *no* drug but may get a placebo—such as a sugar pill. In education we cannot eliminate math study by third-grade students. Thus, we usually compare two or more alternate methods of teaching math, using one or more comparison groups rather than a control group of students who experience no alternative learning experiences.

The concept of natural maturation may be generalized to studies of organizations, teachers, principals, parents, and to most other settings that are studied. When teachers first encounter a new program, they will not be as effective as they will be after using it for three months or three years. Schools grow and change even when no special program or predetermined modification occurs. When someone studies a school or a classroom, the changes that are caused by "natural" ongoing processes versus those brought about by the program or modification implemented intentionally are difficult to differentiate. That is one reason why researchers implement a change in one school (or classroom) and not in a similar situation. The one left alone represents the "natural" changes or maturation; the one in which the program or modification was implemented represents both the natural progression *and* the effects of the program. This allows control of the variables that are modified in the new program to be controlled to some extent in the other setting. Some of the variables may also change "naturally" in the comparison situation. One of the greatest difficulties in education is the complex nature of the situation and the inability to control the numerous alternative explanations in a study.

Testing. In many studies, participants are measured before the treatment begins (pretest) and again after it is completed (post-test), as in Figure 6.1. The scores on the post-test may have been affected by the knowledge or skills gained from experiencing the pretest. Young children (4 to 8 years old) who have had little or no experience with paper and pencil tests may do better on the post-test because of what they learned about taking such a test during the pretest. To estimate the effects of a pretest on both their experiencing the treatment and on their post-test scores, a comparison group of students who did not take the pretest is used. This requires at least three groups to be studied (1, 2, and 3 in Table 6.1), but most researchers would use four, as indicated in the design presented in Table 6.1. Two groups (1 and 2) would experience the treatment, and two (3 and 4) would not. One of the two groups in each case would take the pretest (2 and 4), and one would not (1 and 3). By comparing the differences among the four groups, the effects of both the pretest and the treatment can be measured on the outcomes assessed by the pretest and post-test at times T_1 and T_2, respectively.

If the results came out as indicated in Table 6.1, they would illustrate both an effect resulting from the pretest and an effect resulting from the treatment. The mean post-test scores for both groups that took the pretest (2 and 4) were 6 points higher than those of the similar groups that did not take the pretest (1 and 3, respectively). The mean scores for the two groups that experienced the treatment (1 and 2) were both 14 points greater than for the two similar groups who did not experience the treatment (3 and 4, respectively). In this research design, the effects of the pretest are controlled, assuming that all four groups are equivalent initially. That is, the pretest is *not* confounded with treatment.

TABLE 6.1. CONTROLLING FOR PRETEST EFFECTS

Group	Pretest ($\overline{X}$)	Treatment	Post-test ($\overline{X}$)
1		X	T_2 (60)
2	T_1 (46)	X	T_2 (66)
3			T_2 (46)
4	T_1 (46)		T_2 (52)

Instrumentation. Scores on measures that require some judgment or choice on the part of the researcher may change over time, or the measure may favor one group over another in a research study. Such scores result in instrumentation as an alternative explanation in the study. Persons grading essay tests may give different scores for essentially the same answers. This may occur over time, particularly from the beginning to the end of scoring, and it may become a problem when, for example, a teacher compares the effects of two methods of teaching writing in two classes. The teacher may have no strong bias about which method should result in better writing (although this is rare). If the teacher grades all essays from one class first and then all from the second class, the grading may change from the beginning to the end of grading. If the grading becomes more lenient, the second class would get higher scores. The teacher would conclude erroneously that the method of teaching used in the second class was better, when in fact the only difference was the increasing leniency in grading their essays.

Instrumentation problems have occurred in many studies in which a norm-referenced test, such as the MAT, is used to study the relative effects of alternative methods for teaching reading. Tests only sample the skills and knowledge taught at each grade level, and despite the developer's best efforts, they often emphasize material taught in one classroom more than in another. As discussed in the Garfield study, the test may include more items taught in the phonics than in the meaning class. The significant differences between groups may be a result of instrumentation (the test used) and not of the differential effects of the two instructional methods. Such a difference in achievement tests would explain why the weight of evidence today shows higher reading achievement for students using phonics methods rather than other methods. This instrumentation issue requires more in-depth study.

Regression. In gathering data from unusual groups, such as gifted or remedial groups, researchers have noticed that on repeated testing scores tend to regress toward the mean. That is true for many human characteristics. Children tend to move toward the mean on IQ, height, weight, and other variables when compared to their parents. When using a test to assign students to a program such as remedial or gifted classes, a second testing of these same skills will cause the scores of these groups to regress toward the mean. This is particularly true when these scores are compared with the entire population, or when students near the bottom (remedial) or top (gifted) of the distribution of scores are assessed.

These two extreme examples can be explained by what is called a "floor" or "ceiling" effect. As students' scores become closer to the lowest possible score on the test or to the highest possible score, they cannot move further in that direction. Stated differently, the students' error scores (E) have a greater likelihood of moving their observed scores (X) toward the middle of the distribution, rather than further to the ends of the distribution. This phenomenon has been observed in many situations with many measurement instruments. It also occurs when comparing two or more groups that began the study at different levels of the dependent variable. Any time two or more groups differ initially on a pretest, the regression effect will occur.

Documenting the effects of either remedial or gifted programs is very difficult, in part because of the regression effect. As with history and maturation, regression can be controlled by using a comparison group. The regression effect should be the same for two groups of similar remedial students. This requires that the special program be withheld from some students who may really need it, which raises ethical questions that are difficult to answer. In practice it is difficult to identify a comparison group that is comparable to the remedial (or gifted) students who participated in the program, but that is a problem of selection, not regression.

Selection. To compare two or more groups of people in a study, you must assume that the groups are equivalent in all ways related to the study. In truth, this almost never occurs. There are reasons to believe that groups can be similar enough on important variables such that the other variables do *not* meaningfully affect results on the dependent variable—that is, the other variables are not alternative explanations for the results. Assume that the science achievement of fifth-grade students in Johnstown School District, which uses more decimal problems in math, are compared to that of fifth-graders in Pekin School District, which uses more fractions. Differences in science achievement are more likely to depend on the characteristics of the fifth-grade children than on the type of math taught in each district. One community may be upper class, and the students may have higher intellectual ability. As a result, that group is more likely to evidence higher science achievement, regardless of the math used. Equivalence is a major problem with using preexisting, or intact, groups for a study, and it is why a researcher tries to form the groups in ways that make them as similar as possible on both known and unknown variables.

Randomly assigning 25 students to one group and 25 students to another group eliminates many of the problems that occur when intact groups are used. The two groups will differ on abilities, values, and other relevant variables only by chance. Randomization does not make the two groups equivalent, but it does increase the probability that they will be similar. Table 6.2 illustrates differences between intact groups and randomly formed groups.

Two schools could be selected because they show similar levels of math and reading achievement, as well as IQ (see Table 6.2, Intact Groups). The students in each school have other characteristics that may affect their motivation or ability to learn. These other characteristics are not usually recorded on students' school records and are often difficult to measure. Examples of such variables are parent's salary, parents graduated from college, books checked out from library, and vandalism in the school. If we could measure these variables in the hypothetical example, large differences such as those in Table 6.2 would be likely to occur. The researcher has no control over these unknown variables and is unlikely to measure them in a study.

TABLE 6.2. INTACT GROUPS COMPARED TO RANDOM SELECTION AND ASSIGNMENT

Variable	Intact Groups		Random Selection and Assignment	
	School A	School B	Classroom A	Classroom B
Math Achievement	62.4	61.9	66.1	62.0
Reading Achievement	59.1	60.3	61.8	60.0
IQ	101.1	102.0	105.0	103.0
Salary of Parents	$18,500	$28,000	$24,000	$23,800
Percentage of parents college graduates	22%	34%	29%	25%
Books checked out from library	25	352	53	48
Vandalism	$10,000	$300	$1,000	$1,000

When students are randomly assigned to two classrooms (Table 6.2, Random Selection), the two groups will differ by chance on all variables. There is a possiblity that the two groups will vary greatly on some of the variables, including the important ones. In Table 6.2, Classroom A students show higher levels of achievement than do those in Classroom B. On the "unknown" variables there may also be differences, but they will be chance differences and not the systematic differences that occur in intact settings, which are likely to be much larger.

The strengths and weaknesses of random selection and assignment are discussed further in later sections of this chapter. At this time, the most important point is that selection problems arise when groups that are compared in a research study differ in meaningful ways, regardless of how they were selected or assigned to groups in the study.

Mortality. A seventh alternative explanation for results that arise in studies, particularly those that extend over several years, is the nonrandom loss of subjects. In a 30-year study of the changes in mental functioning, a researcher may begin with 3,000 subjects and have complete results on only 100 after 30 years. Can we have confidence that the results for these 100 represent the changes that occurred in the other 2,900? In most cases we cannot, and there is no easy way to logically address what is essentially an empirical question.

We can compare the characteristics of the 100 in our sample with the other 2,900 who started the study to see if there are any glaring differences among them. We can compare the results from the 100 with whatever incomplete results we have for any of the other 2,900. Of particular interest is the similarity of results for those most like the 100 with complete data, as well as for those least like these 100. The greater the similarity in results for all these groups, the more confidence we have that the results represent what would have occurred if we had complete data on all 3,000 who began the study.

In experimental studies, differential mortality also causes logical problems when you compare two or more groups. If a study begins with two groups of 25 and ends with groups of 22 and 15, do the results for the 22 and 15 represent what would have occurred with the 25 who began the study in each group? In other words, are the 15 in one group comparable to the 22 who are left in the second group? To make them more comparable, you could drop seven subjects from the first group of 22 to make the two groups of 15 as comparable as possible, and then analyze the results for these two groups. Or you could compare the characteristics of the dropouts with those of the subjects who remained in each group. You should do both (and anything else that seems reasonable). Then you can draw conclusions that reflect the consistencies and inconsistencies in the results.

Other authors have identified various ways in which these seven problems occur in studies and ways they interact with aspects of the treatment, or innovation, that is implemented, with characteristics of the people involved, or with the setting in which the study is carried out. Cook and Campbell (1979) described a number of such examples and methods for addressing these internal validity problems in field settings. They also expanded the concept to include construct validation studies of the operational definitions used by a researcher to investigate relationships among variables. In some studies, particularly basic studies of psychological or sociological variables, this investigation of the relationships among variables can be an important consideration. Cook and Campbell's in-depth discussion is useful when more complex relationships are studied in field settings.

In all empirical work, you must gather the information you need to best describe important relationships in a setting. Whether you do research in laboratories, in schools, in classrooms, or in the United States, Japan, or Mexico, you must try to control alternative explanations. You can accomplish this in various ways through design decisions or logical explanation based on whatever evidence you have available or that you can identify. You can exercise greatest control through experimental manipulation of variables in a laboratory. The fundamental problem with such laboratory research in education, and social sciences generally, is the applicability of such laboratory findings in the natural settings of schools or classrooms. A discussion of such issues of applicability, or relevance, follows.

EXTERNAL VALIDITY

In a sense all research is historical. Even the study of an experimental manipulation describes results that occurred at a specific time and place. Any discussion of the implication of a research study must take into account the assumptions that must be met for the results of the study to be relevant in a new setting at a different time. These assumptions are always problematic. In many cases, we are not aware that societal changes or activities in other areas of the world (such as the war in Vietnam) may have meaningful effects on local educational practices and programs (Meade, 1988). In addition to the changes in the broader context, specific differences between aspects of a study and those of the situation of concern to a researcher, or reader of research, affect the relevance of the study.

The specific aspects of a study that affect its relevance to a specific problem in a setting are unique to that situation. Some examples are discussed to illustrate how the characteristics of the population, variables, measures, and setting of a study may affect its applicability to another situation.

Population Validity. Researchers want to gather empirical evidence in a study that describes relationships among variables that typically occur in other settings. The specific situation studied and the persons included in the study determine the situations and groups to which the results should apply. The two Garfield teachers and the principals were interested not only in the results obtained with the 50 second-graders presently in their classrooms but also in how to apply the results to second-graders in the following years. School district administrators and the school board may decide that these results should apply to all first- and second-grade students in their district. Population validity in this situation is determined by the degree to which the 50 students included in the study are equivalent to, or representative of, the other first- and second-graders in Garfield School in the following years, and to first- and second-graders in district schools to which they want to apply the Garfield School findings.

In planning a study, researchers must identify the group they want to draw conclusions about. Many educational researchers want to understand how elementary school students learn reading or math. They are primarily interested in relationships that exist for the "typical" students. Special education researchers often study the unique learning process of learning disabled or hearing-impaired children. The particular group they want to learn more about is called the *target population* for a study. The target population includes all individuals who fulfill the description of the group the researchers want to study. It is the group to which they want to generalize the results. In the Garfield School case, that would include "typical" students in regular classrooms: Such a definition would exclude all special education, remedial, and gifted students. It might also exclude students in private schools.

In planning the study, researchers must select a *sample* of students (or subjects) who will be representative of the target population. Almost never are the researchers able to select from the entire target population. If they are in New York City, there may be many ways to select a representative sample. Researchers in Fairbanks, Alaska, or Jackson Hole, Wyoming, would have greater difficulty obtaining a sample of students who would be representative of "typical" elementary students in the United States. This is because each researcher must select a sample of participants from those who are accessible.

The *accessible population* is the group from which you actually select the study participants. It includes all persons you could have selected to participate in the study. For example, in a survey of third-grade teachers in a county, the list of all county teachers from which you selected the sample would be the accessible population. If you make arrangements to do a study with the only two third-grade classes in your school, then the sample and the accessible population are the same. There are no other third-grade students who could have been included in the study.

In making inferences about the applicability of findings from one sample to other populations, you must keep in mind the relationships among all three groups: (1) the target population, (2) the accessible population, and (3) the sample. The *sample*, strictly speaking, includes only those people who provided the data on which the findings and conclusions in the study are based. To decide on the population validity of this study for *your* situation, you must have as comprehensive a description as possible of both the persons in the sample and the procedures used to select them.

If you are studying learning disabled (LD) middle school students (grades 6 to 8) in Pittsburgh, Pennsylvania, you need to know how similar they are to the LD students in the study you are reading. Age, ability level, school situation, socioeconomic status, and initial skill or achievement level are all needed to make an assessment of the comparability of the two groups on academic, or cognitive, learning tasks. These characteristics are often included in descriptions of the sample.

It is useful to know as much as you can about the accessible population from which a sample was drawn and the process of selection. This information may indicate that this sample has some unusual characteristics that decreases the population validity, or it may call into question the applicability of the study in your setting. If, for example, no special effort was made to include LD students with above-average IQs, they may be underrepresented in the sample. If all LD students were selected from regular academic classes in which they were mainstreamed, the sample may include only the highest-achieving LD students because fewer lower-achieving LD students are mainstreamed. If special schools for LD students with other handicaps were not included in the accessible population, the sample is more clearly defined—and more limited. The specific characteristics of the sample that should concern you will be somewhat different if you are concerned with math instead of reading skills. The characteristics that concern you may be totally different if you are studying interpersonal skills and relationships or other aspects of social development.

The degree to which the accessible population is representative of the target population is often unclear (see Figure 6.2). The degree to which the sample is representative of the accessible population depends on the researcher's method of selecting the sample. Random selection of 60 LD students from a population of 100 LD students in a school district should result in a representative sample. The two most important facts are (1) random procedures were used, so that local selection processes did not operate to overrepresent one type of LD student, and (2) 60 students were selected randomly from the accessible population. If all 100

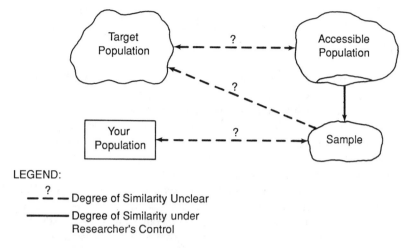

Figure 6.2. Target Population, Accessible Population, Sample, and Population Validity

LD students had been selected, the sample would become the entire accessible population. As Figure 6.2 shows, when 100% of an accessible LD population in a specific setting is selected for study, the population validity of this study for a different population must still be assessed.

Size and representativeness are two important sample characteristics. In most studies, 30 is considered a large sample size. Samples of 60, 100, or 3,000 usually provide more confidence in results than will smaller sample sizes—all other things being equal. The larger samples provide better estimates of characteristics and relationships among variables in the population than do smaller sizes. Some problems, however, must be studied with small samples using case study methods, which provide in-depth information that cannot reasonably be obtained from a large sample.

Variable and Measure Validity. Understanding the variables included in a study and how they were operationally defined (implemented or measured) is essential for assessing the applicability of results to your situation. Clarifying the variables that were actually studied is extremely important in any type of study in any discipline. Each author tends to use terms in unique ways. For example, reading-related terms such as comprehension, achievement, and ability are almost meaningless because specialists in different areas, or disciplines, define and measure them in different ways. In every academic area there is much debate about the variables important to that area. Standardized, norm-referenced tests of reading generally include a common array of variables, such as vocabulary, decoding, spelling, and comprehension. In assessing reading abilities in the elementary schools, these measures do not assess many of the reading-related skills that are taught or learned. Oral reading, including pronunciation of words, is an obvious example. Is writing a reading-related skill? Is that measured in a study? We could continue such questions in most areas of education.

The essential point is to identify the variables included in each study and to clarify the extent to which different studies measured the same variables (regardless of what that author called them). This is done by analyzing as precisely as possible what occurred in the study and what was measured. The necessary information is often not available in a journal article. Measures and materials must be obtained from commercial vendors or from the researcher personally. It is impossible to define the variables described or measured without knowing as precisely as possible the measurement process used. Reading comprehension in a study *is* the process, or processes, used to assess it. The specific test items define the variable. The skills needed to answer an item correctly are always complex. Background knowledge, vocabulary, decoding, reasoning, and related skills contribute to a student's response.

Another aspect of variable validity is whether all relevant variables are taken into account in the study. Are there some potentially important variables in your situation that these studies do *not* address? Do the results provide any suggestions about likely results in those areas not addressed? The variables measured in a study and the variables to which inferences can be made with confidence is the essence of *variable validity*. To synthesize research and identify the present state of our knowledge about a problem, you must go beyond the terms used for the variables and identify the knowledge and skills represented by the results of a study.

An important part of this process is to delineate results that occur when one measure of a variable is used that does not occur when another measure of the same variable is used. In other words, the results do not generalize to situations in which a different measure of the same variable is used. An example of this occurred when we evaluated the effects of a new math curriculum in the second and third grades. One district used the Stanford Achievement Test (SAT), and a second district used the Metropolitan Achievement Test (MAT). The two tests contained subtests with the same names: math concepts and computations. The skills required by the test items looked similar. After analyzing the test results at the end of the school year, we found that our new program did significantly better than the usual curriculum in District 1, but there was no significant difference in District 2. These results recurred over a number of years in various school districts. There was some unique relationship between the content of our new math program and the SAT that resulted in significantly higher scores. With other tests of the same skills (such as the MAT), the new program was never shown to be significantly better than what those districts had been using.

This example illustrates the caution required in assuming that any reasonable measure of a variable will generalize to other measures of precisely the same variable, even other norm-referenced tests with outstanding technical characteristics. Such generalization occurs in the literature more often than you would expect—particularly when an in-depth understanding of any teaching-learning process is needed. The applicability of the results of numerous studies to your own situation depends on the extent to which the variables and measures included in the studies are similar to those used in your setting. An important implication of reading or planning research is that multiple measures of important educational variables are needed to generate confidence that results are not unique to a specific measure.

Setting Validity. What constitutes the important characteristics of a research setting or of your setting? There is no way to answer that question precisely. It is everything that affects the generalizability of results that were not included under population or variable and measure validity. Some authors divide external validity concerns into populaton validity and ecological validity (Bracht & Glass, 1968). The term *ecological* includes any variable that occurs in the milieu that is not a characteristic of the sample studied.

For example, if positive results are consistently obtained with a program that uses an aide, will they also occur in your school, which has no aides? The studies of the program when an aide was used are internally valid because similar results recur consistently. If the results do not generalize to settings where no aide is present, the studies have low external validity. A historian may study governmental relationships in ancient Rome that were not applicable in eighteenth-century England, in part because of the many differences between the two settings.

When school districts hired outside contractors in the 1970s to be responsible for their lowest-achieving students, many of these contractors installed carpeting on the classroom floor and provided background music. They also used new instructional programs. They were successful at times in increasing the students' academic achievement, but often these results did not generalize when only the instructional programs were used in other settings, which implies that other aspects of that setting contributed meaningfully to the academic achievement of the students.

The Hawthorne studies are another example where characteristics of the situation, or procedures used in the study, were confounded with the variables under investigation and affected the results of a study. Industrial psychologists in the 1930s implemented numerous studies in a Western Electric plant in Hawthorne, Illinois, a suburb of Chicago (Roethlisberger & Dickson, 1940). The study described most often was the effect of changing the illumination in the factory on worker productivity. At that time, the plant was relatively dark and dingy. When the researchers increased the illumination, productivity went up. When they increased it more, productivity went even higher. They did this several times, with productivity increasing each time. Then they decided to decrease the illumination and study the effects on productivity. Surprisingly, productivity went up. Each time they decreased the illumination, productivity went up. The researchers finally concluded that workers were responding to the special attention they were receiving from the researchers and not to the changes in illumination. When people change their behavior in a study because of special treatment they receive, it is called the *Hawthorne effect*.

In most intervention studies, the participants are given special attention. Teachers are paid additional money to attend training sessions. A new program is identified as experimental or innovative, so that teachers and students using it feel "special." Selected principals and administrators attend weekly meetings with university faculty and principals and administrators from other districts to learn how to become better instructional leaders. If positive outcomes occur in any of these situations, it is difficult (if not impossible) to determine whether the training sessions, innovative programs, or feelings of being special (Hawthorne effect) were responsible for the positive outcomes.

A reactive effect that often occurs in comparative research settings has been identified as the *John Henry effect* (Saretsky, 1972). In this situation the control, or comparison, group works unusually hard to show that the experimental or innovative program is no better than (or not as good as) the regular program or procedure. John Henry was a legendary man who challenged a machine in laying railroad tracks. He worked so hard that he died trying to outperform this techno-logical innovation; thus the name for this situation. In a study of Individual Pre-scribed Instruction (IPI), there was some evidence that teachers in the comparison group made an extraordinary effort to maximize the achievement of their students, who were using the regular texts. The IPI program required much additional time and energy of its teachers, as well as additional supervisory per-sonnel and aides in the classrooms. These were major changes in their jobs that most teachers did not enjoy. In addition, some teachers disagreed with the philos-ophy and instructional methods of the IPI program. As a result, there was reason to believe that a John Henry effect was operating in this comparative study.

In comparative studies, it is important to be sensitive to the possibility of both the Hawthorne and John Henry effects. These are issues of external validity because the difficulties arise when results are applied in new situations. As long as the studies are replicated under the same conditions, the studies are internally valid. The results will remain the same as long as the conditions that support the Hawthorne or John Henry effects are present. When the comparative setting or special attention is dropped, levels of achievement or productivity will return to the level consistent with the regular effort of the teacher or other subject of research.

Another effect of setting occurs in studies in education that use only teach-ers who volunteer. Time after time, results that consistently occurred with volun-teer teachers (such as extremely positive results for an innovative curriculum) did not occur when that curriculum was used with *all* teachers in a school district. Exactly why these results with volunteer teachers do not generally occur when nonvolunteer teachers are used is not clear. The setting, or ecological, validity of studies using volunteer teachers should be examined carefully.

TYPES OF RESEARCH STUDIES

Research studies are classified in many different ways by various authors. The types of settings and purposes for the research as well as the methods used all affect the structure and content of the various classifications. Psychologists classify studies differently from anthropologists or economists. Historians classify them differently from sociologists or psychiatrists. Psychologists have been the primary researchers in education, so studies are commonly classified along dimensions that they find most useful. Their primary concern has been the extent to which the evidence in a study allows the researcher to make causal inferences (internal validity). The simplistic view is that causal inferences are possibly *only* in experiments when variables are systematically manipulated and subjects are randomly assigned to treatments.

It is important to keep in mind that the primary purpose of all research is to gather information about aspects of our universe in order to predict, or gain some measure of control over, our future. Research is always purposeful—even if the purpose of a research study is to investigate or solve a theoretical puzzle. Learning how leaders and their followers behaved from 1770 to 1776 in the United States or in 200 B.C. in Greece may help us understand human and group behavior in 1987 or in 2010. Describing changes in citizens' opinions about the U.S. president from 1980 to 1987 may help us build theories or models about the relationships between opinion changes and the variables that affect them, such as the status of the U.S. economy or local unemployment. Manipulating instructional variables in a classroom may provide information about relationships between teaching and learning variables. All research contributes to our understanding of the world and the people in it.

In education, research studies can be classified as follows:

1. Historical (gather data from the past),
2. Descriptive (assess natural situation),
   a. Descriptive
   b. Correlational
   c. Causal-comparative
3. Experimental (manipulate independent variables).

The three major classes represent different kinds of situations, each with different problems in drawing causal inferences from empirical data. *Historical* research involves the collection of data from the past. *Descriptive* research is done in the present, but no variables are manipulated. Relationships among variables that occur naturally are simply described. In *experimental* research, the researcher decides who experiences which treatment. Rather than describing relationships between Variables 1 (instructional method) and 2 (academic achievement) as they naturally exist, an experimenter tries to set up two situations that are equivalent in all ways except for the nature or degree of Variable 1 (independent variable). The researcher then measures the differences that occur on Variable 2 (dependent variable). In the Garfield School example, instructional method was the independent variable that was manipulated: one group received the phonics approach, and the other received the meaning approach. The dependent variable was reading achievement.

Examples of the different types of studies are presented to illustrate the major logical and methodological problems that occur in each type of research. These vary from sampling methods and measurement processes to procedures used and comparisons needed. The fundamental problem in each area is how evidence is gathered, organized, and analyzed to draw conclusions in a study.

Historical Research

As illustrated throughout this book, the fundamental issues in empirical research are essentially the same in all disciplines. The relative importance of each issue may change, and the difficulty in ensuring the accuracy or representativeness of a study may vary.

In historical research, the primary logical problems relate to the quality of the information used in a study. The first issue is whether the most relevant data for studying the problem are available. Over time (decades or centuries) many records are lost or destroyed. When archaeologists unearth past civilizations, we can never know for sure how these artifacts they find relate to all the other information and artifacts that have been collected in the past. We do not know what is missing. For example, the Nazi leaders in Germany destroyed evidence of their wrongdoing. As a result, much historical information about Germany and the countries it governed from 1930 to 1946 may never be known.

Earthquakes and floods destroy records and artifacts. Fires and thieves remove other records that cannot be replaced. Records of some eras and places are more nearly complete than others. A historian or reader of historical studies must be aware of the somewhat sketchy information that is available. The identification of the most likely sources of information for the study of a problem is the most important part of a historical study. A major part of the study involves learning more about the quality and value of the data sources.

Historians classify sources as *primary* or *secondary*. Primary sources include original materials or documents written by someone who participated in an event of interest. For example, the audiotapes that were made of President Nixon's conversations in the White House that pertained to the Watergate Affair are *primary sources*. The writings or reports of others about what participants said during those meetings are *secondary sources*. A research report describing a study the author carried out is a primary source. A report about research done by someone else, such as a review of literature, is a secondary source.

Historians know that errors or inaccuracies often occur through the translation process, making data from secondary sources more suspect. In reviewing literature, I am consistently surprised when I read how secondary sources erroneously describe studies that I know well.

Two other concerns about historical information are (1) the authenticity of the data source, and (2) the accuracy of the information obtained from the source. Processes of *external criticism* are used to assess the authenticity of a source. If the data source is a written document, such as a letter, a deed, or a will, methods to assure the authenticity or genuineness of the document are used. When the Dead Sea Scrolls were discovered, some scholars identified them as chapters of the Christian Bible that had been lost and never included in the Bible. To investigate that possibility, the age of the paper was estimated, the chemical makeup of the ink was analyzed, and the period of the urns in which the scrolls were found and identified. All results confirmed that the scrolls were produced during the same period that the New Testament of the Bible was written. These procedures of external criticism provided evidence about the authenticity of the documents, or data sources. Whether the information in them was what it was hypothesized to be was assessed by identifying the authors of the chapters, learning their relationships to writers of the Bible, comparing the substance of what was written, and looking for any other evidence relevant to the belief that their content is related to that of the Christian Bible. These are procedures of *internal criticism* to assess the accuracy or validity of the information.

Descriptive Research

The purpose of descriptive research is to estimate the nature and degree of existing conditions. A primary concern in such studies, as in historical studies, is the quality of the information used. The issues deal with the reliability and validity of the measurement processes used. When gathering data in the present, a researcher has much more control over decisions about which data to gather from which sources under what conditions.

An ethnographer or sociologist may act as a participant observer to learn (and describe) how a culture or other identifiable group seems to operate. The situations and individuals studied depend on the aspects of the group that concern the researcher. Other researchers may be interested in Americans' attitudes toward education. They may ask a cross section of U.S. citizens the same questions every five years to document changes that occur.

To study relationships between variables more directly, correlational and causal-comparative studies may be used. Many correlational studies of relationships between IQ and reading achievement, between IQ and creativity, and between socioeconomic status and success in school have been carried out. Identifying such characteristics of people or events that tend to exist together helps to describe some of the complexities of a society. Such studies also provide the information needed to develop models or theories of the causal relationships between variables. Few doubt that something about the experience of low economic status decreases the likelihood of school success. It is probably not the fact that persons of low economic status have less money but that some other social or personal variables have a negative effect on school success.

Whenever the relationships between two variables are studied in their natural setting, the study is classified as correlational. If one school district uses a phonics approach in the second grade and another uses a meaning approach and the reading achievement of the two groups is compared by a researcher, the researcher is doing a correlational study. There is no manipulation of instructional method, as was done in Garfield School; the differences in reading achievement that occurred in the natural setting are simply described.

Causal Inferences in Correlational Data. There is a common misconception that causal inferences can be made only when an experiment is carried out and that they cannot be made from correlational data. There are situations in which causal inferences cannot be made with confidence from experimental studies, *and* there are others in which they can appropriately be made from correlational data. The hypothetical example that follows illustrates how a causal inference can be made from correlational results. Problems with causal inferences in experimental studies are discussed in the next section of this chapter.

Assume the following conditions: A psychologist, interested in knowing whether the level of physical maturation of adolescent boys affects their self-concept and other personality characteristics, sampled randomly from a broad geographical area of the United States 5,000 15-year-old boys. The psychologist obtained accurate information about each boy's present level of physical maturation: height, weight, facial hair, and level of testosterone (a newly validated measure of a male's physical development). These data allowed for a reliable classification of each boy as early maturer, average maturer, and late maturer. The psychologist administered reliable and well-validated measures of self-concept, motivations, and interpersonal skills. The analyses of the data resulted in consistent and strong relationships between level of maturation and self-concept, motivations, and interpersonal skills. For example, the mean self-concept of early maturers was 71.3 (out of 90), 60.1 for average maturers, and 43.6 for late maturers. These differences were statistically significant ($p < 0.01$). Can the psychologist attribute differences in self-concept to differences in the subjects' rate of maturation?

The three conditions required for making such a causal attribution are the following:

1. The change in physical maturation occurred before the present level of self-concept. (A reasonable assumption but worthy of discussion.)
2. The level of physical maturation is statistically related to self-concept. (Condition 2 is met by the large significant differences in self-concept among the boys at three levels of physical maturation.)
3. Other variables did not cause the differences in *both* levels of physical maturation *and* self-concept for these adolescents. (The central issue to be met if level of physical maturation is to be identified as a cause of adolescent boys' self-concept.)

The extent to which the present level of physical maturation of the 5,000 boys, relative to the others in the sample, existed long enough to have an effect on the boys' self-concepts is not documented in this study. The fact of consistent large differences among the three groups is evidence that some variable seems to be operating that is related to self-concept. Because the groups were formed after random selection on the basis of their level of physical maturation, that variable or one closely related to it occurred in such a way in the past to affect differentially these boys' self-concepts.

What variables might be closely related to, or affecting, the level of physical maturation that would also have an impact on self-concepts in ways consistent with the results obtained by the psychologist? There are few, if any, variables that might have occurred in this study that would affect a child's level of physical maturation, which is determined primarily by genetic characteristics. There is little or no evidence of variables that have major effects on physical maturation that are likely to have occurred among 5,000 boys in widely disparate geographical and residential situations.

The only variable that might affect the rate of physical maturation is nutrition. Only in cases of severe undernourishment has physical maturation been affected. It is unlikely that such levels would consistently occur across a broad geographical area of the United States.

Numerous variables that might affect a boy's self-concept can be identified: socioeconomic status, success in school, a loving, supportive family, good teachers, and so on. There is no reason to believe, however, that these are systematically related to, or affect, the level of maturation. Late-maturing boys are just as likely to have experienced each situation that would result in higher (or lower) self-concepts as are average-maturing and early-maturing boys. Thus, there is no third variable that theory or previous research would indicate caused the relationship between level of physical maturation and self-concept to be obtained in this study.

Another factor that provides a basis for making a causal inference from correlational data is a well-documented theory that explains how increased physical maturation is likely to cause more positive self-concepts and slower maturation to result in lower self-concepts.

If a boy is valued by friends, family, teachers, and others who are meaningful to him, he is more likely to have a positive self-concept than if he receives negative responses from these people. Positive male stereotypes generally include large size and athletic prowess. Boys who are sophomores in high school (15-year-olds) vary extensively in physical maturation. Some boys are more than six feet tall in seventh grade, and others already have facial hair. These larger, more mature, boys are more likely to be successful in sports, which is also valued highly in a large part of U.S. society. Those boys who are most like the positive stereotypes commonly held in society are more likely to obtain positive responses from others and that results in more positive self-concepts. Therefore, given the results of this study, the psychologist should conclude that the level of physical maturation does have a causal effect on the self-concept of 15-year-old boys.

The psychologist would be likely to follow up this study with another correlational study of early- and late-maturing boys that investigated directly the responses of the significant others. If consistent differences in responses of significant others consistent with those hypothesized were obtained, the psychologist (and readers of the psychologist's research) would be even more confident that the level of physical maturation was the cause of these different responses that resulted in more positive (and negative) self-concepts.

In other situations, the strength of a causal inference can be increased by a causal-comparative study (by controlling more of the possible alternative explanations). The relationship between smoking and lung cancer can be studied by identifying a large number of people who have lung cancer. A comparison group is formed with people who have similar demographic characteristics, such as age, occupation, ethnic heritage, and so on, but who do not have lung cancer. Then, the amount of smoking of the people in each group is measured and compared. In general, the results show that more people with lung cancer smoke and that they smoke more than those who do not get lung cancer. In this way, a causal link between smoking and lung cancer is demonstrated.

This type of design can be used to investigate likely causes of many outcomes. We compared relatively high-achieving classrooms using IPI with low-achieving classrooms (holding initial ability of students constant) to identify good instructional practices. Many other relationships can be studied with this type of design.

The fundamental logical flaw in descriptive studies, including correlational and causal-comparative, is that a third variable not identified in a study may be the causal variable. When that occurs, the relationship is said to be spurious, rather than causal. One example is the well-documented relationship between teachers' salaries and liquor consumption in the United States. As teachers' salaries go up, so on the average does liquor consumption. Does the increase in teachers' salaries cause the increased liquor consumption? Probably not. An increase in economic conditions is the accepted cause of the rise and fall of *both* teachers' salaries and liquor consumption. Under such conditions, everyone receives more money, *not only* teachers.

Another example of a third variable that is the causal variable could occur in the study of smoking and lung cancer. A sixteenth-inch polyp on the pituitary gland may cause both the smoking and the lung cancer. The polyp, because it is so small, may never be discovered. We may never know that it is the actual cause of lung cancer (if it were). We would continue to build models and theories that show how smoking is the cause of lung cancer until evidence that it cannot be the cause is obtained. Because we can never know truth, a relationship must be interpreted cautiously; there is the possibility that some other variable is the cause of the relationship.

This logical problem with all descriptive studies is called the *post hoc fallacy*. The existence of such third variables that might be the cause of relationships between variables means that the third condition required for causal inferences is not met. Does this mean that using descriptive or historical evidence to support a causal model is inappropriate? No! That would remove science from the realm of rationality to one based on authority. We must use the evidence and reason that are available to support or not support whatever causal explanations for relationships that are obtained. The strength of the experiment is that, in the long run, the effects of third (or fourth) variables are controlled to a much greater extent than they are in other types of empirical studies.

Experimental Research

When a researcher decides who receives each treatment in a study, such as phonics (decoding) and meaning in the Garfield study, the study is classified as experimental. Because one of the main reasons for classifying research into these categories is to show the relative strength of evidence they provide for making causal inferences, the manipulation must be done in a way to control the post hoc fallacy by minimizing all other alternative explanations. As a result, some authors require that the subjects studied be assigned to groups through the use of random processes. When subjects are assigned to groups randomly, as was done by the Garfield School principal, the two groups should not differ on variables that might affect their reading achievement. Whatever differences that do occur between groups in one study are only random, or chance, differences. When several studies of the same variables are carried out, the likelihood that the two groups will differ in the same way each time on unknown causal variables (such as polyps on the pituitary) may become minuscule, but it is never zero.

Two examples of experimental studies, one in the laboratory and one in a school setting, are presented and discussed. They illustrate the value of the experimental method when other variables can be controlled, and they illustrate its weaknesses in terms of causal inference when reasonable control of other valuables is not possible. In the first hypothetical example, a learning specialist compares two methods of teaching reading to 5-year-old children in a laboratory. In the second, a school superintendent compares these same general methods of teaching reading in inner-city urban elementary schools (grades 1 to 5).

The learning specialist, Dr. E, believes that a decoding (phonics) method of teaching reading will work better than a meaning approach in teaching 5-year-olds a larger, more useful vocabulary, and comprehension of sentences and paragraphs. Dr. E identifies 80 5-year-old children, 40 boys and 40 girls, who are a representative cross section of such children in that city. Dr. E. uses a table of random numbers to assign half of the boys and half of the girls to decoding instruction and the other half of each to meaning instruction. Each child comes to one of four small rooms at the university for a half hour of instruction each day, Monday through Friday, for two months. The four instructors each spend half of their time using the decoding approach to teach the students assigned to that treatment and the other half of their time using the meaning approach to teach the students assigned to that treatment. This procedure controls the quality, or effectiveness, of the teacher because each instructor teaches the same number of students using each method.

The times that students attend is scheduled so that equal numbers of students in the two treatments participate at the same times. Dr. E compares the students in the two groups on initial reading skills, IQ, and socioeconomic status and documents that the two groups are essentially equivalent on these characteristics. Dr. E implements other procedures to ensure that the only differences between the reading-related experiences of the two groups of students during this two-month period deal with the decoding and meaning instruction in reading. These procedures include strict control by parents of the students' TV watching and reading during each day.

After the two months, several measures of vocabulary and reading comprehension are given. The group who used the decoding approach got significantly higher scores on vocabulary and some aspects of reading comprehension, whereas those who used the meaning approach scored significantly higher on other aspects of reading comprehension. To what extent can these differences between the two groups be attributed to the type of reading instruction?

Because the study compared two equivalent groups in the same context—the controlled conditions of a "laboratory"—there should be no systematic differences between the two groups that are possible alternative explanations for the results. There is some concern that over a two-month period one group of students may have had more relevant reading experiences away from the study. Random assignment of the students to the two instructional treatments provides some confidence that the two groups vary on this characteristic only by chance, but we can have no assurance (or proof) that such differences did not occur.

Given the procedures used and the related concerns, we can have a great deal of confidence that the differences in vocabulary and reading comprehension can be attributed to the differences in the type of reading instruction that each group received. If the entire treatment in a study could be given in a single setting, such as some basic psychological studies or Skinner's studies of a pigeon's responses to stimuli in a Skinner box, the contamination that can be caused in a study when the subjects leave the laboratory between treatment sessions is eliminated (one form of control), increasing the internal validity of the study.

This study may be severely limited in external validity if the specialist wants to apply the findings to a kindergarten setting where 20 children are taught by a single teacher. Results of one-to-one teaching are usually much greater than when the same instructional methods are applied in a classroom setting with a one-to-twenty teacher-student ratio.

In a second experimental study, a superintendent of a school district compared the effects of decoding and meaning approaches to teaching reading in four elementary schools that broadly represented the children and schools in the district. Each of these schools had two teachers at each of the five grade levels (1 to 5). In each school, one teacher at each grade level was randomly assigned to teach decoding and the other was assigned the meaning approach. The students also were randomly assigned to each teacher at each grade level so that the two classes at each grade level in every school differed only by chance.

The degree to which the two classes were similar on initial reading, IQ, and socioeconomic status was documented from the permanent records. Parents were informed about the superintendent's study of the relative merits of the two programs and asked not to carry on additional reading activities with these children and to inform the school district of such activities in which their children might participate.

Within the limitations of the school requirements and the characteristics of the participating teachers, the superintendent attempted to make the two classes at each grade in each school as similar as possible. Similar attempts were made to control systematic differences in the other reading-related experiences of the two groups of students in order to minimize the likelihood that alternative explanations for the vocabulary, reading, and other language knowledge and competencies would occur.

During the year several students left school, others were sick for various periods of time, a teacher using the meaning method was in an accident and could not teach for three months, one principal died, and 20 new students entered each of the four schools during the year at various times in various grade levels. A "Right to Read" program was implemented in November across the school district. Two of the four schools in the study implemented the program enthusiastically, with many of their students participating. The teachers who were most involved were primarily teaching the meaning approach.

At the end of the year, various measures of vocabulary, reading, and language skills were administered to all students in the four schools. The numbers of students in each class at each grade level differed in various ways from the numbers of students who initially began each class. The superintendent analyzed scores from only those students who had remained in the same class over the entire year. Students absent more than 15 days were also eliminated from the analysis of the outcome data.

There was a great deal of variability in the scores from the various schools, but there was some consistency in the differences between the two groups at the various grade levels. In grades 1 and 2, students who used decoding scored consistently higher on the average on spelling, vocabulary, and grammar. The meaning group performed better on reading comprehension, except in the classroom taught by the substitute for the injured teacher. In grades 3 through 5 there were no differences in vocabulary or spelling, but the decoding group did better on grammar. The meaning group did better on reading comprehension in three of the four schools. Can the superintendent be confident in attributing these results to the differences *only* in the two instructional methods?

There are, of course, many variables operating in the relatively uncontrolled context of an operating school. A few occurrences were listed to indicate the kinds of problems that can arise in such settings. Each time something occurs in one classroom that does not occur in the comparable classroom, it becomes a potential alternative explanation for the results obtained at the end of the study. The superintendent must be aware of all important events that might have an impact on student learning—such as the teacher's accident and extended absence requiring use of a substitute. Addition and loss of students in a classroom may have positive or negative effects. All these things must be taken into account.

As a result, the superintendent will be less confident than the learning specialist in the laboratory about attributing differences in the outcome data to the type of instructional method. In most practical settings, results from four different schools are not as consistent as reported in this hypothetical example—giving us even less confidence in our interpretation of the study. Thus, an experiment carried out over an extended period in an operational setting, such as a school, will tend to be less internally valid.

The results have greater external validity than a laboratory study because they were obtained from the same type of situation as the one in which the results were applied. In general, the more a researcher modifies a situation to gain control of possible alternative explanations for the results, the more dissimilar it becomes from the setting to which the results are to be applied. As a result, there is a tendency to decrease external validity as internal validity is increased, as is usually done in basic, or disciplinary, research; and as external validity is increased, there is a tendency to decrease internal validity.

Given that conclusions from a study, particularly causal statements, are always based on the weight of evidence available, and no method assures that other variables are not operating, it is inappropriate to indicate that causal statements can be made from experimental studies. And they cannot be made from correlational or causal-comparative studies.

There is always some possibility that another variable (that we may never learn about) is the true causal variable in any study. If cause is viewed as the "necessary" connection of events, we can never solve the problem of Hume: All we can ever observe are covariations among the variables we study.

What is important in the interpretation of all empirical research is to use fair, objective processes in all studies and to document logically the evidence for and against the specific interpretation. We can only investigate the probability that such a causal relationship explains the observations that have been obtained by empirical researchers. In this way we can develop better theories and conceptual maps to understand and make decisions about the small aspects of the universe that concern us at the moment.

SUMMARY

Research design considerations deal with the quality and relevance of research results for your purpose in doing or reading research. The degree to which conclusions are based on trustworthy (valid) data is the most important element of the quality of a study. The applicability of the findings to other settings determines the relevance of the study. These considerations are usually discussed as internal validity and external validity, respectively.

A way of classifying studies as historical, descriptive, and experimental is used to emphasize differences in the types of data collected and the methodological considerations in these three situations. The inherent strength of the experimental method in controlling alternative explanations is illustrated. The conditions required to make causal inferences from any set of data, whether it comes from a historical, descriptive, or experimental study, are discussed. The fact that we use causal models regularly in our professional decision-making and will attempt to interpret available information in causal ways is indicated also. It is important that you recognize that general rules—such as "You cannot make causal inferences from correlational data" and "You can make causal inferences from experimental data"—are usually inaccurate when applied to a specific study.

In the next chapter, ways to analyze data to most meaningfully address the problem statement and to fulfill the researcher's purpose are presented. Uses of descriptive and inferential statistics, which are useful in most educational studies, are emphasized.

SUGGESTED ACTIVITIES

1. A study was conducted to determine whether books printed in red ink or in green ink were more readable for all tenth graders in River City. Two groups of 30 tenth-grade boys were formed by randomly assigning boys to each of the groups. One group received a selection printed with green ink on white paper, while the other group read a selection printed in red ink on white paper. The size of the type was the same for both groups. An achievement test that measured their knowledge of the selection was administered. This test was printed on white paper with black ink using the same size type as the previous selections. Results indicated that the red ink group had significantly higher criterion scores. No student dropped out of the study.
   a. Identify the independent and dependent variables.
   b. Identify the operational definition of the dependent variable.
   c. The sample studied was _____?
   d. The population to which the study can be directly generalized is _____?
   e. What type of study is this?
   f. Identify the alternative explanations for the obtained results that are *not* controlled in this study (if any).
   g. In what way did the study *not* address the author's purpose for doing the study?
   h. What is the most defensible conclusion that should be drawn from the study?
2. Discuss how the *post hoc fallacy* is controlled in experimental studies using random assignment of participants to treatments and how it is not controlled in correlational or causal-comparative studies.
3. In this chapter, internal validity and external validity are defined and discussed. Is there any situation in which internal validity is increased and external validity is also increased?

RELATED SOURCES:

Blalock, H.M., Jr. (1964). *Causal inferences in nonexperimental research*. Chapel Hill, NC: University of North Carolina Press.

In the 1950s and 1960s the value of the experimental paradigm was well established. By controlling other possible explanations for results obtained in a study, researchers could draw causal conclusions with confidence. In applying these same rules of causal inference to "uncontrolled" observational studies, Blalock explores causal models used to make causal inferences. He proceeds in an informal manner, although he uses some mathematical models. He also uses a number of practical examples to illustrate the issues. It is a somewhat more advanced treatment of the issues, but it is informative for readers concerned with the fundamental issue of causal inference.

Goetz, J.P., & LeCompte, M.D. (1984). *Ethnography and qualitative design in educational research*. Orlando, FL: Academic Press.

Goetz and LeCompte attempt to integrate the terms used by anthropologists, psychologists, and sociologists who do naturalistic studies. They tend to use terms in ways that are similar to those used in this text. Methods for carrying out ethnographic studies that maximize the quality concerns of reliability and validity are emphasized with specific details from various studies. The book is valuable to educators and researchers whose background has been primarily in either the quantitative, positivistic tradition or the interpretive, constructivist tradition because it shows the relationships between the two approaches to educational research.

Haney, W. (1977). *The Follow Through planned variation experiment (Volume 5): A technical history of the National Follow Through evaluation*. U.S. Department of Health, Education and Welfare.

This volume reviews and critiques the evaluation of the National Follow Through (FT) Program, which was designed as an experimental comparison between classrooms that used Follow Through and those that did not. The difficulties that occur when researchers attempt to identify two or more comparable groups in a field study are illustrated in several studies related to the FT evaluation. More complex issues of statistical analysis and problems that resulted from the use of the analysis of covariance are discussed extensively. The book is an advanced treatment of some statistical issues, but the basic logic of research design should be clear even to readers with limited research knowledge and experience.

Spindler, G. (Ed.). (1982). *Doing the ethnography of schooling*. New York: CBS College Publishing.

This edited book includes numerous examples of education-related ethnographies in U.S. schools, as well as discussion of methods. The five sections are: Self Appraisals: Concerns and Strategies, Communication and Interaction, Cultural Transmission and the "Hidden Curriculum," Five Diverse Ethnographic Studies, and Methods and Issues: A Review. The many articles illustrate the kinds of education questions ethnographies are used to investigate and ways such ethnographies are carried out. These methods are not meant to replace correlation and experimental research but to supplement other types of information.

REFERENCES

Bracht, H.G., & Glass, V.G. (1968). The external validity of experiments. *American Educational Research Journal, 5*(4), 437–474.

Campbell, D.T., & Stanley, J.C. (1963). Experimental and quasi-experimental designs for research on teaching. In N.L. Gage (Ed.), *Handbook of research on teaching,* (pp. 171–246). Chicago: Rand McNally.

Cook, T.D., & Campbell, D.T. (1979). *Quasi-Experimentation: Design and analysis issues for field settings.* Chicago: Rand McNally.

Meade, E. (1988). Interview of an evaluation user. *Evaluation Practice, 9*(1), 32–41.

Roethlisberger, F.J., & Dickson, W.J. (1940). *Management and the worker.* Cambridge, MA: Harvard University Press.

Saretsky, G. (1972). The OEO P.C. experiment and the John Henry effect. *Phi Delta Kappan, 53,* 579–581.

CHAPTER 7

Organizing, Analyzing, and Summarizing Empirical Information

In trying to learn more about the world and the people in it, we gather much data. The U.S. government gathers census data every 10 years about every person residing in the United States. Pollsters assess the opinions of U.S. citizens on a regular basis. Researchers gather information to answer important questions, such as the factors that cause wars, characteristics of illiterate adults, and ways to improve public education. To simply provide all the individual bits of information, or data, is not very informative. It must be organized, analyzed, and summarized to have meaning in most situations.

Statistics is the body of mathematics that deals with organizing, analyzing, and summarizing data. Measures of central tendency and measures of variability are two mathematical techniques that are useful in describing and summarizing a set of data. Other statistical tools are correlational techniques, which are used to estimate relationships among variables. Graphs and charts are used to display summaries of data. When these techniques are used to describe a set of data, such as census information, school enrollments, economic indicators, or students' scores on the history unit test, they are called *descriptive statistics*.

When doing empirical studies, researchers are *not* interested in describing only the data that were collected from the respondents in their studies. They want to make inferences about the populations that their samples represent. Scientists use the concept of probability to decide whether the results obtained in a study are likely to represent the situation hypothesized to be in the population. The procedures used to calculate those probabilities are called *inferential statistics*.

In this chapter a number of methods for describing data are described. Examples of methods for analyzing data in order to address specific research questions and hypotheses are presented and discussed. Finally, the logic of statistical inference using z, t, F, and χ^2 as test statistics is illustrated. The perspective taken throughout this chapter is that the most important data obtained in a research study are the empirical information obtained from the sample on the measures used in the study. Tests of significance, as well as other conditions of the study, aid in interpreting the meaning of the results in terms of the problem and purpose of the study.

DESCRIPTIVE STATISTICS

Many decisions in society are made primarily on the basis of descriptive statistics. For example, allocations of funds from Congress to various states are determined often by the results of the census that indicate the proportion of people residing in each state. School boards make decisions on the basis of enrollments, budgets, taxes, student achievement, and other descriptive data. Teachers make instructional decisions on the basis of students' behaviors in class, responses to questions, success on math or reading assignments, test scores, and other descriptive information about their present level of skills. How best to organize and summarize information to understand what it means for a decision that is to be made is not usually trivial.

Some ways of organizing, analyzing, and summarizing information are better than others for a specific purpose in a particular situation. For example, to make personnel decisions principals and other school district administrators usually need to know how achievement levels in different schools compare to one another and how they have been changing over time. Reading supervisors are concerned about the specific reading skills that many children are *not* learning, or the differences in achievement in various classes that are using different materials or instruction. To make instructional decisions, teachers need detailed information about the reading or math knowledge and skills of students. Information needed by one group may be totally useless to another.

Familiarity with various methods of describing data is needed to analyze and summarize information most appropriately in a specific setting. Some of the most informative ways to represent the data are often the simplest. The math achievement of students on a 20-item unit test can be described well by a frequency distribution, as in Table 7.1.

The number of people who obtained each score is given under the frequency column. In this example, the scores ranged from 11 to 20, and 14 was the most frequent score (mode). Although not always included in a frequency distribution, the percentage of people who obtained each score and the cumulative percentage of people who scored at that level or lower on the scale can be very useful. The cumulative percentages show that 70% of the students answered 15 or fewer of the test items correctly. This means that only 30% of the students answered more than three-fourths of the items correctly. The reader of a frequency distribution often wants to know the percentage of scores within a specific range of the scale. For example, 50% of the scores fall from 14 to 16. The

TABLE 7.1. FREQUENCY DISTRIBUTION OF 30 FIFTH-GRADE MATH SCORES ON A 20-ITEM MATH TEST

(X) Score	(f) Frequency	Percentage	Cumulative[a] Percentage
20	1	3.3	100.0
19	0	0.0	96.6
18	1	3.3	96.6
17	3	10.0	93.3
16	4	13.3	83.3
15	5	16.7	70.0
14	6	20.0	53.3
13	4	13.3	33.3
12	4	13.3	20.0
11	2	6.7	6.7

[a]In this presentation of cumulative percentage, the concept "real limits of a score" is not used. The individual scores (X = 11 through 20) represent an entire interval, and the cumulative percentage includes all persons who obtained that particular score.

individual percentages can be summed (20.0 + 16.7 + 13.3) or the cumulative percentage figures can be used directly (83.3 − 33.3) to see that 50% of the students scored either 14, 15, or 16.

Such frequency distributions can be easily pictured with frequency polygons or histograms (see Figure 7.1). The frequency polygon is a straight line graph that connects the frequency of each score. In this case, there were two scores of 11, four scores of 12 and 13 each, six scores of 14, five of 15, four of 16, and so on. Because all scores in an interval are assumed to be equally distributed across that interval, the frequency of the score is placed in the middle of each interval. Another way to picture the distribution of scores is with a histogram, or bar graph. If the scale drawing is consistent and the width of each bar is the same, the relative heights of the bars show the relative frequency of the scores. In the histogram (bar graph) shown in Figure 7.1 there are twice as many 12s as 11s in this distribution. The bars extend across the entire interval of the scale represented by each score, from the lower real limit to the upper real limit.

In general, line graphs tend to be better for showing trends, or the general shape of a distribution (symmetric or skewed). Bar graphs give better representation of relative amounts of something, such as differences in achievement between groups using different materials, or changes from year to year.

Another graph that is extremely useful for presenting proportions of a whole is the pie chart. Each year when the federal budget comes out, newspapers and magazines usually present a pie chart to show how each tax dollar is to be spent (Figure 7.2). If drawn to scale, the pie chart gives a visual, as well as a quantitative, representation to illustrate the way each tax dollar is allocated. By using a single dollar, the number of cents spent in each area represents the proportion of the budget that is spent by that unit of the government.

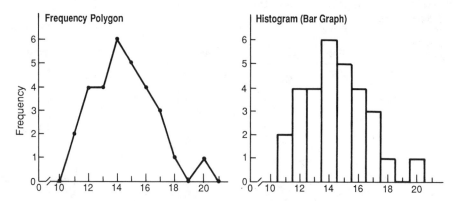

Figure 7.1. Frequency Polygon and Histogram of Student Math Scores

Relationships among variables can be shown in various ways. The Pearson Product Moment Correlation Coefficient (r), used to calculate stability of test scores in Chapter 5, shows the extent to which persons' scores on one measure (or variable) are related to their scores on another measure. When the data are not measured on interval or ratio scales, other techniques are used to estimate relationships between variables. For example, do women drive more carefully, resulting in their having fewer accidents, than men?

Fictitious results, presented in Table 7.2, show that a larger proportion of men than women have at least one accident in a given year (44% versus 32%).

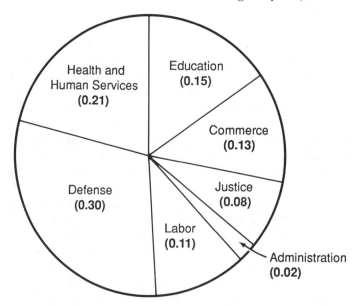

Figure 7.2. Distribution of Federal Tax Dollars to Various Departments and Administration (Hypothetical)

TABLE 7.2. ACCIDENT RATES OF MALE AND FEMALE DRIVERS

	Driver	
	Male %	*Female %*
No accidents	56	68
At least one accident	44	32
(Number of cases)	(9,556)	(9,421)

This implies that men do not drive as safely as women, but the driver's gender may not be the important variable. When number of miles driven is taken into account (Table 7.3), the *proportion* of male and female drivers who have accidents is exactly the same. Of those who drive more than 10,000 miles per year, 52% have at least one accident regardless of whether they are men or women. Because more men drive more than 10,000 miles per year, more men have accidents. The variable that is most highly related to having an accident is miles driven, not the gender of the drivers. In this way relationships among variables can be analyzed in simple ways to describe complex relationships.

These methods of data analysis are also used in doing research. Which methods to use with which types of data in order to investigate a problem comprehensively and insightfully are described in the following section. In the final section of this chapter, the logic of statistical inference and the mathematical foundation of the most commonly used tests of significance are presented and discussed.

RELATIONSHIP BETWEEN RESEARCH QUESTIONS (HYPOTHESES) AND DATA ANALYSIS PROCEDURES

When planning a study, as discussed in previous chapters of this book, a specific problem in a particular context is studied for a primary purpose. Methods that others have used to conceptualize the study, to measure relevant data, and to identify (or design) a particular context in which to study are reviewed. Procedures to be implemented to study the specific research questions, or hypotheses, that are most relevant to the specific problem are prespecified to assure that the

TABLE 7.3. ACCIDENT RATES OF MALE AND FEMALE DRIVERS BY AMOUNT OF DRIVING

	Male Drivers		Female Drivers	
	More than 10,000 miles	*10,000 miles or less*	*More than 10,000 miles*	*10,000 miles or less*
At least one accident	52%	25%	52%	25%
(Number of drivers)	(6,727)	(2,829)	(2,440)	(6,981)

most objective (unbiased) methods are used and that the researcher does not focus on idiosyncratic aspects of the specific situation studied. This includes precise delineation of the ways that the obtained information (data) will be organized and analyzed to address the research questions (hypotheses).

The problem and associated research questions are stated to clearly delineate the problem under investigation. The most appropriate research questions are specified in order to investigate the question as comprehensively and as insightfully as possible. It is important that the data collected and the data analysis procedures result in the most appropriate and accurate answers to each research question or test of each hypothesis. This applies to qualitative as well as quantitative studies. Historical and ethnographic research is carried out in a similar manner. One difference between these kinds of studies and the more quantitative studies is that an important part of the qualitative study is the search for appropriate sources of data. As a result, such researchers are unable to precisely specify at the beginning of the study the most appropriate research questions to investigate or hypotheses to test, or the most appropriate data to answer the questions or test the hypotheses. During the data collection process these questions or hypotheses are identified, and the most appropriate data are identified, collected, and analyzed in a manner similar to that of more quantitative research.

To illustrate these relationships, specific research questions and hypotheses are presented, and the relative strengths and weaknesses of alternative methods for analyzing different types of data are discussed. There is never a single way that data must be collected and analyzed in order to be valid and relevant, but there are important strengths and weaknesses of alternative methods that make some methods more valuable for some purposes and problems and other methods more relevant for others. The characteristics (such as nominal, ordinal, interval, or ratio) of the data collected determine the types of analytic procedures that are appropriate in a particular situation. From those alternatives, the best combination of analyses are selected.

Illustration One

A researcher was interested in whether more sophisticated management information systems (MIS) in small liberal arts colleges are used more often in short-term or long-term decision-making. The following two research questions were investigated:

1. To what extent does the level of sophistication of the MIS implemented in small liberal arts colleges relate to the degree of use in making short-term decisions?
2. To what extent does the level of sophistication of the MIS implemented in small liberal arts colleges relate to the degree of use in making long-term decisions?

By asking the question, "To what extent does the level of MIS sophistication relate to degree of use?" the researcher is required to analyze the data in ways that indicate the extent of the relationship. If no relationship is found, that finding can be reported. If only highly sophisticated MIS systems provide data that are used regularly for decision-making, that finding can be reported.

If the researcher had asked the research question, "Is there a relationship between the level of MIS sophistication and the degree of use?" that question could be answered yes, no, or maybe. The more useful information is the nature and extent of the relationship. Researchers tend to define things very precisely, and that precision is important in matching the data analysis procedures to the research question.

To investigate this problem, 12 small liberal arts colleges within 100 miles of Pittsburgh, Pennsylvania, agreed to participate in the study by completing questionnaires about the level of sophistication of their MIS and the degree of use of data from the MIS in making short-term and long-term decisions. The first questionnaire was completed by the business officers of each college, describing their college's MIS. The second questionnaire was completed by the president of each college, describing the degree of use of MIS data in short-term and long-term decision-making. Each questionnaire included 10 questions.

If the data obtained from the questionnaire allowed the researcher to place both the level of sophistication of the MIS and the degree of use in each type of decision-making on an interval scale, such as from least (1) to most (50), the research questions could be answered by calculating two Pearson Product Moment Correlation Coefficients (r)—one for short-term decisions and one for long-term decisions. If the correlations were significantly different from 0 (no relationship), then degree of use is related to level of sophistication. That is true whether the correlation is positive or negative. If the correlations were positive, then greater sophistication of the MIS would appear to result in greater use for decision-making. If they were negative, greater sophistication of the MIS would seem to result in less use and less sophistication in greater use.

This analysis allows a direct test of the relationship between sophistication of MIS and use of MIS data in decision-making. It does not provide any data concerning how the relationship occurs for these 12 colleges. Do one or two colleges with very sophisticated MIS also tend to be the greatest users of the data and the other 10 somewhat inconsistent in their relationships? Or do two or three colleges with very unsophisticated MIS tend to be the least users of MIS data, whereas the other nine are inconsistent in results? The summary statistic, r, provides little or no help in knowing the position of the individual colleges on the two characteristics, sophistication of MIS and use of data.

This analysis is more appropriate for answering the second type of research question, "Is there a relationship. . . ?" Without further analysis of the data, the nature of the relationship is unknown. That is one difficulty of statistics that provide averages. Even though they simplify the data and more clearly describe overall characteristics, the individual scores that are combined are often unknown to the researcher. In this example, the types of MIS systems that provide data used most for decision-making is not clear.

The use of this correlation coefficient requires that the data on both variables be measured on interval scales. With only 10 questions on each questionnaire, the researcher may not be confident that both the level of sophistication of the MIS and the degree of MIS data use in decision-making are being measured on interval scales. Given the few colleges studied (12), the concern that the measurement scales may not be interval, and the problem that was addressed in the study, it might be better to classify each college as high, average, or low on both the level of MIS sophistication and the degree of data use. Then each college could be identified on a three-by-three table, as illustrated in Table 7.4. The results reported show that five colleges had sophisticated MIS, four were average, and three were low. Six colleges made high use of data, five made average use, and one made low use. A perfect positive relationship was not obtained. A perfect positive relationship would require that all colleges fall in the diagonal boxes of the table, which are High-High, Average-Average, and Low-Low. That would occur only when every college with high level of MIS sophistication would make high use of MIS data in short-term decision-making, those with average MIS would make average use, and those with low MIS sophistication would make low use of the data for short-term decision-making. The actual scores, or classifications, for each college are the empirical results of the study. Do these results indicate whether a relationship exists? Can the nature and extent of the relationship between sophistication of MIS and use of the MIS data for short-term decision-making be described with confidence for the target population of small liberal arts colleges?

There are six colleges in the diagonal boxes representing High-High, Average-Average, and Low-Low and six that fall outside those boxes. The three colleges with low levels of MIS sophistication make high, average, and low uses of the data, whereas none of the colleges with more sophisticated MIS made low use of the MIS data in their short-term decision-making. Three colleges is a small sample of colleges with low sophistication of MIS, however, and may not represent the degree of use most such colleges make of their MIS data. With only 12 colleges in the sample, it is difficult to interpret the somewhat inconsistent data because legitimate arguments can be made for or against the existence of a relationship between the two variables.

A decision rule used most often to decide among these two alternatives is a test of significance. An appropriate test statistic, such as χ^2, could be used with frequency (nominal) data to decide between the two alternatives. It addresses the question: If there is no relationship between the level of MIS sophistication and the use of MIS data for short-term decision-making, how likely is it that the results would have occurred by chance alone? If that chance is low (e.g., less than 0.05), then the results indicate that a relationship between the variables does seem to exist. Appropriate statistics *do not always exist* to test precisely the relationship obtained. When they do exist, they often are not able to identify that a relationship exists when in fact it does exist. In this example, the assumptions

TABLE 7.4. LEVEL OF MIS SOPHISTICATION AND DEGREE OF MIS DATA USE FOR SHORT-TERM DECISION-MAKING BY 12 SMALL LIBERAL ARTS COLLEGES

		Level of MIS Sophistication			
		High	*Average*	*Low*	
Degree of MIS Data	High	3	2	1	6
Use for Short-Term	Average	2	2	1	5
Decision-Making	Low	0	0	1	1
		5	4	3	12

required for using χ^2 are not adequately met, and it should not be used. There are several ways that the relationship could be tested for statistical significance, but none of them is very powerful and would not result in significance, given the results in Table 7.4. A researcher would be forced to conclude that the results do *not* indicate that a relationship exists between the level of MIS sophistication and the use of MIS data for short-term decision-making. If *all 12 colleges* had provided responses that could be classified in the diagonal boxes, that would be clear evidence of a relationship between the two variables—even in the absence of a statistical test of significance.

The importance of the test of significance has been overemphasized in educational research, which may be a result of the fact that educational research, particularly in human learning, has been dominated by psychologists who have emphasized the value of experiments and the "necessity" to quantify data. In all research, conclusions are drawn from systematically collected data that best measure the variables a researcher wants to investigate. The variables important to different researchers and appropriate ways to measure them vary tremendously—especially across different disciplines. The extent to which quantification aids researchers by allowing more precise investigation of hypothesized relationships rather than harming researchers' causes by trivializing the complex activities of human beings by analyzing them into relatively disjoint parts that represent little or nothing depends on the researcher's purpose and the context in which data are obtained. This fundamental issue is an ongoing concern that researchers must consider in each study as they carry out their work. For the past 20 years or so, experimental studies using quantified (numerical) data have been commonly viewed as the *ideal* research method in educational research. Today, more qualitative studies that attempt to identify the important complex relationships among educational variables are more generally accepted. Let us hope that the pendulum does not swing further in either direction so that one method becomes the ideal that all competent researchers must use. Each approach has valuable strengths and associated weaknesses that can be overcome to a great extent by using the strengths of the other.

Illustration Two

To illustrate the use of qualitative data in research, a historical study by Lee (1971) titled, "The Child in Pedagogy and Culture: Concepts of American Preadolescence as Revealed in Teaching Theories and as Related to the Culture: 1900–1914," is described. Lee's purpose was to investigate the interrelationships among (1) selected concepts of the preadolescent child, (2) teaching theories, and (3) the culture in which they both appear. The incidence of this problem in any particular period of history, could have been studied because Lee tried to describe how these variables affect one another. She selected a period (1900–1914) that provided the best opportunity to delineate the types of concepts that would allow her to document these interrelationships as clearly as possible. The procedures she used are described in detail so that others can assess their quality and judge the appropriateness of her conclusions.

Lee listed the sources she used to describe the perspectives on creativity, free moral choice, and the individual in society in terms of the preadolescent child at that time, as well as the pedagogical theory and methods that were taught to teachers. Although these were very complex topics and different authors used different words to describe the concepts, she systematically read the materials and developed procedures to identify and classify relevant content in those sources.

Lee meticulously noted the order in which she carried out her activities, including her initial delineation and classification of material into the relevant categories. This helps to clarify her procedures and allows readers to judge the likelihood that her procedures were biased or likely to produce erroneous results. Her findings were specified with extensive documentation of the associated evidence, as well as with her concerns about a few unexplained inconsistencies, or counterexamples. The findings were discussed in terms of theoretical and research literature. She reported the following conclusions:

1. Although the teaching theories reflect individual insights, they are culturally centered.
2. The older accepted ideas are tenacious. New and old ideas existed side by side for long periods before the new ideas became prevalent (when that occurred).
3. The prevalent physical and biological sciences of the time set the direction for the social sciences and the philosophies.
4. The fragmentation of the American culture involved the schools in burdens and tensions. The tensions resulting from cultural pluralism of the U.S. population were of particular importance. (pp. 32–35)

Although these conclusions are not easily understood without the extensive evidence Lee obtained and reported in her dissertation, they are included to provide a sense of the relationships that her historical methods provided. The description presented here should make it clear that good historical research is at least as meticulous as experimental research in documenting the quality and relevance of the information (data) gathered and in determining the relative weight of evidence for alternative explanations for the relationships obtained in the study.

Getzels (1978) carried out a similar study to investigate the effects of Thorndike and Woodworth's initial research (1898–1901) about the importance of transfer of training in human learning (rather than treating the brain as a muscle to be exercised with Latin and Greek). He reviewed numerous pedagogical books immediately before and for two decades after the turn of the twentieth century. He found that Latin and Greek decreased in importance and that learning principles consistent with those of Thorndike and Woodworth (1901) increased over time to a primary emphasis in many such books.

These studies provide convincing evidence of the impact of theory in practice. Lee also provides evidence of ways in which basic theoretical concepts of the preadolescent child and of the culture affect pedagogical theory and associated practice as described in the books used to teach future public school teachers. The primary data analyzed in each study were qualitative, although instances were counted in several parts of each study. No statistical tests of significance were used, nor were any needed.

Illustration Three

A teacher of French as a foreign language had reason to believe that pictures representing the word or concept underlying a phrase would improve the speed at which English-speaking students at various levels of proficiency in the French language would learn French. She identified 50 students at each of three levels of proficiency —beginners, intermediate, and advanced. She randomly divided each group of 50 in half and randomly assigned one group to use pictures with the language lessons. The other group used traditional methods that included very few pictures. Both groups studied the same French lessons for the same amounts of time. Her problem statement was that students who used pictures that described the French terms being taught would learn more French language over six weeks than students who did not use the pictures. Her hypothetical results are reported in Table 7.5.

In this illustration, the differences between the two groups is not the same for students at the three different levels of French language study. Overall, the group who used the pictures had a mean score of 42, whereas those who did not use pictures scored an average of 35. As indicated in Table 7.5, this overall difference was significant ($p < 0.05$), indicating that it would have occurred less than five times out of 100 by chance alone if the pictures had had no effect. But is there a consistent, overall effect of the pictures across all three groups? (Tests of significance are discussed in detail in the following section of this chapter.)

The summaries of the data from the study (the six means) are the empirical outcomes of the studies. (In fact, the 150 scores obtained on the six-week test are the empirical data from the study.) All additional summaries and analyses are to aid the interpretation of these empirical results. In reviewing the six means, it is clear that the largest difference, which was significant ($p < 0.0001$), occurred at

TABLE 7.5. MEAN NUMBER CORRECT ON SIX-WEEK TEST FOR BEGINNING, INTERMEDIATE, AND ADVANCED HIGH SCHOOL STUDENTS OF FRENCH (HYPOTHETICAL)

Proficiency Level	Pictures	No Pictures	p
Beginning	38	26	0.0001[a]
Intermediate	42	35	0.01[a]
Advanced	46	44	0.45
Total	42	35	0.05[a]

[a]Significant at $\alpha = 0.05$

the beginning level (38 versus 26). A 7-point difference, which is significant ($p < 0.01$), was obtained at the intermediate level (42 versus 35). Only a 2-point difference, which was not significant, was obtained at the advanced level. An appropriate conclusion would be that the pictures appeared to have the most positive effect at the beginning level, a lesser effect at the intermediate level, and no meaningful effect at the advanced level.

The terms *difference* and *effect* as used in this example can be a basis for a discussion of their meaning in research generally. In observing the six means and the two overall means, average differences in favor of the group who used pictures in their study occurred at each level. Do these differences represent "real," or "meaningful," differences between the two groups? In the context of this study, the differences between the two overall means cannot be meaningfully interpreted because the effects of the pictures were not the same for students at the three levels of proficiency in French. The effect of the pictures is said to *interact* with the level of student. The term *interact* (or interaction) is a technical term and means that the effect of a variable is not the same at all levels of a second variable. When that occurs, the overall means cannot be meaningfully interpreted—as shown in this example.

The large obtained difference between the two groups of beginning students does appear to represent real differences between the two groups. Because the difference is large (12 points), it cannot be explained by the error that exists in the measurement process used (the six-week test). The fact that the difference is significant provides more evidence that the differences would rarely occur by chance alone, if the pictures did not in fact have an effect. For similar reasons, the 7-point difference at the intermediate level can be interpreted as a meaningful effect. That does not mean that the results prove without a doubt that the pictures had an impact at either of these levels. The weight of the evidence is such that the most probable reason for the difference (given these results and everything else we know about these groups and the other things that occurred in these two settings during the study) is the use of the pictures by the one group at the beginner and intermediate levels of the study of French.

At the advanced level, only a 2-point difference was obtained. This relatively small difference may be a result of measurement error. It would be likely to occur by chance alone even if the pictures had no real effect at this level, which is what the test of significance indicates. A 2-point difference would occur 45% of the time when the use of pictures had no educational effect. Therefore, we have no clear evidence that the pictures had an effect on the advanced students.

On the other hand, the 2-point difference may have been a real difference. If 10 more studies were carried out and in each case a small but insignificant difference occurred favoring advanced students who used pictures, and no counterevidence existed, the weight of evidence would be such that a researcher could legitimately conclude that the pictures had a small effect on the learning of advanced students. Such small but consistent differences could be tested statistically using Bayesian or other statistical techniques that are beyond the scope of this book, the difference would, in most cases, be statistically significant. This is what logic would imply and most researchers would expect.

Inferences about the relationship that exists among variables in the "real world" is based on all the evidence obtained in various studies. Statements about these relationships (which are usually called *conclusions*)—whether from experimental data, quantitative data, qualitative historical data, or some combination of various types of data—are based on the thoughtful weighing of all relevant information. They are statements that describe the relationships in ways that have the greatest probability, or likelihood, given all that is known. All empirical knowledge is probabilistic.

In the final section of this chapter, the logical process on which tests of significance are based is presented. First, probability is defined. Next, the normal distribution using the z statistic illustrates how probability values are obtained, and the reasons why they can be used in many educational studies are discussed. The assumptions required by each statistic are presented to illustrate that all tests of significance require assumptions. Examples using z, t, F, and χ^2 illustrate their use in studies and the ways they are used in testing hypotheses and drawing conclusions in empirical research.

INFERENTIAL STATISTICS

As indicated in Chapter 6, the inference process in empirical research is based on gathering data from a sample of people (or situations) that the researcher has confidence represents a "typical" population of people (or situations) of interest. Statistics are used to calculate the probability that, if the sample had been drawn from a population with specific hypothesized characteristics, the obtained results would occur by chance alone. Examples of such statistical tests of hypotheses are given later in the chapter. First, it is important to understand the concept of probability as it is used in research.

Probability is defined as *the ratio of the specified event to all possible events*. For example, the probability of selecting an ace from a deck of 52 playing cards is 4 divided by 52, or 1 in 13. There are four aces (the specified event) and

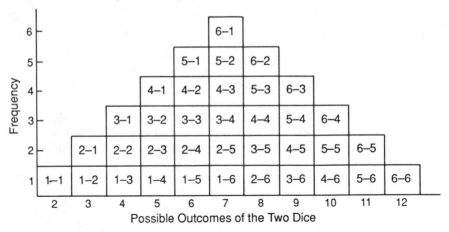

Figure 7.3. The Distribution of Possible Outcomes of a Single Roll of Two Dice

52 cards (all possible events). The probability is the ratio 4 to 52, or 1/13, which equals 0.077. In a similar manner the probability of obtaining a head in one toss of a coin is 1/2, or 0.50. There is one way to obtain a head, and there are two possible outcomes.

The same basic concept is used to calculate the probability that certain results will occur when two six-sided dice are thrown. The 36 ways that the dice can fall are shown in Figure 7.3. The probability of throwing a 7 or an 11 is calculated by adding the six ways of obtaining a 7 to the two ways of obtaining an 11 (8), and dividing by the number of possible outcomes (36), which is 2/9, or 0.222. The probability of throwing a 10 or more is 6 divided by 36, 1/6, or 0.167.

Any known distribution of scores can be used in a similar manner to calculate the probability that a certain outcome would occur by chance alone. In many situations, the normal distribution represents the distribution of scores, or numbers, that a researcher is analyzing. Because the characteristics of the normal distribution are known, the probability of obtaining z scores of a specified magnitude can be obtained directly from a z table. For example, the probability that a z score equal to 2.00 or more would occur in a normal distribution of scores is 0.0228. Another way to state this is that in a normal distribution 2.28% of all possible z scores are 2.00 or above. Because the distribution is symmetric, we know that another 2.28% of the z scores are equal to -2.00 or less.

Logic of Statistical Inference

The basis for statistical tests of significance is that of random sampling from a specific population, or populations. In comparing two educational methods for teaching eighth-grade math, for example, all eighth-grade students could be assigned randomly to one of the two methods. At the end of the term, the math achievement of students in each group is obtained. If there is no difference between the two methods, there should be no difference in achievement between the two groups. The statistical test is based on the hypothesis that there is no difference in the two methods. This is usually presented as:

$$H_o : \mu_1 = \mu_2$$

the null, or statistical, hypothesis (H_o). It states that the mean achievement of the population taught by Method 1 (μ_1) is precisely equal to the achievement in the same population taught by Method 2 (μ_2). If this is true, how likely would it be that in a single study differences as large or larger than those obtained in this study would occur by chance alone? The probability can be calculated in much the same way as the probability for obtaining 10 or greater in a single throw of two dice. If that probability is low, such as 5 times out of 100 occurrences (0.05), or 1 in 100 (0.01), then we reject the statistical hypothesis of no difference and accept as tenable the hypothesis consistent with the data. In this example, if mean achievement for Group 1 $(\overline{X}_1)$, was 65 and that for Group 2 $(\overline{X}_2)$ was 57, the alternative hypothesis

$$H_1 : \mu_1 > \mu_2$$

would be accepted as tenable because the probability of obtaining such a large difference would be less than 1 in 100 (0.01).

The normal distribution is used to calculate the probability in many cases because it appears to represent the distribution of mean scores. It can be shown that when large samples $(n > 60)$ are drawn from populations with mean μ, and variance σ^2, the distribution of sample means approaches a normal distribution. Because of this the standard normal scores can be used to calculate the probability of obtaining specific results in a study. The formula is:

$$z = \frac{\overline{X} - \mu}{\sigma^2 / n} = \frac{\overline{X} - \mu}{\sigma / \sqrt{n}}$$

The same principles hold when comparing two groups. The formula becomes:

$$z = \frac{(\overline{X}_1 - \overline{X}_2) - (\mu_1 - \mu_2)}{\sqrt{\dfrac{\sigma_1^2}{n_1} + \dfrac{\sigma_2^2}{n_2}}}$$

An example of how the normal distribution is used involves a principal who wanted to implement some innovative programs that were developed for high ability students. The principal was convinced that the students in his school were well above average and could gain much from the new program. The superintendent of the school district did not want to spend money on a new program if the students in the school were only average. The principal randomly selected 64 students and administered IQ tests to them. To show that the school population was above average, he used the following test of significance. If the superintendent was correct, the mean IQ for all students in the school should be equal to 100 (average). If the principal was correct, the mean IQ would be greater than 100 (above average). The result was a mean ($\overline{X}$) of 106 and a standard deviation (S_x) of 20. Because the distribution of IQs is normal in the population and sample size is relatively large (64), the theoretical distribution of all possible sample means will also be normal. The normal curve is used to calculate the probability that the mean of 106 would be obtained by chance alone from a school population with a mean (μ) of 100. The formula used to calculate the z value is:

$$z = \frac{\overline{X} - \mu}{S_x/\sqrt{n}} = \frac{106 - 100}{20/\sqrt{64}} = \frac{6}{20/8} = \frac{6}{2.5} = 2.4 \text{ (using } S_x \text{ as an estimate of } \sigma.)$$

The proportion of scores falling at z equal to 2.4 or greater in the theoretical distribution is obtained from a normal distribution table. This value is 0.0082 (see Figure 7.4). This means that less than 1 time out of 100 (less than 0.82%) would a sample size of 64 result in a mean of 106 or greater *if that sample came from a population with a mean of 100*. Because this would rarely occur by chance, the principal and superintendent agree that it is unlikely that the students in the school have only an average IQ, and they accept as tenable the alternative hypothesis that the students are above average (mean IQ above 100).

An illustration of the problem and the normal distribution used to draw that conclusion is illustrated in Figure 7.4. As indicated, 0.9912 of all scores in a normal distribution fall below z equal to 2.4. Only 0.0082 of all scores fall at z equal to 2.4, or above. Using tests of statistical significance, the probability of obtaining results that occurred in a study can be calculated on the basis of a specific hypothesis that the researcher makes about the population from which the sample was obtained.

The same logical process is used in all tests of statistical significance, from the simplest to the most complex. The function such tests serve in all empirical

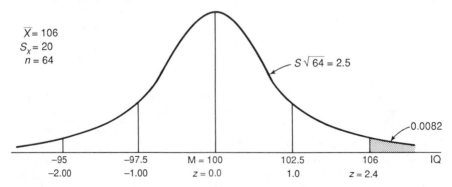

Figure 7.4. Normal Distribution Example for Test of Hypothesis that Population Mean Is 100

studies is to indicate the likelihood that the results would have occurred by chance *if* the original hypothesis is precisely correct. If the results are extremely unlikely to occur by chance alone, the original hypothesis (such as the superintendent's: $\mu = 100$) is rejected and the alternative consistent with the results is accepted as tenable. It is not proven, just accepted as tenable. In this case, $H_1:\mu > 100$ is accepted as tenable.

Statistics Used in Tests of Significance

A number of other statistics are commonly used to test the statistical significance of results in various studies. The most common are t, F, and χ^2. The test statistic that is most appropriate in a particular situation depends on a number of factors. A discussion of some of those factors follows

Inferential statistics used in education are either parametric or nonparametric. The classification is based on whether the statistic requires assumptions to be made about the population(s) from which a sample is selected. Characteristics of populations, such as the mean (μ) or standard deviation (σ), are represented by a Greek letter and are called *parameters*. Characteristics of samples are represented by Roman letters, such as $\overline{X}$ or S, and are called *statistics*.

Parametric statistics, such as z, t, and F, require that the following assumptions be precisely accurate, or true, for the data that are analyzed. Otherwise the obtained probability will not be accurate.

1. Scores are independent observations.
2. Population(s) is normally distributed.
3. Population variances (for two or more groups) are equal.
4. Scores are on an interval scale.
5. Hypothesis being tested (e.g., H_0: $\mu = 100$) is true.

The first assumption is met through random selection of the sample, or random assignment of subjects to treatments (such as experimental or control). Because tests of significance are based on the probability that obtained results would occur by chance alone, this assumption is needed to assure that one person's score is not systematically related to other persons' scores. For example, selecting post positions in a horse race results in an equal probability that each horse could be in any of the starting positions. That is, there is no relationship between the starting position and race-related characteristics of a horse, such as speed or previous record. This procedure meets the first assumption of independent observations.

Similarly, assigning students randomly to a phonics or meaning approach to learning to read assures that the students' scores in the two groups are independent of one another. The common experiences of students in each treatment group produce dependencies within each group. When the normal distribution is used to estimate the likelihood that the obtained differences would occur by chance alone, the extent to which the two treatments have different effects on the dependent variable is tested.

The second and third assumptions concern parameters of the population(s) that the sample(s) represents. The second requires that the characteristic measured in the study, such as IQ or reading achievement, be normally distributed in the population studied. The third assumption is required *only* when two or more populations are studied, and it assumes that their variances on the characteristic measured are precisely equal.

The scores are assumed to be measured on at least an interval scale because of the mathematical operations used to calculate the parametric statistics. Finally, the hypothesis tested (the statistical hypothesis) is assumed to be precisely true.

If any of these five assumptions is not met, the resulting probability will be inaccurate. Rather than 0.05, the actual probability may be 0.132, 0.034, or 0.0481. Both the nature and the extent of the inaccuracy is never known, although it can be estimated at times. The logic of statistical inference in a study is to assure that the first four assumptions are adequately met. If the results obtained in a study are unlikely to have occurred by chance alone (which is usually defined as less than 0.05 or 0.01), then the researcher rejects the statistical hypothesis and accepts the alternative that is consistent with the results.

In practice, the first four assumptions are never precisely met, so the obtained probability value is only an estimate of the actual probability. Even advanced study of statistics does not provide the knowledge needed to measure the extent to which the assumptions are met in the population. What is known about these assumptions is that as long as there are fairly large samples (60 to 100, or larger) and approximately equal sample sizes when two or more samples are used, the probability obtained from a parametric statistic will be fairly accurate, even when the situation deviates a great deal from the assumptions of normal distribution and equal variances of the characteristic in the population(s).

One reason for this is the central limit theorem (CLT), which indicates that in many research situations a normal distribution is an appropriate one for describing a distribution of scores. The theorem states that:

> Given any population with mean, μ, and finite variance, σ^2, as the sample size increases without limit the distribution of the sample means approaches a normal distribution with mean, μ, and variance, σ^2/n (where n is the sample size).

This means that regardless of the shape of the distribution of a characteristic in a population, such as the extremely skewed distribution of annual income in the United States, if large samples such as 500 were selected and the mean income calculated for each sample of 500, the means would be essentially normally distributed. In testing hypotheses in education, a researcher often needs to know the probability of obtaining a specific mean, or the differences between the two means, in a study. This normal distribution of sample means is used to calculate (estimate) that probability.

To understand how such sampling occurs and the effects of sample size on the distribution of means, a population of 168 scores, which are not symmetrically distributed, is given in Table 7.6. A sample of 10 scores ($n = 10$) is drawn randomly from the population and the mean is calculated. The 10 scores are placed back in the population, and the process is repeated indefinitely. All the means form a distribution of sample means. Such a distribution of means will be normally distributed if the population is normally distributed.

If this sampling process were repeated with larger sample sizes, such as $n = 30$, another sampling distribution of means would be obtained. The standard deviation for this second distribution would be less than that obtained for samples of size 10. This is because the sample means tend to be closer to the population mean as sample sizes become larger.

To show how the central limit theorem works in practice, and to illustrate the relationship between the population and the theoretical distribution used to estimate the probability of obtained results occurring in a study, *samples* were selected from a finite population of 168 scores that is *not* normally distributed. Samples of sizes 10 and 30 were obtained, and means were calculated for each sample. The distributions of these sample means should be fairly symmetrical, although the distribution of means for the smaller sample size ($n = 10$) will be shaped more like the population sample than will the distribution of means for the larger sample size ($n = 30$).

Students in several introductory educational research classes calculated the results reported in Figure 7.5 from the 168 scores in Table 7.6. Two important points are illustrated in Figure 7.5. First, the variability of the means is much greater with the smaller sample sizes. Second, a few means for samples of 30 scores differ from the population mean more than those for samples of 10. It is important to note that in a single sample it is possible to select by chance alone the 10, or 30, lowest scores in the population. This sample would produce the lowest mean possible from that population and would deviate a great deal from the population mean. Such a sample would seldom be selected by chance alone, but it is possible.

In practice the population mean (or means) is unknown. The logic of statistical inference is based on the assumption that the statistical hypothesis defines the mean value of the population (e.g., $H_0{:}\mu = 100$). If the probability for the obtained value is very low (less than 0.05 or 0.01), which means that the result would occur rarely by chance alone, the statistical hypothesis is rejected and the appropriate alternative hypothesis is accepted as tenable. It is *not* proven or shown to be a fact; there is always the possibility that this was the one time in a thousand, or one time in a million, that the result occurred by chance alone. Such a possibility can never be rejected totally.

In most cases, the shape of the distribution in the population of scores studied is not known. The central limit theorem and many empirical studies of the distributions used to test hypotheses statistically provide confidence that the probabilities obtained fairly represent the likelihood that the specific results would have occurred by chance alone.

TABLE 7.6. POPULATION OF 168 SCORES[a]

ID #	Scores	ID #	Scores	ID #	Scores	ID #	Scores
1	96	43	67	85	73	127	86
2	67	44	58	86	54	128	72
3	81	45	78	87	95	129	64
4	49	46	88	88	65	130	55
5	93	47	64	89	59	131	62
6	82	48	84	90	58	132	70
7	58	49	79	91	78	133	76
8	60	50	83	92	34	134	79
9	71	51	61	93	61	135	95
10	51	52	79	94	74	136	72
11	61	53	70	95	61	137	46
12	74	54	69	96	66	138	44
13	70	55	79	97	90	139	64
14	93	56	51	98	74	140	78
15	51	57	96	99	52	141	74
16	74	58	58	100	40	142	59
17	76	59	76	101	79	143	76
18	78	60	98	102	71	144	73
19	73	61	72	103	87	145	79
20	51	62	49	104	72	146	78
21	61	63	72	105	77	147	77
22	64	64	73	106	74	148	84
23	60	65	72	107	72	149	70
24	48	66	62	108	95	150	41
25	79	67	82	109	75	151	73
26	85	68	77	110	53	152	83
27	76	69	71	111	41	153	65
28	69	70	65	112	56	154	65
29	88	71	82	113	77	155	60
30	84	72	71	114	61	156	36
31	91	73	61	115	62	157	50
32	65	74	77	116	67	158	85
33	59	75	98	117	77	159	73
34	67	76	88	118	85	160	59
35	89	77	53	119	76	161	85
36	70	78	68	120	81	162	51
37	81	79	50	121	68	163	64
38	65	80	78	122	80	164	92
39	82	81	78	123	58	165	71
40	61	82	52	124	77	166	54
41	80	83	70	125	73	167	64
42	62	84	60	126	64	168	63

[a]Mean (μ) = 70; Standard Deviation (σ) = 13.2; Range: 34 to 98.

The data analyses and tests of significance are aspects of research method that help researchers describe the situations they study and develop confidence in conclusions they reach. It is one way to protect human beings from selectively identifying results consistent with their beliefs and biases, but the results of any

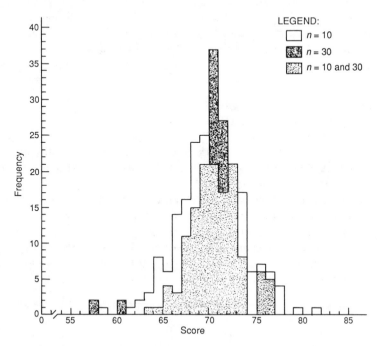

Figure 7.5. Means for 200 Samples of 10 and 160 Samples of 30 Drawn from Population in Table 7.6

one study must be understood and interpreted as part of the broad milieu of information (empirical, theoretical, and experiential) that must be used in a profession to make practical decisions. Only by understanding what statistical tests represent (and do *not* represent) can empirical studies be accurately and appropriately interpreted.

Nonparametric statistics are those that require no assumptions about the characteristics of a population. They are generally used with nominal or ordinal data.

The assumptions required to use a specific nonparametric statistic depend to some extent on the type of data used and other characteristics of the situation. The only two assumptions required by all nonparametric statistical tests of significance are the following:

1. Scores are independent observations.
2. Hypothesis being tested (H_o).

Because there are no assumptions about the type of scale from which the scores are obtained, nonparametric statistics can be used with ordinal and nominal data as well as with interval and ratio data. The primary nonparametric statistic is χ^2, which can be used in many ways. These are described well by Siegel (1956). Most statistics books describe the situations in which each statistic can be used and the assumptions that must be met for the test of significance to provide accurate estimates of the probability for the results of a study. The extent to which those assumptions are met should be estimated each time a statistic is used.

Tests of Significance in Research

In practice the choice of statistic to use in calculating the probability of an obtained result is based on a few primary issues. To illustrate them, some examples of the use of z, t, F, and χ^2 are given.

In the principal and superintendent problem discussed previously, the z score and normal distribution were used. Given that we used IQ scores, which are approximately normally distributed in the population, and that there was a fairly large sample (64), the central limit theorem gives us confidence that a normal distribution would represent the sampling distribution of means and provide an accurate estimate of the probability. The formula for the z statistic is:

$$z = \frac{\overline{X} - \mu}{\sigma / \sqrt{n}}$$

Both μ and σ are characteristics of the population, the values of which we can never know for sure. The value of μ is usually specified in the statistical hypothesis, but σ is not known. In a research study, the only standard deviation available is the one calculated from the sample (or samples). When that value (S_x) is used as an estimate of σ, we find that the resulting scores are *not* distributed normally but are a family of t distributions. The shape of each t distribution is determined by the number of independent scores on which it is based. These t distributions are based on the formula:

$$t = \frac{\overline{X} - \mu}{S_x / \sqrt{n}}$$

The only difference between the z and t distributions is the use of the obtained standard deviation. As indicated, the z distribution can be used with large samples because of the central limit theorem. But keep in mind that these are not magical processes. The more a population distribution varies from normality, the larger the sample size must be for the sampling distribution of means to approach a normal distribution. The t distribution will result in more accurate probabilities than the normal distribution whenever S_x is used to estimate σ.

The z and t distributions can be used to compare the results of two groups in a study. The formulas are:

$$z = \frac{(\overline{X}_1 - \overline{X}_2) - (\mu_1 - \mu_2)}{\sqrt{\dfrac{\sigma_1^{\,2}}{n_1} + \dfrac{\sigma_2^{\,2}}{n_2}}} \qquad t = \frac{(\overline{X}_1 - \overline{X}_2) - (\mu_1 - \mu_2)}{\sqrt{\dfrac{S_1^{\,2}}{n_1} + \dfrac{S_2^{\,2}}{n_2}}}$$

These statistics can be used to test the statistical hypothesis: H_0: $\mu_1 - \mu_2 = 0$. This hypothesis is made when the relative effects of two treatments, or characteristics, are being tested. You can use it to test one of the two alternative hypotheses (H_1: $\mu_1 > \mu_2$, or H_2: $\mu_2 > \mu_1$), or both alternatives at the same time. Testing only one alternative is called a *one-tailed test* (or *directed hypothesis*). Testing both alternatives is called a *two-tailed test* (or a *nondirected hypothesis*).

In carrying out a test of significance, you must decide, before you collect any data, what level of probability you will accept as so rare that you will reject the statistical hypothesis as an accurate description of the populations. There are no strict rules that you must follow in making that decision. Your major concern is the effect of making an error in drawing your conclusion. If you conclude that there is a significant difference between the two treatments when there is not, you may spend a lot of time and money on a treatment that is not better. For example, if the principal in our previous example made such an error, and the students were not above average, or gifted, the students would be unlikely to gain much from the advanced program. To minimize the likelihood of such an error, you can select a low probability for your significance level (α), such as 0.01 or 0.001. Practically, this means that you must obtain in the sample larger differences from the statistical hypothesis before you can reject it. If a 0.001 significance level had been selected by the principal, the obtained mean of 106 would not have been significant (0.0082 is not less than 0.001).

If the greater cost in a study is to fail to discern a difference when there really is one, a higher level of significance would be selected, such as 0.025 or 0.05. Almost never is a significance level above 0.05 chosen, but there are times when 0.10 or 0.15 may be appropriate. The common use of 0.01 or 0.05 may be more a result of history than anything else. When Sir Ronald Fisher (1935) developed the analysis of variance (ANOVA) using the F statistic, he selected the 0.05 level as his operational definition of statistical significance. Later researchers and statisticians have been unwilling to select higher significance levels. Higher levels (greater than 0.05) would result in greater numbers of false effects (concluding that a meaningful difference exists when it does not). An 0.05 level means that a researcher is willing to reject the statistical, usually null, hypothesis 5% of the time when it is, in fact, true. The researcher can never be sure when a statistical hypothesis is rejected that it is *not* one of the 5% that would have occurred *by chance alone*.

All empirical research is based on such probabilistic reasoning. Conclusions that are most defensible from an extensive, objective review of all relevant data are those that can be legitimately made in studies. Truth is never obtained in the laboratory, in classroom studies, or in field observations. Probabilistic reasoning, which recognizes the possibility that the conclusion would be wrong, is the foundation of all empirical research—including history and ethnography. In those nonquantitative studies, precise probability levels cannot be calculated, but the concept is important (see Barzun & Graff, 1985).

Statistical Examples

To gain a further understanding of statistical inference in research, a χ^2 example and an ANOVA example using the F statistic are calculated and discussed. Some important statistical concepts are illustrated by the specific example using χ^2 as the test of significance. The research question is: Does the starting (post) position of a horse on a race track affect the chance of winning a race? The starting position of each horse is random, so the first assumption of independent observations is met. The starting position for the winners of 144 races in a hypothetical example are:

Number of	Post Position							
	1	2	3	4	5	6	7	8
(f_o) Winners (144):	29	19	18	25	17	10	15	11
(f_e) Expected Winners:	18	18	18	18	18	18	18	18

If post position does not affect the chance of winning, the same number of winners should have started the race in each position. The statistical hypothesis is:

$$H_0: f_1 = f_2 = f_3 = f_4 = f_5 = f_6 = f_7 = f_8$$

If that hypothesis is true, then 1/8 of the winners (144/8) should have started from each position. These are the expected frequencies of winners from each post position ($f_e = 18$).

The formula for calculating χ^2 is:

$$\chi^2 = \Sigma \frac{(f_0 - f_e)^2}{f_e}$$

where

$$f_0 = \text{Frequency of observed winners}$$
$$f_e = \text{Frequency of expected winners}$$

To calculate χ^2 the difference between the number of actual winners and the expected number of winners is obtained for each of the eight post positions. This value is squared and divided by the frequency of the expected winners. The eight resulting values are summed to obtain χ^2. In this example:

$$\chi^2 = \frac{121}{18} + \frac{1}{18} + \frac{0}{18} + \frac{49}{18} + \frac{1}{18} + \frac{64}{18} + \frac{9}{18} + \frac{49}{18} = \frac{294}{18} = 16.3$$

The probability of a χ^2 equal to or greater than 16.3 can be obtained from an appropriate table. Selecting a significance level of 0.05, a decision can be made about whether these results indicate that starting position affects the chance of winning a horse race. Since, like t, there are a number of different distributions, we must first decide which χ^2 distribution is appropriate.

The race track had eight starting positions. The expected number of winners was used to calculate χ^2. The expected value (18) was based on the fact that the total number of winners was 144. This means that the number of observed winners must total 144, which is a restriction on the observed scores. Because statistical tests of significance provide probabilities that are based on chance alone, the numbers used in calculating the test statistic must be independent observations. Even though eight numbers were used in this study, only seven of them were independent because their total must equal 144. Once you know the value of any seven of the eight winners from the various starting positions, the eighth number is determined by the fact that they must sum to 144. The number of independent scores in a test of significance is called the *degrees of freedom*. In this example, there are seven independent values, or degrees of freedom.

The probability of obtaining a value of 16.3 for a χ^2 with seven degrees of freedom falls beyond 14.067 ($p = 0.05$) (see Figure 7.6), which means that this result is significant at the 0.05 level. That is, it would occur fewer than 5 times in 100 in a race track where post position was unrelated to winning.

The only conclusion that can be made is that the statistical hypothesis (H_0) is not true. This means that the frequency of winners (f_o) is not the same for each starting, or post, position. Which position is better, or worse, cannot be identified with confidence from this analysis. Practically, a significant result indicates that the difference between the highest position (the first) and the lowest position (the sixth) is probably significant, but the χ^2 test does not show that. In the long run, the number of winners in the first five positions may be essentially the same, whereas those in positions six through eight may be lower. Or, starting in either position six or eight may put the horse at a disadvantage, but starting in one through five or seven does not. To test differences between the number of winners in specific post positions or groups of post positions requires additional analyses. Specific tests applicable to various situations are described by Siegel (1956), Hays (1973), and others listed at the end of the chapter.

In many studies a researcher compares three or more treatments, such as phonics, meaning, and an eclectic method for teaching reading. The results of three such treatments cannot be analyzed at once with either the z or t distributions. In the 1930s Sir Ronald Fisher (1935) developed the analysis of variance to compare the outputs of agricultural plots with various combinations of fertilizers and other additions to the soil. He figured out the sampling distributions of results that would occur by chance alone under various conditions. These are called F distributions in honor of Fisher.

The logic of the analysis of variance is based on the fact that numbers obtained in a study will tend to vary from one another, both within a treatment and across treatments. To calculate the probability that a given set of results would occur by chance alone, if the treatments were in fact *not* different, Fisher di-

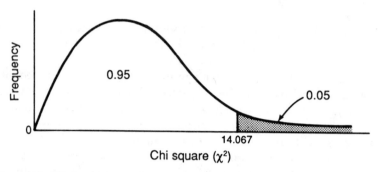

Figure 7.6. Chi Square Distribution with Seven Degrees of Freedom

vided the total variation that exists in a set of scores into that which can be attributed to the treatment that was implemented and that variation in the scores that is random variation, or error. If the treatments are not different, the average variation in the scores caused by treatment should be equal to the average variation in the scores that is random. The F distribution is essentially the ratio of these two numbers.

The way that this is done mathematically is relatively straightforward. Table 7.7 illustrates a study in which six people have been randomly assigned to three different treatments (A, B, and C). After the treatment has occurred, the six people are measured on the dependent variable, receiving the scores of 4, 6, 10, 12, 20, and 20. The variance in this set of scores can be calculated using a modified form of the variance formula:

$$S^2 = \frac{\Sigma(X_i - \overline{X})^2}{n - 1}$$

The denominator of the variance is changed from n to $n - 1$ to account for the fact that the mean is used to calculate the variance—that is, $\Sigma(X_i - \overline{X})^2$. This is called an unbiased estimate of the variance and is required to account for the dependencies in the data. As indicated earlier, when an auxiliary number such as a mean or total score is used in the calculation of a statistic in a test of significance, then the number of independent observations is decreased.

The squared deviations of the scores in the numerator in the previous formula can be divided into the variation caused by treatment and into random variation by adding and subtracting the means for each treatment group ($\overline{X}_G$) as follows:

$$\Sigma(X_i - \overline{X})^2{}_{\text{TOTAL}} = \Sigma(\overline{X}_G - \overline{X})^2{}_{\text{TREATMENT}} + \Sigma(X_i - \overline{X}_G)^2{}_{\text{ERROR}}$$

In this way the total variation is divided into the variation caused by treatment and into the error variation. These are the sums of the squared deviations, which are represented as SS_{TOTAL}, $SS_{\text{TREATMENT}}$, and SS_{ERROR}.

In this case, the squared deviations of the scores from the grand mean *(X)* are illustrated in the fourth column of Table 7.7. The SS$_{TOTAL}$, equals 232. The variation that can be attributed to the treatment each person received is represented in the fifth column as SS treatment, or the variation between groups, and is 228. The error variation is calculated in the last column as the variation within each treatment group, which is 4, the difference between 232 and 228.

In this contrived example, it should be clear that the variation in scores can be attributed almost totally to the treatment that was experienced. The variation in scores within each treatment is logically viewed as random, or error, variation in the scores because everyone in that group experienced the same treatment.

The F statistic is calculated using the following formula:

$$F = \frac{SS_{Tr}/df_{Tr}}{SS_E/df_E}$$

where

SS_{Tr} = sum of squared deviation due to treatment
SS_E = sum of squared deviations due to error
df_{Tr} = number of independent treatments minus one (1)
df_E = number of independent scores within treatments minus the number of treatments

The SS_{Tr} and SS_E are 228 and 4, respectively, as illustrated in Table 7.7. The df_{Tr} is based on the three treatment means: 5, 11, and 20. But these must have the same mean as the grand mean, so only two are independent. The df_E is based on all the individual scores in the three treatments, which is 6, but in each treatment their scores must equal the group mean $(\overline{X}_G)$. Thus, there is only one independent score in each of the three treatments. It can be calculated directly by subtracting the number of treatment means from the total number of scores (6 − 3) to obtain 3 independent scores, or df_E. The value of the F statistic in this example is:

$$F = \frac{228/2}{4/3} = \frac{114}{1.33} = 85.3$$

Because the numerator and denominator of F are expected to be the same when the null hypothesis, $\mu_A = \mu_B = \mu_C$, is precisely true, it should be obvious that large differences among the treatments are indicated in this study. The probability of an F of 85.3 with 2 and 3 degrees of freedom can be obtained from any table of F distributions. It is certainly significant at $\alpha = 0.01$.

These results are usually reported in an ANOVA table, such as Table 7.8. The first column, Source, indicates the source of the sum of squares (SS), which is listed in the second column. The third column usually lists the degrees of freedom (df) for each source. The SS divided by the df is called the

TABLE 7.7. ANALYSIS OF VARIANCE EXAMPLE WITH THREE GROUPS

Groups	X_i	$\overline{X}_a$	$(X_i - \overline{X})^2$	$(\overline{X}_a - \overline{X})^2$	$(X_i - \overline{X}_a)^2$
A	4	$\overline{X}_A = 5$	$(4 - 12)^2 = 64$	$(5 - 12)^2 = 49$	$(4 - 5)^2 = 1$
	6		$(6 - 12)^2 = 36$	$(5 - 12)^2 = 49$	$(6 - 5)^2 = 1$
B	10	$\overline{X}_B = 11$	$(10 - 12)^2 = 4$	$(11 - 12)^2 = 1$	$(10 - 11)^2 = 1$
	12		$(12 - 12)^2 = 0$	$(11 - 12)^2 = 1$	$(12 - 11)^2 = 1$
C	20	$\overline{X}_C = 20$	$(20 - 12)^2 = 64$	$(20 - 12)^2 = 64$	$(20 - 20)^2 = 0$
	20		$(20 - 12)^2 = 64$	$(11 - 12)^2 = 64$	$(20 - 20)^2 = 0$
$\overline{X} = 72/6 = 12$			$SS_{TOTAL} = 232$	$SS_{Tr} = 228$	$SS_E = 4$

mean square, MS. It is the ratio of the mean squares that is the value of the F statistic. Whether the result is significant at some level, such as 0.01, is indicated in every ANOVA table. In this case it is reported with a superscript a. The probability of obtaining these results in a study is often reported as a p value, such as $p < 0.05$. That is different from an α level, which is the significance level selected before any data are collected.

In each of these examples, the test statistic (z, t, and F) is a ratio of obtained difference, or variation, divided by an estimate of the chance, or random, difference in a set of scores. With z and t, the numerator is the difference between the obtained score and the hypothesized value $[(\overline{X} - \mu)$, or $(\overline{X}_1 - \overline{X}_2) - (\mu_1 - \mu_2)]$. The denominator in each case is an estimate of the random, or error, variation in the sampling of means from the hypothesized population ($\sigma/\sqrt{n}$, or $S_x/\sqrt{n}$) for z and t, respectively.

The numerator of χ^2 is the frequency of the observed minus the frequency of the expected, the quantity squared, $(f_o - f_e)^2$, which is the variation, or difference, of the obtained scores from those expected. The denominator is the expected frequency (f_e). When the obtained frequencies are large compared to the expected, or chance, value, the numerator of this statistic becomes relatively large, and the value of χ^2 becomes large. The larger the value of the statistic, the less likely that it would have occurred by chance alone. If it is unlikely to have occurred by chance alone under the conditions hypothesized, then we reject the hypothesized condition (H_0), and accept as tenable one that is consistent with the results obtained empirically in the study. All statistical tests of significance are based on this same logical process.

TABLE 7.8. ANOVA TABLE FOR EXAMPLE IN TABLE 7.7

Source	SS	df	MS	F
Treatment	228	2	114	85.3[a]
Within (Error)	4	3	1.33	
Total	232	5		

[a]$p < 0.01$

Role of Tests of Significance in Research

In an empirical study, the quality of the data, the characteristics of the sample, the conditions under which data are collected, and numerous other considerations affect both the confidence you have in conclusions reached in the study and their applicability in other settings. These two issues are based primarily on knowledge about and experience with the variables that exist in the two situations. Tests of statistical significance are only a decision rule to help the researcher (and the readers of the research) to decide whether the results indicate that a relationship exists among the variables studied—either in the situation studied or in other similar situations. It is simply another piece of descriptive information that should be useful when making that decision.

It is discouraging when only the results of the significance tests are reported in a study and the obtained values on the dependent, or outcome, variable are not included. Both the practical and the statistical significance of the obtained results are important for interpreting the meaning of a study, and these are often not synonymous. With very large sample sizes (100 or more), relatively small differences may be statistically significant, which may or may not have practical significance. It is also important to remember that means and standard deviations are averages that can occur in an infinite number of different ways. In most studies, the *types* of differences between two groups who experienced different treatments is more meaningful than the difference between means. For example, when we compared mean achievement of students in an individualized curriculum with that of students in traditional curricula, we found consistently statistically significant results in favor of those in the individualized curriculum. Many people thought the individualized program allowed more able students to move ahead more rapidly, as well as having other positive effects with average and low-achieving students. When we looked at the frequency distributions of the students' scores, we found that the bottom 25% of the group was affected most. There was no impact on the achievement scores of high-achieving students as a result of using the individualized curriculum. Simply applying standard data analytic methods to data, such as comparing the mean achievement of the two groups using the *t* test, may do as much to mislead as to inform. Mathematical operations do not produce truth. They are simply another tool to use in trying to understand human beings and their environments by analyzing and interpreting data.

Methodological concerns, such as the reliability and validity of data, controlling alternative explanations, and using statistical tests of significance, are primarily tools to keep us from misleading ourselves. Our belief in our hypotheses, theories, and ideologies are so strong that we can usually rationalize whatever empirical results that are obtained in a study in ways that keep those beliefs intact.

Assuring that variables are measured as accurately as possible, designing studies that allow fair and objective assessment of relationships among variables, and prespecifying the level of significance needed to gain support for our theories help to protect us from ourselves. Mitroff (1974) illustrated this human characteristic when he studied leading astronomers, astrophysicists, and other scientists before and after the first space vehicle returned from the Moon with samples of rocks. He found that the scientists whose theories were least supported by analysis of the rocks tended to cling most energetically to their theories.

You and I are no different. Methodological tools are there for us to use, but they are not magical nor should they be used dogmatically. Tests of significance provide an estimate of the likelihood that results obtained in a study would have occurred by chance alone—if the statistical hypothesis was precisely true. That is all that it provides, which is a very small part of the logical process of interpreting research results.

SUMMARY

Obtaining meaning from data is not a trivial activity in most situations. Methods for summarizing large amounts of data were illustrated and discussed. Frequency distributions, percentiles, means, medians, modes, quartile deviations, standard deviations, variances, and correlation coefficients provide different descriptions of a set of data. Graphs, such as frequency polygons, histograms, and pie charts, are useful in ferreting out meaning from data and succinctly communicating it to others.

The methods of data analysis that are most meaningful for different purposes and contexts were illustrated. One of the most harmful outcomes of past teaching of data analysis techniques has been the communication to students that there is one, and *only* one, "best" way to analyze data. In fact, each method of data analysis has strengths and weaknesses, and a combination of techniques is most informative.

The logic of inferential statistics and the meaning of probability were described and illustrated. Although highly mathematical and complex, tests of statistical significance provide *only* the likelihood that an obtained result would occur by chance alone *if* the statistical tests were *precisely* true. In most situations, this information can be used to test hypotheses or answer research questions. The process protects us from our natural tendency to interpret results of a study as supporting our theories and beliefs. In practice the assumptions are never precisely met, so researchers must interpret the results on the basis of all available evidence.

In Chapter 8 an example using both descriptive and inferential data is used to show how the researchers' purpose affects all elements of a study and to illustrate how the various types of information obtained in a study can be used to draw conclusions and make inferences. The principles illustrated transfer to other types of empirical studies.

SUGGESTED ACTIVITIES

1. From the population of scores in Table 7.6, randomly select 10 scores and calculate the mean. Repeat the process four more times. How much variation was there among the five means calculated? Were most of the sample means close to the population mean? Randomly select a sample of 20 scores from the same population and calculate the mean. Select two more samples of 20 (or more) and calculate the mean score for each. How variable are these means? How do they compare to the five means obtained above?

2. Calculate the means and medians for each of the following distributions of scores. Subtract the median from the mean in each case. How is that score related to the skewness of the distribution? (**Hint:** Drawing a graph would be useful.)

A	B	C	D	E
20	10	5	20	24
24	24	24	24	26
28	28	28	28	28
32	32	32	32	30
36	46	46	66	32

3. Place the following set of scores into a frequency distribution. Graph the distribution using (1) a frequency polygon, and (2) histogram.
   16, 18, 21, 17, 17, 19, 18, 20, 18, 19, 18, 20, 19, 18

4. Performance scores are given for an experimental group, (X_1), and a control group, (X_2). At the 5% level, using a two-tailed test, test the hypothesis of equal means of the populations from which the samples were drawn: $(t_{0.05} = 2.101)$.

Experimental Group (X_1)	Control Group (X_2)
11	8
6	4
7	6
8	8
11	9
7	5
8	6
9	7
7	4
6	3

5. In a study, first grade children were asked to identify the students being spoken to when the teacher says, "Sit up," or "Pay attention." Assuming the data had come out as below, calculate the χ^2 value and see if the difference is statistically significant at $\alpha = 0.05$.

	Boys	Girls	$(\chi^2_{0.05} = 3.841)$
Frequency of Selection	40	10	

HINT: The H_0 being tested is that there is no difference between the frequency with which boys and girls would be identified.

RELATED SOURCES

Bruning, J.L., & Kintz, B.L. (1977). *Computational handbook of statistics*. Glenview, IL: Scott, Foresman.

   This book is a fine companion for Jaeger's nonmathematical text. It provides in easy-to-follow steps the computational procedures for statistical techniques commonly used. The logic of the computational formulas is often not easy to follow. They provide "correct answers" with the fewest and easiest calculations.

Hays, William L. (1973). *Statistics for the social sciences* (2nd ed.). New York: Holt, Rinehart and Winston.

   One of the best reference books on statistical methods, this book includes both formulas and discussion of most statistical procedures. Some basic knowledge of statistics and the symbols used in the book are needed to use it successfully. It is only for those who desire an in-depth understanding of both the theoretical and mathematical bases of a statistical technique.

Jaeger, R.M. (1983). *Statistics: A spectator sport*. Beverly Hills, CA: Sage.

   Developed as a consumer's guide to statistics, this book contains no mathematical equations. It is designed for people who want to "learn what statistics are, what they mean, and how they are used." It covers the usual statistical topics: averages, variations, correlations, statistical inferences, estimation, one-way and two-way ANOVAs, and some advanced topics. It is a good book for master's level students who are reading empirical research. Other texts would be needed in order to do calculations, although computers do most calculations today.

Patton, M.Q. (1980). *Qualitative evaluation methods*. Beverly Hills, CA: Sage.

   Qualitative Evaluations Methods gives practical information on using qualitative methods. The author discusses conceptual issues, the collection of qualitative data, and data analysis. It is not a "how to" book but, rather, a book that proposes different ways to produce, understand, and interpret information for decision-making. The same basic principles apply to the use of such methods in research and the meaningful interpretation of qualitative data in other settings.

Siegel, S. (1956). *Nonparametric statistics for the behavioral sciences*. New York: McGraw-Hill.

   Nonparametric statistics are needed for research using small sample sizes (less than 25 to 30) or for research having variables that are not normally distributed in the population studied. Nonparametric statistics require no assumptions about population characteristics (or parameters). Each statistical technique is clearly explained in the book. The conditions required for its use and an example are provided for each statistical technique in the book. It can be used by relatively inexperienced researchers with little mathematics background, but it is more than a "how to" book. It is still the best single source of useful nonparametric statistical techniques despite its publication in the mid-1950s.

Tukey, John W. (1977). *Exploratory data analysis.* Reading, MA: Addison-Wesley.

Tukey describes new ways to analyze and interpret data to describe more comprehensively and meaningfully the variables that are measured. Classical methods, such as those presented in Chapter 7 of your text, emphasize hypothesis testing and single numbers such as means and standard deviations to describe a set of scores. Tukey emphasizes the shape of distributions, such as "stem and leaf" descriptions to describe groups of scores. This book is for more advanced students and requires more in-depth knowledge of mathematics.

REFERENCES

Barzun, J., & Graff, H.F. (1985). *The modern researcher* (4th ed.). San Diego: Harcourt Brace Jovanovich.

Fisher, R. (1935). *The design of experiments.* New York: Hafner.

Getzels, J. (1978). Paradigm and practice: On the impact of basic research on education. In P. Suppes (Ed.), *Impact of research on education* (477–521). Washington, DC: National Academy of Education.

Hays, W. L. (1973). *Statistics for the social sciences* (2nd ed.). New York: Holt, Rinehart and Winston.

Lee, A. (1971). The child in pedagogy and culture: Concepts of American preadolescence as revealed in teaching theories and as related to the culture, 1900–1914. In I. J. Lehmann & W. A. Mehrans (Eds.), *Educational research: Readings in focus.* New York: Holt, Rinehart and Winston.

Mitroff, I.I. (1974). *The subjective side of science: A philosophical inquiry into the psychology of Apollo moon scientists.* Amsterdam: Elsevier.

Seigel, S. (1956). *Nonparametric statistics for the behavioral sciences.* New York: McGraw-Hill.

Thorndike, E. L. & Woodworth, R. S. (1901). The influence of improvement in one mental function upon the efficiency of other functions. *Psychology review, 8,* 247–261.

CHAPTER 8

Interpreting Results of a Study

INTEGRATED NATURE OF A STUDY

As indicated in the first seven chapters of this book, the quality of a study depends on the following aspects of the study and the interrelationships among them:

1. Identifying a problem that is at the forefront of knowledge in a particular type of setting.
2. Specifying the problem statement and research questions, or hypotheses, that are the most important aspects of this problem and that can be meaningfully addressed with data at this time.
3. Selecting an appropriate setting and sampling of subjects that are representative of the population and setting to which the researcher wants to generalize.
4. Identifying or developing instruments and procedures to gather the most appropriate data for addressing the problem and for fulfilling the researcher's purpose for doing the study. The instruments and procedures must be those that provide the greatest confidence in the conclusions and their generalizability to other settings.
5. Organizing and analyzing the data in the most appropriate ways to answer the research questions and knowledge needs that the audience has in the context studied.
6. Using appropriate methods of statistical analyses (and tests of significance, when needed) so that results are reported as accurate and objective as possible.

7. Making accurate and appropriate interpretations of the findings of the study.

Even though this is a rudimentary list of important aspects of a study, it should be clear that the quality and value of a study depend on *every* aspect. Their relative importance will vary from one study to another, but all must be met at some minimal level in any study. In some studies, additional issues may arise; these seven aspects are minimal. The purpose of this list is simply to identify important aspects of a study that affect its quality or value. The important point is that the interrelationships among the various aspects of a study, if it is to be a good educational study, are an integrated whole.

That point must be kept in mind when learning methodological principles (such as in measurement, research design, statistics) or other data analytic techniques (such as content analysis, hermeneutic interpretation, or processes for "bracketing" educational phenomena). The various procedures have different strengths and weaknesses. When procedures are taught in the abstract, students often learn that only the most powerful methods should be used; even more troubling, they learn that good research cannot be done when weaker or more subjective methods are used. The important words in the list of seven important aspects of a study are "most appropriate for the purpose of the study."

In reading a study, it is important to examine carefully the purpose, the problem, the research questions (or hypotheses), the setting, the sampling, the data-gathering instruments and procedures, the organization and analysis of data, and the interpretation of results. Interpretation is not as important as the others, in the sense that if you understand the principles on which the study is based (the first six items of those previously listed), you can make the most appropriate interpretations of the study—even if the author did not.

ANALYZING AND INTERPRETING QUANTITATIVE DATA

Some important principles in interpreting quantitative data, particularly when tests of significance are used, are needed before examining how the interrelationships among the various aspects of a study affect the interpretation of the findings. After the data are collected in a study the researcher analyzes them as preplanned in the proposal and derives frequencies, means, medians, standard deviations, and other summaries of the data. These data and associated summaries are the findings in a study. They indicate the extent to which the theories or beliefs on which the study is based describe the situation studied. The data usually show differences on most variables studied, such as the achievement of males and females, or phonics versus meaning approaches to reading. These differences must be analyzed to see if they represent meaningful differences, and interpreted in order to answer the problem statement or to increase our knowledge about the relationships among variables in a situation studied—such as in an ethnographic or historical study.

The concept of precision, or accuracy, of a number is not generally under-stood. We all have the general notion that there is some error involved in any measurement process, particularly in measurements of such human characteris-tics or behaviors as IQ, math achievement, "ego," or attitudes toward education. Yet, when numbers are obtained from individual measures or in studies, they are often viewed as being precisely accurate. For example, if Bobby's IQ score is 115 and Erin's score is 113, many people would conclude that Bobby's IQ is higher than Erin's. That conclusion is not legitimate in either daily life or in empirical research. The error involved in any IQ test is such that differences of a few IQ points on the measure would be likely to occur quite often (60% of the time or more) on repeated testing. The most accurate interpretation of these two scores is that they represent similar IQ levels for Bobby and Erin. The normal distribution is used to indicate when two IQ scores are likely to indicate real differences in a person's "true" IQ.

In a similar manner, various pollsters obtain on a regular basis the attitudes or opinions of the American public about such topics as their satisfaction with the U.S. president or with public education. When problems arise, such as the huge drop in the stock market that occurred in October 1987, they have an im-pact on the attitudes toward the president or confidence in the economy that can be assessed by the pollsters. If 52% of the public were satisfied with President Reagan before the stock market drop and 49% were satisfied with him after the drop, does that mean that the American public had lower satisfaction after the drop? To answer that question, a number of concepts must be kept clearly in mind. First are the characteristics of the variables and the subject that may lead to errors. In this case, there is no way to know whether a person is satisfied with the U.S. president. All we can obtain is their self-report of their satisfaction. Many variables affect a person's willingness, or ability, to report their satisfaction accurately. For example, if a person has just expressed to a friend or spouse un-happiness with the economy and the government, that person is more likely to report to a pollster a level of satisfaction that is lower than it really is. If the person has just received a raise or gotten a new job, or if other positive things have happened, then the pollster is likely to receive a report that is more positive than it really should be.

A second consideration is the error involved in the measurement process itself. Two kinds of errors are likely to occur in any measurement: systematic and random. Systematic errors arise from the way that the question was worded, the context in which the question was asked, or other reactive aspects of the data-gathering process that might have affected the responses given. If the question was worded as, "Given the recent drop in the stock market, how satisfied are you with the performance of President Reagan?," the introductory phrase would point out something negative and respondents would tend to report lower levels of satisfaction. Stopping people on street corners during a hurried lunch hour or interrupting their family life when they are busy at home also tend to lower reported levels of satisfaction. Such characteristics of the interviewer as gender, size, and dress can affect responses.

When concerned with changes in satisfaction, as we are in this case, rather than in the precise level of satisfaction, these systematic errors will be less important if the wording of the question, the procedures used in gathering the data, and the characteristics of the interviewer are the same in both situations. The consistency controls their effects for the use that is made of the data. Even though the precise percentages, 52% and 49%, may be too low or too high because of systematic error in the procedures, the nature and degree of the systematic error should be approximately the same because the same procedures were used both times.

In additon to the systematic error, random error occurs in any measure. This type of error is usually estimated in any measurement process and is reported with the results. Most polling results tend to report about a 3-point error. Assuming that the errors are approximately normally distributed (which they may not be), the difference between 52% and 49% is only 3%—the same as the error of measurement. That means that there is more than a 30% chance that these two results could have come from populations that have essentially the same level of satisfaction. In this hypothetical example, it is unlikely that the levels of satisfaction of the American people actually differed before and after the 1987 drop in the stock market. The difference of only 3 percentage points is not enough to have confidence that the actual levels of satisfaction with the president decreased after the drop in the stock market.

On the other hand, the evidence was in the direction that we would expect and provides no support for the hypothesis that satisfaction increased. The difference of 3 percentage points, although in the direction expected, was not large enough to conclude with confidence that the satisfaction of the U.S. population had gone down.

In a similar manner, the actual data in a study must be examined carefully and thoughtfully—even when a test of significance was carried out. If a study of two methods of teaching fifth-grade mathematics results in a difference between the two means of six items on a 40-item achievement test, that is a meaningful difference in math achievement. If that difference is *not* significant at the 0.05 level, the researcher should identify the reason(s) why such a large difference was not significant. It may be a result of one or two unusually high or low scores in each group, or to consistently wide variation in the scores of individuals in one or both groups.

When a test of significance shows that the differences obtained in a study, such as the six items on the 40-item test mentioned earlier, would occur fewer than five times in a hundred (0.05) by chance alone if the statistical hypothesis was precisely true, it is important to know *how* that 6-point difference was obtained. A mean difference of 6 points between two groups, such as in the math example, could be obtained many different ways. For example, a few top students in one group could have obtained extremely high scores, or a few low-achieving students in the other group could have obtained extremely low scores. When there are large differences between two groups, most of us have a tendency to think that the increased achievement was obtained by most, or all, students in the higher group—such as in the ANOVA problem in Chapter 7, where scores for Treatment *A* were 4 and 6, for *B*, 10 and 12, and for *C*, 20 and 20. Seldom do such consistent results occur in any data-gathering process. What actually occurred in the situation studied must be understood as completely as possible in order to make accurate, meaningful interpretations of the results.

In education, the overall effects of an instructional strategy or specific curriculum materials on academic achievement, as represented only by a mean for the entire group who experienced the strategy or materials, is not very useful generally. Seldom do high-achieving and low-achieving students show similar outcomes from educational processes. Again, one method or approach has particular strengths and weaknesses. One approach is never terrific in all ways, nor is the other one consistently inferior. The goal of research should be to clarify the relative strengths and weaknesses, rather than to set up studies that are supposed to show which method is best.

In studies conducted with Individually Prescribed Instruction (IPI), for example, we found that the mean achievement gains for students who used IPI was consistently higher in grades 1 through 3 than the mean achievement of students using traditional basal tests and group instruction. When these results were examined with frequency distributions, it was clear that the major impact was on the lowest-achieving group (Eichelberger, 1974). This was an important finding because these are the students who are most at risk in our educational system. It was not the effect that most supporters of individualized instruction expected, however. If we had examined only the means for the two groups, these people would have continued to assume that the effects of IPI were consistent for students at all achievement levels.

Thus, an important consideration for interpreting results in a study is to assure yourself that the findings are reported at a level of specificity that accurately represents what is most relevant to the professional or academic group most affected or concerned by the results. In reading the study, look carefully to see whether the procedures and results are reported in enough detail to identify the relationships among variables that are most relevant to concerns in this setting. The data from a study should represent the state of nature in the setting studied and are the best estimate of the relationship among important variables. The analyses that are carried out on the data serve to further identify or clarify the extent of the relationships among the variables that are likely to occur in similar settings.

STUDY EXAMPLE AND INTERPRETATION

The following example is used to illustrate the importance of integrating the many parts of a study into a tight, logical whole that is focused on the researcher's purpose. In the example, educators' perceptions of differences between a previous pull-out supplementary reading program for elementary school students with reading problems and the present in-class program were obtained. The changes in roles and activities of both the reading specialists and classroom teachers, particularly those viewed as important to effective functioning of reading specialists, were investigated. The relative strengths and weaknesses of the two approaches were examined to help those involved in, or contemplating, a change from a pull-out to an in-class use of the reading specialist. This national issue was of concern to most educators responsible for the supplementary reading programs.

EXAMPLE 6   ANALYZING AND INTERPRETING QUANTITATIVE DATA (BEAN AND EICHELBERGER STUDY)

Changing the Role of Reading Specialists: From Pull-out to In-class Programs*

The role of reading specialists is affected by a number of factors, such as size and type of school, personality of the individual specialist, even financial exigencies. Perhaps a useful perspective is to consider the role on a continuum: On one end, the specialist has immediate and direct contact with students; on the other, the specialist serves only as a resource to teachers.

Although various groups—teachers, administrators, and specialists themselves—have different perceptions about the amount of time the specialist should devote to student instruction versus resource responsibility (Pikulski & Ross, 1979; Mangieri & Heimberger, 1980), several authors recommend that specialists work with both students and teachers (Garry, 1974; Bean, 1979; McMurtrie & Askov, 1982). Most reading specialists, however, emphasize instruction with students who are removed from the classroom to receive supplemental reading instruction in a "pull-out" program. In this type of program, specialists generally have little time for contact with teachers.

The research concerning the effectiveness of the pull-out program is equivocal and limited, and there is some criticism and concern about the effects of separate programs on achievement and emotional and social outcomes (Glass & Smith, 1977; Bean & Wilson, 1981; Leinhardt & Pallay, 1982). Indeed, there appears to be a trend to encourage direct instruction with students in the classroom in what can be called an in-class program.

Most of these in-class programs are voluntary—specialists work in the classroom on teacher request and on an informal basis. There is little empirical data about the effectiveness of such programs or their strengths and weaknesses.

---

*This article was written by Rita M. Bean and R. Tony Eichelberger and appeared in the March 1985 issue of *The Reading Teacher*, pp. 648–653. Reprinted with permission.

An opportunity to study the role of the specialist in an in-class program arose when a large city school district changed from a pull-out program to one in which the specialists worked with students in the classroom under the direction of the classroom teacher. The change was based on the beliefs that (1) more cooperation between classroom teachers and reading specialists would occur, (2) continuity between the developmental program and the remedial program would increase, (3) classroom teachers would benefit professionally from the close interaction with the reading specialists, and (4) greater student achievement in reading would result.

In this context, the present study was carried out. Its purpose was to identify the changes in roles and activities of reading specialists in the in-class program as compared to the previous pull-out program, the roles and associated activities that reading specialists and classroom teachers viewed as important to the effective functioning of reading specialists, and the strengths and weaknesses of the in-class program.

Data Collection Procedures

Questionnaires distributed near the end of the first year of the in-class program were returned by 74 reading specialists and 411 classroom teachers from 105 elementary, middle, and secondary schools. Responses from teachers and reading specialists in 22 parochial schools were included. The return rate was approximately 90% for both reading specialists and teachers.

Respondents indicated the emphasis given to various functions or role activities both during the in-class year and during the previous year's pull-out program. They also indicated on a third scale the importance of that function or activity. Each scale ranged from 0 (no emphasis or importance) to 3 (great deal of emphasis or importance).

The 30 descriptors of the reading specialist's role included items pertaining to four categories: student-related functions (diagnosis and instruction), resource-role functions (feedback to teachers, conducted inservice), administrative functions (developing budgets, writing proposals for funding, evaluating teachers), and curriculum development functions (writing curriculum). Descriptors that identified the types of students with whom specialists might work (the gifted, the average, and those with reading problems) were also included.

In addition to the scale described here, respondents answered several open-ended questions on their views about the most and least important role for reading specialists and their perceptions about the strengths and weaknesses of the in-class program.

We conducted follow-up interviews with 10 reading specialists and 13 classroom teachers from seven schools (four elementary and three middle schools) in order to understand better what the reading specialists did and to interpret the questionnaire responses accurately. School district administrators selected representative schools in which we conducted the interviews.

TABLE 8.1 MEAN RESPONSE OF READING SPECIALISTS AND CLASSROOM
TEACHERS TO ROLE EMPHASES DURING IN-CLASS AND PULL-OUT PROGRAMS

	Reading Specialists			Classroom Teachers		
	In-Class Role	*Pull-Out*	*t Values*	*In-Class Role*	*Pull-Out*	*t Values*
Diagnostic role	1.82	2.46	5.58[a]	1.85	2.17	6.00[a]
Remediation with individuals	1.91	2.12	1.75	2.09	2.32	4.22[a]
Remediation with groups	2.54	2.69	1.60	2.21	2.39	3.57[a]
Specific skills teaching	2.09	2.58	4.11[a]	1.91	2.12	3.50[a]
Working with gifted child	0.30	0.14	−1.27	0.35	0.31	−1.67
Working with average child	0.87	0.78	−1.10	0.88	0.81	−2.31
Working with child with reading problems	2.88	2.91	1.00	2.56	2.57	0.16
Providing feedback to classroom teachers	2.19	2.03	−1.43	1.75	1.60	−2.90[a]
Working with content teachers	1.56	1.08	−4.61[a]	1.68	1.31	−6.98[a]
Resource role	1.12	0.95	−2.49	1.08	1.01	−2.09

[a]Significant at $p < 0.05$.

Results

The results of this study, based upon questionnaire responses and interviews, are
divided into three parts: changes in role of reading specialists, perceived importance of various activities, and strengths and weaknesses of the in-class program.

Changes in role emphasis. During the year in which the pull-out program
operated, the specialists reported that they gave their greatest emphasis to the
following student-related functions (see Table 8.1): diagnosis (2.46), remediation
with individuals (2.12) and groups (2.69), and teaching specific skills (2.58). They
focused on working with children experiencing difficulty with reading (2.91)
rather than with the average or gifted student. The specialists also reported that
they gave some emphasis (2.03) to providing feedback to classroom teachers.

Classroom teachers concurred with these perceptions with one exception:
They had perceived less feedback from the specialists (1.60).

When comparing the performance of specialists in their in-class roles with
the previous year's pull-out program, specialists indicated significant changes
($p < 0.05$) in three of their functions: less emphasis on both diagnosis and teaching specific skills in this new in-class role and more emphasis on working with
content teachers. The specialists perceived no differences in the type of students
with whom they worked: that is, they still spent more of their time working with
students experiencing reading difficulties.

Teacher responses also indicated significant changes in the specialists' role: less emphasis on diagnosis, individual and group remediation, and teaching specific skills; more emphasis on working with content teachers and on giving feedback to classroom teachers.

Interview data from specialists from five schools supported a decrease in emphasis on diagnosis in the in-class program. In one school, however, specialists indicated that diagnosis was more effective because of more teacher input; in another school, respondents indicated no change. Note that schools varied somewhat in their implementation of the in-class program because of the different physical and curricular structures, and therefore some differences in emphasis would be expected.

Data from the interviews indicated that reading specialists spent more time teaching groups and less time with individuals during the in-class program. A change in the type of instruction was evident: less use of audiovisual materials, less oral or choral reading and other instructional methods that might create noise in the classroom and affect the functioning of the teacher. Fewer supplementary materials common in a pull-out program were used. Many specialists saw their role as that of reinforcing skills taught by the teachers and used worksheets and practice materials similar to those used by the classroom teachers. Several reading specialists mentioned that difficulties with transporting materials from classroom to classroom also affected the choice of instructional materials.

Although during both years the specialists perceived themselves as giving more feedback to classroom teachers then did teachers, both groups indicated that reading specialists provided more feedback during the in-class program.

Relative importance of reading specialist functions. Information about how specialists and teachers perceived the specialists' various functions was obtained in two ways: Items on the questionnaire asking respondents to indicate the amount of emphasis they felt should be given to each function, and open-ended questions in which respondents indicated the five most important and five least important functions of the specialists.

Teachers and specialists agreed on the five most important functions for the reading specialists: diagnosis, remediation with individuals and groups, teaching specific skills, working with children with reading difficulties, and providing feedback to teachers. Note that four of the five most highly valued functions were student-centered, with one resource-role function listed.

Both groups identified the following four functions as least important: developing reading budgets, evaluating teachers' performance, writing proposals, and working with the gifted. Three roles are administrative, and the fourth is student-centered. Teachers and specialists differed on one function: Reading specialists mentioned disseminating current research findings as a least important function, while teachers listed conducting inservice workshops. Both functions fall within the resource-role category. Overall, teachers and specialists held similar views about the value of the various functions of reading specialists.

Strengths and weaknesses of the in-class program. Teacher interaction and cooperation, the possibility of individualized instruction, and small class sizes were identified by both teachers and specialists as strengths of the in-class program. Both groups also reported increased interaction and cooperation in planning and teaching.

The primary weakness resulted from two teachers sharing the classroom: space problems and differences in teaching style or instructional strategies used. Teachers reported problems with scheduling and inadequate joint planning times. Reading specialists listed lack of teacher interaction, ambiguity of their role, lack of inservice training, insufficient materials, inadequate management, and difficulty in transporting materials.

Conclusions

Although this study is limited by the fact that the in-class program had been in existence for only one year, we can draw several conclusions. Indeed, the high percentage of questionnaire returns and consistency of responses lends credence to these conclusions.

1. Reading specialists changed the manner in which they functioned when they worked in the classroom. Specialists focused more on reinforcing skills taught by the classroom teachers than on diagnosing skill needs. The instructional program then was more focused, despite some concern about the appropriateness of teaching strategies and materials. There was also more emphasis on giving feedback to and working with teachers.

2. Teachers and specialists both valued the specialists' role as it is currently defined, that is, an instructional position in which specialists focus on working with students with reading problems. Neither group saw the reading specialist primarily as a resource to the classroom teacher, although both groups valued having interaction about specific children.

3. Problems in instituting an in-classroom program fell into two categories. Conceptually, both specialists and teachers had difficulty with two instructors in one room, and the problem of leadership, or control, became a real issue. The notion of teaming did not appear to be easy to accept.

Program implementation also created problems, especially in the areas of definition of role functions for teachers and specialists, scheduling, transportation of materials, and use of space.

Because the in-class program has potential for developing a more consistent, focused program for students and for increasing the efficiency and effectiveness of instruction, we support the notion. However, an in-class program is apparently not easy to institute. Therefore, we would like to discuss some issues that we believe must be addressed by any school district in developing an in-class program.

1. **Preparation of staff.** Reading specialists, teachers, and administrators must be aware of the possible advantages and problems in an in-class program, and must consider whether specialists and teachers have the necessary training. The specific functions of each group must be clearly specified. Staff development efforts may be necessary to help personnel grapple with the changes in role definition and functioning.

2. **Degree of implementation.** Although we believe that an in-class program has many advantages for students, some balance between an in-class and pull-out program might be useful. For example, specialists may need the flexibility to conduct diagnosis and some students may benefit from intensive one-to-one or small group instruction away from the classroom.

3. **Instructional concerns.** New programs should maintain the instructional practices, such as identification of specific needs, direct instruction, appropriate pacing, and small instructional groups, which have been effective. In other words, although both specialists and teachers would be working on agreed-upon objectives, both need to use the most appropriate strategies or materials, and this necessitates a schedule that provides for joint planning. The lack of joint planning time may be one of the greatest deterrents to successful implementation of an in-class program.

In summary, we think the trend toward an in-class program is an important one that will have a great deal of impact on reading achievement of students. Furthermore, in-class programs may require alterations in the training of reading specialists. Continued investigation of the roles of the specialists, ways in which they are effective, and the relationship between those various roles and student learning must accompany the implementation of a new role for the reading specialist.

References

Bean, Rita M. (January 1979). Role of the reading specialist: A multifaceted dilemma. *The Reading Teacher, 32*, 409–413.

Bean, Rita M., & Wilson, R. M. (1981). *Effecting change in school reading programs: The resource role.* Newark, DE: International Reading Association.

Garry, V.V. (May 1974). Competencies that count among reading specialists. *Journal of Reading, 17*, 608–613.

Glass, Gene, & Smith, Mary Lee. (1977). *Pull-out in compensatory education,* ED 160 723. Arlington, VA: ERIC Document Reproduction Service.

Leinhardt, Gaea, & Pallay, Allan. (Winter 1982). Restrictive educational settings: Exile or haven? *Review of Educational Research, 52*, 557–578.

Mangieri, John, & Heimberger, Mary. (March 1980). Perceptions of the reading consultant's role. *Journal of Reading, 23*, 527–530.

McMurtrie, Ronna, & Askov, Eunice. (October 1982). Role of the reading specialist: A state-wide survey of Pennsylvania reading specialists, reading supervisors, principals, classroom teachers, and administration. Report to the Keystone State Reading Association Delegates' Assembly.

Pikulski, John J., & Ross, Elliot. (November 1979). Classroom teachers' perceptions of the role of the reading specialist. *Journal of Reading, 23,* 126–135.

A study should begin with the background of the problem that is investigated. The specific purpose for the study should also be clear. Bean and Eichelberger immediately identify the central focus of the study: the role of the reading specialist. They use a continuum to view the role of the reading specialist from immediate and direct contact with the student to serving only as a resource to the teacher. This allows the work of previous authors and researchers to be placed, generally, relative to one another. The expected benefits of an in-class program are listed. These beliefs, or hypotheses, are often the basis for a study, but in this case they serve only to set the context for the study. The specific framework used to conceptualize and plan the study were the four functions that the reading specialist is to fulfill as derived from previous literature: (1) student-related, (2) resource role, (3) administrative, and (4) curriculum development functions. The logic of the study is that by carrying out those functions that are most important to the effective operation of the reading specialist, the in-class program will result in the following four hypothesized outcomes:

1. More cooperation between classroom teachers and reading specialists.
2. Increased continuity between the developmental program and the supplementary program.
3. Professional benefits to the teacher from close interaction with the reading specialist.
4. Greater student achievement in reading.

The 30 descriptors that are classified into four functions should have direct implications for the likelihood that the in-class supplementary reading program, as implemented in these schools, will result in these outcomes. The problem statement that is implied, but never stated, is: Does the change from a pull-out to in-class supplementary reading program result in changes that improve the quality of reading instruction?

The specific research questions studied were, operationally, the perceived differences between the pull-out and in-class programs on the 30 descriptors of reading specialists' activities, as the results for the 10 reported in Table 8.1 indicate. These results were interpreted both individually and in terms of the four functions in order to indicate which perspectives of the relative merits of the pull-out and in-class models seem to be most accurate. The specific information is needed by the educators responsible for supplementary reading programs so that they can plan the most effective program possible. If the data had been combined, or aggregated, so that results were reported only for the four functions, practitioners would not be able to use the information as readily. The more general information may be adequate for addressing theoretical issues of which theory or perspective on supplementary remedial programs most accurately represents the reading specialist's role in pull-out and in-class programs.

The use of questionnaires and interviews to gather the data, rather than observation of the activities, requires several assumptions to be met if we are to interpret the perceptions of the teachers and reading specialists who responded as accurate reflections of the differences in the reading specialist's role in the two settings. One of the most important assumptions is that the teachers and reading specialists know the extent to which they are presently carrying out these activities as part of the in-class program, and that they can remember the extent to which they carried them out in the previous year during the pull-out program. A second assumption is that they will report this information honestly on the questionnaire and in the interview. On an individual case, a teacher or reading specialist will probably not remember precisely or always report accurately. In the study they were required only to rank each activity on a 4-point scale from 0 (no emphasis) to 3 (a great deal of emphasis). Confidence in the data is gained when the ratings of the various activities are consistent, both within the groups of reading specialists and teachers and across both groups.

Other aspects that affect the decision to use questionnaires and interviews is that observation of the pull-out program in the prior year was not possible. Comparing two similar school districts, or the same district during two years when they change from a pull-out to in-class program could be valuable, but it would be extremely costly. In addition, many of the important aspects of a reading specialist's role are complex and not amenable to direct observation. Other activities, such as planning with teachers and providing feedback to teachers, could occur in various settings on an irregular schedule. They could even occur as teachers and reading specialists commute to school together.

The important issue in any study is the extent to which the data-gathering process produces information that you can be confident represents what you want it to represent. Because the focus is on the differences in the two education settings that should affect the quality of reading instruction received by students, the use of teachers' and reading specialists' perceptions may be the best data that could be obtained about those processes. The fact that many of these professionals have worked for many years, using different types of materials and instructional methods, in different schools and social settings, under different administrations and principals, gives them a strong foundation on which to make judgments and associated ratings about the relative emphasis of the various roles and activities in the two settings. The questionnaire was developed so that the 30 activities and roles were as clear to the respondents as we could make them. In addition to the consistency of the responses on the questionnaires, the results of the many interviews provided a context in which errors or misunderstandings

could be identified. The general agreement among the various group of participants *on the differences between the two settings*, which was the focus of the
study, generated more confidence that those differences were real. The fact that
more than 90% of both teachers and reading specialists completed the questionnaire is also reassuring that the results accurately reflect the differences between
the two settings.

It is important to point out that there is no requirement that the data be
true, or that there be no error in the measurement or data-gathering process. All
that is needed is the confidence that the data are adequate to document, at some
level of probability, that the conclusions made in a study are accurate reflections
of the relationships among the variables that existed in the situation studied. In
this case, for example, that conclusion was that reading specialists focused more
on reinforcing skills taught by the classroom teacher and less on diagnosing student skill needs during the in-class program.

The data were reported primarily in a single table that included the primary
activities and roles of the reading specialists and the degree of emphasis given to
them during the pull-out and in-class programs. The reasons for reporting the
results at this level of specificity should be clear from previous review of the
purpose, problem, audience, and context for which the study was done. Reporting results for all 30 of the descriptors might have provided even more detailed
information, but authors must make choices about which findings are most relevant and best reflect the important conclusions that can be drawn from a study.
A reader can contact the primary author of an article, who will usually be happy
to share the more complete results. Most researchers are flattered when someone
finds their work valuable and are eager to communicate with other professionals
who are seriously interested in learning more about the problems that interest
them.

The results in Table 8.1 include both the mean rating (the actual outcomes)
and the tests of significance used to help in identifying those differences that are
most likely to represent actual differences in the pull-out and in-class programs.
The means represent both the direction and the amount of change that the reading specialists and teachers perceived as occurring in the two settings. In the
interpretation of data, it is often useful to keep in mind that if the data were
entirely comprised of error and there were no differences between the two situations on the dimensions studied, there would be no consistency in either the
amount or direction of the differences in means. Differences would occur, but
we would expect the differences to be relatively small and inconsistent.

Given that knowledge, results such as those in Table 8.1 would be perused
to identify the largest differences between the pull-out and in-class programs.
When a relatively large difference is identified, such as the change in the diagnostic role from 2.46 to 1.82 reported by reading specialists, the ratings of the
teachers on that variable become very important. The fact that they report a
similar large change in the same direction (2.17 to 1.82) indicates that the
changes in the diagnostic role may be meaningful. The significant t values ($p <$
0.05) for the differences between the pull-out and in-class programs for both the

reading specialists (5.58) and the classroom teachers (6.00) provide additional evidence that this role has changed. The other differences between the means are reviewed and interpreted in a similar manner.

Two additional activities that changed significantly in the views of both the reading specialists and the teachers were (1) less emphasis on teaching specific skills to the students and (2) more emphasis on working with the content teacher. In terms of the relative importance of these two aspects of the reading specialists' role, which is addressed later in the article, the reading specialists' and teachers' ratings were still higher for teaching specific skills (2.09 and 1.91, respectively) than for working with content teachers (1.56 and 1.68).

Three other changes in the reading specialists' role as reported by teachers were also statistically significant. These were (1) decreased emphasis on remediation with individuals (2.32 to 2.09), (2) decreased remediation with groups (2.39 to 2.21), and (3) an increased emphasis on providing feedback to classroom teachers (1.60 to 1.75). In all three cases, the ratings of the reading specialists were nearly the same, both in amount and direction, but they were not significant. The fact that they perceived the same types of changes in their role as they moved from a pull-out to in-class role, supports the interpretation that such a change actually occurred.

But why were the changes in teachers' ratings significant, and why were similar or larger changes in ratings of reading specialists not significant? There are a number of reasons why such apparently inconsistent results would occur, all of which can be understood by reviewing the test of significance. The formula for the t statistic is:

$$ t = \frac{\overline{D}}{\sqrt{\dfrac{\Sigma D^2 - \dfrac{(\Sigma D)^2}{N}}{N(N-1)}}} $$

where

$$
\begin{aligned}
D &= \text{the difference in a person's two ratings (pull-out and in-class)} \\
\overline{D} &= \text{mean of the differences in ratings} \\
\Sigma D^2 &= \text{the sum of the squared difference scores} \\
N &= \text{the number of pairs of ratings.}
\end{aligned}
$$

The numerator of the t statistic in each case would be essentially the same for the changes in teachers' ratings and those of the reading specialists. The change in emphasis reported for providing feedback to classroom teachers, for example, was $1.60 - 1.75$, or -0.15 for teachers and $2.03 - 2.19$, or -0.16 for the reading specialists. The different values for the t statistic (-2.90 and -1.43) must depend on the value of the denominator, which is comprised of the variances of the differences of the ratings of each group for the emphasis given that role in the pull-out and in-class programs, and the number of teachers or reading specialists who responded to both the pull-out and in-class parts of the questionnaire. If the ratings of reading specialists had been much more variable, more very high and very low ratings, the variance of the differences in ratings, $\Sigma D^2 -$ $(\Sigma D)^2/N$, would be much larger, resulting in a larger value in the denominator. Dividing -0.16 by a larger number, such as 0.1118 for reading specialists rather than $.0517$ for teachers, would result in a smaller t value, such as -1.43 rather than -2.90 (see Table 8.1).

A larger value of the denominator would also occur if there were fewer reading specialists than teachers as there were in this study: 74 versus 411. If the variances of the two groups were essentially the same, the more subjects in a study, the smaller the denominator, or standard error of the mean differences, would be. That formula is:

$$\sqrt{\frac{\Sigma D^2 - \dfrac{(\Sigma D)^2}{N}}{N(N-1)}}$$

as indicated in the denominator.

In this study, the numerator of the standard error of the differences in ratings for the reading specialists was 67.52 and for the teachers was 450.41. The denominator for the reading specialists, which is based on the number of pairs of responses, or independent observations on which the statistics are based, is $N(N-1)$, or $74(74-1)$, which equals 5402. For the teachers it is 411 (410), which equals 168,510. This shows that the value of the t-statistic is greatly affected by the number of scores on which it is based. The calculation of the t-value for the reading specialists would be:

$$t = \frac{-0.16}{\sqrt{\dfrac{67.52}{74(73)}}} = \frac{-0.16}{\sqrt{0.0125}} = \frac{-0.16}{0.1118} = -1.43$$

Substituting the appropriate numbers in this formula for the 411 teachers results in a t value of -2.90, as indicated in Table 8.1.

The fact that the number of respondents, or scores, used in a test of significance affects the value of the t statistic is taken into account by the number of degrees of freedom (df). As larger samples are selected, the more likely it is that their mean will be closer to the population mean. This was described more precisely in the central limit theorem, which indicates that as sample size goes to infinity the sampling distribution of means becomes normal with a standard deviation $\sigma/\sqrt{n}$. As n becomes larger, the standard deviation of the sampling distribution gets smaller.

Therefore, the t value that would occur less than 0.05 with 73df is 1.99, whereas that for 410df is 1.97. These t values are not much different because both of these samples are relatively large. It is clear that larger sample sizes tend to result in larger t values, all other things being equal. When several thousand independent scores are obtained, very small differences from those hypothesized will be significant in most cases.

This gives rise to the two concepts of *statistical significance* and *practical significance*. Using an appropriate test of significance will usually provide a good estimate of the former, whereas knowledge of the raw scores and what they represent in terms of the knowledge, ability, attitude, or other dependent variable that is measured is needed to determine practical significance. Before addressing that issue directly, we should clarify the use of tests of significance.

Some researchers use the test of significance as a strict decision rule. That is, the only differences that can be identified as representing real differences are those that are found to be significant. This is a good basic foundation from which to work, but it is not a rule that should replace thought. Consistencies and inconsistencies that occur within the raw data or between different tests of significance are usually relevant. Given that each researcher is trying to learn as much as possible about a particular problem in a given context for a specific purpose, all results, significant and nonsignificant, that are relevant to that problem for that purpose must be analyzed carefully and interpreted comprehensively. That is what the authors tried to do in the present study, reporting both the mean ratings and the tests of significance.

In the initial reporting of results under "Changes in Role Emphasis," the aspects of their role that reading specialists reported as occurring in the pull-out program are listed in the order of mean ranking. No tests of significance were used to see which differences were large enough to be called significant. The ratings above 2.00, out of a possible 3.00, were listed as those given greatest emphasis. The order of importance was irrelevant to the authors and to the purposes of the study.

Next, the three significant changes in emphasis from pull-out to in-class on which both the reading specialists and teachers agreed were identified. In addition, the other three significant changes reported by teachers were listed. Consistencies and inconsistencies between those results and the interview results were then discussed to figure out the most appropriate interpretation of the study. For example, some interviewees indicated that there was less emphasis on diagnosis by the reading specialists but that the diagnoses were more accurate because of increased teacher participation. In another school there was no change in diagnosis.

Throughout the presentation of results, the authors used the mean ratings, tests of significance, and interview data to describe the changes that seemed to be occurring in the various schools. First, we report the level of emphasis given the various roles and how they changed. Then the relative importance of these activities are presented. The most important findings from these two areas are reported under, "Strengths and Weaknesses of the In-Class Program."

After analyzing and synthesizing all the data obtained in the study, the authors wrote three short paragraphs of conclusions that dealt with the major changes that occurred, the perceived importance of the reading specialists' role, and problems that arose in implementing the in-class program. These were viewed by the researchers as the most important results of the study for the audience and for the purpose for doing the study.

Given that purpose and the nature of the results, issues that persons responsible for planning or implementing an in-class program should address were delineated. These are not, strictly speaking, results of the study, nor are they implications based on the results alone. They deal with preparation of staff, degree of implementation, and instructional concerns. The one direct implication of the study was the last point made under "Instructional Concerns." That was, "The low level of emphasis on joint planning time must be viewed negatively if the two professionals are going to plan their individual activities to reinforce one another and help the students gain the skills."

The other suggestions were based more on the authors' expert judgment and interpretation of the many questionnaire and interview responses that stemmed from their knowledge and experience. This type of information can be extremely valuable in a profession. In administration journals, for example, administrators report their experiences, the lessons they think they learned from them, and what they would do if they were faced with a similar situation. Many complex aspects of a profession do not lend themselves to tight, formal experimentation or systematic study (Meade, 1988). What is important is to clearly identify results and conclusions based on the data-gathering instruments and associated analyses. When you as a researcher go beyond that systematic study and the legitimate conclusions based on them, you should make it clear to the reader (and to yourself), documenting the basis for such statements or recommendations.

Some research methodologists argue that researchers should stick strictly to the preplanned study, obtained data, and the appropriate conclusions based on these data. It is certainly important that the study clearly do these three things, but it would be a loss to us all if researchers did not share some of the insights they believe that they gained (with associated documentation of the basis for them), the modifications they would make if they were to repeat the study, and the issues that deserve very strong consideration by others who plan to do similar kinds of activities.

The conclusions that the researcher views as legitimate on the basis of the results of the study must be clearly separated from other points of interest to the reader. When everything is presented in an unorganized way, or when the researcher claims that the data "show" something that they clearly do not show, the value of the study is greatly decreased and the researcher and reader gain little from the extensive expenditure of time and other resources.

SUMMARY

Seven characteristics that affect the quality of a study that were addressed in previous chapters were listed. Some basic principles used when interpreting quantitative data were illustrated by Bean and Eichelberger (1985) in a study of pull-out and in-class use of reading specialists.

Ways in which the seven characteristics listed initially in the chapter are discussed in the study and rationales for the particular decisions that were made were presented. The roles that each characteristic played in the study and their interrelationships in terms of the quality and relevance of the study were discussed.

Differences between statistical significance and practical significance were presented as part of the rationale for using the descriptive results in addition to the results of the tests of significance. The ways in which all this information is used to draw conclusions and make recommendations were identified.

The roles of the various characteristics of a study are delineated in more detail and illustrated further in the next chapter. The content of the research report and ways that it is often structured are presented. Why specific content is included in particular sections of the report and how the parts relate are discussed and illustrated. Specific hints for writing a research report are also given.

SUGGESTED ACTIVITIES

1. Identify a problem area that is relevant to your area of specialization and experience.
   a. Identify a problem statement and associated research questions (*or* hypotheses) that would be useful in addressing the problem in that setting.
   b. Select the theoretical framwork(s) and associated disciplinary basis that would be most useful for investigating the problem. Briefly discuss your rationale for using this framework. Identify and discuss two assumptions that must be made to use this theory for this particular purpose.
   c. Identify the specific research approach(es)° and associated methods of data collection that you would use to study the problem in a selected setting. Discuss your rationale for choosing both the setting and the research procedures.
   d. Specify the information that you would use to answer *each* of your research questions (or hypotheses). List two assumptions that you must make to use the data in this way, and indicate why these assumptions are necessary.
   e. Indicate the primary strengths and weaknesses of your proposed study, particularly those areas you view as most important.
2. List the strengths and weaknesses of the Bean and Eichelberger study reported in Chapter 8 in terms of *their* identified purposes. What additional information should have been reported to alleviate some of the weaknesses, or to answer questions that you have after reading the research article?

°Research approach deals with types of study: for example, experimental, correlational, causal comparative, descriptive, historical, or ethnographic, using case study, surveys, observation, or participant observation methods to carry out the study.

RELATED SOURCES

Huck, S.W., & Sandler, H.M. (1979). *Rival hypotheses: Alternative interpretations of data based conclusions.* New York: Harper & Row.

   This book was developed to help readers recognize rival hypotheses in situations in which empirical evidence is used. The authors provide 100 situations in which conclusions have been made based on evidence. Their discussion of each situation identifies alternative explanations for results. The research design and other methodological principles they use are identified so that the reader will be able to recognize them in new situations.

Lehmann, I.J., & Mehrans, W.A. (1979). *Educational research: Readings in focus* (2nd ed.). New York: Holt, Rinehart and Winston.

   This book of readings classifies educational research studies into five categories: historical, descriptive, correlational, ex post facto, and experimental. The characteristics and major methodological issues are described in introductions to each section of the book. Five or more examples of each type of study are provided. Comments and questions for students follow each study. Critiques of some articles are included as are several conflicting studies of the experimenter bias effect and responses by the various authors. The book is a useful adjunct for traditional research methods courses that emphasize methods rather than research studies.

Light, R.J., & Pillemer, D.B. (1984). *Summing up: The science of reviewing research.* Cambridge, MA: Harvard University Press.

   In this excellent book on reviewing literature, the authors discuss appropriate interpretations of empirical evidence. They also indicate how quantitative, nonquantitative, and theoretical information can be combined to draw appropriate conclusions. This is one of the few sources that discuss this complex process explicitly. Although it assumes a somewhat sophisticated understanding of some methodological principles and techniques, it should be valuable to individuals who are faced with questions of data interpretation and synthesis in an applied situation.

REFERENCES

Bean, R.M., & Eichelberger, R.T. (March 1985). Changing the role of reading specialists: From pull-out to in-class programs. *The Reading Teacher, 38*(7), 648–653.

Eichelberger, R.T. (1974). The evaluation of on-going instructional programs. In G.D. Borich (Ed.), *Evaluating educational programs and products.* Englewood Cliffs, NJ: Education Technology Press.

Meade, E. (1988). Interview of an evaluation user. *Evaluation Practice, 9*(1), 32–41.

CHAPTER 9

Content and Structure of the Research Report

The purpose of this chapter is to facilitate your understanding of research reports and your ability to identify aspects of a study that affect its quality. You need this knowledge to do research, such as a thesis or dissertation, and to report it clearly. The specific form of a report and rules on style are often unique to a particular setting. There are a number of books that deal more directly with writing a thesis or dissertation (e.g., Borg & Gall, 1983; Castetter & Heisler, 1984). Preliminary materials, such as acknowledgments, preface, and a table of contents, usually appear in a report. Similarly, all sources cited in a report must be listed at the end of the report as the "Bibliography," or "References." Other related sources that were not cited are often listed as "Related References." Material essential to the research study but not needed in the body of the report is usually included as "Appendixes."

STRUCTURE OF THE REPORT

A typical organization for a research report is as follows:

1. Introduction to the Study
   a. Background of Problem
   b. Purpose of Study
   c. Problem Statement and Research Questions (or Hypotheses)
   d. Limitations/Delimitations of the Study
   e. Conceptual Definitions of Terms
2. Review of Related Literature
   a. History of Relevant Theory and Research

    b. Implications for Study of the Problem
    c. Conceptual Framework for Study
3. Description of Method Used to Study Problem
    a. Subjects Studied (Sources of Data)
    b. Measurement Instruments Used
    c. Procedures Carried Out in the Study
    d. Data Analyses for Each Research Question or Hypothesis
4. Findings From the Study
    a. Description of Findings
       i. Answer Each Research Question as Planned
      ii. Additional Analyses That Were Needed
    b. Other Findings (if any)
5. Discussion of Findings and Conclusions of Study
    a. Discussion of Findings and Other Aspects of Study
    b. Conclusions That Address Problem Statement
    c. Relate Conclusions to Theory and Previous Research
    d. Implications for Practice (if any)
    e. Recommendations for Further Research

This structure is often used for empirical studies that use data collected in the present, such as surveys and correlational, causal comparative, and experimental studies. Historical, ethnographic, case studies, and other studies for which it is more difficult to prespecify the specific problem statement and research methods are usually organized in ways that emphasize the substantive (or methodological) issues central to that particular study. Even educational psychology studies often require a somewhat different structure. In some fields, the problem statement and research questions, or hypotheses, are placed in a short chapter that follows the "Review of Literature" and precedes the "Methods" chapter.

The headings (1 to 5) and subheadings (a to e) indicate the important elements of a study that must be addressed somewhere in a research report. Do not view the foregoing outline as the only acceptable structure for a report or even as the *best*. It is simply a way to identify important elements of a study and the relationships among them.

Within education there are many areas of specialization, such as administration, reading, math, science, special education, and physical education. In each specialization, there is a generally accepted structure for a report that is commonly used and taught to neophytes in the field. This structure is often learned in a rote manner, so that many students perceive it as a form to be learned that has no underlying substantive base.

The relevance of the various elements in a research study, as indicated in the first eight chapters of this book, determines the placement and emphasis given to each element in the report. For example, if a researcher addresses two major questions in a study, such as the academic and psychological changes of first-graders during their first year in school, with extensive data analyses carried out in each area, the findings could be reported in two chapters rather than one.

If extensive knowledge of the literature is needed to understand the purpose and problem for a study, the "Introduction" and "Review of Literature" could be combined into a single chapter and no separate "Review of Literature" would need to be included.

When writing anything, you are attempting to communicate something to someone else. The message you are sending is the one the reader is to receive and comprehand. Writing about research, the purpose, procedures, findings, conclusions, and implications, is no different except that everything should be as precise as possible. There should be as little ambiguity as possible in a research report.

CONTENT OF THE REPORT

The outline presented earlier represents a comprehensive research report, such as a thesis, dissertation, or report to a funding agency. The specific content presented in the various parts of the report are described in this section using the headings and subheadings from the outline.

Introduction to the Study

The background of the problem, purpose for the study, and problem statement and research questions (or hypotheses) were previously described. The background provides the historical and/or societal context for the problem. Choosing an appropriate level of specificity is very important. For example, assume that your problem statement is the following:

> What are the relative effects of various methods of sex education for decreasing teenage pregnancy?

The general societal problem is teenage pregnancy. Data indicating the level of teenage pregnancy among the population to be studied and the detrimental effects of pregnancy on the teenager are probably worth mentioning as background of the problem. Two or three pages of such information would be misplaced emphasis because the study is an investigation of the relative effects of different methods of sex education on teenage pregnancy. The audience for the study will be persons who design, develop, or implement such programs. The problem deals with planning, developing or delivering such knowledge, which *must* be the focus of the entire introductory chapter. The dimensions of the problem that are investigated directly in the study are delineated in the research questions (or hypotheses). These must also be emphasized in the background to the problem and purpose for doing the study.

The purpose for doing the study is to clarify some knowledge need that a specific audience has concerning the problem. That purpose *can never be* "to provide information not previously available," which is true of *all* studies. Professionals and academics always use theories, beliefs, experiences, previous research, and other similar information as their basis for what they do. Seldom, if ever, is there a total vacuum that the research will fill.

A research study is usually carried out because there is something faulty, incomplete, or unverified about the basis for knowledge that many professionals are using to make decisions. Elementary school teachers may assume that mainstreamed learning disabled (LD) students will function like other students in their classrooms. A principal may believe that pulling special needs students out of their regular classes provides the most effective instruction. If you believe that either of these assumptions is false or should be investigated, your reason would not be "to provide information not previously available," but to provide this specific information about relationships between variables in this context so that teachers will gain information that they can use to modify their classes, to better meet the needs of the LD students.

One method for delineating the relationships among specific variables is to describe the situation as a typical representative of the audience, such as the teacher with mainstreamed LD students, would describe it. Researchers often conceptualize a problem too generally. To make a contribution to knowledge, you must plan your research and carry it out at the level on which the audience needs the information. The purpose of a study is to provide the most appropriate information at that level of specificity.

The problem statement and research questions (or hypotheses) were discussed in Chapter 3. An important point to keep in mind when writing the statement and questions is that they must relate to, or describe, relationships in the target population and not be merely descriptions of the situations found in the study. The specific methods used to operationalize the independent, dependent, and other variables are not relevant (usually) to the conceptualization of the problem. The methods used to carry out the study, including such operational definitions, are described later in the report—usually in a chapter that describes the methods.

Other sections of an introductory chapter often include the limitations and delimitations of a study. A *limitation* of a study is *an aspect of the study that limits the confidence you would have in fulfilling the purpose for the study*. For example, a study may occur in one large city school system, which limits the population to which the study can be generalized. Specific characteristics of the data-gathering procedures, such as self-reports on a questionnaire, may limit the confidence of the researcher in accurately measuring the variables in the study.

Every study requires numerous assumptions. The degree to which those assumptions are met in a study affects the confidence you can have in the conclusions you reach. Particularly important assumptions, such as those needed when using self-reports, are often included in the limitations. Seldom are the assumptions adequately identified and written in the research report. As a result, the logic on which a conclusion in a study is based is often not very clear. Some underlying assumptions used by both the researcher and the reader of the study in drawing such conclusions as: "The norm-referenced achievement test measures pertinent reading skills," are not recognized. Most researchers recognize the value of identifying underlying assumptions and investigating them when possible, but such identification and investigation have not become typical.

Delimitations are *those modifications in the research procedure that the researcher made to increase the quality of the study.* A delimitation is usually made to decrease the error, or noise, in a study. For example, you may be interested in the relative effects of three different approaches to teaching math skills in elementary schools. If you use the three methods across three or four grade levels, the effects of method will be confounded with the effects of varying math content and with maturation of the students. To limit the effects of these other variables and to more clearly investigate the effects of the three teaching methods on math achievement, you may decide to delimit the study to one grade level, such as fourth grade. You may have good reason to believe that results obtained in grade 4 should generalize to grades 3, 5, and 6. If that is true, your modification will not limit your ability to generalize the results to any great extent. In a more precise sense, this delimitation does limit somewhat your ability to generalize to the other grade levels. The primary difference between a delimitation and a limitation in a study is whether you plan it to improve the quality of the study (delimitation) or whether it occurred despite your best efforts (limitation).

A final section of the introductory chapter is usually a definition of terms. There is some ambiguity as to the purpose that the definitions serve, but a useful way to think about them is as an aid to communication with the reader. Most terms in education have somewhat different meanings to different researchers, particularly if they come from different disciplines, theories, or ideologies. What should be clear to the reader is your meaning when the term appears in your report.

The part of the report where such ambiguity is most likely to occur is in the "Review of Literature." Therefore, you should define near the end of the introductory chapter the important terms in your study, particularly those that have several meanings. The definitions needed at that time are the conceptual meanings, and not the operational definitions of variables in the research questions. In rare cases, these may also be needed to gain a clearer understanding of the study. But that is an independent decision. The conceptual definitions are almost always needed.

Other terms that you should *not* define are those that you use as they are commonly defined. That is, if you use the most common, or preferred, definition that appears in the dictionary, you should *not* define the term in your report.

Usually, only three to 10 terms, or concepts, require conceptual definitions. Discuss most of these terms rather than giving them a single definition. For example, *reading* is a term that has numerous meanings, and researchers use it in various ways. In your report, give the three or four primary ways that the term is usually used. Then select one of those definitions as the definition that you will use in your report. This decision is often strictly pragmatic. By selecting the most common definition, you can identify easily the few times that researchers use it in other ways.

Program evaluation is another concept with many definitions. A conceptual definition presented before the "Review of Literature" could be as follows:

> *Program Evaluation.* Some authors, such as Tyler (1942) and other objectivists, equate program evaluation and measurement. Others, such as Scriven (1967) and Worthen and Sanders (1987), identify the essential aspect of evaluation as judging the merit or worth of a program. Stufflebeam and his colleagues (1971) define it as providing information useful for decision-making. This latter definition is used in this report because it is most widely accepted, particularly in a decision context such as we are studying.

The definitions are provided as aids to the reader in understanding the report. The "Introduction" and "Review of Literature" should provide an accurate picture of the background and present status of the problem. The various ways in which terms and concepts are defined and used is usually an important part of that picture.

Review of Literature

The fourth chapter of this book is devoted to the functions of the review of literature and analyzing and synthesizing research. Before you attempt to write any section of the review, develop a comprehensive outline of the chapter. The outline should be an integrated whole that clearly communicates to the reader the important concepts and their relationships. You can develop such an outline in many cases by reporting chronologically the changes in the research results and associated theory most relevant to the problem. You must always consider the order in which changes occurred, even when your review is not organized chronologically.

A review of literature in a study of the practice effects of repeated testing could be organized as follows:

1. Reliability
2. Practice Effects of Repeated Testing
   a. United States
   b. Great Britain
3. Characteristics of Respondents
   a. Socioeconomic Status
   b. Academic Achievement
   c. Gender
   d. Intelligence
   e. Test-wiseness

Reliability is addressed first because that knowledge is required to understand the technical aspects of change scores, which represent the practice effect of repeated testing. Research and theory concerning variables that affect the reliability of scores and the differences between two scores on the same, or different, measurement instruments are analyzed and synthesized.

Next, previous research on repeated testing using the same form, or alternative forms of the same test, is reviewed. In reviewing this literature, the researcher realized that the results were very different when studies were carried out in Great Britain rather than the United States. In the United States, the scores usually increased significantly the second time a test was administered —whether the same form with exactly the same test items or a test with different items was administered. On rare occasions, a significant increase in scores also occurred in the third administration but never after that. In Great Britain, scores continued to increase significantly over 10 to 15 administrations of a test.

Many possible reasons for these results were described in the review. The differences in both the results obtained and the functions such tests serve in the two societies were the primary reasons for presenting the studies in different sections. It helps the reader understand the previous research by more accurately separating studies that are not comparable in purpose or results.

Given the increased scores, on the average, that occurred in all studies from the first to second administration of such tests, it would be useful to test developers to know if some types of student gained more than others. Previous research indicated that increased scores, or learning in general, were related to the five characteristics listed in the outline: (1) socioeconomic status, (2) academic achievement, (3) gender, (4) intelligence, and (5) test-wiseness. Research and theory concerning these characteristics as they relate to practice effects (or learning) are presented and discussed in the last section of the review. Alternative ways to measure these variables is an important part of this presentation.

The review ends with a list of the five variables that should be included in a study of the practice effects of repeated testing (1 to 5 above) and the conditions that would be most appropriate for studying this phenomenon in order to aid test developers in designing norm-referenced multiple choice tests—particularly issues of alternate forms and types of students who show the most or least change in repeated testing. This list of characteristics and their relationships to practice effect forms the conceptual framework for the study. The description of methods used in the study usually follows the review of literature, although some authors place the problem statement and research questions after the review.

Methods

You must describe the methods, or procedures, you use to study a problem in enough detail to enable your readers to interpret the findings and conclusions of the study. If your sampling process was biased, the participants in the study may not be representative of other populations. If your measurement instruments do not measure accurately the variables, meaningful interpretation may not be possible. If you do not adequately control other alternative explanations, neither you nor a reader of your report can draw conclusions from your study with any degree of confidence. A well-designed study includes the identification of likely weaknesses that would raise such concerns and describes the steps that you took to assure its quality. If you become aware of weaknesses after the study is implemented that you can do nothing about, you must report these concerns *and* your reasons for the concerns. A research report must be an accurate, honest report of the research process that includes both the strengths and weaknesses. You can then base your conclusions on the most defensible interpretation of the results of your study. There are no perfect studies. Researchers attempt to strengthen those areas most important to the problem studied and the purpose for doing the study, and they allow weaknesses in less important areas.

The methods of most research studies include (1) the sources of the data, (2) measurement processes used, (3) procedures carried out by the researcher (which may include a formal design), and (4) the analyses of the information collected that were used to test the hypotheses or to answer the research questions. In addressing each decision about method, you will be faced with several realistic alternatives. Given the problem and purpose for the study, you must determine the combination of methods that will produce the most valuable answer to your research questions or tests of your hypotheses.

You must clearly delineate the major alternatives that you consider and your reasons for choosing the specific methods you used for each of the four aspects of method. This should be done in every research study, whether it is in psychology, anthropology, chemistry, physics, history, or economics.

The types of data sources, measurement processes, procedures, and methods of data analysis may be totally different in the various disciplines or in different studies in the same discipline. For example, the data from an ethnographer's participant observation will be totally different from those of a psychologist's laboratory study of artificial intelligence, which will be different from those of an existential psychologist's investigation of the human experience of intimacy. Researchers are responsible for describing their methods in enough detail to allow readers to assess the confidence that they can have in the conclusions reached in the study. If there is no assurance that the data sources are representative or that the measurement procedures are valid, readers must be cautious about the accuracy or representativeness of the conclusions.

These four aspects of method are usually described in the order listed here. After the necessary introductory materials in the methods chapter, the methods used to select the data sources, which are the study participants or subjects in most educational research, are described. Often the participants are selected from a larger population of possible participants. The characteristics of this population of all possible participants (the accessible population) and the procedures used to select the actual participants (sample) must be delineated. This information allows readers to determine the relationship between that population and the population that concerns them. The selection process determines the likelihood that the sample of subjects who actually participated in the study was representative of the accessible population and that the target population was of concern to the researcher or reader.

In a similar manner, historians describe the methods used to select the historical documents from which they drew the data used in a historical study. An ethnographer identifies the informants and other data sources and the methods used to select them. A knowledgeable historian or ethnographer can judge the quality and representativeness of the data source used on the basis of previous research and experience with similar sources and variables.

In these latter two examples, the data sources and measurement procedures are often described in the methods section because they are difficult to separate. In studies that use identifiable measurement instruments, the instruments are usually described and discussed in a separate section of the chapter. The quality and value of the data produced by the instruments as they were used in *this* study are addressed as issues of reliability and validity. The more quantitative measurement processes usually produce reliability indexes, such as $r = 0.68$. As indicated previously, quantitative estimates of validity are more difficult to obtain; and logical, theoretical, and other reasonable arguments are used to investigate and document validity.

It is important to remember that reliability is not an inherent characteristic of a measurement instrument that is the same for all uses. It will usually vary with different populations, such as gifted or remedial students, and administration conditions. Seldom are the reliability estimates reported by the developer of an instrument directly applicable in a research setting—even those produced for norm-referenced tests such as the Metropolitan Achievement Test of the Stanford-Binet Intelligence Test. In most studies, the relatively smaller number of participants are unlikely to be representative of the group of subjects used to obtain the reliability estimates. An instrument with a reliability of 0.91 in the general population may have a reliability index of 0.60 with a remedial reading group, LD students, or gifted students. It may even be 0.71 in a study of 100 subjects in regular classrooms of a suburban school district. The important issue in a study is the reliability and validity of the data produced by the measurement process in this *study*. The fundamental issue is always the confidence that one should have in the results obtained and associated conclusions reached in the particular study.

A researcher must be aware of those aspects of the measurement process that are problematic. In survey research, the quality of the survey instrument and the procedures used to identify and generate responses from a representative sample are the two most important elements. Procedures used by the researcher to assure that responses to the instrument represent the variables and dimensions studied must be described honestly and accurately.

A researcher always has some questions or concerns about an instrument and administration procedures that cannot be totally alleviated by the most comprehensive development efforts, such as distinguishing activities of a principal that result from personal initiative rather than from a superintendent's management style, when that is an important element of the study. The nature of the concern, the ways in which the concern has been addressed to produce the best information possible, and the unsolved aspects of the concern should all be clearly delineated. This cannot be done for every minute element of a study, but it should be done for the most important areas that are problematic.

Ethnographers, historians, sociologists, economists, psychologists, physicists, and other researchers are always aware of those areas that are most problematic in their studies. Researchers who are familiar with the fields they are studying and the contexts in which they are working should be able to identify the most problematic aspects of a study—particularly when they also understand the basic methodological principles identified in this book and the results of previous research of the problem they are studying. These must, of course, be addressed in planning the best possible study of that problem for this purpose at this time. The steps taken to address these problematic areas and the degree to which they are solved must be presented and discussed. Usually these are included in the "Methods" chapter of a report.

The important procedures in a study are those activities that are carried out to do the study—particularly those that affect the researcher's ability to draw conclusions from the findings or results. The characteristics of the population studied and of the measurement processes used are certainly important aspects of a study. In addition, how the participants were selected, when they were selected, who had which specific experiences at what times, and when the measurement processes were implemented and under what conditions are also important. Some of this information is often provided in the discussion of data sources and measurement processes, but much of it is included in a description of the entire study.

The procedures are often described chronologically to aid the readers' understanding of the entire study. A schedule, as illustrated in Table 9.1, is a useful planning and communication device. The important steps are listed in chronological order, providing a comprehensive picture of the study as well as the amount of time that each activity required and the order in which each was executed. In some studies, such as experiments, a drawing of the design is also a useful description of the study. The complexities of a research study can often be described with a "picture" rather than with prose. A study of the relative effects of three methods of teaching reading on students with different levels of initial reading ability might be visually represented by Table 9.2. This design indicates not only the three teaching methods (phonics, meaning, and eclectic) and three initial reading levels (high, average, and low) but also the number of participants who experienced each method (75) and the total number of participants in the study (225).

In studies in which no formal design can be pictured in easily separable cells, the prose description, the schedule of activities, and other aspects described in the methods section of a study comprise the "design" of the study. A formal design, such as the one illustrated in Table 9.2, usually describes the statistical analyses carried out in the study. Some developers of statistical tests even give them names, such as a Latin-square design, which can be useful to experts in statistical analysis but are rarely meaningful to practitioners. The important issues in research are the logical ones that allow researchers and readers to draw

TABLE 9.1. SCHEDULE OF ACTIVITIES FOR STUDY OF DRUG AND ALCOHOL ABUSE AMONG THE ELDERLY

Activity	Week									
	1	*2*	*3*	*4*	*5*	*6*	*7*	*8*	*9*	*10*
Sampling										
1. Meet AAA	x									
2. Diversified service	x									
3. Senior times	x									
Design and Construct Instruments										
1. Write interview		x	x							
2. Pretest			x							
3. Get sample		x	x							
4. Post cards			x							
5. Train interviewers		x	x							
Interview Phase				x	x	x				
Data Procedures										
1. Code				x	x	x				
2. Computer input					x	x	x			
3. Analyze data							x			
Report										
1. Write reports								x		
2. Disseminate for comments									x	
3. Revise final report and disseminate										x

meaningful conclusions about relationships among variables in a particular setting. One such setting is identifying the relative effects of three methods of teaching reading in the second grade on students with varying reading levels.

The final aspects of methods used in a study is the specific analysis of data carried out to answer each research question or to test each research hypothesis. All methods used in research help protect researchers from their own biases and other human frailties. We seem to do whatever possible to cling to our favorite theories, beliefs, and ideologies. Mitroff (1974), for example, studied physicists,

TABLE 9.2. DESIGN OF A STUDY OF THREE TEACHING METHODS ON STUDENTS WHO DIFFER IN INITIAL READING ABILITY

Initial Reading Level	Teaching Method *Phonics*	*Meaning*	*Eclectic*	*Total*
HIGH	25[a]	25[a]	25[a]	75
AVERAGE	25	25	25	75
LOW	25	25	25	75
TOTAL	75	75	75	225

[a]Number of participants in each catagory.

astrophysicists, astronomers, and others whose scientific knowledge and beliefs would be affected by the data obtained from the first rocks brought back to Earth from the Moon. He found, in general, that those scientists who held to their theories and beliefs the strongest were those scientists whose theories were supported *least* by the objective analysis of the rocks. You and I are no different.

To protect ourselves we design studies that allow us to gather, analyze, and interpret data (information) to investigate theories, beliefs, or hunches that we have about the relationships among important variables. That is the most important function of prespecifying the methods used to study a problem and clearly delineating the rationale for using the methods. In no area is this prespecification more important than in the data analysis.

By indicating the most appropriate ways to gather and analyze results solely on the basis of previous research, associated theory, and experience, you need not be affected by the specific data you obtain in your study. Once you collect the data, you must carry out all analyses that you have prespecified. Only when unusual circumstances arise, such as no respondents who identify themselves as having a particular characteristic (e.g., being classified as gifted), can you make modifications in the analyses. In this case, you would have to modify all prespecified analyses that include a gifted group because you have no respondents who can be so classified. And you must give the rationale for the modification.

The description of the data analyses should specify precisely how the data that were actually analyzed were obtained from the measurement instruments. In many cases the individual responses are counted to produce frequencies. The relative frequencies of responses by one group to one item on a questionnaire are compared with those of a different group. It is also common to use the individuals' scores on an achievement test and compare mean raw scores. If transformed scores, such as standard scores, or grade equivalent scores are used, that must be clear to the reader. Each type of score has different characteristics and distributions that affect the analyses that can be carried out with it. A reader cannot make that assessment without the necessary information.

Participants' responses are often combined in specific ways to measure a particular variable, or dimension of a variable, more adequately. Precisely which responses to which items are combined in what ways must be clear. The question is not whether something is right and something else is wrong. There are always advantages and disadvantages to each alternative method of data analysis that a researcher might do. The reader must know precisely the sources of the information (data) that were actually analyzed to be able to interpret the results meaningfully. The relationship between the hypothesis that is tested, or the research question addressed, and the specific data that are analyzed in the study must always be clear. As indicated in Chapter 7, the important information in a study is that which is obtained directly from the measurement processes used in the study. Statistical analyses, including tests of significance, are tools to help interpret the meaning of the results. The data analyses section of a report is neither a list of statistics, such as means, medians, frequencies, and *t* scores, nor a selection of the "right" test of statistical significance to use in analyzing the data. Both types of information may be needed, but the more important issue is: Which data were analyzed in what ways to most adequately investigate the problem addressed and directly answer the research questions of hypotheses posed?

Findings

After the data are collected and analyzed, the findings of the study, which are the results of all the preplanned activities, are reported. A researcher should not deviate from the purpose for which the study was planned. It is an integrated whole. Studies are not always successful, but when results do not come as expected, the purpose of the study, problem statement, and data analyses cannot be modified after the fact to be consistent with the idiosyncratic results of a single study. The "Introduction" (purpose, problem statement, and research questions), the "Review of Literature," and the "Methods" were all planned to best address the problem stated for the purpose specified. The literature most relevant to that purpose was reviewed. The wording of specific test or questionnaire items was best for the purpose specified. The data analyses were delineated to maximize the value of this particular study for the purpose delineated. The answers to the initial research questions or hypotheses posed must be provided, even when they are not the most valuable or interesting outcome of a study. The prespecified problem statement and research questions are the only relationships for which a researcher can draw conclusions from the results of that study, because those were the bases of all activities.

There are always surprises in research studies. Sometimes they are small surprises; other times they question the relevance of the entire study. These surprises (such as having few respondents in an important category or the illness of a teacher or principal) may require modifications in planned procedures during the study or in specific analyses after the data are collected. These modifications do not replace the planned analyses, which should be carried out if possible, but are additional. The most relevant additional analyses are carried out to describe more accurately, or comprehensively, the findings in the study, For example, one or two students may have refused to respond to a test, or one person in one group may have scored 20 points higher than anyone else in the study. Those scores cannot simply be discarded, but the data can be analyzed both with and without the unusual scores, and the reasons for those unusual scores can be investigated. Several children may have missed more than half of the experimental (or comparison) treatment, or a teacher may not have implemented important aspects of a treatment. Such situations may lead to additional analyses.

In some studies, additional variables that arise during the study may seem to be more important than those identified in previous research and theory. You as the researcher should investigate these variables, particularly if they are likely alternative explanations for your results. Even if they are not logical problems for you in investigating the problem and associated hypotheses of the study, you should attempt to obtain all relevant information that you can about these other variables. But this does not change the focus of the study! Nor are these additional variables legitimate *findings* of the study. They can be no more than "interesting information" that may have implications for a future study. This is an example of the hypothesis-generation function of research.

Meanings of the terms, *findings, results*, and *conclusions* as they are used in empirical research are often confusing. Definitions that help distinguish the three terms follow. Most researchers agree that a *finding* is the outcome of the prespecified procedures and data analysis to answer one of the research questions. It includes the test of significance if one is used. For example, if two instructional methods are used to teach math and one research question addresses their relative effects on math computation, the difference in mean achievement between the two groups on a math computation test is a finding. The fact that one group did significantly better than the other on the math computation test is also a finding.

Many researchers use the terms *finding* and *result* interchangeably. Others consider results to mean more than just the findings. It may be useful to think of *results* as all the outcomes of the study. There is no single consistent definition of results. The term is used most often by researchers as it is defined in dictionaries: a consequence of a particular action; an outcome.

There is general agreement that a *conclusion* of a study is the most defensible statement of the extent to which expected relationships, or hypotheses, seem to exist. In the example given two paragraphs earlier, "Method *A* is significantly better than Method *B* in facilitating math computation skills" would be an appropriate conclusion if there was no alternative explanation for the significant differences in math computation results. When other activities and procedures that occurred in the study are reviewed and it is unlikely that other variables caused the significant math computation findings, the foregoing statement is an appropriate conclusion.

Alternative explanations arise in most research: One teacher may get sick, randomly selected groups are not equivalent on IQ, a test was not administered on time (or not correctly administered), one teacher hated her supervisor (or the researcher), four students consistently disrupted one classroom, *ad infinitum.* Given the findings, additional analyses and other results, as well as the investigation of other uncontrolled variables in a study, a conclusion is the statement that can be legitimately defended on the basis of the findings and all other results of this study.

It is usually best to organize and report the findings by research questions, or hypotheses, in the same order that they are listed in the statement of the problem section of the report. A research study is extremely complex. Most researchers find it impossible to keep in mind the various research questions and activities carried out to address each part of each question. One of the easiest ways to simplify the study, both as it is planned and as it is reported to others, is to focus on one research question (or hypothesis) at a time.

Limit this section of the report to findings. Meaningful interpretation of the findings depends on many other aspects of a study in addition to the findings—as indicated. It is usually best to point out uncontrolled alternative variables or other mediating concerns that are addressed more fully later in the study. This alerts the reader to read this specific finding with particular caution. Without such information, the reader may accept all findings as equally relevant and organize them meaningfully into a whole. When inconsistencies or problems are identified in the discussion, it is more difficult for the reader to understand or assimilate them if indications have not been given previously.

The findings may be organized in many different ways. They are most often placed in a single chapter with a short introduction and a listing or summary of findings at the end of the chapter. When many findings are presented and there are two or more distinct foci in a study, the findings can be presented more effectively in two or more separate chapters. This is done to simplify a complex set of issues and findings so that the findings for each issue are as clear as possible to the reader.

Discussion and Conclusions

The discussion of the study focuses on the most meaningful interpretation of the activities carried out and the findings that were made. It must focus on the initial purpose for doing the study. That purpose should be to inform the audience about the relationships among the variables studied that are most relevant to the problem studied in their context. That problem may be teachers who have several learning disabled students in their classrooms and must plan the daily schedule to meet the academic needs of all students. It may be principals who want to involve teachers in setting academic policy in their schools. Identifying the relationships that seem to exist among the most important variables and their implications in that context (if any) is the most important function of drawing conclusions and discussing the results and their meaning.

In the final chapter of research reports, the findings are discussed in the context of other relevant facts about the study. The most relevant facts are those which indicate that a finding cannot be interpreted at face value. The groups of subjects may differ on initial ability or other relevant characteristics, for example. Even though Group A evidenced significantly higher achievement on the dependent variable, that difference may be a result of their higher initial ability. If any of the teachers of the group with lower achievement were often absent because of illness, the significantly lower achievement may be a result of teacher absence rather than of the type of instructional treatment the students experienced. All such problems must be pointed out, investigated, and their effects thoughtfully assessed in order to draw defensible conclusions.

The conclusions are the most important of everything that occurred in the study that is directly relevant to the problem statement. The three or four most important conclusions are all that should be reported in most studies. There is no reason to write a conclusion for each research question, although it is often a useful way for the researcher to begin to understand the possible conclusions.

The conclusions must be based directly on data that were systematically collected to address one or more of the research questions. Conclusions cannot be based on information that arose unexpectedly during the study. Such information can be used to question findings and possible conclusions, and it is the basis for recommending future studies that will allow adequate investigation of the new information.

A discussion of the relationship between the findings and associated conclusions in a particular study to those in the literature is an essential part of a research report. This discussion can be done mechanically by simply listing those studies that obtained similar results and those that obtained different results. How they differ can also be described mechanistically. Identifying such similarities and differences is a necessary step in delineating contributions of this study to the knowledge base in the literature. Such a discussion is inadequate if it does not provide the most meaningful interpretation of the results of the study for the audience and context for which it was planned.

To achieve such a meaningful discussion is very difficult, particularly for researchers not intimately familiar with previous research and associated theory and their applications in the context studied. The balance between describing findings obtained and identifying assumptions needed to draw inferences about both the relationships among variables studied and their implications for practice is difficult to achieve. Too often, researchers believe that they have fulfilled their responsibilities by simply listing the various views and findings, and they make no attempt at meaningful interpretation. On the other hand, some authors write as conclusions relationships among variables that *cannot* be defended with data from their studies. Their beliefs and biases are so strong that they report their beliefs as conclusions, even when the data do not support them.

Conclusions must be clearly differentiated from implications for practice. In any practical setting, many variables that affect decision-making will not have been included in the study. The primary concerns of the audience may be very different from those of the researcher. For example, a researcher concerned about improving the instruction of mainstreamed LD students may not take into account the teacher's concern about educating *all* students in the classroom. When a researcher presents a list of implications for practice that includes activities that require a teacher's time, which of the present activities in the teacher's overfilled schedule should be dropped? The extent to which conclusions obtained in a particular setting have reasonable implications for practice vary tremendously from one study to another. Most studies provide only food for thought rather than clear implications for practice. Seldom do results of a study imply that a teacher or principal "should" do something. Instead, the results indicate variables, or activities, that should be useful for teachers or principals to consider as they carry out related activities with similar purposes in mind.

Recommendations for further research should be an important part of a research report. Each researcher gains some insights during a study about additional variables that appear to be more promising, other ways to obtain relevant data, or new approaches to the problem area. Each of these insights, or lessons learned, has implications for ways the problem could be studied more precisely or comprehensively.

As a result of doing a study, particularly after attempting to interpret the meaning of the results, a researcher knows what information is still needed. In a study of principals, for example, the respondents may be identified by highest degree earned, grade levels of school, and geographic location of school, but their years of teaching experience and administrative experience may not be obtained. Differences in their responses seem to be related to their years of experience, but there is no way to investigate them. A recommendation for further research should be to collect data on experience. In other studies using questionnaires, researchers often need explanations of the responses and the follow-up questions that are based on the questionnaire responses. Too often, this need is not recognized until it is too late to do anything. Such researchers should recommend follow-up interviews. If there are particular questions that should be asked or a specific sampling procedure that seem most valuable, these should be part of the recommendations.

Researchers who indicate only that their study should be replicated with a larger sample or with a sample that represents a different population are not sharing their lessons or insights with others interested in the same problem. We all lose when such experience and insights are lost from future consideration.

WRITING THE RESEARCH REPORT

Knowing the structure and context that are required in the report and the functions that each part serves helps the author to organize the report. Most studies last at least eight months from beginning the review of literature and preparation of a proposal to writing the final report. Many studies take more than a year to complete. A number of hints can help in this process, and they include the following:

1. Write the appropriate section of the report at the time the activity is carried out.
2. Outline each section before trying to write it. (The outline may change somewhat as the report is written, but the outline helps to simplify the topics and show relationships among them.)
3. Write a rough draft of a section or chapter and set it aside for a few days.
4. When precisely the same thing is identified in various sections of the report, use precisely the same words.
5. A table or figure in a report must stand alone; do not attempt to put too much into it.

When these hints are most relevant and how they are applied in writing a research report follow.

Write Up Activity While Doing It

The first three chapters of a master's thesis or doctoral dissertation are often required as a proposal or overview of the proposed study. These chapters include all the material discussed under "Introduction," "Review of Literature," and "Method." When these three chapters are required before the implementation of the study, the researcher must write these sections as the activities occur. If the specific instruments used are selected, or modified, during the study, be sure to obtain and organize the sources of information and other data or information that was the basis for their selection or modification. If possible, write the material needed for the final report at this time. You are intimately involved in it; the information is fresh in your mind and available. If you wait until after all data are collected to write the methods section of the report, it will take an incredible amount of time to gather, reorganize, and identify the steps carried out and the rationale for each. Or, even worse, much important information may be lost and not included in the report.

When the sample is selected, document everything that occurred and write it up *before* sending out the questionnaire or implementing the study. Changes and additions that occur during the study can be added at the time you become aware of them. When questionnaires are returned, there are often questions of percentage of return and completeness of each questionnaire. Decisions are made daily about each specific questionnaire, as well as about more general rules. You need a procedure to keep track of these as they occur. When all questionnaires have been returned or when you begin to analyze them, write the section on the return rate and the decisions you make about the data. Detailed information is usually placed in the "Appendix," but it is needed *somewhere* in the report.

Some ethnographic or other more qualitative studies have phases. In one phase, certain information is collected from specific sources. Based on this phase, a second phase is planned, which can lead to a third phase. It is tempting to move to the next phase without adequately documenting and writing the findings and interpretations of the earlier phase.

These examples should be useful in helping to identify the sections of the report that can be written during the planning and operating phases of the study. The specific activities that occur at particular times during a study will vary from one study to another. The report should document everything that occurred and the reasons for each decision that is made.

Outline Each Section of the Report

The problem statement, purpose, and general procedures in a study determine the emphases that different activities require. Each section of the report should be written with that in mind. A major misunderstanding of some students is that a research report should have a specific form, one that they view as "research." They attempt to organize and write their reports to resemble in form other research reports they have read. There is some value to this approach for a neophyte, but the emphasis on form must be moderated by the knowledge of function and the purpose for doing the study.

In preparing an outline for an instrument description section of a report, for example, issues of reliability and validity of each instrument used must be adequately addressed, including reliability coefficients in most cases. An abstract description of the psychometric characteristics of a measure, such as the reliability in the general population, is of limited value in a research report. What were its qualities in *this* study with *these* respondents? The outline should clearly focus on issues specific for this study, and organize the relevant topics in order to write a first draft of the section.

Write Rough Draft and Set It Aside

The first draft is usually produced a few pages at a time. When you write something, you know precisely what you mean; so whatever you write tends to look all right. After three or four days of other activities and other writing, return to the earlier pages. You will have a fresh perspective and be able to more clearly read the message written on the paper. The sentences that are unclear or awkward can be identified and revised. Material that is missing can be added.

Very few people write well. Most of us have to work extremely hard to write research reports that others can read with understanding. This is a more difficult task if you believe that research must be written in a particular style—using the researcher's jargon. I attempt to write so that my parents, who are not researchers, can read the report with understanding. In education, research reports should *not* be written only for the enlightened. If it does not make sense to the teacher or principal, it will probably not be used or understood.

Another writing tip is to give examples. Most of us write very abstract sentences. We know what we mean, but others may have to select among various meanings—all of which come from their experience. Examples clarify the meaning of the most abstract sentences. This book is filled with examples. I am sure that there are sentences that you think need even more examples.

There are other things to look at, of course, when reviewing your rough draft. Writing well is a desirable goal in all areas. Most of us never reach such a level. The best we can do is work hard to improve.

Use the Same Words for the Same Meaning

The precise wording of the problem statement and research questions is an important part of a research endeavor. An investigation of the relationship between socioeconomic status and school achievement, for example, is different from a study of socioeconomic status as a cause of school achievement. Obtaining evidence that one variable is a cause of a second variable is more demanding than showing how these variables vary together within some population.

In a similar manner, a study of fifth-grade students' reading comprehension is somewhat different from a study of such students' understanding, or knowledge, of what they read. A research report should indicate accurately the relationships among variables that the researcher is studying. If you believe that your study is addressing all three aspects of reading comprehension indicated earlier, and that is the important aspect of the study, you must take the time and space needed to make that point and document the rationale for it. Even after that point has been made, using the same phrase for each aspect of that variable makes the report easier to read and comprehend.

Tables and Figures Must Stand Alone

It is a good practice to prepare each table and figure in such a way that it is easily understood—even if it were taken out of context and handed to someone on a single sheet of paper. If this is not done, the reader must move back and forth from the table or figure to the prose in the report, which is often confusing and time-consuming.

Developing good tables and figures is a skill that requires a clear purpose for including each one. Some authors place all their data, or findings, into a single table. In their study of pull-out and in-class remedial reading instruction reported in Chapter 8, for example, Bean and Eichelberger (1985), included only 10 of the 30 questionnaire items in the table in their article.

Reporting findings by research question helps to identify the most relevant data to be included in a table or figure. It also facilitates the reporting of the obtained results, such as frequencies or means, not simply the tests of significance. After the analyses are carried out and the findings for each research question are clear, the most important data that best document the findings should be included in a table or graph. If there is some inconsistency or complexity in the findings, two or three tables and figures may be needed to describe the results.

SUMMARY

The research report is a comprehensive description of a study. *All* its parts should be focused on the problem statement and the researcher's purpose for doing the study. The author should organize and write the report so that it is as clear and unambiguous as possible to a relatively naive reader. The problem studied and the purpose for studying that specific problem is the focus of the first two or three chapters, or sections, of the report. The methods used in the study and the researcher's reasons for using each specific method are accurately and honestly presented. The findings that were obtained when these methods were implemented are reported separately from any interpretation of them. These findings are discussed in the context of other aspects of the study, with confounding variables and other alternative explanations for the findings being clearly identified. Conclusions are drawn from all these results with respect to the problem statement and the purpose for doing the study. Interpretation of the meaning of these results in terms of other research and theories in the literature, considerations about implications for practice, and implications for future research complete the research report.

In writing the report (1) write each section at the time the activity is carried out, (2) outline each section before writing it, (3) put the first draft of the report aside for a few days before revising it, (4) use the same words when you mean the same thing, and (5) make sure that tables and figures can stand alone.

In Chapter 10 relationships among theory, research, and practice are discussed using several illustrations. Issues presented in Chapters 1 to 3 are particularly relevant as you attempt to apply theory and data to practical decision-making. Knowledge of measurement, research design, and statistics are assumed as educators identify the underlying theories and associated assumptions required to apply research results in their situations.

SUGGESTED ACTIVITIES

1. Review the "Table of Contents" of at least five dissertations or theses in your area of specialization. How do they differ in terms of:
   a. Number of chapters?
   b. Order of material?
   c. Where the problem statement and associated research questions (or hypotheses) fall? How many of the five use hypotheses? Are they hypothesis-testing studies or research-question studies?
2. Read the introductory and final chapters of one or more dissertations or theses.
   a. Do the conclusions all relate to the problem statement and purpose?
   b. Are the recommendations for future research based on questions or knowledge that arose from this study?
   c. Are there implications for practice? Do they imply that *on the basis of the results of this study* practitioners *should* do something? Do they imply that specific variables or activities should be considered by practitioners? Which type of implication seems more defensible in the specific study you read?
3. Read the "Methods" chapter or section of a dissertation or thesis.
   a. Are the procedures used to select the sample described so that you know what population the sample represents?
   b. Are the measurement instruments described adequately? Are reliability indexes or indications of their validity appropriate for the data that were collected in the study?
   c. Are the data that were collected from each subject clearly identified? Are the conditions under which the data were collected complete enough to enable you to replicate the study in another setting? If not, what is missing?

d. Are the analyses that were used to analyze the data clearly delineated for each research question or hypothesis? You may not be able to judge the appropriateness of the analysis, but what the analysis was should be clear. (It may be described more fully where the results are reported.)

e. What perspectives arise as you read this chapter that:
   (1) Gives you confidence in the quality or relevance of the results?
   (2) Cause you to question the quality or relevance of this study in your situation?

RELATED SOURCES

Borg, W.R., & Gall, M.D. (1983). *Educational research: An introduction* (4th ed.). White Plains, NY: Longman.

This comprehensive text provides a more general discussion of the sections of a research report than does this textbook. It includes much practical information about writing style, preliminary materials, and preparing papers for publication. It should be useful for most students to read both descriptions, even though there is much overlap between this text and Borg and Gall. Different texts present material in different ways, which helps readers of various descriptions to identify the essential characteristics of research reports. Reliance on only one textbook to learn most aspects of research methods usually results in students' misunderstanding of some essential elements. Borg and Gall's book is one of the most authoritative and comprehensive texts on research methods in the classic tradition.

Castetter, W.B., & Heisler, R.S. (1984). *Developing and defending a dissertation* (4th ed.). Philadelphia: School of Education, University of Pennsylvania.

This clearly written monograph specifies the important issues in planning a research study. It does not address issues of interpretation, but it is one of the best sources for information about the first three chapters of a proposal or research report. These chapters include the introduction, review of literature, and methods used in a study. A number of tables and figures illustrate useful techniques for organizing past research and communicating your plans to the reader.

Mauch, J.E., & Birch, J.W. (1983). *Guide to the successful thesis and dissertation*. New York: Dekker.

This guide provides much practical advice, particularly in the human aspects of getting a thesis or dissertation through the faculty review and final approval process. It is clearly written with an extensive bibliography. The most important elements of the research process are identified, particularly in terms of present practice and faculty perspectives. It can be used easily with this text even though Mauch and Birch's perspective is more traditional.

REFERENCES

Borg, W.R. & Gall, M.D. (1983). *Educational research: An introduction* (4th ed.). White Plains, NY: Longman.

Bean, R.M., & Eichelberger, R.T. (1985). Changing the role of the reading specialists: From pull-out to in-class programs. *The reading teacher, 38*(7), 648–653.

Castetter, W.B., & Heisler, R.S. (1984). *Developing and defending a dissertation* (4th ed.). Philadelphia: School of Education, University of Pennsylvania.

Mitroff, I.I. (1974). *The subjective side of science.* Amsterdam: Elsevier.

Scriven, M. (1967). The methodology of evaluation. In *Perspectives on Curriculum Evaluation*, AERA monograph series on curriculum evaluation (Volume 1). Chicago: Rand McNally, pp. 39–83.

Stufflebeam, D.I., Foley, W.J., Gebhart, W.J., Guba, E.G., Hammond, R.I., Merriman, H.O., & Provus, M.M. (1971). *Educational evaluation and decision making.* Bloomington, IN: Phi Delta Kappan.

Tyler, R.W. (1942). General statement on evaluation. *Journal of educational research, 35,* 492–501.

Worthen, B.R., & Sanders, J.R. (1987). *Educational evaluation: Alternative approaches and practical guidelines.* White Plains, NY: Longman.

CHAPTER 10

Theory, Research, and Practice

PRACTICAL VALUE OF THEORY

Relationships among theory, research, and practice are presented and discussed throughout this book. These discussions have tended to be very detailed, relating conclusions directly to data collected in a particular study. Empirical, or scientific, information is only one kind of information available to decisionmakers in education, and it must be interpreted within the complex context of the education setting. Many professionals in various fields, such as teachers and principals in education, regard the emphasis on scientific knowledge and associated theories as "ivory-tower games" that have little use in practice. There is some evidence for such a view because major changes, or fads, do occur in education with negative effects. One such fad was the new math implemented in the 1960s, which emphasized more theoretical math concepts and de-emphasized practical skills. Nearly a generation of Americans became adults without many practical math skills. Such fads usually have a logical and empirical basis, however, and produce some positive effects. As a result of the "new math" experience, for example, many teachers gained new theoretical math knowledge, some students gained insights into math that would not have occurred with traditional methods, and teachers learned methods for teaching base two and other math concepts that many continue to use.

In this book, the central role of theory in research and practice has been emphasized. Einstein (1936) said, "Physical concepts are free creations of the human mind, and are not, however it may seem, uniquely determined by the external world (p. 221)." Theories determine which aspects of this infinite universe that a person attends. An operant conditioner, a cognitive psychologist, and a Piagetian theorist would "see" different things if they observed the same classroom at the same time. The theories that each believes best describes the most important variables and relationships operating in a classroom determine the aspects of the classroom that each attends. You and I are no different! Each of us has theories and models in our heads that affect the way we perceive the world as professionals, scholars, and human beings. Are these theories unrelated to practice, "ivory-tower" conceptions of the world, or are they necessary parts of our daily lives? There is much evidence for the latter view. Dewey (1929) aptly summarizes this perspective: "Theory is in the end . . . the most practical of all things (p. 17)."

In a National Academy of Education volume on the impact of research on education, Getzels (1978) presented several examples of basic research that had major impacts on education in the past century. One of the most compelling and best-known examples is the work of Thorndike and Woodworth (1901) at the turn of the century. Before their work, education was viewed as training the mind in much the same way as training the muscles of the body. This was in part the rationale for including Latin, Greek, and other repetitive and "mind-exercising" coursework in the curricula of a school.

Thorndike's and Woodworth's studies indicated that the mind did not seem to work that way. Their research provided the foundation for theories of transfer of training, or generalization of learning. Their work implied that the more elements that are common to what is learned and to the new situation, the greater the transfer to the new situation. As a result of these studies and the acceptance of their new theory about the way human beings learn, textbooks and curricula changed. Less Latin and Greek was included. Today these languages are still taught in some schools, but the rationale often given for doing so is to improve understanding of English words that have a Latin base, rather than for exercising the brain.

Another example of the practical impacts of basic research is that of Lewin, Lippitt, and White (1939). They observed the behavior of young childen under democratic, autocratic, and laissez-faire leadership. They found that the children continued to function effectively when the leadership was absent only under democratic leadership. When the autocratic leader left, the group activities tended to stop. The laissez-faire group never functioned effectively.

At that time, most teachers (and parents) believed that children learned best when "controlled by" an adult. This was the age of "spare the rod and spoil the child" and "hickory-stick" education. It was also the age of the one-room schoolhouse in rural areas and other education conditions that differed greatly from those of the 1980s. After publication of Lewin, Lippitt, and White's research, a number of authors translated the meaning of these studies into education. More democratic methods of teaching were included in textbooks used to prepare teachers. Results of research, such as that of Lewin, Lippitt, and White (1939), became an accepted part of the education curricula used to prepare future teachers.

These examples do not imply that such profound changes in American education arose from a single study. Many important aspects of the education process as well as characteristics of U.S. society affect educational decision-making: the purpose of education, citizens' satisfaction with present practice, the needs of U.S. business, the United States' role and activities in the world, and other changing perspectives in a dynamic society. The examples do indicate that basic research about human beings and how they function in groups, which was designed to address theoretical issues within a discipline (sociology), can be translated quickly and applied to education in very practical ways.

EXAMPLE 7   IMPACT OF RESEARCH ON EDUCATION (GETZELS STUDY)

Getzels (1978) reported a study of the configurations of classrooms in schools that were constructed in different periods of the twentieth century (1900–1970) and related them to educators' conceptions of the learner at those times. At the turn of the century, the classrooms were rectangular with pupils' desks and chairs bolted to the floor in straight lines directed toward the teacher's desk. In the 1930s, the classrooms were square. The students' desks and chairs were movable, as were the teacher's. The classrooms of the 1950s had the same square shape. Students' desks were trapezoidal to facilitate their forming a circle, and there was no desk for the teacher. With the open classrooms of the 1970s, the classrooms became four times larger with no furniture for students or teachers, being filled instead with learning materials—particularly those manipulable by the students.

These classroom configurations are related by Getzels to the conception of the child as a learner that was more prevalent at each period. At the turn of the century, children's learning was equated with animal learning. Each student was an "empty" organism responding to a stimulus in ways controlled by rewards and punishments. The teacher, front and center in the classroom, promoted learning by controlling the stimuli and administering the rewards and punishments.

Researchers in the twentieth century found that human beings experienced stimuli in combination, rather than in single entities, and the incomplete figures and words were perceived as complete. The learner was viewed as a combination of dynamic conscious and unconscious forces. Researchers studied relationships between children's personal characteristics and their learning. Teachers attempted to address an individual student's needs. Movable desks allowed for more flexibility in addressing the unique needs of each learner.

Getzels (1978) indicated that during the third period (1950s), "Experimenters in the laboratory were concerned with such matters as interpersonal cohesion and communication networks, and teachers in the classroom with sociometric structure and group processes" (p. 35). The child was viewed as a social organism operating within a larger group. The circular arrangement of desks emphasized this view, forcing each pupil to learn in such a group context.

The large change from these three types of classrooms with furniture ar-
ranged in various ways to the huge open space with little or no furniture and
numerous learning areas of the open classroom was based on a fundamental
change in the conception of the child as a learner. Previous learning theories were
based on drive-reduction views of human beings, whereas the open classroom
assumed that learners were innately curious, seeking out meaningful stimuli. The
most appropriate types of learning environments for such learners are inquiry-
centered with various types of settings and materials for the students to explore
in each classroom.

Getzels reported that in doing the study he was struck by the changes that
present teachers made when teaching in the four types of classrooms.

> The movable chairs are often placed in straight rows, the trapezoidal desks are
> lined up behind one another, the open classroom is partitioned into separate
> closed-off spaces. In one renovated classroom I visited, the movable chairs were
> placed exactly on the bolt marks left by the fixed chairs they had supplanted,
> and woe to the child who moved his chair off the bolt mark. Despite the usage,
> the design of the altered classroom and furniture had obviously been *not* to have
> straight rows. Why then the reversal? In a paradoxical way, this is a rather nice
> demonstration of the impact of conception on practice in the classroom. The
> usage conformed to one conception of the learner, or at least to the methods the
> teachers had learned within the conception; the design of the classroom con-
> formed to another conception. The discrepancy between usage and design is a
> reflection of differences in the conceptions and cannot be understood apart from
> these. (pp. 496–497)

This example illustrates the tremendous effect on daily practice of theories
about the learning (and teaching) of children. It also illustrates the inconsistencies that result when the theories, or conceptions, of the designers are different
from those of the users. This occurs too often in education. Two different situations help to explain such inconsistencies. In the first, designers do not understand the many important practical variables that teachers have to deal with. The
design, or plan, is based totally on a theory that the designers (and decision-
makers) believe is applicable in a particular setting and that will improve the
effectiveness, efficiency, or value of what occurs. In these classrooms, for example, the designers expected improved learning by the students. In many cases of
planned change, the theory is not an improvement over previous practice.

In a second situation, the theory would be an improvement if the teachers
were adequately prepared to make the change. Teaching in an open classroom
requires different skills from teaching with a basal textbook. It may even require
some modifications in teachers' values about which behaviors or characteristics
in a classroom are good. For example, most of us value order and quiet in classrooms, which are nearly impossible to implement in open classrooms. Human

beings need some degree of consistency in their lives. Few of us can change from teaching a small, self-contained class with textbooks to a vastly different physical and psychological setting without preparation and training. Change is facilitated by preparing those who must implement the change.

In making education decisions, it is difficult to differentiate the two situations when an innovation does not have the expected effect. Is it because the theory is too limited or inaccurate, or is it because too little training and preparation were given? There are, of course, many other reasons for failure, but this fundamental distinction is always an important one when doing applied research or making decisions about program or policy changes in education.

RELATIONSHIP BETWEEN RESEARCH AND THEORY

The relationship between empirical research results and theory is difficult to discern precisely. For decades scientist have emphasized the building block view of science. In this view, each researcher adds some small piece of knowledge or technique that the next researcher can use to move forward in a linear fashion.

In his book, *The Structure of Scientific Revolutions* (1962), Kuhn was one of the first to question this view. He provides evidence from his historical study of science that the major gains in knowledge result from what he calls paradigm shifts. A paradigm shift occurs when a fundamental theory is rejected or a more comprehensive theory is developed. Two examples in this century are Einstein's theory of relativity and Skinner's behavior modification perspective. Skinner argues that he has developed a science of behavior that is not a theory. Although this is an interesting question, for purposes of this discussion his work has resulted in major changes in the variables psychologists study and the methods they use to study them. These are two major characteristics of a paradigm shift.

Neither Einstein nor Skinner added another block of knowledge to those provided by previous researchers. They developed entirely new schemas. Einstein posited direct relationships between velocity, mass, and time. Skinner rejected all variables that could not be objectively observed by others. Others had developed the basic ideas on which behavior modification is based; Skinner expanded this work and was more broadly accepted. Internal states of human beings, except those such as hunger, thirst, or deprivation that can be operationally defined and measured (such as time since food was eaten, liquid drunk, or stimulus experienced), were rejected as irrelevant to a science of behavior.

The use of these theories has resulted in numerous impressive results in our ability to predict and control our environment and the behavior of people in it. They also provide new concepts and relationships among concepts that each of us uses to experience and explain our world.

To understand the relationship between research and theory it is useful to be aware of both perspectives. At a particular time various people working on the same array of problems make small contributions that others can use to move forward in a somewhat linear fashion within a particular theory, or paradigm. At other times a person can develop a new set of concepts, as did Sigmund Freud did with the id, ego, superego, and others. Or one can develop new ways to think about old concepts (as did Einstein in relating time to mass and velocity) that result in paradigm shifts. These shifts result in both new ways of viewing the world and new ways of studying it.

EXAMPLE 8   RELATIONSHIP BETWEEN RESEARCH AND THEORY (TEACHER EXPECTANCY EFFECT STUDIES)

A practical example of the building block approach to knowledge is provided by the study of the teacher expectancy effect (TEE), initially identified by Rosenthal and Jacobson (1968). They carried out a study of 320 children in grades 1 through 6 in a school district near Cambridge, Massachusetts. The description of their study that they shared with participating teachers indicated that they were developing a test of inflected acquisition that would identify children who were about to blossom academically. The following is a letter that they shared with teachers describing their study, which was supported by both Harvard University and the National Science Foundation.

STUDY OF INFLECTED ACQUISITION
(HARVARD/NATIONAL SCIENCE FOUNDATION)*
All children show hills, plateaus, and valleys in their scholastic progress. The study being conducted at Harvard with the support of the National Science Foundation is interested in those children who show an unusual forward spurt of academic progress. These spurts can and do occur at any level of academic and intellectual functioning. When these spurts occur in children who have not been functioning too well academically, the result is familiarly referred to as "late blooming."

As a part of our study we are further validating a test which predicts the likelihood that a child will show an inflection point or "spurt" within the near future. This test, which will be administered in your school, will allow us to predict which youngsters are most likely to show an academic spurt. The top 20% (approximately) of the scorers on this test will probably be found at various levels of academic functioning.

The development of the test for predicting inflections or "spurts" is not yet such that *every* one of the top 20% will show the spurt or "blooming" effect. But the top 20% of the children *will* show a more significant inflection or spurt in their learning within the next year or less than will the remaining 80% of the children.

Because of the experimental nature of the tests, basic principles of test construction do not permit us to discuss the test or test scores either with the parents or the children themselves.

Pygmalion in the Classroom by Robert Rosenthal. New York: Holt, Rinehart and Winston, pp. 66. Copyright © 1968. Reprinted by permission of the publisher.

TABLE 10.1 MEAN GAIN IN TOTAL IQ AFTER ONE YEAR BY EXPERIMENTAL AND CONTROL GROUP CHILDREN IN EACH OF SIX GRADES

Grade		Control		Experimental	Expectancy Advantage	
	N	Gain	N	Gain	IQ Points One-tail	$p < 0.05$[a]
1	48	+12.0	7	+27.4	+15.4	0.002
2	47	+7.0	12	+16.5	+9.5	0.02
3	40	+5.0	14	+5.0	−0.0	
4	49	+2.2	12	+5.6	+3.4	
5	26	+17.5(−)	9	+17.4(+)	−0.0	
6	45	+10.7	11	+10.0	−0.7	
Total	255	+8.42	65	+12.22	+3.80	0.02

[a]Mean square within treatments within classrooms = 164.24.
SOURCE: *Pygmalion in the Classroom* by Robert Rosenthal, p. 75. Copyright © 1968. New York: Holt, Rinehart and Winston. Reprinted by permission of the publisher.

Upon completion of this study, participating districts will be advised of the results.

The ostensible reason for the testing done by Rosenthal and Jacobson in Oak School was to perform a final check on the validity of the test, which was presented as already well established. Actually, the Harvard Test of Inflected Acquisition was a standardized, relatively nonverbal test of intelligence, the Test of General Ability (TOGA) (Flanagan, 1960).

A small number of students at each grade level were randomly selected and identified to their teacher as students who are about to blossom or to show the academic spurt identified by Rosenthal and Jacobson. At the end of the year, the students were retested with the same test (the TOGA). The results obtained are reported in Table 10.1.

In the first and second grades, those students identified showed significantly higher increases in IQ scores than did the remainder of the students in their respective grade levels. At the other four grade levels, there were no significant differences in IQ score changes between those identified by the researchers as about to blossom and those who were not identified. The average change across all grade levels indicated that the identified students gained 3.8 IQ points more than those not identified, which was also significant ($p < 0.02$). Rosenthal and Jacobson interpreted these results to mean that the indentification of these students as about to make academic spurts developed an expectancy on the part of the teacher that led to increased IQ scores for these students.

This general interpretation of the expectancy effect, even for those of us who believe in it, seemed somewhat excessive because it occurred in only two of the six grade levels. But the results did seem to indicate that the expectancy was related to significantly greater scores for identified students in grades 1 and 2.

A few years later, two researchers who questioned the existence of the teacher expectancy effect (TEE) attempted to replicate the procedures in grades 1 and 2 (José & Cody, 1971). They focused on the first two grades because children in these grades showed the greatest evidence of the TEE in Rosenthal and Jacobson's research. They carried out the research in the relatively rural area near Southern Illinois University. In addition to the TOGA, they also analyzed math and reading scores from the Metropolitan Achievement Test (MAT). In all their analyses, they obtained no significant differences in the IQ or achievement score changes between the two groups at the end of the year.

The researchers also asked the teachers at the end of the year about their expectancies for the children who were identified as about to experience an academic spurt and whether the information given them at the beginning of the year had modified their expectancies. Only seven of the 18 teachers said that they expected these children to show greater improvement, and only four teachers indicated that they believed these students had shown improvement. In those four classrooms, the identified students had actually shown less improvement than had the comparision group.

A third researcher (Finn, 1972), who was somewhat confused about the inconsistent results (both these and those in other relevant research), analyzed and synthesized all available relevant literature. From this review he developed a model that would explain the inconsistent results and could be used as a framework for further research (see Figure 10.1). He called it a "Network of Expectations."

The various expectations that relate to a student's outcome behavior, such as IQ or achievement, occurs within a general milieu of cultural traditions and demands, which affect the way that a person's characteristics are perceived. The four general types of expectations that most affect self-expectations are identified as (1) expectations of peers, (2) expectations of parents, (3) expectations of teachers, and (4) expectations of others. The relationships among the different dimensions of the model are illustrated with arrows in Figure 10.1. The final set of expectations, expectations of others, does not affect the student's self-expectation or outcome behavior according to Finn's model.

Using this model to explain previous research results, Finn (1972) argues that persons' expectations are part of their complex, pervasive cultural milieu and that it is unrealistic to expect the introduction of one abstract piece of information (scores on the "Test of Inflected Acquisition") to affect the teachers' expectancies about the academic promise of a pupil. The fact that Rosenthal and Jacobson (1968) obtained such a result for pupils in grades 1 and 2 was extraordinary in Finn's view. This result can be attributed to the fact that there were aspects of their study that increased the likelihood that it would affect teachers' expectancies, particularly when compared to José and Cody's study. The fact that Rosenthal and Jacobson were funded by the National Science Foundation and were associated with Harvard University, both prestigious organizations, was clearly noted in the description that they gave to teachers. Their study occurred near Boston, where families and teachers are relatively transient. Most teachers would not know the children or their families before the children were assigned to their classes.

José and Cody carried out their study as José's dissertation with little or no outside funds, and they were associated with Southern Illinois University (from

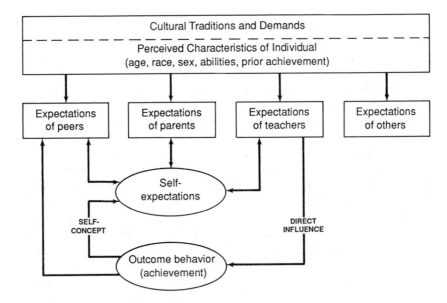

Figure 10.1. "Network" of Expectations.
SOURCE: "Expectations and the educational environment" by J. Finn (1972). *Review of Educational Research*, 42 (3): 387–310. Reprinted with permission.

which many of these teachers had earned their teaching degrees). The communities they studied are extremely stable. Many of these teachers grew up in the town and attended the same schools as did the students. They knew most of the students' families and had known them most of their lives. They had much prior experience on which to base realistic expectations for these students. As the researchers indicated, the identification of students as about to spurt academically did not affect the expectations held by most teachers. (There is no information from the teachers studied by Rosenthal and Jacobson about the extent to which their expectations changed. It would have been useful, but it was not an essential part of the study. Researchers cannot be expected to do everything that is possible in a study.)

As a result of these differences in the two studies, their differential effects are reasonable. Finn does not have the evidence he needed to show that this is exactly what happened, nor does any other researcher. But he has built a model with an associated rationale that explains the obtained differences in the results in a reasonable manner. It is a model that other researchers who want to know more about teacher expectancies can use to conceptualize their studies and interpret the meaning of their results. This is called the model's *heuristic value*—that is, the value of the model or theory for planning and carrying out research in ways that test directly the applicability of the model in the setting studied. Freud's theory of interrelationships among the id, ego, and superego does not have much heuristic value because it is so difficult to operationalize the variables and obtain situations that clearly differ on these variables.

Scholars in every field of human endeavor are attempting to develop theories or models that explain the apparent inconsistencies in research results, as Finn did in this example. As further testing is carried out, the model will be supported, modified, or replaced by a more meaningful or useful model. This is an ongoing, never-ending process of knowledge production. What we are able to do in this century compared with what people were able to do in previous centuries is clear evidence of the increasingly useful knowledge that is gained. We can send a person to the Moon, operate with laser beams, send messages through silicon threads, store millions of bits of data on a small computer chip, and many other wondrous things. Our being able to do these things does not mean that our present theories are accurate descriptions of even the smallest part of this infinite universe. Will we ever be able to describe anything precisely as it is? Einstein (1938) said, "He [mankind] will never be able to compare his picture with the real mechanism and he cannot even imagine the possibility of such a comparison" (p. 221). In a similar vein Bertrand Russell stated, "When a man tells you that he knows the exact truth about anything, you can be safe in inferring that he is a very inexact man."

RESEARCH, EXPERIENCE, AND PRACTICAL DECISION-MAKING

Theoretical versus Practical Knowledge

With the realization that we cannot know the exact truth about anything should come the understanding that *all* relevant knowledge for making the "right" decision is seldom, if ever, available. Even under the best conditions teachers, principals, supervisors, superintendents, and school board members must make numerous assumptions about not only the available information and associated theories but also the applicability of that knowledge in the present situation. In addition, different people will weigh the available evidence in different ways. Some want to see increased achievement test scores, whereas others want more realistic experiences for students through field trips and hands-on experiences, which may not be the most efficient or effective way to teach the knowledge and skills addressed by norm-referenced tests but may have other positive educational effects.

This realization also means that educational decision-making requires more than the information provided by available systematic research. Many good adminstrators plan their activities so that past research and associated literature can be reviewed, and data are systematically collected to monitor and study present activities so that the administrators are well informed when decisions must be made. But the inherently limited nature of such data and the theories and models associated with them are well recognized by experienced, knowledgeable administrators, researchers, and scholars.

The present discussion of these limitations and associated concerns is presented in the context of the importance and value of theory for personal, professional, and academic purposes. Theory provides the variables and relationships that we use to experience and understand the world. The teacher expectancy effect research and Finn's model are useful tools to use when such issues arise. For example, I may be concerned that I have different expectations for different students in my course. How likely is that to affect their learning? What can I do to increase the likelihood that I give all students equal opportunity to learn in this course? The research and model presented in Example 8 should be useful to me in addressing these questions.

A superintendent of a school district is no different. Wanting to improve the elementary reading program in ways that will lead to increased reading abilities and attitudes of students, the superintendent applies theories that are relevant to this problem to the extent possible in attempting to meet that goal. The utility and value of research and theory in this type of setting are emphasized throughout the education process. The concern raised here is that theory is often perceived as being a precise description of the important variables in a setting and the path to school improvement as being the implementation of the theory or the generally accepted conditions as quickly as possible in precisely the ways recommended by researchers.

Many problems in education may lie not in the failure to apply the latest theory but in applying them too quickly with too little piloting in the local setting and with limited use of practical experience. The best way to understand and use available research and associated theory is to be aware of the assumptions needed in order to apply them and to critically assess both the conditions under which they have been successfully applied and their value and relevance in your present setting.

The first nine chapters of this book describe the tools commonly used to do research and the logical basis for drawing conclusions from empirical data. The assumptions the tools require and the procedures useful in critically assessing the information they provide were described in relatively detailed fashion. When these tools are combined in doing a research study a number of more general concerns become important due to complexities that arise. Similarly, teaching one child is much simpler than teaching an entire class. The researcher must, as does the teacher, learn to work successfully in extremely complex settings. The examples in this section are provided for the purpose of applying the research and theory in the more complex educational and societal context.

Robert Nisbett (1975) wrote an article in the *New York Times Magazine* that points out some problems that occur when scientists and scholars use their discipline-based research and theories to advise decision-makers to make major changes in policies or programs, often overlooking its inherent limitations, the importance of the practical knowledge gained from years of experience, and the need to obtain new empirical information in the setting where changes are implemented. Nisbett wrote that many scientists and scholars in the past several decades who have become advisers to U.S. presidents, congressmen, and other important decision-makers in our society, have made promises (or encourage expectations) about programs that would eliminate poverty, reduce crime, end urban blight, and solve other equally complex societal problems.

Some of these programs have been in place for more than 20 years (Head Start and Follow Through, for example), which should be time enough to judge fairly their effects. Many of these programs have had positive results, although there are counterexamples. Head Start was described by President Reagan as a successful social program, and he continued to support it. Many economically disadvantaged children and their families have gained much from this national program. But is poverty or illiteracy being eliminated in the U.S. by this program and others that address these problems? Not enough so that anyone can notice it. Why? Because in part our present theories are too limited and inadequate for dealing successfully with these major complex problems. The theories may be useful for investigating why the problems were not affected extensively and for proposing new ways to address them. Also, the fact that research and scholarship are divided into the various disciplines of psychology, sociology, economics, history, anthropology, physics, chemistry, and so on may affect our ability to study complex human problems. This issue is discussed later in this chapter. The important point is that professionals must be cautious in applying theories that have not been adequately tested in situations similar to the one in which they are to be applied. Practical decisions affect the lives of human beings. Most experienced decisionmakers are acutely aware of this fact and make changes cautiously.

Another example that illustrates this point occurred when leaders of the United States of America met to rewrite the Articles of Confederation and produced the United States Constitution. These men were all experienced politicians, even though some were scholars and researchers, such as Benjamin Franklin and Thomas Jefferson. They discussed whether to be guided by reason or experience. They unanimously agreed that reason can easily mislead, so that they must be guided by experience. Accounts of the process describe their use of history and lessons learned from the experiences of other countries when certain governmental structures or policies were implemented. Their knowledge of England's experiences in governing different cultures and their own experiences with England were often used in arguments. These lessons from experience were far more important than individuals' theories or ideologies unsupported by data or experience.

Nisbett (1975) pointed out that every civilized language except English has two common words for knowledge: that resulting from experience and that resulting from systematic, sustained study. He cited *connaitre* and *savoir* in French.

[The first word means] knowledge-by-acquaintance (knowledge-of), the knowledge one finds in every occupation, skill, profession or role.... The second, "knowledge-about," is the result of sustained systematic study, of reflection, logic and abstract thinking. It is the kind of knowledge that we associate with science and scholarship. (p. 39)

When these two types of knowledge are in conflict, the educator tends to talk about "ivory-tower academics," and academics talk about "uninformed practitioners." In most situations, each could learn a great deal from the other. Practitioners must make informed decisions that are based on all types of knowledge (information) available to them, so that the most positive educational outcomes result. This means that they must learn as much as possible about relevant research and theory, and to trust their own practical experience and that of others in their profession.

This chapter addresses the relationship among theory, research, and practice. The practical value of theory, some ways that theories are developed from research, and conflicts between theoretical knowledge and practical decision-making were discussed. In the next section, an example that illustrates two fundamental limitations of theory when applied to education is presented and discussed. Those limitations relate to (1) the identification of all variables that have an impact on the educational outcomes we want to affect (such as student learning), and (2) the other outcomes that occur when we make changes in the variables that we believe affect important educational outcomes, such as teaching practices or curriculum.

Unknown Variables in Research and Theory

When researchers study problems, they know that two sets of variables exist, but they are not sure how to deal with them. Every theory includes predictor variables and criterion, or outcome, variables. A researcher who uses a theory can include only a limited number of variables. One unknown set of variables includes all unmeasured variables that affect the outcomes addressed by the research. The researcher will have made every effort to include the most important variables but is aware that other variables are in the setting and that these other variables may turn out to be more important than those included in the study. The researcher does not believe that is true but is aware that it is a possibility.

A second set of unknown variables (unintended outcomes) includes all the other outcomes, not measured, that arise in a setting when changes are made in educational procedures or policies. These unintended outcomes are particularly important when an agency or institution, such as a school district, school, or classroom, implements change. New curriculum materials, teaching methods, or personnel policies are implemented to improve educational processes. Even when the expected outcomes are achieved, other unintended outcomes may also occur. The results of research on effective schools reported by Edmonds (1982) are used to illustrate the two unknown sets of variables not addressed by the research.

From much study of school effectiveness, which is usually identified as high scores on norm-referenced tests, Ronald Edmonds (1982) identified five characteristics of effective schools:

1. Strong leadership by the principal with substantial attention to the quality of instruction.

2. An instructional focus that is broadly understood in the school.
3. A safe, orderly climate conducive to teaching and learning.
4. Teachers convey the expectation that all students will learn.
5. Assessment of student achievement is used as the basis for program evaluation. (p. 582)

These five characteristics have been broadly disseminated and are widely accepted as characteristics of effective schools. Many universities are even changing their programs for principal certification to emphasize the principal's role as the instructional leader in each school building.

When administrators try to implement these five conditions in their schools, what are the effects on student achievement, and what are the unintended outcomes? Increasing the extent that these five conditions occur in a school may increase achievement test scores, but what are other possible outcomes? Aid for Dependent Children (ADC) may, for example, provide adequate money to feed and house children of unemployed single mothers, but it may also lead to more pregnancies in unwed mothers.

In a similar vein, a principal who wants to provide strong leadership to improve instructional quality may, in a dictatorial manner, declare that all teachers will teach in a specific, prescribed manner. The teachers, who had been able to vary in their approaches and had developed what they felt were effective methods for teaching various subjects, may not be as effective under this mandate. Even if the required methods increase students' test scores, many teachers may find teaching less satisfying and leave the profession, or retire early. These are only two of numerous possible unintended outcomes. The one truth that we can count on is that such unknown variables will occur whenever change is implemented in a new setting. These variables are not necessarily important in all situtations, nor are there always negative unintended outcomes, but this is almost never an empty set. Practitioners must be alert to them and be ready to respond when they occur.

A second set of variables consists of those that exist in the setting but that are not included in the research. In the present literature, a characteristic of effective schools that Edmonds does not list is community and parent support for the instructional program in the school. Other characteristics are the intellectual climate of the school and the students' belief that doing well in school is important. I am sure that several other variables Edmonds did not list should be important to school effectiveness. Researchers try to include the most important variables for studying relationships in a particular setting for a particular purpose. The characteristics not addressed appear to them to be relatively unimportant at that time. Later, some previously omitted variables may become more important and researchers will begin to include them in their studies.

These two sets of unknown variables are illustrated in Figure 10.2 in a hypothetical relationship among variables U, V, and W to predict Y. Ways in which the unmeasured variables that affect Y actually operate are also unknown. Some

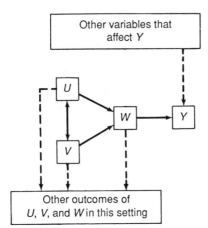

Figure 10.2. Hypothetical Relationship among *U, V, W,* and *Y* with "Other Possible Variables" and "Unintended Outcomes" Illustrated

may affect *U, V,* or *W* directly and affect *Y* indirectly; others may be unrelated to *U, V,* or *W* and affect *Y* directly. Other outcomes of *U, V,* and *W* in this new setting may not result from their inherent characteristics but may result from the way that they are implemented. Good policies may fail because of poor planning or inadequate preparation for the implementation of change. A person must be aware of the various possible causes of failures, or good policies that would improve education will be rejected as inappropriate because they are poorly planned and implemented. Often the cause of a failed policy or theory is difficult to discern.

MULTIDISCIPLINARY NATURE OF EDUCATION

As indicated previously, knowledge has been artificially divided into various disciplines, which has allowed scholars to focus on limited aspects of the universe and the people in it. Some sensational successes in the production of knowledge have resulted from both natural and social scientists. Practitioners in most professional fields learn the theories and research from various disciplines that are most important to their professional field. In education the primary discipline is psychology, with some sociological knowledge of organizational research and group behavior included. Multicultural issues, when addressed, often use anthropological theories and associated research evidence.

Human activities, such as those in education, affect and are affected by variables commonly studied in nearly all disciplines. (Geology, astrophysics, and nuclear physics are a few exceptions that come to mind.) Some important disciplines with which educators are not usually familiar are political science, economics, anthropology, and sociology. The heavy emphasis on psychology too often gives the impression that educational issues can be comprehensively, or at least adequately, addressed using only psychological theories and associated variables. In practice, the dimensions of an educational activity do not fall neatly into the various disciplinary categories. Some tools, such as cost-benefit analysis, have been developed to systematically describe the nature and degree of a program's benefits and to specify the costs of producing those benefits. In education, the primary benefits are usually delineated as learning (knowledge) gains based on psychological theories, and the costs are derived from economic theories.

Regardless of which specific discipline or combination of disciplines is used to study an educational problem, it is important to realize the limited nature of empirical study. Singleton (1967), in the postscript to his ethnographic study of a Japanese school that was based on anthropology theories and methods, made this point well:

> Each observer brings special competencies to a study, just as each setting has certain unique features. If an anthropologist, an economist, a political scientist, a sociologist, a social psychologist, a social geographer, a historian, a communications specialist, an educator, or another specialist within the behavioral sciences compare notes on observations of the same educational institution, each will perceive and describe a different order of relationships between the school and its setting. The specific questions which they ask and their perceptions of observed human behavior will be conditioned by their disciplinary background. This is as it should be. The important error to avoid in all of these methods of study is the claim that any one discipline or model can give a complete analysis of a particular situation. (p. 120)

As an evaluator educated as an educational psychologist, I became acutely aware of the multidisciplinary nature of education as I evaluated operating programs in school districts and was involved with adminstrators and school board members responsible for deciding the future of these programs. The evaluations carried out were based only on psychological theories relevant to students' learning the knowledge and skills taught in the elementary school programs. Such learning was measured exclusively with standardized, norm-referenced tests, which were viewed as the most reliable and valid way of measuring the important outcomes of educational processes.

The evaluation results were generally viewed as valuable and informative and could not be ignored by decisionmakers. But these competent, responsible decisionmakers who directed the programs, administered the schools, or sat on school boards always discussed other considerations not addressed by the evaluation (or research) study. They were always concerned about cost, and they usually wanted to know how well the program was integrated with the remainder of the school curricula and the personnel and administrative problems that the alternative decisions would have on the educational process. An example of an elementary school program with documented evidence of effectiveness that was discontinued is briefly discussed to illustrate the complex multidisciplinary nature of educational decision-making.

An individualized program was in two local schools with money from the federal government. It included the curricula for math and reading in the first through the sixth grades. Aides were required for record-keeping and other clerical tasks in the classrooms. The additional cost of the program over what the district would have spent without these curricula and the aides was about $60,000 per year.

After more than 10 years of the program's operation, the school board requested an evaluation of it. I analyzed the academic achievement results in math and reading that were available on norm-referenced tests. The superintendent of the school district gathered extensive information on the effects of the individualized instruction approach on later academic and extracurricular activities of students who had attended these classes. In all instances, there was consistent, believable evidence that students had gained both academically and personally from the program. The amount of federal funding for the program had decreased during previous years, and the district had been paying all educational costs in these schools for several years. The school board decided to discontinue the program and to use the same instructional materials in all elementary schools. They did not question the accuracy or validity of the evaluation results. Their concerns did not relate to the effectiveness of the instructional program. In fact, their concerns were not related to variables that usually concern educational psychologists. Some of their concerns included the following:

1. *Equal treatment of students in all schools.* The board could not afford to provide the same amount of additional money to all schools without a large tax increase. With a large tax increase they could implement this more effective program in all district schools. Not all parents or teachers wanted this individualized program in their schools. They would rather have the additional money to improve their educational program in other ways if the board could provide it. Many board members felt that each school should operate with the same per-pupil costs, using the same instructional materials and following the same district-wide policies.

2. *Hiring additional aides and the likelihood that they would form a labor union.* The major costs in a school district's budget are personnel costs. Also, much administration and school board time and energy are spent on personnel issues. Principals, supervisors, teachers, special educators, janitors, cafeteria workers, bus drivers, secretaries, clerks, and other employees are covered by numerous laws and have legitimate concerns that must be addressed. If the individualized program were extended to all schools, another employee group would be formed that would take up more time and lead to increased costs over time.

3. *Other aspects of the individualized program were not universally valued.* The individualized program required that each student be given a unique set of math and reading assignments each day. These were usually based on curriculum-embedded tests that were adminstered and scored daily —usually by the aide. The time required of teachers was much greater

than that required by more traditional educational approaches. Many teachers, including some in the two schools already using the individualized curricula, were not eager to use these programs and lobbied for their removal.

These and other concerns were all operating while the decision about the individualized program was being considered. Exactly which argument was most persuasive for each board member is impossible to know. All these issues and associated variables from various disciplines were important in the deliberations. How such variables interact in the education setting is probably different from how they interact in a business or other setting, making research carried out from a single disciplinary perspective even more suspect when making educational decisions.

What can we learn from such examples? One is to become more aware of the variables operating in the present situation that are not addressed adequately by psychological theories. We must learn how these variables are studied in other disciplines so that we can use appropriate theories, or conceptual maps, to understand more about how these variables may be affecting important educational processes or outcomes. We usually read magazines and journals that are too limited, often dealing only with psychological issues. When studying a problem, we can get a more comprehensive picture of the problem and the setting in which it occurs by also reading research and theory in sociology, social psychology, and anthropology. Critically analyzing and synthesizing this literature to provide the best way to conceptualize the problem in a particular setting, as described in Chapter 4, is one useful process. Simply reading broadly is useful, but it is not nearly so useful as organizing it all in writing, as in a formal review of the literature.

SUMMARY

The purpose of this book is to help develop a better understanding of the research process and how research and theory relate to educational decision-making. A broad definition of science is used to include all systematic attempts to gather, analyze, and interpret empirical data in order to investigate a problem. The relationship among problem identification that is based on a comprehensive review of literature, the procedures used to investigate the problem, and appropriate conclusions based on the results of the study are described and illustrated with various practical examples. Detailed presentation of the research (scientific) procedures are included to make clear the assumptions required to use the procedures appropriately and to understand the logical process that underlies the conclusions drawn from empirical results.

Numerous examples illustrate the problems that can arise when these assumptions are not met or when a critical analysis of the results and their applicability in a new setting is not carried out. The belief that quantitative measurement of variables that have been manipulated will lead to valid theories has been over-emphasized in research courses. This book has emphasized the problems that can arise when science is viewed too simplistically.

The value of doing experiments that compare equivalent groups and common settings is well recognized, and they should be used when appropriate in research. Similarly, all researchers desire to measure as accurately as possible the most important variables in a study. Important questions about *how* best to obtain and analyze the most relevant information to draw valid conclusions have arisen in the past decade. Multiple choice norm-referenced tests may not be the best measure of important human knowledge and skills. They are certainly a valuable tool, and one that we must all learn more about. They are no longer viewed, however, as the *only* important measure of educational outcomes that can be used with confidence in educational research. Knowing both the strengths and weaknesses of the methods used to study education is an important outcome of studying this book.

Campbell and Stanley's (1963) purpose for writing the chapter, "Experimental and Quasi-Experimental Designs for Research on Teaching" was to establish, ". . . a cumulative tradition in which improvements can be introduced without the danger of a faddish discard of old wisdom in favor of inferior novelties" (p. 172). They were committed to the experiment as the only means for meeting that purpose. In trying to fulfill that same purpose, researchers today are concerned about the adequacy of a single analytical technique and are using more wholistic methods, such as case studies and ethnographies, to investigate variables important for improving education practices.

Whatever methods are used by a researcher, the conclusions drawn from a study and their implications for practice require scrutiny. That scrutiny is based on knowledge of (1) the methods used, (2) the theory on which the study was based, and (3) the practical context in which the study is to be applied.

SUGGESTED ACTIVITIES

1. Read an article in the *Review of Educational Research (RER)* that is particularly relevant to your professional role or area of specialization. Read the seminal, or most important, article on which the review article is based. (This is often the oldest article quoted.) Read the second most important articles and as many of the other articles that you feel would be valuable. Do you believe that the author of the *RER* article gave an accurate review of these articles and their relationships to each other? If not, what changes would you make in the *RER* article?
   a. What was the most important knowledge you gained by reading these articles?
   b. Do you find the empirical articles more valuable than the theoretical or experiential ones? Defend your answer with reasons and associated documentation.

2. Read an article of particular interest to you from a journal that is read regularly by practitioners in your field.
   a. On what types of evidence are conclusions drawn?
   b. What underlying theory is the author using in the article?
   c. Is that theory applicable in the setting?
   d. What assumptions must be met for the theory to apply in (1) the setting described by the author? (2) your setting?
   e. What are the greatest weaknesses in the article in terms of the quality or relevance of the conclusions or recommendations provided? What are the greatest strengths of the article?

RELATED SOURCES

Boyan, N.J. (Ed.). (1988). *Handbook of research on educational administration.* White Plains, NY: Longman.
    This handbook is similar to the three handbooks of research on teaching. It is also a product of the American Educational Research Association (AERA). The chapters review research and theory in four areas related to educational administration: "The Administrator," "Organizations," "Economics and Finance," and "Politics and Policy." A fifth section of special topics includes: Technical tools of decision-making, Evaluation, Collective bargaining, Legal aspects, Comparative educational administration, Quantitative research methods, and Fieldwork methods. It does not provide as much methodological information as the other AERA handbooks, but the individual chapters synthesize research and theory so that you can gain substantive knowledge about the topic and see how research results are meaningfully interpreted. The handbook illustrates better than most sources the relationships among theory, research, and practice.
Suppes, P. (Ed.). (1978). *Impact of research on education.* Washington, DC: National Academy of Education.
    This book is one of the best sources of analysis and synthesis of past work that shows the impact of research and theory on the practice of education. Nine topics are addressed in detail by authorities in that field:

   1. On the theory-practice interface in the measurement of intellectual abilities, by John B. Carroll (pp. 1–105).
   2. Words for schools: The applications in education of the vocabulary researches of Edward L. Thorndike, by Geraldine Joncich Clifford (pp. 107–198).
   3. The contributions of B.F. Skinner to education and some counter influences, by Robert Glaser (pp. 199–265).
   4. The theoretical ideas of Piaget and educational practice, by Guy J. Groen (pp. 267–317).
   5. Psychoanalysis and American elementary education, by Patrick Suppes and Hermine Warren (pp. 319–396).
   6. The impact of the language sciences on second-language education, by H.H. Stern, Marjorie Bingham Wesche, and Birgit Harley (pp. 397–475).
   7. Paradigm and practice: On the impact of basic research in education, by Jacob W. Getzels (pp. 477–521).

8. Educational research and educational reform: A case study of Sweden, by Torsten Husen (pp. 523–579).
9. Education, social science, and the law: The Rodriguez case and school finance reform, by Marvin Pressler and Joel S. Berke (pp. 581–645).

If you are interested in any of these topics, you will gain much from these outstanding chapters—particularly the historical perspective.
Wittrock, M.C. (Ed.). (1986). *Handbook of research on teaching* (3rd ed.). New York: Macmillan.

Most chapters in the three handbooks of research on teaching are reviews of past research in an area related to teaching. This book, however, is one of the best sources for up-to-date information about a substantive area. By reading various chapters, you will also see how past research is analyzed and synthesized to reach conclusions in each chapter. The first section of each handbook deals with theory and methods of research on teaching. Each handbook is produced by a committee of AERA and does not repeat material presented in previous handbooks. Educators should be familiar with the chapters that relate to their professional responsibilities or expertise.

REFERENCES

Campbell, D. T. & Stanley, J. C. (1963). Experimental and quasi-experimental designs for research on teaching. In N. L. Gage (Ed.), *Handbook of research on teaching* (pp. 171–246). Chicago: Rand McNally.

Dewey, J. (1929). *Sources of a science of education.* New York: Liveright.

Edmonds, R. (1982). [Working Paper]. East Lansing: Michigan State University, Center for School Improvement, cited in T.L. Good & J.E. Brophy, School effects, in M.C. Wittrock (Ed.), *Handbook of Research on Teaching* (3rd ed.). New York: Macmillan.

Einstein, A. (1936). On physical reality. *Franklin Institute Journal*, p. 221.

Finn, J. (1972). Expectations and the educational environment. *Review of Educational Research, 42*(3), 387–410.

Flanagan, J.C. (1960). *Tests of general ability: Preliminary technical report.* Chicago: Science Research Associates.

Getzels, J. (1978). Paradigm and practice: On the impact of basic research on education. In P. Suppes (Ed.), *Impact of Research on Education.* Washington, DC: National Academy of Education.

José, J., & Cody, J.J. (1971). Teacher-pupil interaction as it relates to attempted change in teacher expectancy of academic ability and achievement. *American Educational Research Journal, 8*(1), 39–49.

Kuhn, T.S. (1962). *The structure of scientific revolutions.* Chicago: University of Chicago Press.

Lewin, K., Lippitt, R., & White, R.K. (1939). Patterns of aggressive behavior in experimentally created social climates. *Journal of Social Psychology, 10*, 271–299.

Nisbett, R. (1975, September 28). Knowledge dethroned. *The New York Times Magazine*, pp. 36–43.

Rosenthal, R., & Jacobson, L. (1968). *Pygmalion in the classroom.* New York: Holt, Rinehart and Winston.

Singleton, J. (1967). *Nichū: A Japanese School.* New York: Holt, Rinehart, and Winston.

Thorndike, E.L. & Woodworth, R.S. (1901). The influence of improvement in one mental function upon the efficiency of other functions. *Psychology review, 8*, 247–261.

Index